D0554520

DATE DUE

THE POLITICS OF KNOWLEDGE

Also by Ellen Condliffe Lagemann

A Generation of Women
Nursing History (editor)
Private Power for the Public Good
Jane Addams on Education (editor)

Ellen Condliffe Lagemann

THE POLITICS OF KNOWLEDGE

The Carnegie Corporation,
Philanthropy, and
Public Policy

Wesleyan University Press
Middletown, Connecticut

Chapter 1 originally appeared, in somewhat different form,
in *History of Education Quarterly*
(Volume 27, Number 2, Summer 1987).
Chapter 6 originally appeared, in somewhat different
form, in *Minerva* (Volume 35, Winter 1987).

All inquiries and permissions requests
should be addressed to the Publisher, Wesleyan University Press,
110 Mt. Vernon Street, Middletown, Connecticut 06457

Library of Congress Cataloging-in-Publication Data

Lagemann, Ellen Condliffe, 1945–
  The politics of knowledge : the Carnegie Corporation,
philanthropy, and public policy / Ellen Condliffe Lagemann.—1st
ed.
    p.   cm.
  Includes bibliographical references.
  ISBN 0-8195-5204-6
  1. Carnegie Corporation of New York. 2. Endowments—United
States. 3. United States—Social policy. I. Title.
HV97.C3L34   1989
361.7'632'0973—dc20   89-16634
                                                                CIP

Manufactured in the United States of America

FIRST EDITION

For my mother
Jane Condliffe Morris

Contents

Preface

WHEN I BEGAN this book, I had no intention of writing as broad a history as this one has become. Although I had planned to consider Carnegie Corporation grant-making in relation to public policy, I had not yet realized how far that would take me from a straight institutional plot line of people and events. In fact, I began fully to appreciate the scope of what I was attempting only as I wrestled with the difficult "so what" questions implicit in the record of Carnegie Corporation grants and administrative processes, questions having to do with what the Carnegie Corporation did not as well as did finance, and with the history, social location, and subsequent comparative development of the organizations, ideas, movements, and individuals involved. The logic that took me from those questions to what I have described as "the politics of knowledge" is explained elsewhere in the book; here, I should like to acknowledge a list of debts that has lengthened with the scope of the book.

My first debt is to the Carnegie Corporation of New York. In 1983, I completed a history of the Carnegie Foundation for the Advancement of Teaching, entitled *Private Power for the Public Good*. I had begun that book while Alan Pifer was president of both the Carnegie Corporation and the Carnegie Foundation—two distinct and very different foundations, which are often confused in public perception, having sometimes shared officers though never full boards of trustees. It had grown out of Pifer's interest in history and his wish to have a historian look at the Foundation from a critical, external perspective; and, on my side, out of a curiosity about progressivism and its large, design-level influence on American education and society. Although Pifer and his associates at the Corporation and the Foundation did not concur in all the interpretations and judgments advanced in *Private Power*, they nevertheless invited me to undertake a second book. In a way, therefore, even though this book is not a sequel to *Private Power*, it did grow out of that earlier work. Also, as was true when I wrote *Private Power*, my work was partially financed by grants from the Carnegie Corporation, and I was given full and free access to all Corporation records. In addition, Corporation officers and staff members made time to talk with me and to answer queries, while carefully not intruding into any and all interpretive matters. In fact, no one currently or formerly associated with either the Carnegie Corporation or the Carnegie Foundation saw the manuscript until after it went to press. I can think of few organizations that would allow a historian the unrestricted access and freedom that the Carnegie Corporation has granted me, and I am very grateful.

I am particularly indebted to Alan Pifer for having created the opportunity to write this book and for having been so supportive (and laissez-faire!) in his attitude toward it throughout the years it has taken to complete. I am also grateful to John W. Gardner, Barbara D. Finberg, David Z. Robinson, Sara L. Engelhardt, E. Alden Dunham, Frederick A. Mosher, and Avery Russell for many helpful conversations. Florence Anderson died before the book was finished, but she was tremendously helpful in the early stages, and I learned a good deal about the Corporation from her. Idalia Holder, Patricia Haynes, Evelyn Nieders, and Helen C. Noah always found a desk and a Xerox machine for me to use.

People familiar with Carnegie philanthropy may notice that, contrary to internal usage, I have consistently referred to *the* Carnegie Corporation rather than Carnegie Corporation (with no prefatory "the"). I am aware that this is jarring to insiders, but common usage seemed the best choice for a general audience. I should remark, too, that the documents and records cited as "Corp. Files" in the notes were located in the Carnegie Corporation offices when I used them. However, as this book went to press, plans were being made to move them to a university archive. I regret the difficulties this may create for scholars who wish to follow the notes I have supplied.

While writing this book, I was lucky enough to have had a number of research assistants who contributed in important ways. Mary Ann Dzuback helped me find many of the initial sources and did some of the research on the behavioral sciences and area studies. As a result of her own work on Robert Maynard Hutchins, she was also able to point me toward studies of legal realism, which proved relevant to my work on the American Law Institute. Henrietta Mosher worked with me throughout a year of research leave (1985–86). She read oral histories, tracked down elusive books and journals, and checked quotations and footnotes. Her energy and interest sometimes surpassed my own, and I shall always owe her thanks for the persistence and intelligence with which she approached small and large research questions. Daniel Humphrey did much of the library work necessary for chapter 9 and helped me with all the final tasks involved in finishing the manuscript, in the process giving up a much-needed Christmas vacation. He and Andrea Walton checked more quotations and footnotes than either would like to recall, and did so with consistent care and good cheer. For brief periods of time, Mara Gross, Deborah DeSimone, and Jonathan Penders searched libraries for books I needed.

As the notes will indicate, this book is based largely upon primary source materials. For permission to quote from the papers for which they serve as custodians, I am grateful to the following libraries and individuals: Ann Stouffer Bisconti (for Samuel A. Stouffer Papers, Harvard University Archives); the Carnegie Corporation of New York (for all materials cited as Corp. Files); the Joseph Regenstein Library, University of Chicago (for Beardsley Ruml Papers and Interview with John Dollard, Department of Sociology Interviews); the Moorland-Spingarn Research Center, Howard University (for Alain Locke Papers); the Harvard University Archives (for Clyde Kluckhohn, Department of Social Relations, Talcott Parsons, and the Russian Research Center Papers); the Observatories of the Carnegie Institution of Washington (for George Ellery Hale Papers); the Oral History Research Office, Columbia University (for Carnegie Corporation of New York Oral History, Interviews with Florence Anderson, Vannevar Bush, Morse A. Cartwright, John W. Gardner, Devereux C. Josephs, Gunnar Myrdal, Frederick Osborn, John Russell, and Donald Young); Alan Pifer (for Carnegie Corporation of New York Oral History, Interview with Alan Pifer); the Rare Book and Manuscript Library, Columbia University (for Frederick P. Keppel Papers); the Rockefeller Archive Center (for Laura Spelman Rockefeller Memorial Collection); and the Social Science Research Council (for Hanover Conference Transcripts).

Somewhat different versions of parts of two chapters were published previously: parts of the Introduction appeared as "The Politics of Knowledge: The Carnegie Corporation and the Formulation of Public

Policy" in the *History of Education Quarterly* 27 (Summer 1987): 205–20; and some of the material presented in chapter 6 appeared as "A Philanthropic Foundation at Work: Gunnar Myrdal's *American Dilemma* and the Carnegie Corporation" in *Minerva* 35 (Winter 1987): 441–70. I owe appreciation to B. Edward McClellen and William J. Reese of the *History of Education Quarterly* and to Edward Shils of *Minerva* for editorial comments and assistance.

Over the years I have benefited from conversations with colleagues working on similar or related topics, especially Martin Bulmer, Stanley N. Katz, James A. Smith, Paul J. DiMaggio, Steven C. Wheatley, Roger L. Geiger, and Kathleen D. McCarthy. Francis Keppel talked with me at length about his father (Frederick P. Keppel), Frederick Osborn, J. B. Conant, and the educational legislation of the 1960s. Francis X. Sutton shared his wealth of knowledge about the Ford Foundation and area studies. Bruce A. Ackerman helped me understand the history of American law. Jeannette Hopkins made available her fine sense of the written word in the form of careful, incisive editing, while her colleagues at the Wesleyan University Press moved the book through the production process with dispatch.

My work has been facilitated by a number of colleagues at Teachers College and in the Department of History at Columbia. John A. Garraty arranged for me to work in Fayerweather Hall for a year while I was on leave (1985–86), and Alden T. Vaughan was kind enough to lend me his office. Jane P. Franck, director of the Milbank Library at Teachers College, presides over a wonderful library that I have used almost every day; she also lent me materials on the Ford Foundation from her personal collection. Lambros Comitas has been a model department chairman, always firmly supporting scholarly commitments regardless of other institutional pressures. He has encouraged my work in many small, daily ways and has read and commented upon a number of chapter drafts. My greatest debt is to Lawrence A. Cremin, with whom I have often taught since 1978. He has read every draft of this book and has listened to ideas still only half-clear. Over the years he has shared my excitement in new research and made me laugh when despair set in and I thought the book would never be finished. Most important, he has taught me an extraordinary amount through his profound knowledge of American educational history and his wise and humane approach to American educational policy. I am fortunate to have such a generous colleague and friend. Finally, I should like to acknowledge the financial support for my research and writing that has been generously provided by the Institute of Philosophy and Politics of Education.

My husband, Kord Lagemann, and our son, Nick Lagemann, know how to combine encouragement with distraction in wonderful ways. Their affection and patience with my scholarly preoccupations are great, and my thanks to them are profound.

E.C.L.

THE POLITICS OF KNOWLEDGE

The Politics of Knowledge

T HE CARNEGIE CORPORATION OF NEW YORK was the last and largest of the various philanthropic trusts established by the Scottish steel magnate Andrew Carnegie. Organized in 1911 and endowed with $125 million, to which $10,336,867 was added at Carnegie's death in 1919, the Corporation was chartered "to promote the advancement and diffusion of knowledge and understanding among the people of the United States." In pursuit of that broad mandate, over the century it has helped to establish or endow institutions as varied as the Carnegie libraries, the National Research Council, the American Law Institute, the Russian Research Center at Harvard University, and the Children's Television Workshop. It has supported research into business cycles, the description of adult intelligence, and the development of cognitive science. It has financed the writing of innumerable books, including, among the most noted, Gunnar Myrdal's *An American Dilemma*, David Riesman's *The Lonely Crowd*, John W. Gardner's *Excellence*, and Christopher Jencks's *Inequality*. And it has provided funds for conferences and international exchanges, radio shows and art exhibitions, legal proceedings and serial publications, and many other knowledge-related activities. Through such means, the Corporation has contributed a great deal to learning and scholarship, and in the process has frequently had an important, if usually indirect, influence upon public policy. The history of this foundation from 1911 until 1982 is the subject of this book.

But the book is also about a politics—the politics of knowledge.

This is a politics that has been central to our lives. It involves the creation, organization, development, and dissemination of knowledge. Emerging in the United States in conjunction with the development of a large-scale national state at the end of the nineteenth century, this politics crystallized as knowledge of various kinds became more and more essential to economic activity and to the formulation, implementation, and evaluation of public policy.

As the United States moved from a preindustrial and industrial state to a postindustrial state, knowledge joined land and capital as a critical national resource. It served as a basis for invention, and hence for the development of new products, services, technologies, and markets. It was a resource the possession of which could make a worker more valuable economically. As the people of the United States increased in number and in diversity of background and interest and as the social geography of the country became denser, with more and more crowded cities, and more interconnections between cities, management acquired a major significance. Professions began to manage the delivery of human services through varied and complex processes of education and licensure. Governmental agencies began to manage conflict through the regulation of commercial activities in which private interests in profit were often at odds with public interests in health, safety, and the conservation of scarce resources, or in the protection of civil rights. Universities and research bureaus of an ever increasing number and variety, many financed by private foundations like the Carnegie Corporation, as well as by public foundations like the National Science Foundation and public agencies like the Department of Agriculture, began to manage the development and diffusion of knowledge through the award or denial of support for research, dissemination, and training activities. Management, no less than the production of goods and services, required knowledge: both specialized, expert knowledge to guide and justify the forecasts ventured, the choices made, and the policies established and revised, and popular intelligence to facilitate active participation in management on one end of the spectrum, or passive acquiescence on the other.

With the principal economic, demographic, geographic, and social trends affecting the United States throughout the century combining to move knowledge to an increasingly critical place in public life, the emergence of a distinct politics of knowledge is not at all surprising. This politics involved (and still involves) three large questions. The first had to do with which fields of knowledge and which approaches within different fields would become more or less authoritative and therefore closely associated with the expertise considered relevant to policy-making. Leaving aside the large secular trends that resulted in greater authority for knowledge gained through experimental science and less authority for either the revealed insights of religion or the common-sense perceptions of experience, questions of what knowledge would influence policy were essentially questions of whose approach would gain priority—which groups would become the key knowledge-producing elites, those most able to exercise significant influence on decisions about public problems.

A second set of questions central to the politics of knowledge involved issues about how experts would communicate with nonexperts. These were questions of who could and should govern, in general and within the separate domains of public concern. Should those governing be immediately responsible managers, that is, members of the elites, or everyone affected by public policies? Obviously, these matters concerned enfranchisement and participation in public affairs, and as such they had vital political consequences. It is always useful to recall that for the Greeks the opposite of a "citizen" was an "idiot," one who did not have a place in the polis. Decisions about access to knowledge concerned the role of citizens who could make informed judgments about public matters, about how decisions would be made and by whom, with implications for the distribution of power and knowledge.

Finally, there was the question of who could and would gain entrance to the knowledge-producing elites that emerged and proliferated as the United States became a more nationally and bureaucratically organized society. To a large extent, these elites were related to professions. The professions and knowledge elites developed simultaneously. Access to knowledge-producing elites often came through access to one of the professions, which in turn was granted by access to educational credentials. Educational credentials were not, however, sufficient. Rather, personal acquaintance, professional colleagueship, styles of research, political views, even manners, and other presumed measures of merit determined access. Such access was often limited to those already considered potential elites, and hence many were excluded on the basis of race, gender, ethnicity, or social class.

Chartered to advance and diffuse knowledge and understanding, the Carnegie Corporation was quickly caught up in all these questions and, through them, in the shaping of public policies. As for other large foundations, the politics of knowledge was, for the Corporation, a vehicle for influence. The resources the Corporation could command were vast: at the time it was established with an endowment of roughly

$125 million, the Corporation was reputed to be the largest philanthropic trust in the world. But within a society where a politics of knowledge was emerging and intensifying, a foundation so chartered could exercise power beyond that inherent in its extraordinary wealth. The Corporation's self-imposed mandate to define, develop, and distribute knowledge was, in a sense, a franchise to govern, in important indirect ways.

To hold a franchise, however, is not necessarily to exercise it. It was the interests, knowledge, circles of acquaintance, and personalities of the Corporation's trustees, officers, and staff that determined how and to what extent its potential was realized. The Corporation's influence on public policy waxed and waned and even, to some extent, altered in direction with changes in personnel and with the experience, acquaintance, and professional and personal styles that individuals brought to it. Circumstances outside the Corporation as well as luck necessarily influenced what was attempted, and the sometimes conflicting or even contradictory results. In looking at the first seventy-odd years of the Corporation's history, one finds four different periods. These periods provide the framework of this book.

The first period, treated in chapter 1, spanned the eight years from 1911 to 1919, when Andrew Carnegie was president of the foundation. The special character of this period derived from Carnegie's unshakable belief in a liberalism of the late nineteenth-century British variety and from his broad approach to grant-making, an approach entirely consistent with nineteenth-century conceptions of distributive rather than regulatory policy-making. His gifts to build libraries, purchase pipe organs, and otherwise increase opportunities for the release and development of individual talent, kept the Corporation from aligning itself with the more scientific assumptions that were coming to dominate effective social initiatives. In consequence, the full extent of the Corporation's potential to influence public policy was obscured during these early years.

Soon after Carnegie's death, all this changed. The heretofore restrained ambitions of the Corporation's two most interested, active, and effective trustees, Elihu Root and Henry Smith Pritchett, began to guide internal operations. Root and Pritchett were convinced of the nation's need to increase scientific management under private, voluntary auspices. Both could be described as progressive conservatives.[1] They hoped to foster moderate reform in order to ensure traditional American values and liberties. They expected science to inform such efforts. In collaboration with James R. Angell, president of the Corporation for one year (1920–21) before moving on to the presidency of Yale, Root and Pritchett reorganized the Corporation to foster this goal. As the Corporation itself sought to become a center of scientific expertise—that is, of "scientific philanthropy"—large institution-building grants, intended to establish centers of public policy expertise, became the order of the day. During this brief but important period in the Corporation's history, 1919 to 1923, decisive intervention in contests between groups that were attempting to develop and apply knowledge to public matters was characteristic of Corporation grant-making. This occurred in the natural sciences, in economics, and in the common law, each of which is the subject of a chapter in Part I, on "Scientific Philanthropy."

The third period, which spanned the years from 1923 to 1942, was in some ways like the first period. The Corporation was again dominated by a single individual, Frederick Paul Keppel, a genial and energetic man of unswerving integrity and character, of wide personal acquaintance and eclectic interests. Grant-making during his long presidency was, at least technically, organized into programs, although it was actually directed more by hunch, coincidence, opportunity, friendship, and a wish to help than by clear, specific, consistently applied "scientific" goals or principles. As in the early years, too, awards tended to be modest, usually most significant at the local rather than the national level, and relatively diverse in range of recipients.

The Keppel years did manifest a consistent concern, however—a concern to find ways to disseminate traditionally elite culture to a larger number of people. Great books, classical styles in the fine arts, and the habits and sensibilities associated with them, were seen as essential to character and to taste, especially as culture became more susceptible to commercial standards and interests. Although they were certain of the benefit to be derived for most citizens from acquaintance with great works and traditions of Western civilizations, the Corporation's trustees were nonetheless not certain of their relevance to the education of blacks. Gunnar Myrdal's *An American Dilemma* is best known for its clear discussion of the isolation of blacks within American society and for its influence on public policy. But it was initiated with questions in mind about the education of blacks and about appropriate similarities and differences between the education of blacks and whites. Thus it derived from the same concern with "cultural philanthropy" that ran through all Carnegie Corporation grant-making during that era.

In the years between the Second World War and the early 1980s, the unifying theme of Corporation policy was an emphasis on "strategy," on finding maximally effective means to achieve agreed-upon ends. This emphasis was a result of three influences. First and most important was the perception that the issues facing American society were critical in ways public issues had never been before. Whether it was the threat of nuclear Armageddon, of Soviet expansionism, or of persistent domestic inequality, a sense of peril pervaded these years. Second, Corporation grant-making was predicated upon the realization that the foundation's capacity to influence public policy had declined, at least in relative terms. After the Second World War, the Corporation operated within a domain that included new public agencies like the National Science Foundation, new and larger private organizations like the Ford Foundation, and, generally, a growing number of philanthropic foundations. Finally, the "strategic philanthropy" of this period resulted from a growth in staff and collaborative staff planning that marked the presidencies of Devereux C. Josephs, Charles Dollard, John W. Gardner, and Alan Pifer. In combination, these influences produced an aspiration to public influence and a style of operation that resembled the 1919–23 period. Yet there were also important differences. Significantly, a sure faith in progress through science had been replaced by a less confident, more cynical, if still determined, optimism. There was also a greater realization of the limitations involved in relying exclusively upon education as a means of pursuing liberal goals. Comparisons aside, carefully thought-through, articulated, and criticized rationales for action were now in evidence, as the Corporation sought to foster more useful knowledge for foreign policy, greater excellence in education, and more equal access to the rights, responsibilities, and privileges of American life.

If the potential for public influence of the Corporation's wealth and purpose, heightened by a milieu congenial to a politics of knowledge, was fulfilled so differently at different periods, two constant themes nevertheless ran throughout the Corporation's history. The first was a commitment to liberalism, and the second, a tendency to reflect and supplement, by its own activities, changing federal policies and administrative styles.

Newton D. Baker, the prominent lawyer and secretary of war under Woodrow Wilson who served as a Carnegie Corporation trustee from 1931 to 1937, once defined liberalism as "a sure feeling that things get better in this world rather than worse and have their best chance of improvement when they rest for approval upon the informed conscience of the common man."[2] This belief was consistently evident at the Carnegie Corporation, from the earliest days when Carnegie's buoyant optimism—"all is well, since all grows better"[3]—still reigned, into the 1980s, when Alan Pifer, while expressing "considerable sadness" about a "short-sighted and uncharitable spirit [that] seems to be abroad in the land," affirmed his hope that a society that was "humane, caring, and provident in developing the talents of all its people" was still possible.[4] That hope for a better future has been a consistent thread through all Corporation undertakings for more than seventy years.

The Corporation's commitment to liberalism was also manifest in constellations of values sustained through time. First, there was a belief in the individual's efficacy and in the need for freedom to strive, to improve oneself, and to advance through education; second, a recognition that liberty without equality, at least in the sense of equal opportunity, would result in an unstable and oppressive social situation in which liberty itself would be insecure; and third, a conviction that individualism, liberty, and equal opportunity could best be preserved and advanced in a society where voluntary action and a consensus about national direction would preclude a monopoly of power under the auspices of official agencies of government. However these constellations of values changed in details as they were built into changing grants and programs, they remained, in their essential forms, the touchstone for all the Corporation stood for, supported, and did.

If an allegiance to liberalism was the first constant theme in the Corporation's history, the second was a tendency to support government policies. Indeed, each period of the Corporation's history demonstrated resonances between foundation and government concerns, activities, and style. From 1919 to 1923, the era of "scientific philanthropy," the concerns about efficiency, organization, and prosperity so dominant within the Carnegie offices were not unlike the concerns that led Herbert Hoover to favor an "associative state" system of government. And if the Keppel years were marked by a relatively informal, pragmatic, ad hoc style of operation, that orientation resembled that of FDR and the New Deal in the 1930s. Finally, if "strategic philanthropy" was the leitmotif of the post-Second-World-War period, so strategic action was also seen as a necessity of public policy-making in the tense atmosphere of the Cold War, urban riots and the civil rights movement, and, later, the Vietnam years.

Beyond these resonances across lines dividing private and public agencies interested in public policy, the Corporation's policymakers sometimes assisted government policymakers in realizing a program or plan. They provided funds for presidential projects like Hoover's

Committee on Recent Economic Trends, and supported the personal or political interests of a particular president, as in the case of the proposal of the Carnegie Commission on Educational Television for the establishment of a Corporation for Public Broadcasting, which meshed well with Lyndon B. Johnson's long interest in (and ownership of) educational radio stations. They even offered national leadership in public policy arenas outside the boundaries of federal authority, such as the leadership provided by James Bryant Conant, with Corporation support, to reform the nation's public schools, in the late 1950s and early 1960s, a time when federal leadership in education was still neither expected nor acceptable.

Relationships between the Carnegie Corporation and federal officials and policies have not been one way, of course. The federal government often invited the Corporation to participate in policy-making or implemented the recommendations of Carnegie-supported groups. What is more, in any number of situations, although there was no direct communication or even awareness of a supportive, reciprocal relationship, a reciprocity resulted from a shared climate of opinion on social conditions, public problems, and ameliorative actions. The Corporation has also helped and been helped by many private groups and agencies active in public policy-making.

Always an advocate of liberalism, and often both directly and, via the politics of knowledge, indirectly a participant in the making of public policy, the Carnegie Corporation has reflected and illuminated certain crucial American dilemmas of the twentieth century. For example, in fostering high levels of specialized knowledge, the Corporation has also at times failed to encourage, and indeed has discouraged, the participation of a wider public in matters of public policy. The dilemmas associated with this tension are evident throughout the Corporation's history, as are others associated with other tensions: between excellence and equality in and through schooling; between the missions of an educational or cultural institution and the realities of that institution's need for clienteles and for a market; and even between the politics of knowledge and democracy. These tensions and dilemmas are central to the story told in this book.

Although many of the major grants and activities of the Carnegie Corporation are discussed here, many others are not. This had to be, given the extent of the Corporation's undertakings. More important, careful selectivity was needed if the Corporation's history was to serve as a lens through which to examine the larger questions that have made foundations politically significant and, to some extent, also politically problematic. And since these larger questions have to do, I believe, with the politics of knowledge and the consequences of foundation involvement in this politics, the book deals primarily with the sorts of awards that best illuminate that politics and those consequences, usually those large grants or sets of grants that have had relatively clear, and often quite decisive, effects.

This approach has inevitable limitations. For example, it focuses on the Corporation's domestic programs, even though the Corporation has also made important awards to Canada, the United Kingdom, and the countries that were British colonies at the time of Andrew Carnegie's death. Although vitally important to developments in countries abroad, to the transfer overseas of American patterns of social organization, and to international politics, these grants to British Commonwealth nations tended to be extensions of the Corporation's domestic grant-making and of the politics of knowledge within the United States, and thus, for my purposes, not identifiably different from the domestic grants I have chosen to treat. Curiously, too, there has been more writing by others on the international dimensions of philanthropy than there has been on the domestic dimensions—a point I shall discuss at somewhat greater length in the bibliographic essay.

Being interested in the politics of knowledge, I have dealt with a relatively few outstanding grants, so as to recreate contests among groups and to grasp both the alternatives taken and those not taken. This has made the book a work of "high" history, by which I mean history that features the atypically influential and the publicly prominent. Whether one could write a history of foundation philanthropy from the bottom up, so to speak, and what that would be like, is a question worth exploring. That many people, including that half of humankind that is female, do not appear prominently in this book will be readily apparent, and I shall discuss that problem directly at the end. Still, since the politics of knowledge is a rather "high" politics in which most people do not participate, such an elite focus makes sense.

CHAPTER ONE

Liberal Commitments

ANDREW CARNEGIE WAS seventy-six years old and weary of philanthropy by the time he established the Carnegie Corporation of New York in 1911. Giving away the millions he had accumulated in the extraordinary career that had taken him from a job as a bobbin boy in a cotton factory to the principal owner of the largest steel company in the world, had proven far more difficult than he had anticipated in 1889, when he had published his famous essay, "The Gospel of Wealth." Indeed, after giving away $180 million, he still had almost that much remaining and was now in danger of failing in his pledge to divest before death. Encouraged by his wife, Louise Whitfield Carnegie, and by his lawyer, Elihu Root, he therefore decided to transfer most of his remaining funds to a foundation. He hoped that in doing so he could continue personally to supervise the distribution of his fortune as long as he was able, and still die assured that his millions were no longer his own.

Carnegie expressed great relief after the papers establishing the Corporation were drawn. "Now it is all settled," he wrote to a friend. "We are off for Florida."[1] But of course it was not all settled. In creating the Carnegie Corporation and endowing it with $125 million (to which $10,336,867 was added after his death), Carnegie had established what has been described as "the greatest endowment ever given to a group of men for the promotion and diffusion of knowledge and understanding amongst the people of a nation."[2] He had suggested that the income from this endowment be used to aid "technical schools, institutions of higher learning, libraries, scientific research, hero funds, [and] useful publications." But, recognizing (in the simplified style of spelling that he favored) that "conditions upon the erth inevitably change," he had also given the Corporation's trustees the freedom to change policies as they thought wise and prudent.[3] Exercising this freedom, the trustees involved the Corporation in a politics the founder himself had not envisioned: the politics of knowledge.

From Politics to Philanthropy

The beginnings of the unprecedented campaign of benevolence that led to the creation of the Carnegie Corporation date from December 1868, when Carnegie, sitting alone and reflecting upon his life, wrote a private memorandum setting forth his intentions for the future:

Thirty three and an income of 50,000$ per annum. By this time two years I can so arrange all my business as to secure at least 50,000 per annum. Beyond this never earn—make no effort to increase fortune, but spend the surplus each year for benovelent [sic] purposes. Cast aside business forever except for others.

Settle in Oxford & get a thorough education making the acquaintance of literary men—this will take three years active work—pay especial attention to speaking in public.

Settle then in London & purchase a controlling interest in some newspaper or live review & give the general management of it attention, taking part in public matters especially those connected with education and improvement of the poorer classes.

Man must have an idol—The amassing of wealth is one of the worst species of idolitary [sic]. No idol more debasing than the worship of money. Whatever I engage in I must push inordinately therefor should I be careful to choose that life which will be the most elevating in its character. To continue much longer overwhelmed by business cares and with most of my thoughts wholly upon the way to make money in shortest time, must degrade me beyond hope of permanent recovery.

I will resign business at Thirty five, but during the ensuing two years, I will spend the afternoons in securing instruction, and in reading systematically.[4]

This memorandum was a vital document to Carnegie. Even as a relatively young man, he was a person of considerable complexity and many contradictions. Both Puritan and Yankee, he was worried that he would be tainted by the money he had worked so hard to earn, and he was urgently seeking salvation. Yet at the same time his worldly ambitions were compelling; business engrossed him, and he relished and thrived on the entrepreneurial quest he was now promising to renounce. Curious, eager, energetic, and intense, Carnegie would not retire from business for another thirty-three years. Long before that, however, he did, as promised, concern himself with the "education & improvement of the poorer classes." Above all else other than business ventures and, later in life, international peace, the cause of education of the poor seems to have stirred the imagination of this pugnacious but idealistic and peace-loving man.

Carnegie believed that—unlike the United States, a land of un-bounded promise that had given him opportunity, wealth, and happi-ness in abundance—Great Britain was a declining society, bogged down in authoritarian traditions, unequal and unfair privileges, and social-class constraints. Hence it was to Great Britain that he turned first in his effort to instruct the poorer classes. Needless to say, it was convenient for an American industrialist, bent on containing costs and wages in his own works, to promote reform on the other side of the Atlantic. But his actions sprang more from enthusiasm than from self-interested calculation. What he described as "the BELOVED REPUB-LIC under whose laws I am made the peer of any man, although denied political equality by my native land," was, he believed, an inspiring model of progress Great Britain would do well to follow.[5]

To encourage English workers to agitate for change, Carnegie in the early 1880s bought a number of half-penny daily and weekly newspapers, creating a syndicate in the most densely populated and industrialized sections of the country. The syndicate supported the parliamentary program of William Gladstone's Liberal government, but went far beyond that to advocate the abolition of the monarchy, the House of Lords, and the Church of England. The positions it took were sometimes an embarrassment to Gladstone and to Carnegie's many other friends in the Liberal Party; because he was not a British subject, they were especially open to criticism. But this proud and convinced descendant of Scottish Radicals and Chartists explained himself with forceful conviction. He once told a critic: "Holding these opinions I should not have been honest had I not admitted that I would destroy, if I had the power, every vestige of privilege in England, and give to every man equal and exact privileges; but at the same time I would not shed a drop of blood, nor violate a law, nor use violence in any form, to bring about what I so much desire. It is not necessary to do so. It will all come in good time, and come the more quickly and the more surely from the gradual spread of education, and by peaceable discussion, than by any other means. . . . The weapon of Republicanism is not the sword, but the pen."[6] His belief in equal rights for all men and in political reform through "the gradual spread of education" was abundantly clear. Nor did these convictions lessen when, following the defeat of Gladstone's third ministry in 1886, Carnegie became disillusioned with direct, political journalism of the polemical kind. Partly to limit his own financial losses, he sold the newspaper syndicate he had built. Soon thereafter he told W. T. Stead, editor of the *Review of Reviews*, that "the same money paid in advertising our views in the ordinary periodicals would, in my opinion, have a much greater effect."[7]

Whether Carnegie's foray into British politics would have been more satisfying if he had stood for Parliament as an advanced Liberal (which, despite problems of citizenship, he did in fact contemplate) is impossible to know. But it is certain that, still committed to liberal ideals, he shifted strategies after 1886. He turned, first, from political journalism to lengthier writing for general audiences. *Triumphant Democracy*, a boastful description of the United States, characterized by his biographer Joseph Wall as "a Fourth of July oration with statistical tables," appeared in that year.[8] "The Gospel of Wealth" was published three years later in the *North American Review*. In all, when collected after his death, Carnegie's writings filled eleven volumes.

The "star-spangled Scotchman," as he was often called, also turned increasingly to the distribution of his "surplus." Hoping to build institutions to foster the "education & improvement of the poorer classes," his goal, as described in "The Gospel of Wealth," was to create the "ladders upon which the aspiring can rise."[9]

His essay began by an insistence that a man of great wealth has an obligation to act as steward for his less fortunate brethren. He must regard all his funds, save those necessary for modest and unostentatious living and for the needs of his dependents, "as trust funds" that, given the exceptional talent that had made him rich, he was "called upon to administer in the manner which, in his judgment, is best calculated to produce the most beneficial results for the community." That calculation would require that he avoid "indiscriminate charity" to "the slothful, the drunken, the unworthy," and instead "provide part of the means by which those who desire to improve may do so." Intended to address the problems of community associated with industrialism, the essay dealt with the need to maintain the freedom of action and accumulation that in Carnegie's opinion inspired talent, hard work, and progress. It also dealt with the need to ensure that the "rigid castes [which] are formed" would not block efforts at individual betterment. The essay made clear Carnegie's wish to justify his own plutocratic life, but it also reflected the classical liberal values in which he sincerely believed, among them the necessity for equal opportunities for all, protection of the individual's right to exercise initiative, and the promotion of popular enlightenment as a means to social reform. "The Gospel of Wealth" provided a rationale for the divestment he would now undertake on a large scale.[10]

Providing funds to build libraries became the first and best-known of Carnegie's many philanthropic projects. It fit logically within the guidelines he had developed in his creed. Actually, he had already begun to build libraries. In 1881, he had built one for the town of Dunfermline in Scotland, where he had been born in 1835. His mother, whom he adored and called "the Queen Dowager," had laid the library's cornerstone. He saw something of "the fairy tale" in this. She "had left her native town, poor, thirty odd years before, with her loved ones, to found a new home in the great Republic and was to-day returning in her coach, to be allowed the privilege of linking her name with the annals of her beloved native town in one of the most enduring forms possible."[11] Philanthropy, he was discovering, could be heady stuff.

In the same year "The Gospel of Wealth" appeared, Carnegie donated $481,012 to build a library in Allegheny, Pennsylvania, the town to which his family had moved from Dunfermline in 1848. Once again, his satisfaction was great. He wrote to his wife on September 26, 1889: "Yesterday I strolled out with Henry Phipps and walked over to see the Library in Allegheny. If ever there was a sight that makes my eyes glisten it was this gem. A kind of domestic Taj. Its tower a pretty clock, so musical in tone too, for it kindly welcomed me as I stood feeling— 'Yes, life is worth living when we can call forth such works as this!' I saw many people standing gazing and praising and the big words Carnegie Free Library just took me into the sweetest reverie and I found myself wishing you were at my side to reap with me the highest reward we can ever receive on earth, the voice of one's inner self, saying secretly, well done!"[12] In a sense, libraries had been one of the "ladders" upon which Carnegie had risen; he hoped they would do for others what they had done for him.

Carnegie had read widely in libraries as a youth. He found in them both pleasure and an education in works he had never before read— Shakespeare, Burns, Macaulay, and many others. He took pride in telling people that his father and other poor Dunfermline weavers had pooled their scarce resources to purchase books from which one of their number read aloud as they worked. That his father, who had died a broken man in a foreign country without marketable skills or vocation, had been a founder of the town's first circulating library was important to him. As a young man in Pittsburgh, Carnegie frequently borrowed books from the private library of a Colonel James Anderson. Later the library was transformed into a "mechanics and Apprentices' Library" and, since he was neither mechanic nor apprentice, he was required to pay a $2.00 fee. He wrote outraged letters of protest to the Pittsburgh *Dispatch*, and the rules were changed: all working boys now were granted free privileges. As Joseph Wall noted in his biography of Carnegie, "nothing else that he had known in the way of recognition by others had been quite as exhilarating as this experience."[13] So it was hardly surprising that he should have made libraries a principal object of his benevolence. He hoped, in vintage liberal fashion, that they would help "make men not violent revolutionists, but cautious evolutionists; not destroyers, but careful improvers." He provided more than $56 million over the years to build 2,509 libraries in the United States, Canada, Great Britain, Ireland, and other British Commonwealth countries like Australia, New Zealand, and South Africa.[14]

Administered by James Bertram, his Scottish secretary, Carnegie's library-giving quickly fell into a routine. Communities requesting funds received a "Schedule of Questions" to determine the town's population, whether it already had a library and, if so, what kind (Carnegie did not want his buildings to house private subscription libraries), and whether the community could meet Carnegie's two major grant requirements: a town-owned building site and a willingness to pledge annual maintenance funds, to be raised through taxation, equivalent to 10 percent of the sum Carnegie would donate, which was usually calculated at the rate of $2.00 per inhabitant. After 1908, standard architectural plans were distributed, since Bertram had become convinced that libraries in "Carnegie Classic" style would be more aesthetically pleasing, and also would minimize earlier problems of building function and cost. Once a grant was approved, a simple letter such as this one to F. S. Thompson, president of the public library in Albion, Nebraska, was dispatched:

Dear Sir,
    Responding to your communication on behalf of Albion,—If the City agree by resolution of Council to maintain a Free Public Library at a cost of not less than Six Hundred Dollars a year, and provides a suitable site for the building, Mr. Carnegie will be glad to give Six Thousand dollars to erect a Free Public Building for Albion.
    Respectfully yours
    [James Bertram]
    P[ersonal] Secretary[15]

When construction began, Carnegie's treasurer, Robert Franks, began to make small, intermittent payments on the grant to meet immediate costs. That was it, except for one last, small, significant detail: Carnegie requested "that there should be placed over the entrance to the Libraries I build a representation of the rays of a rising sun, and above 'LET THERE BE LIGHT.'"[16]

Sweetness and Light

Fond of mottoes like the Biblical injunction "Let there be light," Carnegie also associated his library gifts with the phrase "Sweetness and Light." This was the title of the first chapter of *Culture and Anarchy* by Matthew Arnold, the British liberal essayist and poet. Introduced to Arnold at a London dinner party in June 1883, Carnegie had found him "the most charming man" he had ever met.[17] *Culture and Anarchy*, which was published in 1869, one year after Carnegie wrote his private memorandum of benevolent intent, had helped him as he considered what to do about his enormous wealth.

To Arnold, culture was "a pursuit of our total perfection by means of getting to know, on all matters which most concern us, the best which has been thought and said in the world."[18] Thus conceived, culture was a pursuit to which Carnegie was certainly dedicated, as seen in his wish of 1868 "to get a thorough education." Arnold argued further that "the men of culture" were "the true apostles of equality."[19] That was precisely what Carnegie wanted to be. Finally, Arnold said that "the great men of culture are those who have had a passion for diffusion, for making prevail, for carrying from one end of society to the other, the best knowledge, the best ideas of their time; who have laboured to divest knowledge of all that was harsh, uncouth, difficult, abstract, professional, exclusive; to humanise it, to make it efficient outside the clique of the cultivated and learned, yet still remaining the *best* knowledge and thought of the time, and a true source, therefore, of sweetness and light."[20]

It was somewhat ironic that Carnegie should have been inspired by Arnold. Carnegie approved of utilitarian plans of education, whereas Arnold did not. Carnegie thought education should be purposefully designed to prepare students for the everyday social and vocational occupations of their communities; Arnold thought education should enable people to transcend, stand above, and criticize the humdrum, "philistine" daily pursuits of their neighbors as a result of exposure to "the best which has been thought and said."[21]

Carnegie greatly admired Ezra Cornell, the founder of Cornell University in Ithaca, New York—he so admired the man, in fact, that he placed Cornell's widow on his private pension list and described the university Cornell had founded in 1868 as "the university of triumphant democracy."[22] It was linked to the common school system, Carnegie explained, and allowed students to choose their studies; it did not require religious tests of its faculty members and it admitted women, a wise step, he thought, since their learning would improve the conduct of men. Arnold, who was highly disdainful of the United States, which he visited as Carnegie's guest in 1883, saw the university as "a really noble monument" to Cornell's "munificence," but he believed that "it seems to rest on a misconception of what culture truly is, and to be calculated to produce miners, engineers, or architects, not sweetness and light."[23] Eager to be conversant with liberal intellectuals like Arnold and willing to be selective in his borrowing, Carnegie was not troubled by divergences of view such as these, although they may have been more fundamental than he recognized. He was better able to shift his liberal commitment from politics to philanthropy after reading Arnold. First through "library-planting," and then through other schemes, he dedicated himself as a philanthropist to "the advancement and diffusion of knowledge and understanding."

Straightforward and efficient, Carnegie's library-planting was increasingly combined with other kinds of giving. Believing that music was a source of "Sweetness and Light" and, more particularly, that "the organ is one of the most elevating voices," he gave approximately $6.25 million for 7,600 or more organs for small churches like the Swedenborgian chapel his father attended after the Carnegie family emigrated.[24] At odds with the increasingly common belief that schooling was the only means to an education, Carnegie was nevertheless concerned to promote access to schooling, especially for those who had previously been deprived of the privilege. Contrary to Arnold, he hoped to encourage more practical and useful programs of study, and he took pleasure in giving to institutions like Cooper Union and the Stevens Institute of Technology. The education of blacks particularly interested him. Recalling his first encounter with the South, he said: "Preconceived ideas of liberty and equality, ending in the sublime privilege of the suffrage, were rudely shaken, and I was forced to see that it was not enough to say that 'a slave cannot live in the Republic; he breathes our air, his shackles fall.' That necessary act performed, the task does not end; it only begins. We have destroyed one bad system, but constructive work is needed."[25] Viewing Booker T. Washington as "the combined Moses and Joshua of his people," and convinced that Hampton Institute and Tuskegee Institute were leading the "constructive work" now required, Carnegie gave generously to both.[26] In all, his gifts to colleges, universities, and schools (not including the funds given to the Carnegie Foundation for the Advancement of Teaching) came to between $15 and $20 million.[27]

In 1901, Carnegie finally retired from business, selling his steel interests to J. P. Morgan for $480 million, of which more than $225 million was profit. That year, while continuing his other kinds of giving, he began also to establish the various perpetual trusts that bear his name. Sometimes portrayed as an important departure from his previous philanthropy, these gifts were actually continuous with it, representing to Carnegie a large-scale and perpetual capitalization of what had been his smaller, more tentative, experimental undertakings.[28] Among the trusts created were the Carnegie Trust for the Universities of Scotland, a scholarship fund; the Carnegie Institution of Washington, a scientific research center; the Carnegie Foundation for the Advancement of Teaching, a professional pension fund that also conducted educational studies, and that in 1917 organized the Teachers Insurance and Annuity Association; and the Carnegie Endowment for International Peace, intended to "hasten the abolition of international war . . . [and thereafter to] consider what is the next most degrading remaining evil or evils whose banishment—or what new elevating element or elements if introduced or fosterd, or both combined— would most advance the progress, elevation and happiness of man, and so on from century to century without end."[29]

"Sweetness and Light." So long as the project might inspire, inspirit, ennoble, instruct, foster equality, or promote international peace, Carnegie was likely to support it. Indeed, within the broad guidelines that bounded his giving, he financed anything and everything he could think of. He created "Hero Funds" in the United States and Great Britain, hoping that rewards to those who had been injured, or to relatives of those who had been killed, while performing noble, daring deeds, would stimulate courage in others and promote peace rather than war. He supported the Simplified Spelling Board, hoping that the streamlining of words like "altho," "pedagog," "demagog," "thru," "erth," and "thoro" would enhance communication, especially across national boundaries, thereby promoting the international understanding necessary for peace. He built "palaces to peace"—the Pan American Union Building in Washington, D.C.; the Central American Court of Justice in San José, Costa Rica; the International Court of Justice at The Hague—hoping that these forums for friendship and discussion would lessen the strife that led to war. He even wished to give pensions to ex-presidents of the United States. His friend Lord Bryce had observed in *The American Commonwealth* (1888) that the best men did not run for public office; Carnegie doubtless hoped that, as with pensions for professors, pensions for former presidents might reward and exemplify the nobility of selfless public service. That such an action undertaken by a private citizen was inappropriate did not occur to him. "'The way of the Philanthropist is hard,'" he once told Harvard's president, Charles W. Eliot, "but I don't do anything for popularity . . . just please my sel' [*sic*] do what I think is useful."[30] Carnegie's philanthropy was carried out with a buoyant optimism that sprang from confidence, determination and a sense of humor. It also was influenced by the insights he gleaned from his brief and disappointing earlier foray into British politics, when his newspaper syndicate's advocacy embarrassed the Gladstone government.

In search of new ideas, Carnegie wrote to his friends asking how they thought $10 million could be spent, adding with characteristic ebullience, "P.S. Prize for the best!"[31] Much sought after by the public and the press, he talked gleefully to reporters, posed for photographs, and attended innumerable luncheons and dinners in his honor; gave speeches and sent greetings to library committees all over the United States; and in Great Britain accepted the "Freedom of the City" whenever it was offered. The publicity caused him to be spoofed and criticized as often as he was praised. Cartoonists drew him in tartans leaving the golf links to plant yet another library in yet another town.[32] Finley Peter Dunne's Mr. Dooley ordered, "Come on, Andhrew, an' paint ye'er illusthrees name on me."[33] And one commentator declared he "would have given millions to Greece had she labelled the Parthenon Carnegopolis."[34] But Carnegie ignored the critics, trying to listen only to those who praised his endeavors. He saved letters of praise and thanks in a special desk drawer labeled "Gratitude and sweet words."[35]

The fanfare and notice, which he called "the Hallelejuh business," was to Carnegie a form of useful "advertising."[36] When he had explained his retreat from direct political advocacy to W. T. Stead, the British editor, in 1886, he set forth his belief that general statements of general principles would serve the liberal cause more effectively than propaganda; this was what he was offering as he traveled the countryside giving speeches and making toasts. His boastfulness, humor, and vanity may have given his philanthropy something of "a Peter Pan quality," but to Carnegie himself it was a crucial quest.[37] It marked penance for "idolatry" and progress toward a world of reason, beauty, prosperity, and peace.

The Administration of the Carnegie Corporation

"Our nation faces sharp, pressing, insistent questions concerning which the people stand in urgent need of knowledge and understanding," Henry Pritchett, president of the Carnegie Foundation for the Advancement of Teaching, wrote in 1916. "It seems clearly the duty of the Trustees [of the Carnegie Corporation] to inquire if there are means by which this Trust may come to closer grip with these questions than through the giving of library buildings and church organs."[38] Pritchett, who believed Carnegie's philanthropic practices were often wasteful, launched a campaign for change.

A scientist and former president of MIT, Pritchett had a keen intuition for new trends and developments and an almost Machiavellian sense of politics. Tall and rather sternly handsome, he was as different from the short, elfin philanthropist in appearance as in personality. In contrast to Carnegie's sense of humor, Pritchett offered an earnest and self-righteous sense of honor. He professed earnestly that whatever he believed was "true" and "sincere." In contrast to the older man's spontaneity, he offered careful forethought, even calculation. He was as precisely competent as Carnegie was impulsively imaginative.

Having won Carnegie's confidence through the assistance he had provided for the establishment of the Carnegie Foundation, Pritchett had been appointed president of that trust in 1905. He transformed an organization Carnegie had expected to be a single-purpose professorial pension fund into a pension fund that would also, in Pritchett's words, aspire to be "one of the Great Agencies ... in standardizing American education."[39] As president of the Carnegie Foundation for the Advancement of Teaching, created in 1911, he had gained a seat on the board of trustees of the Carnegie Corporation. This allowed him to press his belief that Carnegie's money should be used, not merely to develop and disseminate knowledge, but, more important, to organize it.

Pritchett said later, "When Mr. Carnegie formed the Carnegie Corporation, he simply incorporated himself."[40] Even Carnegie's authorized biographer, Burton J. Hendrick, described the Corporation as "Andrew Carnegie, Inc."[41] And no wonder. The Corporation was chartered by the state of New York to promote "the advancement and diffusion of knowledge and understanding."[42] The means designated as initial vehicles for this purpose—libraries, technical schools, hero funds, useful publications, and the like—were those that Carnegie had already relied upon. The Corporation's trustees were all, like Pritchett, close associates of Carnegie. Two, James Bertram and Robert Franks, were personal assistants; the remaining five held office in Carnegie's U.S. trusts. William N. Frew was president of the Carnegie Institute of Pittsburgh; Elihu Root was a trustee of the Carnegie Endowment for International Peace, as well as Carnegie's lawyer; Charles L. Taylor was president of the Carnegie Hero Fund of Pittsburgh; Robert S. Woodward was president of the Carnegie Institution of Washington; and Pritchett was, of course, chief executive of the Carnegie Foundation for the Advancement of Teaching. As intended, these arrangements ensured that there would be few modifications in priorities or procedures when the funds were placed under the authority of the Corporation's trustees.

As before, public libraries remained a major undertaking, and library bequests continued to entail few requirements. Assuming that places of culture were by definition places of "light," Carnegie tried to organize his library gifts so that as many people as possible could pursue an autonomously defined search for culture, for "perfection." With this in mind, he refused to stock libraries with books or to provide funds for maintenance. He hoped that these limitations would foster what he called "proprietorship." He once wrote: "I do not think that the community which is not willing to maintain a Library had better possess it. It is only the feeling that the Library belongs to every citizen richest and poorest alike, that gives it a soul, as it were. The Library Buildings which I am giving are the property of all members of the community which maintain them."[43] He wanted citizens to be "joint" proprietors. As he had told a crowd at the 1890 opening of his much-beloved Allegheny library, he wished

that the masses of working men and women, the wage earners . . . will remember and act upon the fact that this is their library. . . . The poorest man, the poorest woman, that toils from morn till night for a livelihood, as thank Heaven, I had that toil to do in my early days, as he walks this hall, as he reads the books from those alcoves . . . equally with the millionaire and the foremost citizen, I want him to exclaim in his heart, "Behold, all this is mine. I support it, and I am proud to support it. I am joint proprietor here."[44]

Naive and romantic, Carnegie's admonitions on proprietorship often fell on deaf ears. Indeed, some people resented his gifts. "Who told Mr. Carnegie that we were worthy objects of charity," a correspondent to the *Detroit Journal* asked in 1901 in a heated controversy over the wisdom of accepting a Carnegie library gift.[45] Others thought he should have "distributed his money among his employees while he was making it."[46] And labor leader Eugene V. Debs went so far as to urge refusal of Carnegie library grants, insisting to his fellow workers that there would be libraries "in glorious abundance when capitalism is abolished and working men are no longer robbed by the philanthropic pirates of the Carnegie class. Then the library will be as it should be, a noble temple dedicated to culture and symbolizing the virtues of the people."[47] In some instances, too, his grant stipulations were violated. Libraries were sometimes sparsely used and even then predominantly by the already more educated and affluent members of the community. Books were not always bought for a library, or if bought, not made generally available. Library buildings were frequently used for purposes other than culture, and annual maintenance pledges were sometimes not met and often not exceeded.

Unperturbed by criticism and by increasing stories of abuse, Carnegie left all problems to James Bertram to deal with as he chose. He never answered his public critics himself. He preferred to attend only to the happy letters, like the one he received from Charles H. Allyn of Corsicana, Texas, telling him that in the eight years since its construction, the Carnegie library there had increased its book stock from six hundred to nine thousand volumes and regularly employed one librarian and an assistant, who kept the building open from 10 a.m. until 9 p.m., to serve the 60 percent of the town's residents who had taken out library cards, and who withdrew thirty-five thousand books each month. "We have nothing to fear in our great Republic because of our Free School System and the Free Libraries," Carnegie replied to Mr. Allyn. "A reading people are of course an active people, full of new ideas and anxious to test them, which ensures peaceful development."[48] Apparently assuming that many people would not be able to rise to the challenge of culture, Carnegie was delighted when people like those in Corsicana, Texas, appeared to do so. But trying to find more active and possibly even coercive ways to prod other communities and more people to strive for perfection did not seem wise to him. To have acted this way might violate natural laws, he feared. He was a student of Herbert Spencer, albeit as selective in his borrowing from the English liberal philosopher of social Darwinism as he was in his borrowing from Matthew Arnold. When attempting to do good, Carnegie also feared doing harm and steadfastly refused to act in ways that might have been more interventionist. His famed insistence on avoiding charity was part of this, as was, for example, his unwillingness to stock or to supervise the libraries built with his funds.

If Henry Pritchett understood Carnegie's scruples, he certainly did not share them. And when Carnegie fell into a state of melancholy upon hearing the news of war in Europe in August 1914—"Men slaying each other like wild beasts!" he wrote; "I dare not relinquish all hope"—Pritchett was ready to enter the breach.[49] Because Pritchett worked in the Carnegie Foundation offices in New York City and lived near the Carnegies on East 92nd Street, he was better informed about daily Corporation operations than most of the other trustees. He was fully aware, therefore, of problems with library gifts that Carnegie insistently chose to ignore. If these problems were confirmed, there would be reason for the trustees to consider a change in Corporation patterns of giving. Pritchett was convinced of the wisdom of such a change. In an increasingly complex, densely populated, and industrialized society, there had to be ever greater specialization, he believed, and the men responsible for this, "the greatest endowment ever given to a group of men for the promotion and diffusion of knowledge and understanding amongst the people of a nation," must acknowledge as much in the awarding of funds. To go on building libraries routinely made no sense to him.

With this in mind, Pritchett got in touch with Alvin Johnson, a Cornell University professor of economics who was working part-time for the Carnegie Endowment for International Peace. (Johnson later became president of the New School for Social Research.) "What Pritchett wanted of me," Johnson recalled in his autobiography, "was ten weeks of my time, to go through the country on a sort of sampling tour, to take a look at the operations of as many libraries as I had time to visit. I thought a professional librarian could do a better job, but Pritchett didn't agree. What the corporation needed," Pritchett apparently told Johnson, "was not a comprehensive report but a series of impressions of libraries and their place in the community."[50] Pritchett, who had organized the Flexner Report, the influential 1910 Carnegie Foundation survey of medical education, may have been hoping to initiate a similar Corporation study of libraries. Because he did not seek formal trustee approval of the project until after the survey had been completed, it is difficult to know for certain, but the Flexner analogy seems plausible. Perhaps Pritchett hoped that Johnson could produce a study with the clarity, color, and muckraking outrage of the Flexner Report. At Cornell he had written a novel about academic life; he was also a regular contributor to the recently launched *New Republic*. Did Pritchett want a study to help establish the Corporation as an agent of standards? Certainly that was the role that the Carnegie Foundation had been able to assume after Flexner's medical bulletin appeared.[51]

Whether the Johnson report that survives is the report as Alvin

Johnson submitted it is not clear. The day after it was discussed by the trustees, Johnson called at the Corporation's offices to retrieve it, but was told by a secretary that "Mr. Bertram had it destroyed." The report that exists, a printed copy of which Johnson was finally given fifteen years later, was, he claimed, "edited somewhat."[52] The surviving version argued that "the only justification for investing philanthropic funds in the provision of library buildings is the prospect of efficient library service."[53] Better library service would help solve problems of financial support, since "more generous appropriations will follow upon more active service"; and adequate local support would ensure that the free public library would serve as "an essential part of a system of universal public education" thereby playing a significant part "in advancing popular intellectual progress."[54] For these reasons, the report concluded, "the character and spirit of library personnel" and the professional training of librarians, and not the essentially reactive and random building of libraries, should become primary Carnegie Corporation concerns.[55]

The Johnson survey caused a stir within the Corporation's boardroom, but never really went beyond. The study was presented at a trustees' meeting, where it was immediately challenged by James Bertram. Pritchett often referred to Bertram as one of "the clerks," but his vote was equal to Pritchett's and, at least in this instance, his argument was correct and for a time decisive. Were the study's recommendations accepted, he claimed, the Corporation would contravene Carnegie's clear and known wish "to give libraries to communities and [to] leave the communities absolutely free to manage them any way they might see fit."[56] The trustees apparently felt unable to take overt, positive action on the report, although Chairman Elihu Root quietly informed Johnson: "We are all for your report . . . except Bertram. . . . However, you will see, your recommendations will presently be in force."[57] And so they were. Using the emergency created by the nation's entrance into the First World War as the pretext, the Carnegie Corporation discontinued its grants for library buildings in 1917 and after the war did not renew them.

Obviously, the recommendations made in the Johnson report were continuous with earlier Carnegie library-giving, in that they were intended to foster "popular intellectual progress." Obviously too, however, they differed in two key assumptions: first, the assumption that the benefits to be derived from a library could be extended and enhanced if library use were properly guided; and second, the assumption that such guidance required professional personnel of appropriate "character," which in actuality, as would be revealed later, meant

career-oriented, highly trained men, as opposed to benevolently inclined, often moralistically motivated, "amateur" women. Carnegie
had hoped to distribute resources widely to provide opportunities for
talent to emerge, but Johnson advised the Corporation to concern itself
with expertise and with helping to organize the sets of institutions
and interpersonal relationships such expertise required. Carnegie was
convinced that a sense of proprietorship would encourage community
support for a library; Johnson, that professional service would best
serve that function. Johnson envisioned library readers becoming "clients" of the expert librarians they would hire, rather than, as in Carnegie's dream, "joint proprietors here."

The Johnson report was as representative of "progressive" thought
as Carnegie's speeches were of an earlier, laissez-faire liberalism. Carnegie and Bertram on the one hand, and Pritchett and Johnson on the
other, were caught up in a conflict evident in many different arenas as
the United States moved gradually, unevenly, and yet decisively into a
new era. The shift would likely have occurred in any case, but the
Johnson study pushed the Corporation to a critical juncture. It helped
move it out of alignment with a nineteenth-century conception of
policy-making and into alignment with a conception more widely held
in the twentieth century—from a belief in positive but loosely coupled
associations between the collective good or national destiny, the free
exercise of individual initiative, and the absence of a strong, central
executive power, to a belief in expert decision-making and leadership,
combined with the wide and deliberate transmission of expertise from
"the best men" to "the people." Within the domain of government, the
nineteenth-century view had fostered reliance upon ad hoc, essentially
distributive policies as a means of encouraging economic growth,
whereas the twentieth-century view would foster an increasing reliance
upon more purposive and planned legislative and administrative acts,
designed to coordinate and mediate among competing interests, claims,
and rights.

As the Johnson report suggested, the more regulatory conception
of the Corporation's functions raised a host of difficult and divisive
questions that earlier had been less germane. What knowledge and
skill should librarians possess to be considered professionals? Where
should they acquire this knowledge and skill? At what price? For
what return? According to whose standards? And to acquire which
credentials, if any? What was library service, and how, if at all, did it
relate to library "science"? How should librarians, as experts, serve
and instruct the public, their clients? Carnegie had believed that, since

all knowledge was good and all individuals differed, no one, not even he, should attempt to determine what knowledge would best serve different individuals and different purposes. Questions of this kind implicit in the Johnson study had not been explicit in the politics Carnegie had known. But after the Johnson report, questions like these would become central in the affairs of the foundation that served as his philanthropic heir. And it was, of course, the Corporation's involvement in questions of this kind that enmeshed it in the politics of knowledge.

I

Scientific Philanthropy

I F A L V I N J O H N S O N ' S survey of Carnegie libraries augured fundamental changes at the Carnegie Corporation, a 1919 grant of
$5 million to the National Academy of Sciences-National Research
Council (NAS-NRC) initiated the new era. In a narrow sense, the
grant was intended to provide the Academy and the Council with a
headquarters and an endowment. In a broader sense, it represented
Corporation support for a more elevated place for science and scientists
in national policy-making. It was the first of several large grants made
by the Corporation during the early 1920s to help establish research
institutes and research-coordinating councils that would be accessible
to the federal government but not controlled by it.

The Corporation's willingness, even eagerness, to capitalize private
organizations that could fulfill public policy functions was notable for
a variety of reasons. First, the Corporation's interest in developing
such institutions derived from a somewhat contradictory mix of attitudes that was widely held at this time. Within this, a concern for
increasing the capacity of different groups and localities in the United
States to act in concert was central, as was an equally urgent concern
for preserving a relatively limited sphere for governmental action. In a
sense, the hope was to increase the nation's capacity for *governance*
without enlarging the *government*. The development of fair, objective,
expert knowledge would enable all Americans voluntarily to coordinate and rationalize their actions. The ideal of an "associative state,"
in which leadership and the wide dissemination of information would

enable all people without coercion to do their part in promoting prosperity and stability, has been well described by many historians; this was the governing ideal within the Carnegie Corporation after the First World War.[1] Most of the Corporation's trustees were Republicans; most admired Herbert Hoover; and most shared Hoover's belief that scientific expertise and public education could advance the international interests of the United States, even against totalitarian societies, while safeguarding the nation's traditions of liberty and individualism.

Mobilized by these political sentiments—now considered conservative, but then rather forward-looking and "progressive"—the Carnegie Corporation's trustees were also guided in their grant decisions by an acknowledged wish to protect Anglo-Saxon prerogatives, customs, and genes. Most of the trustees believed, as did many of their social peers, that everything from intelligence to business initiative was transmitted over generations through biological inheritance. While endorsing the Carnegie Institution of Washington's financing of research in eugenics, they also favored the development of institutions that could preserve power for people of white, Anglo-Saxon, Protestant lineage. In a recent study of the history of "national administrative capacities," Stephen Skowronek has maintained that after 1900 "the central question in institutional development was . . . no longer a question of whether or not America was going to build a state that could support administrative power but of who was going to control administrative power in the new state that was to be built."[2] Carnegie Corporation actions indicate, not only that Skowronek's reading of the history is correct, but also that assumptions about race avowedly determined how some people, including the Corporation's trustees, answered this question. Racial thinking played a prominent part in the early years of Carnegie Corporation grant-making, thereby providing dismaying but significant evidence of the reinforcement "science" could and, in this case, did bring to the exclusionary sentiments of a relatively small, culturally based elite.

Stimulated by discernible ideals, values, prejudices, assumptions, and interests, the Corporation's investment in scientific research and coordinating institutions also reflected clear and related trustee preferences for specific individuals, groups, and disciplines—those that tended to be business-oriented, as well as dominated or backed by people of white, Anglo-Saxon, Protestant descent. Although grants were announced in terms of what they were positively intended to foster and encourage, in actuality they were often also authorized in opposition to one or several alternative views. The Corporation's willingness thus to intervene in contests between different individuals, groups, and views, and to do so in relation to vitally important public questions—the organization of science, the study of the economy, and the formulation of the common law—early made it an important force, more accurately a powerfully partisan force, in the politics of knowledge. But politics is a continuing process; and, however unusual the Corporation's power to capitalize institutions may have been, it could not fully control or forever forestall the claims and challenges of the alternatives it acted against. Ironically, in some of its early grants to research institutions, as in its grant-making throughout the century, agencies it helped establish or support often ended up providing vital assistance to people and views of which the Corporation's trustees and officers had not and would not have approved.

In the end, therefore, it was the Carnegie Corporation's capacity to build institutions that would serve as arenas for the politics of knowledge that was most enduringly significant. James Rowland Angell, who was chairman of the National Research Council in 1919 and then briefly president of the Carnegie Corporation, once pointed out that research is "the organized technique of science itself for its own propagation. It is, so to speak, the reproductive process of science."[3] Building on that, one might even argue that, by helping science through grants in support of research, the Carnegie Corporation and increasingly other foundations helped decisively to shape American politics. They did not cause the transformation from a party politics to a politics of knowledge that occurred at the turn of the century, as both cause and outcome of a shift from distributive to regulatory policy-making. But they did solidify this transformation through grants such as those made to capitalize what George Ellery Hale, the tireless promoter of the NAS-NRC, and others called "the new world of science."[4]

CHAPTER TWO

A Clearinghouse of American Science

The National Research Council

G EORGE ELLERY HALE , chief architect of the National Research Council, claimed in 1920 that "one of the most striking results of the war is the emphasis it has laid on the national importance of science and research."[1] He was not suggesting that science was more important in war than in peace. Rather, he was suggesting that science was "fundamentally important to the welfare of the United States," because it could help "reduce the cost of living" and advance knowledge "without thought of any industrial applications," while also helping to perfect "the means of national defense."[2] Ever the promoter of science, he was eager that the gains of the war years become permanent. He was concerned that the United States begin "as a state to respect and be guided by scientific methods and scientific men."[3] The Carnegie Corporation became his ally in the effort.

George Ellery Hale and the National Academy of Sciences

Hale was a fascinating fellow. An enthusiast who was also persistent, clever, and effective, he lived the advice he often gave to others: "Make no small plans."[4] He was "the J. P. Morgan of the scientific community," Nathan Reingold has aptly observed: a master in the formation of "intellectual pools, trusts, and conglomerates."[5] While engaged in important research in astronomy and astrophysics, Hale invented,

33

among other things, the spectroheliograph, which made it possible to photograph and analyze the gaseous clouds over the sun's surface. He also established the *Astrophysical Journal*, organized the International Astronomical Union, helped to found the California Institute of Technology, planned the Huntington Library and Art Gallery, and raised the funds to support the Yerkes Observatory in Chicago, and later the Mount Wilson Observatory in Pasadena.

Born in Chicago in 1868, Hale had been reared in a cultivated family of considerable means and was educated at MIT. He had grown up with an almost reverential regard for science. While recognizing its practical value as a basis for economic development, he also believed it had "cultural value." Science could "stimulate the imagination no less profoundly than the best works of art or literature," he once said.[6] To a man who had spent his childhood reciting Keats aloud as he watched the stars, science was not merely a means for understanding natural phenomena, but also a commitment to reason, beauty, truth, and order as preeminent human values. For him, the advancement of science was virtually equivalent to progress in a civilized world.

According to many measures, of course, science had progressed tremendously in the United States during the half century between the Civil War and the First World War. Although no Ph.D.'s in science had been awarded in the United States before 1861, by 1910 2,513 degrees had been granted. Reflecting this growth, the American Association for the Advancement of Science (AAAS) quadrupled in size between 1900 and 1914, when its membership passed 8,000.[7] Opportunities for research had also increased, though hardly in step with demand. Research universities had grown up alongside the undergraduate colleges, and industrial laboratories, sponsored by AT&T, General Electric, Eastman Kodak, and Westinghouse, among others, had developed alongside the older but also expanding government bureaus involved in scientific research. A few privately endowed centers of science had been established, notably the Carnegie Institution of Washington and the Rockefeller Institute for Medical Research.[8]

Hale was certainly aware of these gains, but he was also aware of several disturbing aspects of post-Civil War developments in science. He knew for example that, as science had become more specialized, its appeal to the public had lessened, and that scientists had lost their once assured place within the pantheon of popular Chautauqua heroes. A chemist or an astronomer might once have been paired on the lecture circuit with a literary star, but as chemistry and astronomy became more specialized and abstruse, the natural scientist was likely to be replaced by a social scientist, perhaps a sociologist like Albion Small or an economist like Richard T. Ely.[9] As the "hard" sciences lost status in this way, they also lost standing within the curricula of many of the older, private New England colleges. Although institutions like Amherst, Wesleyan, and Yale had once been respected centers of science, after the Civil War that distinction increasingly passed to the newly founded universities; the older colleges, partly to appeal to an upper-class clientele, chose instead to focus more exclusively upon the more mannerly, if less practical, liberal arts,[10] a development of which Matthew Arnold would have approved. Advance had thus ironically undermined the once certain social and cultural prestige of science, which in turn threatened the high social status that Hale thought scientists should have. This did not augur well for gaining financial support for research.

Finally, there was the possibility that the utilitarianism that had yielded such significant technical advances through practical tinkering would now stand in the way of more abstract, theoretical investigations. Members of Congress were inclined to ask "what in the name of common sense a physicist is?"[11] They might be willing to support research in physics if it could be described as an experiment in electronics that would foster, for example, the development of radio; not comprehending the worth of theory, however, they would not otherwise look with favor on the "pure" research needed to understand the atom, gravity, or energy. "Pure" research of this kind was being undertaken in Europe by the turn of the century; as Hale knew from his extensive European contacts, this gave scientists there a significant edge over their brethren in the United States. Clearly, then, despite considerable growth, not all prospects for science were pleasing at the beginning of the twentieth century, when Hale, the J. P. Morgan of American science, began actively to interest himself in the affairs of the National Academy of Sciences.

The NAS had been organized in 1863 by fifty prominent scientists and incorporated by an act of Congress that directed it "whenever called upon by any Department of Government [to] investigate, examine, experiment, and report upon any subject of science or art." It provided a means by which, "as a state," the United States could seek the advice of scientists.[12] In fact, however, as federal (and state) bureaus of science grew in number and size after the Civil War, the advice and assistance of the Academy was rarely solicited. Instead, the NAS spent most of its time defining and redefining the organizational apparatus that would govern its small, self-perpetuating, and relatively aged

membership, which tended in any case to be out of touch with developments in the most rapidly advancing special fields of science.[13]

Elected to membership in 1902, Hale was bound to find the inactivity
of the NAS dismaying. Unlike the public, he saw science as the bearer
of cultural and creative, and not only practical, advances. If the NAS
was "ever to occupy its proper position in the scientific world," he
remarked to a colleague, the Academy would have to "acquire a commanding influence of a favorable character, favorable alike to the
development of research and the public appreciation of science."[14]
Hoping to make the Academy the executor of his ambitions for science,
he developed a far-reaching set of reform plans and presented them in
November 1913 to a meeting in Baltimore. Hale said that the Academy
should fulfill a variety of functions for a variety of constituencies:

To the government it should make itself necessary by the high standards of its
work, the broad range of its endeavors, and the sane and scientific spirit
underlying all of its actions. To its members it should offer stimulus and
encouragement in their investigations; due recognition of their advances; financial assistance and the use of instruments at critical periods in their work;
the advantage of listening to papers ranging over the whole field of science,
bearing suggestions of principles or methods likely to develop new ideas;
contact with the greatest leaders of research from all countries and opportunities to listen to descriptions of their work; access to books and manuscripts
not easily obtainable from other sources; and participation in international
cooperative projects in every field of investigation. In the public mind it should
rank as the national exponent of science, and as the agency best qualified to
bring forward and illustrate the latest advances of its own members and of the
scientific world at large. To representatives of manufacturers and industries,
the Academy should serve to promote the appreciation and widespread use of
the scientific principles and methods which have built up the great industrial
prosperity of Germany. With other societies devoted to various branches of
science, it should cooperate in harmony with the best interests of American
research. Toward local bodies for the encouragement of investigation and the
diffusion of knowledge, it should act as an inspiring example and a reliable
source of support. And in the broad field of international cooperation, it should
unite with the leading academies of the world in the endeavor to perfect the
organization of research and in the use of all agencies contributing to its
advancement.[15]

It was truly an extraordinary and all-encompassing mission Hale
had proposed for the NAS, and to accomplish it he suggested a variety
of activities ranging from the publication of *Proceedings* and the sponsorship of lectures to support for original research. He recommended
an increase in membership, to include more young scientists and repre-

sentatives from engineering and archaeology; and he urged the construction of "a suitable building . . . commanding public appreciation and support . . . [for] The Academy . . . as a living and active body."[16] In presenting his program, Hale continued to sound this central theme: to gain support and respect for the pure, applied, "cultural and imaginative value of science," the Academy should provide the nation with the intellectual center it had never had and now, owing to "the rapid development of original research," needed more than ever before.[17] With his sights set upon the "exceptional opportunity to impress its influence upon the future scientific work of the United States," he announced his bold and, given the decentralized traditions of American science, revolutionary scheme.[18]

Hale hoped for immediate acquiescence but found little support. Only seventy-five of the Academy's 122 domestic members offered their views when asked, and only fifteen of these expressed overall agreement with his plans.[19] Undaunted, he pressed on. In April 1914 he defended his program at an NAS business meeting, where, as Ronald C. Tobey has put it, "his vision grew grander as he spoke. It seemed amenable to indefinite elaboration."[20] Still failing to gain his colleagues' support (except for his suggestion that the NAS publish a *Journal*), Hale was also blocked—at least initially—in his other avenue of approach. In May 1914 Carnegie rejected his request for $950,000 to construct a building for the NAS.[21] To a less determined man, this would have been a devastating blow.

Hale knew Carnegie personally—he had met him on a trans-Atlantic voyage in 1907—and had been a beneficiary of the philanthropist's largesse. Like so many other scientists, he had been thrilled by the 1901 announcement of Carnegie's gift of $10 million to establish the Carnegie Institution of Washington. "The provision of a large endowment solely for scientific research seemed almost too good to be true," he remembered thinking at the time. "Knowing as I did the difficulties of obtaining money for this purpose and devoted as I was to research rather than teaching, I could appreciate some of the possibilities of such an endowment."[22] Hale immediately set to work to get a solar observatory where he could mount a new sixty-inch refractor telescope. Aided by various scientists associated with the Carnegie Institution of Washington, including its secretary, Charles D. Walcott, head of the U.S. Geological Survey, who told Carnegie that "in Professor George E. Hale you have an exceptional man," he managed to secure CIW funds for what became the Mount Wilson Observatory.[23]

Long interested in astronomy, Carnegie was delighted with this investment. He visited Mount Wilson in 1910 and in the following year he doubled the original endowment, combining in his letter of gift general praise for "the success of the Institution" and an expression of "hope [that] the work at Mount Wilson will be vigorously pushed."[24] He told an interviewer: "The Institution discovered a young genius in Professor Hale. . . . The whole world is going to listen to the oracle on top of Mount Wilson. . . . I hope I shall live long enough to hear the revelations that are to come."[25]

Carnegie nevertheless would not assent to Hale's request for an Academy building that could serve "as the clearing house of American science, and its official center in both a national and an international sense."[26] Indeed, during one of Hale's visits to press his suit, Carnegie described the NAS mockingly as "just one of those fancy societies," and as Hale saw it, on another visit rebuked him "savagely," saying, "It is Sunday, and no time for such a matter!"[27] The First World War had recently erupted and the aging philanthropist was often irascible. His irritation with Hale may have been exacerbated by depression caused by the toll the war was taking. And yet, in his charge that the NAS was a "fancy society," Carnegie was probably expressing a genuine sympathy for proponents of a fundamentally different approach to the problem of organizing science, an approach championed from within the AAAS by the psychologist James McKeen Cattell.

James McKeen Cattell and the AAAS's Committee of One Hundred

The first psychologist elected to membership in the National Academy of Sciences, James McKeen Cattell was both similar to and different from Hale. Eight years older, he also came from a relatively wealthy family. His father was president of Lafayette College in Pennsylvania, where the younger Cattell was educated before moving on to study in Germany and England. Like Hale, he became an outstanding figure in his field. His pioneering application of experimental laboratory methods to the measurement of mental differences helped to establish experimentalism and behaviorism as leading characteristics of American psychology. His early approach to the development of mental tests did not prove durable, but as a professor of psychology at Columbia University from 1891 until 1917 he trained many of the leaders of the next generation of experimental psychologists, Edward L. Thorndike among them. A founder of the

American Psychological Association and its president in 1895, Cattell was the owner and editor of a long list of scholarly and popular journals, including the *Psychological Review*, *Scientific Monthly* (previously called *Popular Science Monthly*), *Science*, the *American Naturalist*, and *School and Society*. Certainly he was Hale's peer as an advocate for and organizer of science and scientists.[28]

At the same time, however, Cattell could be acerbic, cantankerous, harping, and difficult to a degree that Hale, for all his persistence, was not. And, in contrast to Hale's romantic and elite view of science, his view was pragmatic and popular. Although he developed the methods for rating scientists that were used in *American Men of Science*, which he owned and edited, he was concerned primarily with applying psychology to everyday problems, and he did not believe that science could or should be insulated from the pressures of the marketplace. Typically, for example, when he organized the Psychological Corporation in 1921, he hoped it would make psychological testing and counseling services more widely available and, through a plan for reinvesting part of the profits, provide money for psychological research.[29] The scheme was consistent with Cattell's interest in "radical democracy," with his 1912 proposal for confiscatory taxes on inheritance, and with his belief that, even though "Mr. Carnegie and Mr. Rockefeller may return some of the millions acquired through the application of science . . . science would be indefinitely richer if a cent were paid to it each time a match were struck or a pin used."[30]

Because Cattell was such a strong believer in wide participation in institutions of democratic governance, it was virtually inevitable that he would favor a model for organizing science different from the one favored by the more elitist Hale. Both men recognized that, with the growth in the numbers of scientists, the increasing specialization and professionalization, and the constantly rising costs of research, a need existed among American scientists for more coordination and leadership. Hale thought the NAS should fulfill these functions; Cattell thought they should be assumed by the AAAS. Although a member, Cattell was even more disdainful in his view of the NAS than Carnegie himself. It is "an exclusive social club for those who have arrived," he charged, "a house of lords" of American science.[31] With characteristic color and bite, he wrote: "The academy has been called on by the government to render only a few reports. Perhaps the most typical of these was to determine whether the ink with which the Declaration of Independence was written can be prevented from fading; for it was not, of course, a question of preserving the sentiments of that document. It may also be significant that the academy holds its annual meetings in a museum and is presided over by our most eminent student of invertebrate fossils. It is said that a representative once asked in the House, 'What does the National Academy of Sciences do?' and the reply was, 'The members write obituaries of each other when they die.'"[32] Of the AAAS, which first met in 1848, he said: "The sixteen sections of the association cover completely the pure and applied sciences. Committees of these sections are formed of representatives of the association and of the affiliated societies. The council of the association and the sectional committees are thus organized on a democratic basis to represent through the association and through the national scientific societies the scientific men of the country."[33]

In line with all this, while Hale worked to prod the NAS, Cattell in 1914 organized a Committee of One Hundred on Scientific Research under the auspices of the AAAS. Not without personal ambition, Cattell had once seen himself, and with some accuracy, as *the* representative of "American men of science." Writing to Carnegie after Daniel Coit Gilman's resignation as president of the Carnegie Institution of Washington had been announced, he had asked: "Do you care to give me an appointment for a few minutes to speak with you in regard to the Carnegie Institution? As editor of *Science* and of *The Popular Science Monthly* I am probably better informed than anyone else as to the views of the scientific men of the country, and it is possible that you might like to ask me some questions."[34] Whether or not he found Cattell's lack of modesty offensive, Carnegie wanted to remain aloof from CIW affairs and seems not to have granted Cattell's request for "a few minutes." To gain a hearing for his belief that the CIW "trustees should not repeat their mistake of three years ago and elect one who has become prominent through a college presidency or the like, but one who may not have the peculiar qualifications needed" to be CIW president, Cattell wrote to a trustee, William N. Frew, again claiming that "as editor of *Science* and *The Popular Science Monthly* I can to a certain extent speak for the scientific men of the country."[35] His bitterness over subsequent events is not difficult to understand. The AAAS's Committee of One Hundred to Promote Scientific Research had been designed to serve a coordinating function through the development of inventories of scientists and of opportunities for education and research. But after war broke out in Europe and preparedness became a preoccupation in the United States and NAS activities increased, the work of the AAAS committee was rendered unnecessary. In the contest to advance their different views, Hale gained and Cattell lost.[36]

The National Research Council

A pacifist, James McKeen Cattell waged a long and bitter fight against Columbia University's president, Nicholas Murray Butler. He saw Butler as encouraging a drift toward autocracy and business management in university affairs that he deplored. Then, in the fall of 1917, using Columbia University stationery (he was, after all, on its faculty), he wrote to several congressmen urging that consent be obtained from draftees before they were sent to fight in Europe. Butler used the incident as a reason to ask the trustees to fire him. They did so. This was a serious violation of academic freedom on Butler's part; but Cattell's often arrogant, even mean, behavior, combined with his unpopular stand against preparedness and war, had helped to erode his standing with other members of the Columbia faculty. He was therefore vulnerable to Butler's attack, despite the respect accorded him by scholars elsewhere. The principles Cattell stood and fought for were often unpopular, though important. He was an admirable historical figure, but a difficult person to deal with. His discharge from Columbia and his inability to gain an institutional affiliation elsewhere damaged his credibility and capacity to lead in his profession.[37]

At roughly the same time, Hale's own stature was increasing. Ever vigilant in his concern for the NAS, he was both distressed and alarmed when he discovered that Secretary of the Navy Josephus Daniels had established a Naval Consulting Board to help develop defensive military technology and had asked no members of the NAS to join it. Daniels's action was entirely understandable in light of the aged and inactive state of the NAS. There is also no evidence to suggest that the action was pointed in its exclusion of NAS members. Having read a statement made by Thomas Alva Edison after the May 1915 sinking of the *Lusitania*, to the effect that the United States should be ready for war and "ought to have on hand equipment for an army," Daniels had hastened to ask the popular inventor to head an advisory group.[38] He wanted to set up a "department of invention and development" and thought Edison's great popularity and public prestige would be helpful in securing the necessary congressional approval.[39] After visiting Edison at his laboratories in West Orange, New Jersey, and securing his cooperation, Daniels had then asked various engineering societies to elect representatives to the board. As would also have been the case if he had turned for assistance to Cattell and the AAAS's Committee of One Hundred for Scientific Research, the engineering societies could select representatives from among a much larger number of scientists than were represented in the NAS. What is more, they represented sciences Daniels could understand and appreciate because they were practical. Like most of his countrymen then and now, he might have joined in the congressman's query concerning "what in the name of common sense a physicist is?"

However sensible Daniels' actions may have been, they were alarming to Hale, who was determined to preserve the NAS's unique status as the official adviser to the federal government on scientific affairs. With war ever more likely and in Hale's opinion highly desirable, he prevailed upon his fellow academicians in April 1916 to deputize a small group to call upon President Wilson to offer help in organizing research. Wilson accepted the offer on the condition that his acceptance be kept secret. In June 1916 the NAS established a new subagency, the National Research Council.[40] It was "to bring into cooperation governmental, educational, industrial, and other research organizations with the object of encouraging the investigation of natural phenomena, the increased use of scientific research in the development of American industries, the employment of scientific methods in strengthening the national defense, and such other applications of science as will promote national security and welfare." The Council was based on the premise that "true preparedness would best result from the encouragement of every form of investigation, whether for military and industrial application or for the advancement of knowledge without regard to its immediate practical bearing."[41] Like industrial laboratories such as those at AT&T, GE, and Westinghouse, it was to routinize invention, replacing the previous industrial and military practice of buying up or taking over technological inventions that occurred at random elsewhere.

Acting on his own advice—"Make no small plans"—Hale moved on to lobby for a public endorsement of the NRC from Wilson. Using as leverage a promise of public support from the Republican presidential candidate, Charles Evans Hughes, he won this by July. Thereafter Hale convinced the Council of National Defense, which had been created by Congress to oversee all research, to delegate to the NRC matters related to science. For all intents and purposes, the NRC became what Navy Secretary Daniels had wanted the Edison group to be, a "department of invention and development," while the engineers were left the old function of reviewing inventions offered to the military by the public. Hale and his close colleague, the physicist Robert A. Millikan, one of the wartime leaders of the NRC, were quite forthright in their disdain for old-school inventors like Edison. Cattell, in contrast, believed that "Mr. Edison . . . is the scientific representative of the industrial world."[42] However that may be, there was a tone of triumph in Millikan's immediately postwar claim: "A wise man learns even more from his failures than from his successes. One of the most dismal failures of the war was made in the endeavor by all the principal belligerents to utilize the inventive genius of the *average citizen*. Every major belligerent had a board of inventions and research to which every man with an idea was asked to communicate that idea. All of these boards had precisely the same experience. . . . They all agree that not one suggestion in ten thousand . . . was of any value."[43]

Thus besting the Naval Consulting Board, the NRC also helped render the AAAS's Committee of One Hundred obsolete.[44] Cattell could denounce the NRC—as a pacifist, he found it "militaristic"; but many of the prominent members of the AAAS's Committee stood ready to cooperate with the Council.[45] Beyond that, with a subagency in place able to call upon the services of all scientists, the NAS's small, self-perpetuating, aging, and unrepresentative membership could no longer be said to be unsuitable to serve as the central coordinating agency for American science. Most important, while Cattell could contend that science ought to be supported by a tax on matches, Hale was able to parlay the war emergency into grants of money. He secured funds to operate the NRC first from the Engineering Foundation; then from the Carnegie Corporation (principally, through indirect grants passed through the CIW) and from the Rockefeller Foundation; and finally from the federal government. During the war, the Carnegie Corporation was, in fact, the main financial backer of the NRC; the funds Hale secured from it helped the Council organize a truly extraordinary list of inventions, including listening devices to detect submarines, range finders for airplanes, and intelligence tests to classify army recruits.[46] Cattell later wrote to Hale, charging, "You believe that aristocracy and patronage are favorable to science; I believe that they must be discarded for the cruder but more vigorous ways of democracy." Hale answered simply: "I . . . believe in adopting what appears to me to be the most promising means of advancing science and research under existing conditions. If I am not mistaken, you would not object to an appropriation by the Rockefeller Foundation toward the support of work in which you are interested."[47] The rejoinder may have been mean-spirited, but it was probably true. Cattell's rival was to have his own plans for science capitalized by the Carnegie Corporation. Having been refused $950,000 by Andrew Carnegie in 1914, Hale received $5 million from the Corporation for the NAS-NRC in March 1919.[48]

Elihu Root: Hale's "Valued and Beloved Adviser"

This rather dramatic turnabout was primarily a consequence of the elder statesman Elihu Root's intervention. Probably known to Root through Root's membership on the board of trustees of the CIW, Hale had written to Root about his NAS reform plans even before presenting them to his fellow academicians. Despite Root's own keen enthusiasm, he had been unsuccessful in recruiting Carnegie to the cause. He had nonetheless encouraged Hale: "You are certain to succeed ultimately in bringing about the more comprehensive and effective organization which you have in mind."[49] Root's enthusiasm had surpassed even that of Henry Pritchett, to whom Hale had also turned for assistance.

Although Pritchett, like Hale, was an astronomer by training and very much a proponent of the kind of hierarchical centralization Hale favored for American science, he was not initially certain that Hale's plan to make the NAS the center of American science would work. "The essential question involved," he told Hale in 1913, was whether "the present Academy [can] be developed into an agency which shall touch the national life more directly, which shall help to dignify the calling of the scientific man in the eyes of the American people, and which shall also serve the interests of science at the same time?" To do this the Academy would need to develop "an unselfish, enthusiastic, scientific leadership" that could rally a wide variety of constituencies in support of science, since "many individuals in the country have far more influence both upon public opinion and upon Congress than has the National Academy." Pritchett was not sanguine that this would be possible.[50] Hale, displeased by Pritchett's caution, concurred in a colleague's later description of Pritchett as "a roll top desk sort of man."[51] Root, by contrast, became one of Hale's "most valued and beloved advisers."[52]

Root's eager interest in Hale's plans sprang in part from a respect for science not different from Hale's own. Although he was a lawyer, Root came from a scientific family. His father had been a mathematics teacher. Early in his career he had taught at a school run by Henry Pritchett's father; later he had become a professor at Hamilton College in Clinton, New York. He had been known at Hamilton as "Cube Root," while Elihu's older brother, also a mathematics professor at Hamilton, had been known as "Square Root."[53] Having grown up in a household where the "table talk . . . came naturally from the science department of a college," Root declared that he had early acquired "a subconscious attitude toward science of its being the most important thing in life."[54] This alone would have inclined him to see merit in Hale's wish to place the NAS at the pinnacle of American culture and learning. Furthermore, Root was enthusiastic about Hale's plans to centralize science under the leadership of the NAS, because the scheme made sense within his personal political perspective. A well-known exemplar of the American conservative tradition, Root was a staunch Republican, highly successful as a lawyer, a leader of the bar. He served as a national statesman in various capacities. He was U.S. attorney for the Southern District of New York from 1883 to 1885, and U.S. senator from New York from 1909 to 1915. He was secretary of war for Presidents McKinley and Roosevelt from 1899 until 1904, and secretary of state for Roosevelt from 1905 to 1909. In all these positions, he exhibited both an unswerving expansionist faith in American democracy and a fundamental distrust of popular government. As secretary of war, Root was charged with establishing governments for Puerto Rico, Cuba, and the Philippines after the Spanish-American War; characteristically, he set up regimes that protected individual liberties while severely limiting participation in government.[55] As president of the Constitutional Convention for the State of New York in 1915, he urged adoption of the so-called "short ballot," restricting the number of officials to be elected directly and increasing the number to be appointed.[56] To Root, such an arrangement would make the franchise more effective, because it would limit the degree to which political favors, graft, and even charisma could lead the average man away from principled, intelligent decisions.

More than many individuals, Root fits into a clear historical "type." He was a Mugwump, a "good government" reformer. Individuals of this type in American society had tended to be upper-class business and professional people, who, in Martin J. Schiesl's words, "interpreted democracy in terms of property rights . . . assumed that government should be in the hands of well-educated and 'respectable' people . . . [and were] frightened by the growing social and political influence of immigrants and workers."[57] In need of clients, Root had begun his legal career as a defender of members of New York City's infamous Tweed Ring and had then moved on to make his name and fortune as counsel to some of the nation's largest industrial corporations. He was the descendant of early English settlers. His maternal great-grandfather, John Buttrick, had ordered the shot at Concord Bridge that was "heard 'round the world." A stern Victorian, he always wore well-polished black boots and held "himself as erect as a young West Point graduate."[58] He knew firsthand the abuses of popular patronage

politics and approached his public disputes with a moral rectitude
based upon memories of "a plain old house in the Oneida hills, overlooking the valley of the Mohawk, where truth and honor dwelt in my
youth . . . [and] lessons [were] learned . . . from the God of my fa-
thers."[59] Root would have described himself and the American tradition as Anglo-Saxon, and he thought it crucial to preserve the nobility
and civilization of the "race." He was devoted to "better and purer
government, a more pervasive morality and a more effective exercise
of the powers of government which preserve the liberty of the people."[60] His official biographer acknowledged, however, that he totally
lacked that "passionate sense of grievance . . . which inspired some
popular American leaders."[61] A gentleman, he was to some a "reactionary,"[62] to others "a wise counselor."[63] According to his old friend
Nicholas Murray Butler, the elite (then all-white, all-male) Century
Club in New York City was "the home of his heart and of his mind."[64]

Having worked for "good government" at the local, state, and
federal levels, Root could easily see great promise in Hale's campaign
for the NAS. According to Robert Millikan, Root told Hale that the
NAS was "of greatest importance . . . [because] its members were
to serve the government without compensation, thus eliminating the
terrible menace to free institutions of political patronage."[65] In all
likelihood this meant that Root believed the NAS to be above politics,
more accurately, an institution removed from the favors and barter
of non-Anglo-Saxon, immigrant politics. For Root, corruption and
immigrant politics were causally related.[66] Millikan reported him to
have said, "If we are going to conserve the finest elements in Anglo-
Saxon civilization, we must conserve the method of free private initiative and not depend primarily upon government aid."[67] The NAS
appealed to Root because it was located close to but outside of government. Especially when reformed according to Hale's blueprint, it would
provide a more centralized administration of scientific affairs without
subjecting science to direct governmental control.

Favorably disposed to providing Hale with the funds he needed for
the NAS, Root was initially hampered by his sense of duty to Carnegie,
whose opposition to Hale's grant request was known to both Root and
Pritchett. According to Louise Whitfield Carnegie, Andrew Carnegie's
wife, Root was one of the people who "understood Mr. Carnegie better
than anyone else and . . . had a clearer vision of his deeply affectionate
nature."[68] The two men were very different—Carnegie was romantic,
boisterous, impulsive, and more or less consistently liberal; Root was
measured, disciplined, Puritan-plain in style, and always conservative.

But both men were internationalists in outlook, though Carnegie was anti-imperialist and a pacifist, and both were centrally concerned with the avoidance of war. Mutual admiration led to trust on Carnegie's side and faithful service on Root's. Carnegie thought Root's success in negotiating the treaties that prevented war between the United States and Japan the event of the year in 1908,[69] and Root thought Carnegie's philanthropy made him one of "that great race of nation-builders who have made the progress and development of America the wonder of the world."[70] Even though Root strongly disagreed with Carnegie's view of the NAS and thought his negative reply to Hale's request misguided, Root would not challenge Carnegie by opposing him directly. His counsel as chairman of the Corporation's trustees was patience, as seen in his assurances to Alvin Johnson that, in time, Johnson's recommendations for changes in the Corporation's library grants would be put into effect.

After the NRC was established and the United States entered the war, circumstances changed. As Hale explained in a 1917 proposal to the Corporation, there was by this time—in addition to the NAS, which Hale described as "a scientific body of the highest class, uniting the leading American investigators in a compact group, serving as the official scientific advisor of the Government, and universally recognized abroad as the academic representative of the United States"—a larger, more representative body, operating "under the auspices of the Academy, and enjoying the advantages of its Congressional charter . . . [although] not entirely restricted in membership to original investigators."[71] The members of the NRC were recommended to the NAS by the nation's professional scientific societies, and were then actually appointed to the Council by the Academy. The establishment of the NRC may have answered Carnegie's complaint about the NAS being one of those "fancy societies," and it certainly demonstrated that, contrary to Henry Pritchett's earlier fears, the NAS could provide vigorous leadership. Also, there was a war to be won. Root, for all these reasons, was able to secure Carnegie Corporation grants to the NAS-NRC of $50,000 for 1917 and $100,000 for 1918, both grants payable through the CIW, of which Root also served as trustee chairman at the time.

Then, in May 1918, Hale secured an executive order establishing the NRC on a permanent peacetime basis. The idea of seeking an executive order instead of congressional approval was Root's.[72] Equally important, Hale organized an Advisory Committee on Industrial Research of the NRC, which included prominent industrialists like

Cleveland H. Dodge, George Eastman, Andrew W. Mellon, Ambrose Swasey, and Pierre S. du Pont. Through this committee he began to solicit large corporate contributions. By 1919 Hale could appeal to the Carnegie Corporation, not merely in terms of principle and potential, but on the grounds that "no other body [than the NAS-NRC] has given such promise of securing unified and effective effort among research agencies. The loss of the opportunity to continue and perfect this undertaking would mean failure to profit by one of the greatest lessons of the war. . . . A permanent guarantee of an income of $125,000 or $150,000 per year for general expenses would make the Council a going concern, and enable it to secure additional contributions from the industries."[73]

Andrew Carnegie was probably no longer interested in whether the Corporation did or did not capitalize the NAS. The war had crushed him. He died less than five months after the NAS-NRC grant had been approved. Regardless, Hale's urgent need for operating income and a headquarters that would make the Academy and Council a "going concern" in which private organizations could invest, would have been compellingly appealing to Root. Root sincerely believed that the NAS and NRC were vital to the welfare of the United States. They represented "good government" in and through science. In an address on "The Need for Organization in Scientific Research" delivered in 1918, Root pointed to the great, if despicable, achievements of "the German system of research applied at Charlottenburg and Grosslichterfelde" and then observed: "It remains to be seen whether peoples thoroughly imbued with the ideas and accustomed to the traditions of separate private initiative are capable of organizing scientific research for practical ends as effectively as an autocratic government giving direction to a docile and submissive people. I have no doubt about it myself, and I think the process has been well begun in England under the Advisory Council of the Committee of the Privy Council for Scientific and Industrial Research, and in the United States under the National Research Council."[74]

Presumably linked in Root's mind to the English effort by some notion of Anglo-Saxon traditions, the NRC was actually unique among contemporary scientific research coordinating agencies in having the approval and cooperation of the federal government while not operating under government control.[75] The arrangements governing the NRC were vital, Hale told a colleague following a conversation with Root, because Democratic congressmen tended to oppose grants for "research and advanced study" and to demand "that attention be concentrated on the needs of 'the Little Red School House on the hill,' standing for light and leading to the lowly of the land!"[76] Had the Council been dependent on Congress, it would not have fared well. Equally important, as a leery secretary of agriculture warned Woodrow Wilson when Wilson signed the executive order establishing the NRC on a permanent basis, the arrangements under which it operated meant that it could sponsor "investigations [that] might take a course quite at variance with the policy of the administration."[77] Put otherwise, it could support or try to counteract the will of popular majorities and their elected officials.

For these reasons, the NRC represented just the kind of organization Root thought the United States needed. It expanded the nation's *governing* capacities, but did so without concentrating power in the elected *government*. It was a private center of expertise. The significance Root assigned to it was evident in the NRC press release announcing the Carnegie Corporation's 1919 grant. In it the Council was described as "a democratic organization based upon some forty of the great scientific and engineering societies of the country. . . . It is not supported or controlled by the government, differing in this respect from other similar organizations established since the beginning of the war in England, Italy, Japan, Canada, and Australia. It intends, if possible, to achieve in a democracy and by democratic methods the great scientific results which the Germans achieved by autocratic methods in an autocracy while avoiding the obnoxious features of the autocratic regime."[78]

James McKeen Cattell, one should note in the end, described the NRC very differently. He called it "the Rockefeller-Carnegie Research Council (the R_2C_2)."[79] Before 1919 was out, the NRC had become, not only the recipient of the Corporation's building and endowment grant, which, as a matching grant (a standard Carnegie practice), might serve as a magnet for other grants, but also the administrator of Rockefeller fellowship funds that were the ultimate result of a prewar grant proposal Cattell had initiated on behalf of the AAAS's Committee of One Hundred.[80] As Cattell realized bitterly, first Carnegie grants and then Rockefeller grants had played a decisive role in shaping national science policy and in determining the ways in which it would be formulated in the future. It may be argued, as Daniel Kevles has done, that if "the Council [had] come out of World War I able to write checks against the federal treasury it might have been able to make much more of Hale's program workable."[81] But the point here is that the temporary and then the permanent establishment of the NRC foreclosed the more cumbersome and participatory alternative plan for organizing science Cattell had favored and for a time effectively advanced through the AAAS. It was an early and significant example of the Carnegie Corporation's capacity to intervene decisively in the politics of knowledge, in this instance via institution-building that would preserve unusual power in the hands of a small, expert elite.

CHAPTER THREE

Propaganda or Research?

Creating an Institute of Economics

N O L E S S T H A N their natural science colleagues, scholars in the social sciences emerged from the First World War sensing profound change and wishing for a chance to contribute actively and publicly to postwar reconstruction. "Of the many effects which the war has exerted on the minds of men, one of the most notable is the keener desire which we all now feel to be of genuine public service," the noted Yale University economist Irving Fisher explained in his 1919 presidential address to the American Economic Association. "It therefore becomes each of us, as we pause on the threshold of a possible 'new world,' to consider what are the new opportunities and what the new duties which lie before us. That new world of which we are speaking is still unbuilt. Is it to build itself, unplanned, or is it to have architects? And are we to be numbered among the architects?"[1] To a considerable extent, the answer to Fisher's question would depend on whether the economists could win funds for research.

Even before the war, the importance of empirical investigations had become evident to young economists. It was such investigations, they believed, that would make economics a truly valid and "objective" science, fundamentally different from the prescriptive theories of moral philosophy and capable of informing public action through accurate, factual analyses of real economic behavior and choices. Unfortunately, however, there were few possibilities for undertaking the kinds of investigations this would require. University appointments were still generally intended to support teaching and not research. Economics tended to be a derivative interest at new research foundations like the Russell Sage Foundation, where the main interest was social welfare work, or the Carnegie Endowment for International Peace, where studies of the economic effects of war were intended ultimately to show the futility and wanton waste of armed conflict. And to the extent that the federal and state governments employed economists, this employment tended to involve routine statistical work rather than fundamental research. No wonder, then, that Irving Fisher included in his 1919 speech a call for "an endowment for economics research, in the management of which labor, capital, and economists would, all three, share and which would be a sort of laboratory for the study of the great economic problems before us." This was scarcely an original suggestion with Fisher, but if, as he believed, "the great problems of reconstruction" were largely economic, support for economics research would now be even more vital than before.[2]

Having played an umpire's role in the contest between Hale and Cattell concerning the organization of science, the Carnegie Corporation in this instance assumed a role more akin to that of a broker. It helped economists gain standing within the arenas where public policy was made. It did this directly, by providing funds for research, as well as indirectly, by adopting internal policies that encouraged other philanthropies to support economic research. Seemingly unrelated decisions made by the Corporation at this time also helped to promote acceptance for specialized, professional work in the social sciences, in the process contributing to a related devaluation of older models of social science research. Deriving from assumptions about economics and, far more important, from a conception of "scientific philanthropy" and its role within a large, modern, voluntarily integrated, associative state, the Corporation's policies and actions had far-reaching significance for the organization and conduct of social policy research.

The Early Debates: "Propaganda" or "Research"

The first institute of economics assisted by the Carnegie Corporation was the National Bureau of Economic Research, chartered in 1920. The Bureau emerged from prewar discussions among businessmen, philanthropists, and economists. Against a backdrop of mounting industrial tension and violence and escalating concern in many quarters about how these could be counteracted, the possibility of developing an institute was initially conceived during the summer of 1912 at a conference called by Theodore Vail, the founder and president of AT&T. Vail's purpose was to gather some of the nation's wealthiest and most important industrialists to consider how unrest might be lessened. He believed that "an institute of economics" was needed because "the prevailing unrest and the ill-conceived though possibly honest efforts to relieve it were due chiefly to misinformation and misrepresentation."[3] According to Vail, "popular agitators saw a means of obtaining for themselves position and influence by appeals made, in the manner of demagogues, to the ignorance and class consciousness of the people."[4] To counter this, he thought there should be "a constant chain of correct information, put before the public by a sort of publicity bureau, with the special idea of reaching not so much the better educated members of the community, as the middle and lower classes upon which the demagogues chiefly preyed."[5] Having attended the conference, John D. Rockefeller, Jr., became interested in this suggestion, and Vail's ideas were therefore turned over for study to Jerome Greene, then director of the Rockefeller Institute for Medical Research.

A former secretary of the Corporation of Harvard University, Greene consulted a number of academics, including Edwin F. Gay, a professor of economics and first dean of the Harvard Business School, and Wesley C. Mitchell, a University of California professor of economics, who moved to Columbia University in 1913. Gay, Mitchell, and others reinforced Greene's own sense that what was needed was not "a publicity bureau" but an institute for basic economic research. Writing to his future wife, Lucy Sprague, in 1911, Mitchell had explained the belief that would lead him to take this position. "It is not lack of will that impedes progress, but lack of knowledge . . . sure knowledge of the causal interconnections between social phenomena. . . . The progress of medical science . . . has come from the laboratories, where the issues of life and of death in individual cases are replaced as the immediate object of attention by little problems of chemical reactions and bacteriological detail for which the busy practitioner had neither time nor patience. So must it be in other subjects. If we are ever to have an economics of use in guiding our efforts at social reconstruction, it must come from men who find some way of resolving the vital social problems into simpler elements."[6]

At odds with Vail's diagnosis of and prescription for the problem of "unrest," the views of Greene's economist advisers were opposed within the Rockefeller Foundation by Frederick T. Gates, the chief philanthropic lieutenant of John D. Rockefeller, Sr. "Life is short; time is fleeting," Gates wrote to the younger Rockefeller and presumably also told Greene. "We cannot do everything. . . . The selection of the things we undertake to do is therefore of the first importance. Now, if we are to do something in the field of economics, it seems to me that we ought to select, if we can, that department which is most urgent and of most practical importance. . . . Economics research . . . is not at all urgent, because its results will have no immediate and perhaps not even a distant practical value. What is urgent in economics is . . . a clearer apprehension by the masses of the people and the voters of the United States of the simpler and more fundamental economics laws."[7] For Gates, "the thing needed" was "to get before all reading and thinking people (even a low stratum, vis., the sort of men who have the capacity to get elected to Congress, and demagogues, laborites, socialists, editors, ministers, and other people who know little of practical life and live in a dreamland) a few of the elemental principles of economics." He cautioned Rockefeller, Jr., and Greene: "Beware of an institute of economic research."[8] Doubtless sincere in his warnings, Gates was also eager to preserve Rockefeller Foundation money for his preeminent interest, medicine, and possibly for that reason resisted all ideas that might lead to what was commonly coming to be called "scatteration" of resources.

The differences between the proponents of "propaganda" on the one hand and of "research" on the other were to some extent generational. They had to do with the hopes of social scientists like Wesley Mitchell, not simply to stabilize the social situation, but to achieve this through reform based on the laboratory analysis of empirical data. This hope was at that time a new, still not widely appreciated, possibility recognized by an increasing but relatively small number of scholars. Younger than Gates, Mitchell was in revolt against the established presumption that society worked best when all people understood and aligned their actions with immutable social "laws," the kind of a priori "truths" about how society worked that Gates referred to as "the elemental principles of economics." Mitchell's classic study, *Business Cycles* (1913), fundamentally altered prevalent views of alternations between periods of boom and bust because, as Arthur F. Burns once observed, it offered "a tested explanation of experience instead of an exercise in logic."[9] Mitchell was deeply committed to the belief that, "just as science affords the chief means of improving the practice of medicine, so science affords the chief means of improving the practice of social regulation."[10] Frederick T. Gates thought that was nonsense.

Beyond this, the proponents of "propaganda" and the proponents of "research" differed on how information about society should be used to improve the processes of governance. In line with nineteenth-century conceptions of social science as a form of "advocacy," the former group thought social studies should help shape public opinion rather directly: they should, in a sense, provide norms to guide those people Gates would have described as "low stratum." Research advocates, on the other hand, being more in tune with emerging twentieth-century conceptions of social science as a systematic, empirical, often abstract and particularistic form of investigation, thought social studies should provide an "objective" basis for the improvement of public and private administration, for "scientific management" in the broad sense of the term.

The disagreements evident in prewar discussions of possible Rockefeller financing for an institute of economics were not resolved at this time but were tabled. After the worst and most prolonged battles in American history between state militia and federal troops on one side, and striking workers and their families and sympathizers on the other, the Rockefellers, owners of the principal coal-mining firm involved, the Colorado Fuel and Iron Company, were vilified in the press and held responsible by many for what became known as "the Ludlow Massacre." The Rockefellers responded by retaining William Lyon Mackenzie King, a former Canadian labor minister trained in political science, to investigate the situation; King was to work with Ivy Lee, a public relations specialist, to quiet public alarm. King's research was placed under the auspices of the Rockefeller Foundation, which had not previously granted funds for work in labor relations. Because this gave the arrangement the unmistakable aura of a cover-up, the venture had a boomerang effect: it did not quiet but instead heightened public criticism of the Rockefellers and of the Rockefeller Foundation, and indeed, by extension, of all foundations.[11] King's work was seen by John D. Rockefeller, Jr., as an expensive project of social research that led to public upset. A disappointing report by King lent further credence to Gates's warning: "Beware of an institute of economic research." As a consequence of all this, the Rockefeller philanthropies withdrew from further consideration of assistance for economics and for more than a decade avoided such grants altogether.

Soon after the Rockefeller philanthropists discontinued their own deliberations, discussions of an "institute of economics" began within the Carnegie Corporation. The possibility of establishing an institute had been proposed to the Corporation's board by Henry Pritchett in 1916. Sympathetic to what Vail and Gates, in contrast to Greene, Gay, and Mitchell, had in mind, Pritchett argued: "Americans stand in need of . . . knowing and understanding the fundamental facts involved in their domestic problems. American political questions today are without exception economics questions. Disintegrating forces in the body politic are pulling in one direction and another. . . . A propaganda of socialism, and in some instances of anarchy, is energetically prosecuted. The antidote to these movements must be found in a dissemination among the mass of the people of simple, fundamental economic facts, told in understandable form." Pritchett then launched a diatribe against "the propaganda of misinformation now existing in this country."[12]

According to Pritchett, this propaganda was spread by the Hearst and the Scripps newspaper chains; by "certain representatives of particular factions and organizations" (who remained nameless); and by "the Walsh-Gompers Bureau, at Washington. . . calling itself the Committee on Industrial Relations."[13] This was a lobby, organized by Frank P. Walsh, chairman of the U.S. Commission on Industrial Relations, backed by AFL leader Samuel Gompers, and supported by people as diverse as the journalist Frederick C. Howe, the labor organizer Agnes Nestor of the Women's Trade Union League, and the politician Amos Pinchot. The Committee's purpose was to press for implementation of the Industrial Relations Commission's report.[14] As Pritchett knew, the majority recommendations of that report included calls to investigate and regulate foundations and to counteract their influence through increases in federal funding for social services. In pressing for action on the report, the Committee on Industrial Relations published some inflammatory material, including an attack on Pritchett's close friend Frank A. Vanderlip, president of the National City Bank. In all likelihood, however, it was fear for the Carnegie Corporation's future freedom in grant-making that led Pritchett to recommend the establishment of an institute of economics.

During these years of domestic turmoil, Pritchett was generally concerned with finding ways for the foundation to support dissemination of what he took to be correct, truthful information. Thus, for example, in addition to an institute of economics, he recommended "the purchase and endowment of an independent newspaper." Writing to Elihu Root on July 31, 1916, he explained: "I believe this a fruitful and significant thing for the Carnegie Corporation to do, and that from it might flow enormous results. What I had in mind was the purchase of the Washington Post, the placing of it under a small board of men of high character and ability, and the endowment of it sufficiently to make it independent of advertisers. With such an arrangement, and with an Editor who had both freedom and ability, a profound national and international result might be achieved."[15]

In reply, Root agreed that "of course we do very much need in Washington such a paper as you have in mind, which will convey correct information of what is going on in the world and particularly in our own government, and which will express the kind of opinion that substantially all well informed and thoughtful, decent people are agreed upon but which the ignorant and thoughtless need to have suggested to them." But Root thought the *Washington Post* would be a bad investment: "It would take about a million and a half to buy, much more than its earning capacity justifies." Hence it "would need a very heavy endowment."[16] Presumably for this reason, discussion of purchasing a newspaper was dropped, as was discussion of establishing an institute of economics. Grants to build libraries and purchase church organs still absorbed a large percentage of Corporation income, and in the face of Pritchett's constant press for new grant priorities, Root continued to urge patience.

Forced to withdraw his suit, Pritchett did not give up. His eagerness to support such a bureau was fundamentally related to his larger hopes for the Corporation. He wanted this, "the greatest endowment ever given to a group of men for the promotion and diffusion of knowledge and understanding amongst the people of a nation," to help promote efficient patterns of social organization.[17] Seeing the Corporation as something more than a bank for capitalizing the ideas and wishes of other people, he wanted to be part of the private but public realm of institutions, which he no less than Elihu Root and other proponents of public administration hoped would extend the United States's capacity for governance without enlarging the government. Establishing an institute to diffuse economic knowledge would fit well within this view of the Corporation's function. It was fortunate for Pritchett that, during the years when he was forced to bide his time, the economists earlier consulted by Jerome Greene on behalf of the Rockefellers continued to talk and plan.

The Founding of the National Bureau of Economic Research

As before, these conversations, though not limited to academics, posited research rather than propaganda as the goal of collaborative effort. The participants in the talks were no less concerned with the strife and violence of the pre-First World War era than were the more conservative, propaganda-oriented Vail and Pritchett, but their response was different. They tended to believe that research followed by reform was needed to prevent young people like the McNamara brothers, who had bombed the vehemently antilabor *Los Angeles Times* on October 1, 1910, from growing up believing, as Lincoln Steffens put it, "that the only recourse they have for improving the conditions of the wage earner is to use dynamite against property and life."[18] If they did not actually join, they tended at least to sympathize with, the lobby organized in 1912 by fifty-three prominent lawyers, businessmen, professors, journalists, and social workers, known as the Committee on Industrial Relations. The Committee's purpose was to push for the establishment of the very Commission on Industrial Relations that would be so critical of foundations. Financed by Adolph Lewisohn and Julius Rosenwald, officially supported by the National Civic Federation, but vehemently opposed by the National Association of Manufacturers, the Committee achieved its goal, and, equally important here, served as a vehicle by which Malcolm Rorty, an engineer and chief statistician for AT&T, became acquainted with Wesley C. Mitchell, the University of California economist, later at Columbia University.[19]

Although more closely allied with business, Rorty was much like Mitchell in other respects. He was convinced that "a considerably greater degree of political and industrial stability than exists now could be brought about if certain of the fundamental facts of industry and business were determined with accuracy or within reasonable limits of error."[20] Among these fundamental facts, one was the extent of the national income, which Rorty believed could be measured by using AT&T data on rent distribution. He thought that the amount of wealth to be divided between employers and employed could be thus determined, helping to answer the difficult question of what a fair wage should be. Apparently a dispassionate man of conscience, who was no less determined than Mitchell in his faith in the arbitrating and consensual power of facts derived from careful scientific inquiry, Rorty was convinced that "among those of differing viewpoints who are sincerely seeking for the truth, there is a common meeting ground in the search for the actual, tangible facts which must underly [*sic*] all sound economic reasoning."[21] This conviction was similar to the assumptions evident in Mitchell's 1919 presidential address to the American Statistical Association. Observing that "reform by agitation or class struggle is a jerky way of moving forward, uncomfortable and wasteful of energy," Mitchell asked: "Are we not intelligent enough to devise a steadier and a more certain method of progress?"[22]

Rorty and Mitchell's obviously compatible association in the work of the Committee on Industrial Relations was renewed in 1917 by Edwin Gay, the economist who served as first dean of the Harvard Business School. Rorty had gone to Gay to urge that the Business School undertake a study of the national income question, and Gay, feeling compelled to decline because of a lack of adequate research facilities at the school, sent him to talk with Mitchell. Thereafter the three held frequent discussions, often joined by other scholars and businessmen concerned with studies of the actual workings of the economy. In fact, a "Committee on the Distribution of Income" was about to be launched, when the demands of government war work intervened. Finally, however, planning began again, and in January 1920 Rorty, Mitchell, Gay, and N. I. Stone, another economist interested in labor relations, met and, according to Mitchell's abbreviated notes, "found certain differences in opinions on public policies based on different views concerning fundamental facts rather than on differences of our economic interests. No one could be sure his views were sound or that other fellow's were mistaken. None of us had time and facilities for making sure—though the facts could be ascertained with substantial accuracy. We believed many other men felt same need of a fact-finding agency. . . . National Bureau of Economic Research chartered January 1920 as such."[23]

The decision to establish the NBER marked the successful culmination of prewar talks, but also something of a defeat. During the war, Gay had been director of the Central Bureau of Planning and Statistics in Washington, D.C., set up in June 1918 to coordinate the statistical work of all federal government boards and bureaus. Mitchell, who had served as the Central Bureau's research director, later said of it: "When the Armistice was signed we were in a fair way to develop for the first time a systematic organization of federal statistics."[24] Clearly, as Lucy Sprague Mitchell observed later, the work of the Central Bureau "deepened Mitchell's conviction of the value of social statistics and confirmed his belief that the kind of work he wished to do (what he called 'other things which nobody else cares about as much as I do') was of social significance."[25] Hoping to establish a permanent board, he had urged Gay to try to win Woodrow Wilson's support for the peacetime continuance of the Central Bureau, which Gay had done. But Wilson, who was often unreceptive to his fellow academics' offers of expert service, had not looked with favor on the suggestion, and shortly before the National Bureau of Economic Research was launched, the Central Bureau had been closed down.

Less by choice than by necessity adding to the number of private institutions concerned with public policy, the NBER was organized under the control of a board of directors of economists, businessmen, and representatives of labor, as well as individuals from a number of national associations such as the American Economic Association, the Engineering Council, and the American Federation of Labor. All were known to be of different political persuasions, Democratic, Republican, and Socialist. Paralleling the earlier structure of the Central Bureau, Gay became the NBER's first president, and Mitchell, its first research director. Their hope was that the large and diverse group they had gathered to serve with them on the board of directors would guarantee that the NBER's purpose would remain "fact-finding." Especially because it was private, they did not wish the NBER to be confused with a "publicity bureau."[26] The NBER won early and vital support from the Carnegie Corporation. In light of Pritchett's keen interest in economic "propaganda," the Corporation's willingness to back the NBER was revealingly anomalous.

Carnegie Corporation Grants to the NBER

By 1920, when a request for funds for the NBER reached the Carnegie Corporation, Andrew Carnegie was dead and James Rowland Angell occupied the president's office. The coincidence of Angell's presence at this moment was significant. A psychologist who had served on the faculty of the University of Michigan and the University of Chicago, Angell had spent the war years in Washington, D.C., where he had worked for the Committee on the Classification of Personnel, and then for the Committee on Education and Special Training. After the war, he had returned briefly to the University of Chicago as acting president and then was recalled to Washington as chairman of the National Research Council. His predecessor in the post, John C. Merriam, left the NRC to become president of the Carnegie Institution of Washington. Elected to membership in the NAS at the same time that he became chairman of the NRC, Angell worked closely with George Ellery Hale in raising the matching funds the Carnegie Corporation had required as a condition for the receipt of its $5-million grant.[27] "All this brought me of necessity into some contact with Elihu Root, Henry S. Pritchett, and other members of the Board of Trustees of the Carnegie Corporation," Angell recalled. "Perhaps as a result, I was in the late Winter of 1920 invited to become President of the Corporation."[28]

Henry Pritchett was convinced that the development of the Corporation as an institution that could "take the initiative in seeking out those forces in the social order that promise to be significant and fruitful" depended upon the appointment of a chief executive "of large experience, of vision, of shrewdness . . . a man of education, of refinement, of large views."[29] In all ways—training, previous jobs, family connections, and even what he himself described as "Mayflower ancestry"—Angell met these requirements.[30] The trustees had gone to considerable lengths to recruit him. With Pritchett as their representative, they had promised, among other things, a salary of $30,000 and three months of paid vacation before assuming office. Having finally won their catch, Pritchett and Root, if not all the trustees, were pleased with the appointment.

Agreeing with Root and Pritchett that the development of science was vital to the well-being of the United States, Angell also agreed that the organization and support of science should not be controlled by the government.[31] Beyond these points of agreement, he was a younger man, and more in touch with current scientific views and developments than were the Corporation's two leading trustee science promoters. Not surprisingly, therefore, Angell favored the wider dissemination of scientific research, not so much to impress and instruct the public as to foster communication and criticism among scholars. Equally important, he was concerned with balance among different fields of science and feared that "the support of research is likely, by sheer force of circumstances, to run off onto the lines of the physical and particularly the applied sciences. . . . One is far more likely to be approached by the natural scientists than by the men in the other fields of scholarship . . . for there are more workers in the former, and they are, on the whole, more aggressive in their methods."[32] Familiar with the rapid development of social science research at the University of Chicago, Angell thought that what he called "the social and economics sciences" could benefit greatly if "courageously and judiciously cultivated."[33]

On November 8, 1920, the Corporation's president received a letter from Max Farrand. Farrand was a Yale University historian who later became director of the Huntington Library; at this time, he was serving a brief term as general director of the Commonwealth Fund, a new trust established with Harkness money. "Have you been approached on behalf of the [National] Bureau of Economic Research?" Farrand asked. "If so, I shall say nothing more about it. If not, I should like to suggest your consideration of it."[34] Sympathetic to the NBER, Farrand had convinced the Commonwealth board to support the organization during its first year. But the Commonwealth trustees, who would soon decide to limit the Fund to projects in medicine, had indicated that after their first grant of $20,000 they would provide only an additional $15,000 and would do that for only one year.[35] Introduced by Farrand, the NBER's secretary then wrote to Beardsley Ruml, a psychologist and protegé of Angell's, who served as his assistant at the Corporation. The NBER's secretary told Ruml that "the continuance of the Bureau" was at stake.[36] A month later, the Corporation promised the requested $45,000 over three years and, still following old Carnegie practice, made the grant conditional upon matching funds, in this case amounting to $20,000 a year.[37] This speedy and positive response to the NBER's grant request was clearly a result of Angell's recommendation and of eagerness on the part of the Corporation's trustees to back their new president.

In light of the progress Angell was making in modernizing the administration of the Corporation, Pritchett would not have been likely to jeopardize their collaboration by quibbling over a $45,000 grant. Pritchett was pleased that Angell agreed with his belief that the Corporation should become more initiatory and less reactive in its grant-making. As a "giving corporation," it should be "a human agency seeking out the great and significant causes," and it should not be a "public reservoir to which all applicants are invited to apply."[38] To ensure that this conception was not undermined by administrative procedures instituted or overseen by one of the "clerks," Angell, with Pritchett's advice and assistance, worked hard to concentrate power in the president's office. For example, he sought and secured a resolution that gave the president rather than the treasurer the right to decide whether the conditions of a grant had been met and whether, in consequence, actual payments on that grant could continue. Long favored by Pritchett, who was constantly at odds with James Bertram and with Robert Franks, the Corporation's secretary and treasurer, this seemingly inconsequential bureaucratic change in procedure demoted Franks by precluding him (or Bertram), through the enforcement of technicalities, from blocking grants they thought inappropriate.[39]

Although Angell consistently and effectively supported Pritchett rather than the "clerks" on matters of significance to Corporation policy and administration, he indicated to his assistant Beardsley Ruml that he found it unpleasant to deal with the strained relationships that existed within the Carnegie offices.[40] To Pritchett's chagrin, he therefore gave up the presidency after only one year. In addition to finding the Corporation a difficult place to work, he was eager to follow his father, who had been president of the University of Michigan, and his grandfather, who had been president of Brown, by himself becoming a college president. Having earlier been barred from the presidency of the University of Chicago because, as a Congregationalist, he could not meet the requirement then in effect that the president be a Baptist, he accepted the presidency of Yale University as soon as it was offered to him in the spring of 1921. Pritchett served as acting president of the Carnegie Corporation for the next two years. His hope, and Root's hope, was to prevent any "breach in the continuity of the office administration."[41] By this they meant to block any effort by the "clerks" to undermine the hard-won internal administrative changes that provided the necessary underpinning for the more initiatory policies Pritchett and Angell favored.

Thus it was Pritchett to whom the NBER appealed in 1921, when it sought again to tap the Corporation's coffers. The NBER's second grant was facilitated by no one less than Herbert Hoover, U.S. Secretary of Commerce at the time.[42] Hoover's mediation was a consequence of his belief in the value of science as a basis for management, and in publicity as a means to promote regulation through private and individual action. When the "Great Engineer" entered the Warren Harding cabinet in March 1921, he had already developed a vision of the "Cooperative Committee and Conference System." With unemployment significantly higher in the winter of 1921 than "the normal trend of growth" that economists at the Russell Sage Foundation and elsewhere suggested it should be, he was ready to demonstrate the value of this cooperative system.[43] His scheme involved having President Harding call a conference to develop awareness of unemployment; next, establishing privately funded committees of experts to analyze the problem and formulate remedial action; and finally, through publicity, disseminating recommendations for action based on the committees' studies.[44]

The NBER was involved from the beginning of what became the 1921 President's Conference on Unemployment. Hoover's strategy promised an unparalleled opportunity to test and elaborate Wesley Mitchell's theory of business cycles. Commissioned work for the project could also bring the NBER the funds it needed to match the Carnegie Corporation's 1921 grant, which had proven more difficult to come by than anticipated. Although the NBER had "been asked to undertake a considerable number of profitable investigations which would be financed by the big corporations like the banks," Edwin Gay had told Angell, in discussing the first grant, that these would have to be refused until the NBER's "scientific prestige" was established.[45] As subsequent NBER fund-raising efforts confirmed, translation of "general interest [in the Bureau] . . . into financial support" was found to be virtually impossible.[46] According to its secretary, this was because "the Bureau is a scientific, non-partisan institution, engaged only in fact-finding, and therefore manifestly unable to respond to partisan enthusiasms or appeals to the spirit of the reformer."[47] But that did not prevent the NBER from responding positively to Hoover's call, and since Hoover believed that private funding was necessary for conference committees, Hoover himself approached the Russell Sage Foundation, the Commonwealth Fund, and the Carnegie Corporation for the money to secure the services of the NBER for what became the Unemployment Conference's Committee on Unemployment and the Business Cycle.

From his own correspondence and that of his associates, it is clear that Hoover thought the success of his program would largely depend on committee work that was "technically first-class, and . . . presented to the business public under the auspices of a disinterested group which will carry weight." Generally favoring a system of "private government," in any case, he thought private funding preferable to public, because public funding would require "a personnel paid the [low] salaries set by the government."[48] He also wanted to ensure that the committee's findings were not associated with a political party. His proposal was rejected by the Russell Sage Foundation, which was planning to release staff member time to the Conference, and also by the Commonwealth Fund, whose trustees had already decided against further support of the NBER. The Commonwealth trustees did not believe Hoover's conference system could prevent businessmen from acting "on their own initiative which is chiefly that of getting ahead of their competitors."[49] But the trustees of the Carnegie Corporation greatly admired Hoover. They had wanted him to join the board of trustees, and had more confidence in the Hoover project than did their peers at Commonwealth.[50]

Writing to Pritchett on November 18, 1921, Hoover said: "I am a great believer in investigations of this type as a method of clearing the decks of erroneous ideas and restarting public thought in proper channels. . . . The great quality of such investigations is that they should be carried out under such auspices as guarantee not only the soundness of its [sic] collections but will carry weight with the entire community."[51] Although the NBER was, as Gay told Hoover, "debarred from making propaganda for any policy," a carefully formulated report endorsed by its impartial board of directors might help in "securing agreement upon the question of what ought to be done."[52] Actually, this came very close to being "propaganda" in the old prewar sense of the term; but then again, Hoover's chief publicity man, E. E. Hunt,

could call it "continuing public education."⁵³ Whatever the label—
research as in "fact-finding," or propaganda as in public instruction—
expert research linked to an expert publicity campaign was the purpose
for which the Carnegie Corporation made a second grant of $50,000
in February 1922.

Additional Grants and Indirect Assistance

The Corporation's second grant to the NBER, actually applied as
matching funds to help meet the requirements of the first grant, was
authorized largely out of trustee respect for Hoover. His belief in
voluntary private efforts as the basis for public policy fit perfectly with
Pritchett and Root's wish to involve the Corporation in the establishment of institutions that could enhance governance without increasing
the actual institutions of government. The expectation was that expertise combined with public education would yield progress and prosperity, but without essential social change. What the country needed
was a corporatist social plan, in which unity would be achieved by
leadership from the center, the center to include scientific research
institutes like the NBER, scientific coordinating councils like the NRC,
and scientific philanthropies like the Carnegie Corporation. When
Henry Pritchett spoke of taking "the initiative," or of replacing "routine giving" with something "finer," he meant using the Corporation's
funds to capitalize and sustain a social design of this kind.

It is entirely logical, therefore, that several "institutes of economics,"
not only the NBER, received Carnegie Corporation funds. In May
1921, for example, the Corporation approved grants of well over one
million dollars to establish the Food Research Institute at Stanford
University, an organization Hoover had suggested on the basis of his
wartime work as food administrator. Its official purpose was to study
and educate the public about the economics of worldwide food pro-
duction.⁵⁴

In January 1922, the Corporation also approved grants, again of
more than one million dollars, to establish the Institute of Economics
in Washington, D.C. Proposed to the Corporation by Robert S. Brookings, this institute was affiliated with the Institute for Government
Research, established in 1916 to develop at the national level the
policy-making capacity that municipal "good government" groups
were developing in cities across the United States.⁵⁵ In 1927, the Institute of Economics and the Institute for Government Research were
merged with the Robert Brookings Graduate School of Economics and

Government to become the Brookings Institution. Elihu Root was a trustee of the Institute for Government Research, and it may well be that, when Pritchett proposed that the Corporation establish an institute of economics in 1916, he had had in mind an economic counterpart to this organization.

The backers of the Institute of Economics believed, as the proposal sent to Carnegie indicated, that

the events of the past ten years, and particularly those of the years since the War, have gone far to emphasize the fact that many government questions are, in their essence, economic questions. It is clear today to thinking men that the basis upon which just settlements must be made as between groups of citizens and as between nations must be economic. The ordinary citizen does not fully appreciate the fact that he also, in his daily life and business, is subject to economic conditions that closely affect the business of the individual as well as of the world. . . . The situation [therefore] seems ripe for the inauguration of some agency, competent to collect, interpret, and lay before the country in clear and intelligible form the fundamental economic facts concerning which opinions need to be formed."[56]

Pritchett explained, in endorsing the Brookings proposal to the Corporation's board, that "the publication and distribution of clearly written, simple statements" could have a powerful effect on public opinion, and this was what he and Brookings hoped the new Institute of Economics could achieve.[57]

Pritchett's expectations for the research institutes assisted by the Corporation diverged from those of the economists involved. Both Pritchett and the Corporation's board had hoped the Food Research Institute would convey information directly to the public. The economists who served as directors of the Institute, on the other hand, wanted to try "to affect policy by supplying technical advisors of policy makers with accurate, properly analyzed information."[58] In lieu of simple pamphlets, the scholars employed by the NBER and the Institute of Economics chose to publish monographs, described by Wesley Mitchell as "bulky . . . [and] crammed with statistics and charts." "They are technical," Mitchell wrote, "and their style is more remarkable for striving after accuracy than for grace. To value such 'literature,' readers must have keen interest in a problem and uncommon power to assimilate facts."[59]

Whether Pritchett rued the situation, the institutes of economics supported by the Carnegie Corporation did not become centers of propaganda, as he and others had hoped they would. They became, rather, places for "objective" social study, laboratories for advancing knowledge with no direct links to reform campaigns or to partisan public politics. The almost value-free detachment that characterized the professional aspirations of economists like Mitchell precluded the fulfillment of the moralizing and educating role Pritchett had had in mind. Yet the institutes of economics the Corporation financed did mesh with the corporatist social plan Pritchett and others favored far better than other contemporary centers of social science did.

The social settlements like Jane Addams's Hull House in Chicago, which sprang up in Great Britain and in the United States in the early twentieth century, were examples of such centers of social science. The several hundred settlements that had been established in the United States at the time of the First World War tended to embody an approach to research and reform at odds with the conception of "scientific philanthropy" emerging at the Carnegie Corporation. This was not because settlements were charitable institutions. Their founders and staff thought of them as neighborhood centers engaged in sociological research. However, while the NBER and other institutes of economics were national in orientation, social settlements were purposefully local, indeed, self-consciously affiliated with neighborhoods. The institutes of economics were professional in approach and almost entirely staffed by men; the social settlements were what one might call "preprofessional" and operated usually by "amateur" female college graduates, who lived and worked together for a short time, usually not in pursuit of careers, but of opportunities to study and improve the life of a neighborhood.[60] Advocates of professionalization and professionalism often held the misguided belief that settlements were charitable missionary centers rather than institutes for sociological research.

As initially organized, most of the early social settlements were rooted in liberal, even populist, values and in social feminism. They stood for ideals that had little to do with the brand of progressivism of a man like Pritchett, and they were at odds with the drive toward expertise and professionalism that men like Pritchett favored. A cause and a consequence of this different orientation was increased gender-related occupational segmentation, not only between male school administrators and female schoolteachers, but also between male academic sociologists and female practice-oriented social workers.[61]

Social settlements engaged in "social science" as a combination of study and action that addressed problems holistically. They did not separate what would later be seen as the economic aspects of a problem like unemployment from sociological or political or even anthropological aspects. Their focus was on the comprehensive problems faced by an individual or group or community. Typically, therefore, they collected statistics not in connection with an abstract question, like the extent of national income, but rather as part of an effort to document malnutrition or track the whereabouts of out-of-school youths. The educational surveys organized by Pritchett at the Carnegie Foundation for the Advancement of Teaching were first cousins to this kind of sociological study. What is more, in his interest in "propaganda" Pritchett harkened back to the old nineteenth-century advocacy conception of social science that had originally contributed to the emergence of social settlements. And yet, despite these commonalities, Pritchett could recognize in the new institutes of economics a potential for centralization and national leadership that meshed well with his larger social vision.[62]

Research institutes like the NBER, because they seemed compatible with the perspective that guided it, won early and significant support from the Carnegie Corporation, whereas social settlements were denied funds altogether. Pritchett called for such a denial in a 1919 memorandum, which he sent to Elihu Root, having "shown [it] . . . to no other member of the board." It called for an end to what Pritchett termed "benevolent receptivity"—"the passive sorting out of the innumerable petitions from Colleges, hospitals, Settlements, and all other causes engaged in their judgement at least, in the advancement and diffusion of knowledge"—so that the Corporation could "take the initiative in seeking out those forces in the social order that promise to be significant and fruitful."[63] In May 1921 the trustees passed a resolution stating that, "in view of the impossibility of meeting all the claims from such organizations and the extreme difficulty of determining a just and rational basis of discrimination," the Corporation would consider no further applications from social settlements.[64]

This was a pointed and unusual refusal of access to Corporation consideration. Similar action was *not* taken against other institutions that were associated with "benevolent receptivity" on Pritchett's 1919 list. Colleges always received large sums and so did some hospitals. By providing funds to male-led independent research institutes and denying them to settlements, the Corporation contributed to the demise of these often radical, highly intellectual, and female-led centers of reform. Over time, they evolved into social service distribution centers linked to professional and government bureaucracies.

By helping to eliminate from the field a potentially competing model of social research, the Corporation indirectly helped research bureaus like the NBER become the established model of social science expertise.

It provided further indirect assistance to such centers by developing internal administrative policies and procedures that make philanthropic support of social science less vulnerable to public criticism. In the early 1920s, the specter of the Rockefeller fiasco with William Lyon Mackenzie King and of the U.S. Industrial Relations Commission was still recalled with considerable alarm by foundation trustees and officers. The Corporation adopted a policy of refusing to associate itself with or to give aid to any organization committed to discernible religious, political, economic, or social interests.[65] Even though Pritchett and Root might privately favor "propaganda" in the old meaning of instructing the public in the "facts" of a situation, the resolution could be expected to lend an aura of objectivity and nonpartisanship to organizations the Corporation chose to fund. Beyond this, the Corporation encouraged the institutions whose research it financed in part or in whole to describe and organize themselves as "educational" institutions. Thus when Richard T. Ely, who received a grant of $10,000 in 1922 for the Institute of Land Economics, appealed a subsequent refusal of funds, he said: "You have spoken of the Institute in Washington [the Institute of Economics] and the Laboratory in California [the Food Research Institute] as distinguished from our Institute because they are your children. But our Institute is in the same class. The Carnegie Corporation called us into existence when Doctor Angell was President. Even our form is due to the Carnegie Corporation because he told us that we should be incorporated as an educational institution."[66] Finally, wherever possible, the Corporation indicated that it did not control the work of the institutions to which it had granted funds. Typically, the documents establishing the Food Research Institute explicitly stated that "Carnegie Corporation . . . will desire to abstain entirely from any attempt to direct or control the work of the Institute."[67]

Maintaining distance from the possibly controversial views or findings of economists whose work was made possible by Carnegie funds served as something of a model for other philanthropies. The Corporation's policies, as well as James Angell's belief that the "economic and social sciences" represented a good opportunity for investment, were carried by Beardsley Ruml from the Carnegie to the Rockefeller offices. After Angell's resignation, Ruml had found "the chaotic state of things" at the Corporation intolerable, and since Angell could not raise a high enough salary to bring Ruml to Yale, as Angell would have liked to do, he helped the younger psychologist secure a job with the Rockefeller philanthropies.[68] Early in 1922 Ruml became director of

the Laura Spelman Rockefeller Memorial Fund. Having initially
followed Laura Spelman Rockefeller's interest in financing charitable
organizations, including social settlements, the Memorial under Ruml's
guidance became the chief U.S. funder of more professional social
science research.

A brilliant, colorful, and eccentric character who would later become
dean of the social sciences at the University of Chicago and then
treasurer of R. H. Macy's department store, Ruml was, according
to University of Chicago president Robert Maynard Hutchins, "the
founder of the social sciences in the U.S."[69] Hutchins's claim was
exaggerated, but Ruml was indeed one of the most important early
foundation entrepreneurs for the social sciences—probably the most
important—and the time he spent at the Corporation, though brief,
facilitated his success in that role. During the seven years he served as
chief executive of the Memorial, Ruml directed more than $58 million
for work in the social sciences to Chicago, Yale, North Carolina,
Vanderbilt, and a number of other universities in the United States, as
well as to the London School of Economics, the Deutsche Hochschule
für Politik, and the University of Stockholm.[70] In 1923 he helped
launch, and thereafter helped finance, the Social Science Research
Council, which albeit without official government connection would
seek to provide social scientists with the same kind of national coordinating organization the natural scientists had in the NRC.

Directly and, no less important, indirectly, the Carnegie Corporation
had helped social scientists, especially economists, realize their postwar
aspirations to public prominence. Without the assistance of the Corporation and a few other philanthropies, economics and the social sciences generally might well have remained on a par with the classics,
Egyptology, and other branches of the humanities; that is, they might
have remained interesting to many able people, but not bases for public
policy-making. The fact that the social sciences achieved considerable
prominence during the interwar period, and that a number of social
scientists, including Wesley Mitchell, became important government
advisers, was in part due to decisions by Carnegie and by those other
foundations, notably the Laura Spelman Rockefeller Memorial, that
were influenced by Corporation precedents and policies. Ironically,
however, as its roughly contemporaneous grants for the American
Law Institute would further reveal, Corporation grants did not always
derive from an informed understanding of what professional social
scientists themselves wished to achieve.

CHAPTER FOUR

Conceptualists vs. Realists

An Institute to Restate the Law

O N A P R I L 17, 1923, the Carnegie Corporation authorized a grant
of $1,075,000 to a new organization of legal scholars, corporate
lawyers, and judges established "in response to the growing feelings
that lawyers have a distinct public function to perform in relation to
the improvement of the law and its administration."[1] The American
Law Institute (ALI) had been planned by a committee whose work was
financed by a 1922 Corporation grant for $25,000; it had been for-
mally established in February 1923 at a meeting in Washington, D.C.,
chaired by Corporation trustee Elihu Root. The ALI was intended to
provide a means by which to review, synthesize, and summarize in
"restatements" a proliferating body of court decisions. Confusion resulting from a continuous growth of case precedent threatened otherwise to jeopardize the American legal system.[2]

During the early years of the twentieth century, legal literature grew
at an unmanageable rate. "The industry of legal writers produces
without intermission textbooks and encyclopedias which grow amazingly not only in number but in size," a lawyer from New Zealand told
the Association of the Bar of the City of New York in 1922. "There is
nothing in the records of human literature to equal or approach the
laborious industry of those authors who keep the American legal printing press at work in modern times."[3] According to Samuel Williston
of the Harvard Law School, in the thirty years before the First World
War, American case law nearly tripled.[4]

Reformers further argued that access to justice was unequal. In

Work-Accidents and the Law, for example, a 1910 study published as part of the Russell Sage Foundation's Pittsburgh Survey, Crystal Eastman, the feminist lawyer who drafted New York State's first workers' compensation law, claimed that the inability of workers to gain compensation for injuries and death caused by industrial accidents, which often left widows and young children without money for food, housing, and clothes, was "not hardship alone, but hardship an outcome of injustice."[5] In *Justice and the Poor*, a 1919 study sponsored by the Carnegie Foundation, Reginald Heber Smith, a prominent Boston attorney, argued that one's ability to retain a lawyer and to pay court fees was a major and unequal determinant of one's ability to seek redress for grievances through the law. Smith had investigated the adequacy of the services provided by legal aid societies, which, as private, charitable organizations designed to help the poor settle disputes through legal means, the Carnegie Corporation was eager to encourage. He had concluded that "it is the wide disparity between the ability of the richer and poorer classes to utilize the machinery of the law which is, at bottom, the cause of the present unrest and dissatisfaction."[6]

At the other end of the spectrum, lawyers for large corporations were saying, as Francis Lynde Stetson, J. P. Morgan's lawyer, once put it, that they no longer knew "what to advise as lawful." Corporations were being subjected to suit, he maintained, even "when the Corporation does not know it is violating the law."[7] Lawyers like Stetson often brokered with federal officials to obtain private settlements for their clients; and, according to Elbert Gerry, chairman of U.S. Steel, federal regulation could be seen and understood as "a strong safeguard . . . to the prevention of violent attacks on private rights in general that might otherwise come."[8] Nevertheless, the federal trust-busting that began during Theodore Roosevelt's presidency had caused consternation among corporate lawyers.

The American Law Institute was structured in response to these varied complaints. It was intended to advance the belief that lawyers themselves, as members of a "public" profession, should shoulder the responsibility for bringing an end to a situation both wasteful and dangerous. If "uncertainty as to what the law is" already had resulted in intolerable delays and unwarranted discrepancies in the rendering of justice, ALI organizers argued, the way might be open for calls for legislative clarification in the form of statutory enactments.[9] This could result in a loss of the flexibility inherent in common law and threaten the highly cherished right and responsibility of the legal profession to develop that law through court arguments and decisions. ALI backers therefore believed the need for decisive professional action was urgent. As Elihu Root told the distinguished academic lawyers, practicing corporate attorneys, and judges assembled at the 1923 Washington meeting for formal establishment of the Institute, the alternative was "that we should ultimately come to the law of the Turkish Kadi, where a good man decides under good impulses and a bad man decides under bad impulses, as the case may be." Should that happen, Root warned, "our law, as a system, would have sunk below the horizon, and the basis of our institutions would have disappeared."[10]

Not all agreed that restatements of law developed by a private organization like the ALI were needed or wise. Supreme Court justice Oliver Wendell Holmes was skeptical of what he described as Root's "flamboyant address"; he observed an elite, self-serving motive among "the eminent . . . yearning for the upward and onward—specifically the restatement of the law."[11] His friend and colleague on the Court, Justice Louis Brandeis, simply remarked, "Why, I am restating the law every day."[12]

Like the unusual public yet private arrangement developed to provide nationally coordinated research through the National Academy of Sciences-National Research Council, the ALI was also a recognizably self-interested professional response. It was a means to deal with pressing social problems in ways that would advance the interests and priorities of elites within the legal profession. That this was indeed the case was evident in the concerns that joined the three groups involved in creating the ALI: the legal scholars represented in the Association of American Law Schools (AALS), the corporate lawyers and judges of the American Bar Association (ABA), and the philanthropist social architects on the Carnegie Corporation's board of trustees.

An Alliance of Legal Scholars and Corporate Lawyers

According to an ALI history written by William Draper Lewis, a University of Pennsylvania law professor and dean, and ALI director from 1923 to 1947, the origins of the Institute are to be found in two prewar speeches to the Association of American Law Schools, an organization formed in 1900 to unite "reputable" law schools so as to raise the standards of legal education.[13] The first speech, delivered in 1914 by Wesley Newcomb Hohfeld of Yale Law School, argued that university law schools were not "giving adequate recognition to the constructive science and art of legislation."[14]

[A] few decades ago the humanities, such as the classics, philosophy and mathematics, held the center of the stage in our great universities. During a more recent period natural science, greatly encouraged by the demands from the enormous industrial activities of the country, has had the position of by far the greatest prominence; and thus it is that we now have *separate* university departments of physics, chemistry, zoology, entomology, botany, geology, agriculture, horticulture, etc., *each* with elaborate equipment and with an able faculty frequently larger than that of an entire law school. . . . Just now, however, more than ever before, the political and social sciences are winning their way to prominence and respect; and this movement includes the science of justice according to law. All this being so, there would seem to be at the present moment an unusually great opportunity to persuade men that the kind of institution heretofore most neglected and now therefore most deserving to be fostered in behalf of the public interests is a great school of jurisprudence and law—one with a program more constructive, vital and hopeful than any yet represented in this country.[15]

Hohfeld was expressing a wish to shape public policy through specialized, scientific research rather than through direct, public advocacy, a wish shared by many turn-of-the-century social scientists eager for more assured professional standing. This aspiration, as well as more exclusionary concerns, was apparent in the address that followed Hohfeld's, one by Joseph H. Beale of the Harvard Law School, which was also delivered in December 1914. Like Hohfeld, Beale claimed that there was a pressing need for legal research and its linking to legal reform. Burgeoning concentrations of wealth had "led to a widely diffused feeling with which we must reckon: that those of average intelligence are not sufficiently protected by law against men of more powerful minds."[16] This Social Darwinist explanation of criticisms of economic inequality and American law was followed by the assertion that "within the last twenty years a horde of alien races from Eastern Europe and from Asia had been pouring in on us, accustomed to absolute government, accustomed to hate the law, and hostile above all to wealth and power." The phenomena required study, Beale said, possibly followed by legal reform; and "if the law is to be reformed, that must be done by lawyers of learning, light and leading." Universities should relieve law professors of some of their teaching duties and provide leaves of absence. They should "recognize that law is an all-important and a developing science." Law professors should be permitted "to advance knowledge as well as to teach it."[17]

As ALI director William Draper Lewis recognized, Hohfeld's and Beale's addresses paved the way for the creation in 1915 of "a special committee [of the AALS] on the establishment of a juristic center" probably to be located in Washington, D.C.[18] But not until 1920 was an effort made to reactivate the "juristic center" committee, which had not met during the war. In that year a renewed push was made "to bring into a single organization the law teachers and a select group of lawyers and judges who have a genuine interest in law reform."[19] A complex of issues, touched upon but not fully explicated in either Hohfeld's or Beale's remarks, was involved.

By the early twentieth century, the consequences of profound changes in the social situation of the legal profession were becoming uncomfortably evident. If midnineteenth-century American lawyers had been able to combine statesmanship with legal practice relatively easily, by the 1880s and 1890s this was no longer possible. As law had become more specialized, legal practice itself had become more all-engrossing. As corporation law developed and large law firms serving large corporate clients began to be formed, drawing in more and more of the most prominent members of the bar, lawyers gained wealth but lost the public respect and status they had held when private legal practice and public service had been more commonly combined. Commentators as different as Lord Bryce writing in the 1880s and Herbert Croly writing in the 1900s faulted the legal profession for having given up its tradition of disinterested public leadership. According to Croly, "the retainer which the American legal profession has accepted from the corporations" had placed it in danger of losing "its traditional position as the mouthpiece of the American political creed."[20] Addressing the American Bar Association in 1910, Woodrow Wilson, then president of Princeton and a political scientist, went further: "Lawyers have been sucked into the maelstrom of the new business system of the country." Continuing with criticism of corporations, through which "quite autocratic managers . . . [have] concentrated the resources, the choices, the opportunities, in brief, the power of thousands . . . [and] have accumulated the vast capital they employ," Wilson presented a direct challenge to the bar. "I am simply trying to analyze the existing constitution of business in blunt words of truth, without animus or passion of any kind . . . to recall you to the service of the nation as a whole, from which you have been drifting away; to remind you that, no matter what the exactions of modern legal business, no matter what or how great the necessity for specialization in your practice of law, you are not the servants of special interests, the mere expert counsellors of this, that, or the other group of business men; but guardians of the general peace, the guides of those who seek to realize by some best accommodation the rights of men."[21]

By the time of Wilson's address, this challenge had been accepted, if not by most practicing attorneys, then by at least two groups within the profession. First, there was a small group of reform-oriented practitioners, among them Louis Brandeis and Samuel Untermeyer, counsel to the Pujo Committee that investigated J. P. Morgan and other financiers, who believed that, in Yale psychologist Edward Stevens Robinson's words, lawyers should be "social engineers . . . specialists in social arrangements."[22] Such views posed a direct threat to corporate lawyers, especially those who approved Elihu Root's words in addressing the 1904 graduates of the Yale Law School: "There is one general characteristic of our system of government which is essential and which it is the special duty of lawyers to guard with care—that is, the observance of limitations of official power."[23]

In addition, there was a still relatively small, but increasingly self-conscious and ambitious, band of organized legal scholars represented by the AALS, who believed that lawyers, and indeed the law itself, should and could be restored to public prominence through the teaching and research of law teachers. The legal scholars also posed a threat to their corporate-oriented practitioner brethren, if a less obvious one. They believed and were arguing to this effect within the AALS, that scholars of the law were superior to and more important than practicing attorneys. Thus in 1906 William Draper Lewis had charged that, "in a world marked for increasing efficiency in organization, the lawyers of our country exhibit the anomalous spectacle of a body of persons apparently incapable of efficient co-operation for public ends. . . . If, as a profession, we are awake to our failure to perform our public duties, it is the small class of men who are devoting their lives to legal teaching who must point the way."[24] Lewis was reflecting the concern of academic lawyers with securing ABA recognition and cooperation in their effort to raise the standards of legal education, a concern that grew as nonuniversity, proprietary law schools proliferated in response to growing demand, often indeed from newly arrived immigrants. He shared the sentiment expressed later by his colleague Eugene A. Gilmore of the University of Wisconsin: "those who would lay upon the law teachers the task of law adaptation, improvement and reform do not thereby claim for them any superiority of capacity over the practitioner. It is rather a superiority of opportunity available to the law teachers and a lack of time and inclination on the part of the practitioner. The dominant and absorbing interest of the practising lawyer is in looking after the welfare of the business entrusted to him."[25]

Reluctant to encourage the legal scholars' drive to secure preeminent status within the organized bar, the corporate lawyers who dominated the ABA were nevertheless spurred to enter into an alliance with them. There were two reasons for this. First, in contrast to the agenda and strategy for increasing the profession's public prominence advanced by men like Untermeyer and Brandeis, the agenda and strategy of the legal scholars was less threatening. Second, the academic lawyers' efforts to gain status through acknowledgment of the superiority of the more established and prestigious law schools could offer a seemingly democratic way to foster the wish of many lawyers to exclude immigrants from entrance to the bar.

The troubled and nativist sentiments expressed by Beale in his 1914 address to the AALS were widely held and articulated by lawyers.[26] William V. Rowe spoke for many in a memorandum published in the *Illinois Law Review* in 1917:

Among the foreign stock we find some of our best scholarship and our most thirsty seekers for knowledge and light and material progress—a thirst, however, which, only too frequently, has slight relation to those qualities having to do with morals and character. . . . This foreign element is now largely of the blood of southern, eastern and central Europe. . . . By inheritance more or less hostile to all authority, and with little inherited sense of fairness, justice and honor as we understand them, the earnest striving for knowledge of many of these people is centered mainly upon their selfish advancement. . . . So much for their inherited character and point of view. Of equally disturbing import . . . is the fact that their legal traditions, such as they have, all rest upon a Continental 'ready made' code or system of law, handed down by authority, and that they have no inherited conception of, or capacity to understand, the common law, as the people's law. . . . How are we to preserve our Anglo-Saxon law of the land under such conditions? This is the stock from which our untrained lawyer-politicians will be drawn, and are, in a measure, now being drawn to flood our legislatures.[27]

Echoing these sentiments more succinctly, Harlan Fiske Stone, dean of the Columbia Law School, observed in 1915 that "the deterioration of the bar which has taken place during the past generation . . . has resulted mainly from the lowering of the average by the influx to the bar of greater numbers of the unfit."[28] Sometimes expressing their views in less explicitly racial terms that focused on the need to exclude "the poorly educated, the ill-prepared, and the morally weak," members of the ABA and the AALS were alike in their xenophobia.[29] Hostility to "prospective lawyers who were continental born" facilitated an alliance between members of the two organizations.[30]

Assistance from the Carnegie Philanthropies

Academic lawyers who belonged to the AALS were trying to establish more rigorous and more nationally uniform educational standards for entrance to the bar. This effort was expected to encourage the further development of university law schools, where standards of admission were high and where lawyers interested in a full-time career in teaching could find employment. It was expected to discourage, and eventually force the closing of, the growing numbers of proprietary schools, where standards of admission were lower. Practicing lawyers in need of additional income often worked in such schools as part-time professors at night. Immigrants were, of course, far more able to attend the proprietary schools. The educational credentials required for entrance to a university law school were expensive to procure (if only through forgone income) and, for many who were not young when they arrived, virtually unattainable.

Potentially relevant to the nativist fears and discriminatory wishes of ABA members, the calls of academic lawyers for higher standards in legal education were nevertheless treated with indifference in the first decade of the century. Then in 1910, the year of Woodrow Wilson's address "The Lawyer and the Community," the Carnegie Foundation published Abraham Flexner's noted study of medical education. The study had been commissioned by Henry Pritchett to demonstrate the Foundation's capacity to catalyze movement toward the elevated, scientific standards he believed institutions of higher education should maintain. The Flexner Report had been designed to empower and to be empowered by an already established drive of the American Medical Association for reform of medical education. The Flexner Report was a brilliant success; Pritchett's "technology of influence" worked without flaw. Only 85 of the 155 medical schools in existence in 1910 were still operating ten years later. Those that did not survive tended to be small, local, proprietary institutions of low standards, including six of the eight schools admitting black students. Lawyers were dazzled by the report's apparent effectiveness in forcing proprietary school closings.[31] Having wished earlier to survey schools of law, in February 1913 Pritchett received a letter from the ABA's Committee on Legal Education and Admission to the Bar, stating: "The Committee was greatly impressed by the investigation, made a few years ago under your direction by the Carnegie Foundation, into the conditions under which medical education is carried on in the United States. . . . The Committee of the Bar Association is most anxious to have a similar investigation made by the Carnegie Foundation into the conditions under which the work of legal education is carried on in this country. There is an imperative need for such an investigation."[32]

The study that resulted was written by Alfred Z. Reed, who was not a lawyer, just as Flexner had not been a doctor and Alvin Johnson, the author of the Corporation's unpublished library study, had not been a librarian. Not coincidentally, the study was entitled *Training for the Public Profession of the Law*. It was a brilliant exposition of the divisions that had developed between elite corporate and academic lawyers and jurists on the one hand, and nonelite, local attorneys who both served and preyed upon the poor on the other. Its prescriptions for educational reform did not parallel Flexner's, however. Flexner had called for one model of medical education, whereas Reed called for several models of legal education. He was critical of proprietary schools, but thought they should be acknowledged by the bar and improved. Unlike Flexner, Reed was sensitive to "the poor boy's" need for access to the profession. Reed believed that different kinds of training, to prepare for different kinds of legal work, should be allowed. But this was not the message that ABA lawyers had wanted. They had anticipated a report recommending educational reforms that would help "the old American stock . . . avert the threatened decay of constitutionalism in this country."[33] Before the report was actually published, therefore, copies were given to the ABA's Section on Legal Education and Admission to the Bar, of which Elihu Root had become chairman in 1920. Its recommendations were promptly repudiated. Fearing that the report might be as influential as the Flexner Report, thus undermining the exclusionary intent that had brought academic and practicing ABA lawyers together, the ABA now at last officially endorsed the AALS's long-sought campaign to raise standards. Before *Training for the Public Profession of the Law* reached the public, the ABA resolved that all candidates to the bar should have graduated from a law school requiring two years of collegiate preparation.[34]

The alliance between academic lawyers and corporate attorneys that was institutionalized in the ALI began to emerge with the ABA's request for a legal Flexner Report. It was, ironically, solidified by the possibility that the resulting report might increase, rather than decrease, immigrant entrance into the legal profession. And it was further cemented by support from the Carnegie Corporation, whose leading trustees were also deeply worried about the consequences of immigration.

Speaking to the New York State Bar Association in 1916, Elihu Root presaged the wish to safeguard American traditions that would be institutionalized in the ALI. "Fifteen per cent of the lawyers of this city are foreign born. Fifty per cent of the lawyers of this city are either foreign born or of foreign born parents. And the great mass of them have in their blood, with all the able and brilliant and good and noble men among them—have in the blood necessarily the traditions of the countries from which they came. They cannot help it. They will hold those traditions until they are expelled by the spirit of American institutions. That is a question of time. And somebody has got to look after it. Somebody has got to make the spirit of those institutions vocal. Somebody has got to exhibit belief in them, trust in them, devotion to them, loyalty to them, or you cannot win this great body from Continental Europe to a true understanding of and loyalty to our institutions."[35] In the same year, Henry Pritchett recommended that the Corporation finance a study of "the alien stream flowing into our citizenship." He was worried that "the immigrants of the last twenty years have learned far more slowly than those of former years the elemental ideals of America."[36] At this time, both Root and Pritchett were trustees of the Carnegie Institution of Washington, and the president of the Carnegie Institution was a trustee of the Carnegie Corporation. A leading supporter of eugenics research, the CIW paid for the work of biologist Charles B. Davenport, a prominent figure in the movement to connect experimental work in biology and genetics with efforts to improve what was then commonly described as "the germ-plasm" that controlled human evolution. It also financed the Cold Spring Harbor Laboratory for Experimental Evolution, of which Davenport was director, as well as the Eugenics Records Office there.

Supporters of eugenics believed, as it was expressed in the 1921 Carnegie Institution *Year Book*, that "there is no group of questions more significant in the complicated organization of human society than those concerning the meaning and the possibility of direction or control of inheritance in man."[37] Some supporters of eugenics urged selective breeding and forced sterilization of the "unfit." Others, for example, David Starr Jordan, president of Stanford University and a Carnegie Foundation trustee, called for the end to war, because it killed the bravest first and with them the best germ plasm. Studies sponsored by the NRC, the Carnegie Foundation, and the Carnegie Corporation, as well as other organizations, promoted the development of tests thought to measure innate intelligence and also supported the use of such tests to match people to jobs and educational opportunities.

Needless to say, one could be affiliated with the peace movement or see promise in mental testing without subscribing to the biological

determinism of the eugenicists; obversely, one could support heredi-
tarian explanations of human behavior without depending on the
genetic theories upon which eugenics was allegedly based. Hamilton
Cravens, in *The Triumph of Evolution*, a study of the hereditary-
environment controversy, has suggested that, at a time when many
believed that traditional American institutions were being eroded by
rapid change, it was relatively easy to translate a belief in the importance of individualism into a belief in the importance of what professionals biologists called "inheritance."[38] Whatever the reason, the fact
remains that Carnegie Corporation trustees worried about and financed projects that were intended to help preserve the racial purity
of American society.

Beyond that, Elihu Root endorsed the views of Madison Grant, a vehement anti-Semite and author of *The Passing of the Great Race*, an account of the danger facing the "Nordic race" that popularized the notion
of racial suicide through racial intermixing. Root also testified in favor
of the immigration restriction legislation that was passed in 1921 and
strengthened in 1924.[39] John Merriam, president of the CIW, was also a
close friend and colleague of Grant's.[40] The evidence is as clear as it is
convincing concerning sentiment within the legal profession: the trustees
of the Carnegie Corporation were convinced of the superiority of the
white, Anglo-Saxon "race," and were determined to preserve this, nowhere more so than in the "public profession of the law."

Legal Realists in Dissent

Motivated by nativist beliefs and anxieties that, at least in overt
expression, waned rather quickly as a variety of restrictive measures
were put into effect, the organizers and backers of the ALI had in
common a genuine concern with the adequacy of American law, as
well as a belief that, if "the people and legislative bodies, through
constitutions and statutes, [are] to express the political, economic, and
social policies of the nation[,] it is the province of lawyers to suggest,
construct and criticize the instruments by which these policies are
effectuated."[41] Translating this belief into practice opened the door to
fundamentally different views of what law was and should be as an
instrument of policy, and debates over these differences revealed the
enduringly important purposes and function of the ALI.

According to the "Report of the Committee on the Establishment of
a Permanent Organization for Improvement of the Law Proposing the

Establishment of an American Law Institute," which was accepted at the 1923 Washington meeting chaired by Elihu Root, the object of the ALI was "to promote the clarification and simplification of the law and its better adaptation to social needs, to secure the better administration of justice, and to encourage and carry on scholarly and scientific legal work."[42] To fulfill this objective there were to be studies and surveys of the actual "operation of existing rules of law," so that the law might be better adapted to existing needs, and each "restatement" of a different area of the law developed through a similar four-step process.[43] First, a Reporter, who was to be a prominent scholar and a leading authority on a particular subject, would examine "the present sources of the law" and draft a restatement to include "a complete citation of authorities, decisions, treatises, and articles." This draft was to be reviewed during several days of meetings by a Committee of Advisors made up of scholars, judges, and practicing attorneys. Next, following whatever revisions the Committee of Advisors mandated, the draft was to be reviewed by the Council of the Institute, which again included scholars, judges, and practicing attorneys. From there, the draft was to be returned to the Committee of Advisors for additional review and revision or sent to a meeting of the full membership of the Institute, which encompassed invited representatives from the academic, the judicial, and the elite practitioner segments of the bar. When finally approved by the Institute, an "official draft" was to be printed and "promulgated."[44]

The procedure established for restatements, while obviously a long and expensive one, was considered necessary to gain authority for the documents. After all, as Root explained, an ALI restatement was "not itself made law by any political authority." But ALI members hoped that each restatement "would be accepted as being prima facie a correct statement of the law contained in the decisions examined. Upon such a statement lawyers could safely advise their clients, and judges could safely decide their cases, unless good reason to the contrary should be shown."[45] In other words, the fact that the ALI was a private organization, voluntarily and on its own initiative assuming a public function, made this procedure necessary. Not surprisingly, however, the multilevel review and revision process, designed to encourage discussion and consensus, stimulated discussion and divergence instead.

As ALI director William Draper Lewis explained, it was not so much the question of "what the law was" that was controversial, but the basis for interpretations of law in the explication of cases.[46] When, in the last third of the nineteenth century, the father of the case method,

Harvard's Christopher Columbus Langdell, had set about developing a scientific basis for legal education, he had claimed that "all the available materials of the science [of law]," were "contained in printed books [of judicial opinion]."[47] The claim had been critical to the development of a special vocation for academic lawyers, who were qualified to teach, not because of "experience in the work of a lawyer's office, nor experience in dealing with men, nor experience in the trial or argument of cases," but through "experience in learning law."[48] It had also been helpful in legitimating a place for legal education within the growing university, and in turn had helped justify the superiority of university study as opposed to apprenticeship in a law office as a method of legal training. But the validity of Langdell's conception of legal science was problematic, at best, since different lawyers read the same words differently, depending in part on the knowledge, concerns, and biases they inevitably brought to a case. In consequence, lawyers had great difficulty agreeing on the precise meaning of case authority. In fact, "after a fair trial had been made"—the ALI spent more than ten thousand dollars trying to agree on citations to accompany its restatement of contracts (the first subject the ALI dealt with) and "got nowhere"—it was recognized that the venture would fail, if agreement had to be reached on both the substance of, and the authority for, the law.[49] In consequence, the ALI decided to publish restatements without "treatises discussing authorities," leaving these to be developed independently by Reporters, if they chose (which most, as it turned out, did not), "on their sole responsibility," and then to be published by the ALI separately from the substantive restatements.[50]

This solution to a potentially devastating problem was acceptable to those who believed that doctrine was the basis for common law, but unacceptable to those who believed that psychological and social circumstances—Oliver Wendell Homes would likely have called it "experience"—had to be, were, and should be the basis of common law.[51] Implicit in this disagreement were vital differences about how law should serve as "an instrument of public policy": whether, as proponents of a doctrinaire basis for common law believed, law should reconcile contemporary public policy with traditional views of liberties and rights; or whether, as proponents of an experiential basis for common law believed, law should reconcile contemporary public policy with empirical evidence of how traditional liberties and rights needed to be reformed in the face of new circumstances. The differences between these two groups were not unlike the differences between those who had favored "propaganda" in contrast to "research" as they discussed and then, bridging but not resolving their differences, managed to collaborate in launching not one but several institutes of economics. These differences of view had earlier led Root and other ABA members to resist the concept of "public" duty that reform-oriented practitioners like Brandeis supported. This, combined with nativism, led them into alliance with the academic lawyers in the AALS. By 1932, however, when the ALI's first restatement was published, a progressive, experiential view of law was gaining considerable influence among academic lawyers—far more so than had been the case in 1910 or even 1920.

As Wesley Hohfeld had suggested in his 1914 address to the AALS, academic lawyers were well aware of developments in other disciplines in the universities where they worked. Their colleagues in the social sciences were also struggling with the problem of how to gain public influence, as well as a professional legitimation as rigorous and authoritative as that of the increasingly respected and well-financed natural sciences. The problem faced by social scientists did not differ from that faced by academic lawyers. Academic lawyers also wanted public influence—indeed, more of it than their practitioner colleagues had. To achieve this through teaching and research, they needed a basis for claiming that they had techniques for understanding the law beyond generic skills of analysis. This encouraged legal scholars to accept the ideas and methods being developed within the newly specialized and professionalized social sciences. Increasingly throughout the 1920s and 1930s, therefore, so-called "realist" interpretations of judicial behavior and of the functions of the law were advanced by scholars at such trend-setting institutions as Harvard, Columbia, Johns Hopkins, and Yale. These were interpretations based upon insights and techniques of analysis derived from anthropology, sociology, economics, and psychology.[52]

Not all members of the "realist" movement concerned themselves with the ALI, but many did. The ALI was a well-financed operation engaged in important work, and it was purposefully and brilliantly designed to be influential. Indeed, as Henry Pritchett explained to William Draper Lewis, the Carnegie Corporation trustees thought it "essential that a mass of organized opinion be put behind whatever is done by the organization."[53] Beyond the multilevel review and revision process, which was developed in order to secure endorsements of restatements by a select group of nationally prominent lawyers, it was therefore decided in 1927 that each restatement would be annotated by state bar associations. Lewis explained the logic for this: "The

Restatement states the law as it would be today decided by the great majority of courts. There is always the possibility [however] that a State has followed in the past and will continue to follow a different rule."[54] Although no official state bar association endorsement was asked, willingness to engage in annotation, even annotation noting divergences, reinforced the legitimacy of the ALI endeavor. Later, indices "to take the reader from volume to volume where related subject-matter is treated" were also published, as was a collection of "The Restatement in the Courts," with "a brief paragraph indicating the citation of every appellate court decision which has cited the Restatement and the use made by the court of it."[55] "The Restatement in the Courts" series, combined with the indices, state annotations, and the restatements themselves, which were brilliantly clear, pristine formulations of "black-letter law," gave the ALI's promulgations, as Lewis claimed, "an authority far greater than those of us who organized the Institute to do the work anticipated."[56] In light of its carefully crafted methods for gaining authority and influence, the ALI was difficult to ignore, especially if one's view of the law led one to believe, as did most realist legal scholars, that the ALI was not restating but rather remaking the law.

One person who recognized this from the start was Herman Oliphant, a realist professor at the Columbia University Law School. In 1928 President Nicholas Murray Butler (a founding trustee of the Carnegie Foundation and, beginning in 1925, in his capacity as president of the Carnegie Endowment for International Peace, a trustee of the Carnegie Corporation) thwarted an effort to reorganize the law school according to a functionalist plan developed by Oliphant and other faculty members interested in realist scholarship. One result of the realists' defeat at Columbia was the departure of Oliphant and his close colleague Hessel E. Yntema for Johns Hopkins, where they established a short-lived realist Institute for the Study of Law. At the same time, William O. Douglas and Underhill Moore left Columbia for Yale, where they also promoted legal realism within both the law school and the Institute of Human Relations.[57]

At an Academy of Political Science meeting in 1923 held just five months after the ALI was established, Oliphant announced the realists' challenge to the organization. "There can be no mere restatement of the law. Where will it [the ALI] find a field of law in which there are no questions with conflicting answers, each supported by a line of decisions? It must choose between these two lines of cases and, in choosing, it will state new law in the jurisdiction of the rejected cases."[58]

The impossibility of restatement notwithstanding, Oliphant, at least in 1923, supported the experiment the ALI was about to launch. He thought the Institute's choice of subjects—agency, conflict of laws, contracts, judgments, property, restitution, security, torts, and trusts—was sound. Of particular importance to lawyers interested in preserving the rights of corporations, these subjects were not necessarily of the greatest importance to private individuals concerned with preserving their civil rights. Aware of this, Oliphant remarked that the ALI had "excluded from study . . . such matters as the rights of parties in the struggles of labor and capital and the scope of the due-process clause of the Constitution in fixing the limits of social legislation. . . . The reason . . . is not that they contain debated questions, but that such of their questions as are debated still cut more deeply into the popular mind [than do the subjects chosen for study]. . . . They play on the deep plane of the instincts of self-interest, the plane of prejudice and emotion. For economy of time let such questions be called political questions. They are to be avoided because they involve social-policy judgments having a marked emotional content. These judgments it is distinctly not the business of the Institute to formulate."[59]

By thus avoiding the most divisive questions of policy, Oliphant argued that the ALI could be a source of progress in the law. He favored its efforts to develop "sound" objective methods for basing law and legal decision-making on expert knowledge of business, sociology, and government. This would advance a truly "scientific" basis for law, he believed, substituting for a haphazard reliance upon common sense a "study [of] the business and social structure affected by rules of law."[60] This was necessary, he claimed, for the law more effectively to fulfill its true function, which was, as Oliphant saw it, to make society work better. That the kind of study Oliphant favored could lead to interpretations as different as those evident in existing legal decision-making was a possibility he did not consider. He shared a then typical sense of certainty about what the social sciences could accomplish and reveal. A leading realist, he initially supported the ALI because his view of law led him to assume that the task the ALI had set for itself would, if well done, inevitably contribute to a more valid, scientific "sociological jurisprudence."[61]

Soon after the first volume of the restatement appeared, Oliphant gave up his academic career to join Franklin Roosevelt's brain trust. He suggested to FDR the tax on undistributed corporate profits that was enacted in 1936.[62] This was but one of many examples of the way in which realist lawyers working for the New Deal went outside of institutions controlled by the legal profession to try to make law the kind of instrument for progressive social policy they thought it should be.

Perhaps for this reason, Oliphant did not comment on ALI restatements as they appeared, but his realist colleagues still in academe did. Notable, in relation to the views and hopes Oliphant expressed in 1923, were comments by the professor with whom he had left Columbia for Johns Hopkins, Hessel E. Yntema. Addressing the 1935 annual meeting of the AALS, Yntema agreed with Oliphant's earlier statements about the soundness of the ALI's initial plans and argued that these plans provided "an admirable standard by which to measure the adequacy of the actual Restatement of the Law."[63] The contrast he then developed between projected and actual accomplishments was withering and revealing. Rather than the anticipated "statement of law, analytical, critical, and constructive, embodying whatever improvements in the law itself might be recommended," Yntema declared that "the actual Restatement of the Law purports to be, and is substantially limited to, a statement of the law as it is." Despite promises of "a complete citation and critical discussion of all relevant legal materials," there was none. Studies of "legal procedure and of the administration of justice" having been "explicitly anticipated," only work on criminal procedure had begun, and this was being carried forward as a plan for a model law and not as a restatement.[64]

What Yntema was lamenting in his address to the AALS was that the ALI had been turned, as he saw it, from progressive to conservative ends. First, it had been turned from an effort to improve the law through research to an effort to translate it, "as it is," into codelike form—so-called "black-letter law," without the citations of precedent necessary for continuing legal interpretations and reinterpretation. And second, it had been turned from an effort to deal with legal procedures and the administration of justice in all their ramifications, including those touching upon the availability of justice equally to all, to an effort to deal only with criminal violations of the law, which left untouched civil violations and, as opposed to violations of law, violations of justice itself. Nor would a model law, needless to say, have the authority of a restatement. Implying betrayal, Yntema concluded that these changes would be difficult to explain "except upon the supposition that the policy of securing the public acceptance of the Restatement has affected its content and perhaps even partially diverted the fundamental purpose."[65]

Yntema's criticisms, combined with his thinly veiled suggestion that the ALI had knowingly gone back upon its original promises, were echoed by other critics, none of whom troubled leaders of the ALI more than Charles E. Clark. An ALI member (as Yntema was not), Clark was a realist scholar and dean of the Yale University Law School. Purporting to speak for "that large number of the workers themselves and certainly large numbers of law teachers if not of lawyers [who] recoil from the 'restatement' straitjacket," Clark charged a retreat from initial plans.[66] More important, he claimed that, "caught between stating the law which should be and the law which is," the ALI had ended up "stating only the law that was." Attributing this to "a shift in emphasis from stating the law to stating the conclusions of the experts as to the general situation in the country upon the topics considered," Clark charged that "the Institute seems constantly to be seeking the force of a statute without statutory enactment."[67]

Defending the ALI

Yntema's criticisms were answered by ALI director William Draper Lewis with reasoned explanation of the difficulties encountered in developing agreement concerning case authorities for the restatements. Clark's criticisms elicited a response by George W. Wickersham, a prominent corporate lawyer and former U.S. Attorney General, who was the ALI's president.[68] Although Wickersham's statement was moderated before publication, in draft form it came close to an ad hominem attack. Belaboring the fact that Clark was not only an ALI member but also a member of the Committee of Advisors for the Restatement of Property, Wickersham claimed a high "general professional estimate of the value of this work" based upon the fact that five thousand sets of volumes had already been sold. Following this statement, which confused a measure of potential influence with professional praise, Wickersham dismissed the Yale dean's "charming naiveté" with the following: "Limitations of space prevent a more detailed analysis of Mr. Clark's criticism. It represents a school of thought [i.e., the realist school] which, to the writer, seems one of the unfortunate developments of the time. The academic mind delights in uncertainties. The practical work of the everyday lawyer calls for definite standards by which the activities of business, commerce and industry are conducted."[69]

To be fair to Wickersham, it is true that, regardless of book sales, the ALI's work was highly regarded by prominent members of the legal profession. For example, when asked by Lewis to endorse the ALI's request for additional Carnegie Corporation funds, Benjamin N. Cardozo, chief judge of the New York Court of Appeals, stated:

I appreciate the fact that here and there, in respect of one topic or another, there is room for difference of opinion as to the accuracy of the work or its harmonizing power. I know, besides, that the very greatness of the enterprise has made it difficult for the members of the Council and the general members of the Institute to subject the successive drafts to minute and patient criticism, with the result that the value of the work must rest to a large degree, perhaps larger than we had hoped, on the authority of the Reporters and their advisors, checked and supported none the less by the comment and the suggestion of an informed and expert audience. If I state at the outset these restraints upon eulogy, it is only in the hope and with the desire of maintaining the judicial attitude. When all deductions from panegyric have been made, my residuary conviction is still strong and unabated that no project so important for the simplification of our common law and for its harmonious development has been launched during all the years of its history upon the soil of the New World.[70]

Beyond such favorable endorsements, Wickersham did have a point in noting that practicing lawyers often had needs and interests different from those of academics. Finally, whether legal realism was an "unfortunate development" or not, the radical skepticism of some realists did lead eventually to the legally and socially destructive argument that law could not have integrity since, in reality, it was little more than the authoritative assertion of personal biases, opinions, and neuroses.[71] Still, Wickersham did not appreciate, as William Draper Lewis seems to have done, that Clark (and others) were making incisive comments about what the ALI had and had not accomplished in its First Restatement. This suggests that divergences between the ALI's projected plans as of 1923, and its actual accomplishments as of the mid-1930s, were seen by Wickersham as insignificant and perhaps even predictable. Most likely, this was also the view of Elihu Root.

As in the ALI, where Root was honorary president and senior to him, Wickersham was Root's junior partner in many public undertakings.[72] Indeed, following Root's speech to the 1923 Washington meeting advocating a permanent institution through which members of the legal profession could restate the law, it had been Wickersham who actually made the motion to establish the ALI. The careers and social concerns of the two men were similar. Wickersham believed that immigrants who became lawyers lacked the "full realization of the meaning of our law historically" and were interested only in personal mobility and gain. "To think of some of these men getting into political life, coming ultimately to be judges and interpreting the law, and, with, their imperfect ideas of our political institutions, having an influence upon the development of our constitution, and upon the growth of American institutions," was frightening, he remarked in 1922.[73] Backing the ABA's support for higher educational standards for admission to the bar, which Root had sponsored, Wickersham joined Root in securing ABA support for the ALI. In his reply to Charles E. Clark, he was trying to safeguard that support from a potentially dangerous attack.

So far as Wickersham was concerned, the purpose of the ALI was, as Root had put it in 1923, to provide "a statement of the common law of America which will be the *prima facie* basis on which judicial action will rest; and any lawyer, whose interest in litigation requires him to say that a different view of the law shall be taken, will have upon his shoulders the burden to overturn the statement."[74] The restatement was, indeed, to involve "science." But it was to involve legal science as Langdell had defined it. Writing in the 1870s, Langdell had said:

Law, considered as a science, consists of certain principles or doctrines . . . the growth [of which] is to be traced in the main through a series of cases; and much the shortest and best, if not the only, way of mastering the doctrine effectively is by studying the cases in which it is embodied. But the cases which are useful and necessary for this purpose at the present day bear an exceedingly small proportion to any that have been reported. The vast majority are useless, or worse than useless, for any purpose of systematic study. . . . It seems to me, therefore, to be possible to take such a branch of law as Contracts, for example, and without exceeding comparatively modest limits, to select, classify or arrange all the cases which had contributed in any important degree to the growth, development or establishment of its essential doctrines.[75]

Legal science as sociological jurisprudence was different. It involved using the social sciences and psychology to analyze and guide the evolution of the law. As early as 1916, Root had condemned the misguided conclusions of "half baked and conceited theorists"—law school "professors who think they know better what law ought to be, and what the principles of jurisprudence ought to be, and what the political institutions of the country ought to be, than the people of England and America, working out their law through centuries of life."[76] It would appear, therefore, that the ambitious 1923 plans for the ALI had suggested different kinds of "science" to Wickersham and Root from those it had suggested to Oliphant, Yntema, Clark, and perhaps also Lewis, who had actually drafted the plans for the ALI.

Everything Root did in the realm of law during the later period of his life was intended to strengthen the legal profession. Seeing merit in an alliance with academic lawyers as a means to securing this end, Root could countenance priorities he considered irrelevant and misguided. Thus, he could endorse plans for the ALI that included the aspirations of academic lawyers like Oliphant, Lewis, and before them Hohfeld, because he wanted legal scholars and practicing corporate lawyers to collaborate, and through that collaboration to become the backbone of a stronger, more public, and more homogeneous profession. To endorse plans is not to help fulfill them, however; and having won the collaboration of academic lawyers and presided over the launching of the ALI, Root secured Carnegie Corporation funds to develop restate-ments—a second grant of $1,020,196 was made in 1933—as well as state annotations that state bar associations could not or would not finance. But he did not secure Corporation funds to support the work necessary to illuminate disputes concerning case authority through the kind of social research the realists wanted, even though he most likely could have done so. The Corporation's second grant to the ALI, in 1933, was resisted by at least one trustee, Russell Leffingwell, who had been active in the ALI and thought the restatements not worth the money involved. But in this instance, as in most others, Root prevailed.[77] Throughout his years as a trustee of the Corporation, Root was able to gain funds for virtually any project he favored; it is difficult to believe that would not have been the case with the ALI.

Whether or not more money to provide more time and talent would have realized the hopes for the ALI held by legal realists must remain a moot question. Still, what the Corporation did not support could be as significant in its impact on public policy, and as revealing of Corporation priorities, as what it did support. Hence, the ALI's lack of funds for the kinds of projects the legal realists were interested in, including studies of legal procedure and the administration of justice, was telling. Root was a staunch Republican who had felt most at home in the McKinley era, and he apparently did not think these projects vital. His goals for the ALI derived from his nativism and from his closely related conservative concerns for preserving the social struc-tures of American society. By restating the law "as it is"—or, according to Charles E. Clark, "as it was"—the ALI was designed to preserve the notion that a corporation, without the same extent of personal liability, had rights similar to an individual.

Root could, and on occasion did, acknowledge a need for reforms in the administration of the American legal system. He did this, and did it eloquently, in his foreword to Reginald Heber Smith's *Justice and the Poor*, where he said: "No one . . . doubts that it is the proper function of government to secure justice. In a broad sense that is the chief thing for which government is organized. Nor can any one question that the highest obligation of government is to secure justice for those who, because they are poor and weak and friendless, find it hard to maintain their own rights. This book shows that we have not been performing that duty very satisfactorily, and that we ought to bestir ourselves to do better."[78] Eager to preserve the legal profession's prerogatives, he concluded: "I do not think that we should be over-harsh in judging ourselves. . . . We have had in the main just laws and honest courts to which people—poor as well as rich—could repair to obtain justice. . . . I think the true criticism which we [lawyers] should make upon our own conduct is that we have been so busy about our individual affairs that we have been slow to appreciate the changes of conditions which to so great an extent have put justice beyond the reach of the poor. But we cannot confine ourselves to that criticism much longer; it is time to set our own house in order."[79] This was what the ALI was to help in doing.

Over time, as it moved on to develop additional restatements and a variety of national legal codes, including the Uniform Commercial Code, which were to be adopted through state legislative action, the ALI accepted many of the criticisms made of its First Restatement. For example, its restatements were no longer presented *ex cathedra* without case authorities. After the First Restatement these were integrated with the substantive "black-letter law," although expressed as interpretations developed by the Reporters. And a code like the Uniform Commercial Code was designed to combine principles of law with actual customary practices in the businesses involved.[80] The chief Reporter for the Uniform Commercial Code, Karl Llewellyn, was a legal realist—indeed, one of the most important.[81]

Such changes notwithstanding, the law "as it is," transmitted via the case method of instruction as developed by Langdell at Harvard, still predominates in American law schools. This static, formal view of law has been criticized, as has the case method, which presumes that textual analysis can provide sufficient training for aspiring lawyers apart from other kinds of study and experience. Nevertheless, Langdellian conceptions of law and of legal education have remained essential to the legal profession and to American law. And because ALI restatements have, as planned, set forth simplified, codelike versions of case law, they have in turn provided essential support to these Langdellian views and practices. Whatever else it has accomplished, therefore, the ALI has played an important role in helping a strong profession maintain its exclusive role in legal interpretation and, through that, in the making of common law. As it did through its grants to the NAS-NRC, to the NBER, and to other private centers of economic policy research, the Carnegie Corporation thus again played a vital role in helping organized private groups preserve access to the processes through which essential national policies and agenda were formulated. Not only "what the law is," but how law would (and would not) serve the different and sometimes conflicting interests of different individuals and groups, have remained to a large extent matters for the organized legal profession to determine.

II

Cultural Philanthropy

HELPING TO DEVELOP research institutes and other centers of scientific expertise was a central goal of Carnegie Corporation grant-making during the early 1920s. Promoting public enlightenment became increasingly important thereafter. This had been Andrew Carnegie's goal as a philanthropist, and now, in relation to "progressive" concerns about effective governance, it again became a primary Corporation aspiration. The logic for this return to cultural philanthropy derived from the realization that there could not be general concurrence in the policy recommendations of experts in law, economics, the natural sciences, or other fields, unless the citizenry was prepared to respect and to follow the advice of those who knew more than they. In 1897 Harvard president Charles W. Eliot, in an address on "The Function of Education in Democratic Society," had said: "Confidence in experts, and willingness to employ them and abide by their decisions, are among the best signs of intelligence in an educated individual or an educated community; and in any democracy which is to thrive, this respect and confidence must be felt strongly by the majority of the population." His views were shared by the Corporation trustees.[1]

To foster the attributes of character and mind that would nurture confidence in experts, the trustees did not look primarily to the nation's formal institutions of schooling. Henry Pritchett spoke for many members of the Corporation's board when he said that an "over-emphasis on education, and in particular on higher education, as the sole opening for the youth of the country has not only filled the schools with ill-assorted pupils, but has closed the minds of people to the opportunities offered by agencies other than the school."[2] The challenge was to channel popular interest in education into alternative agencies, among them the library, the adult education center, and the art museum.

In the 1920s more and more Americans were pursuing cultural activities of diverse kinds. According to the Corporation's own estimates, in the mid-1920s 1.5 million Americans were enrolled in correspondence schools; 1 million were attending public evening schools; 150,000 students were taking part in university extension programs; 100,000 adults were participating in YMCA courses and classes; and 100,000 visited the Metropolitan Museum of Art and the Chicago Art Institute at least once a year for a concert or an exhibition.[3] Recent studies by Colin B. Burke have found that private correspondence schools enrolled approximately twice as many students as the regular colleges throughout this period, and that more than one in five American adults were taking part in some form of higher education on the eve of the Great Depression.[4]

No less indicative of popular educational and cultural pursuits were the sales figures for popular publications, which soared during the 1920s. One example was the Little Blue Books of Emanuel Haldeman-Julius. These were small, inexpensive paperback editions of the classics (Shakespeare, Dante, Goethe, Plato, and the like), as well as works about sex, atheism, and radical politics, and how-to-do-it manuals such as *How to Get the Most Out of Walking, How to Make Money in Wall Street,* and *How to be Happy Though Married.* The Little Blue Books went to millions of readers in the 1920s; approximately 300 million copies were sold between 1919 and 1951.[5] Somewhat more middlebrow in its appeal, the Book-of-the-Month Club, which was founded in 1926 and enrolled 60,000 members in its first year of operation, had 110,588 members by 1929.[6]

Within this context, the Corporation's programs were notable, not so much for the encouragement they gave to continuing education or cultural activities outside of schools and colleges, as for the support they provided to organize such education according to standards held by the nation's traditional "custodians of culture." Popular thirst for knowledge and learning was greeted with ambivalence by those custodians, who on the whole were well-to-do, WASP men and women who had long understood culture in moral terms. Heeding Ralph Waldo Emerson as well as Matthew Arnold, they assumed that the pursuit of culture was a means to build "character," that culture nurtured fortitude, resolve, courage, honesty, disinterest, public spirit, and "good taste," this last defined as a preference for simple, muted, symmetrical designs. Charles C. Alexander has observed that men and women of this group were "worried lest the influx of non-Anglo-Saxon peoples, the pursuit of [new] wealth, and the excesses of popular democracy destroy American's artistic potential . . . [and therefore] felt obliged to safeguard the 'fine arts' from popular debasement."[7] They could accept Charles Eliot's justification for publishing a preselected set of classics. With Eliot, they could believe that the so-called "Five Foot Shelf" of Harvard Classics might offer, if not a liberal education, at least a "liberal frame of mind."[8] But they were horrified by claims such as those made by Emanuel Haldeman-Julius in his advertising for the Little Blue Books. "Why are Great Books Simple?" the publisher asked, and then answered: "All great things are simple. That is what makes them great."[9] Here was indisputable evidence of a loss of rationality, discipline, and rigor. Culture was becoming mere amusement, entertainment, and escape. How could character survive?

Confirmed in the belief that exposure to culture was a determinant of the development of virtuous character, the Corporation's trustees turned to Frederick P. Keppel to design programs of grants to popularize access to culture without "debasement." A man of strong personality and pragmatic inclination, well versed in the classical liberal arts, Keppel took over as president of the Carnegie Corporation in 1923 and remained in that office until 1941. The programs he initiated were remarkable for their success in linking the moralistic Victorian concerns of trustees like Elihu Root to emerging patterns of professional organization and professional leadership. The Keppel cultural programs tended to provide reinforcement for the "high" cultural standards of established cultural elites, and to do so without mediating the tension, endemic in American culture, between *mission* and *market*. This tension is best recognized in differences between "good" taste and "popular" taste; between the edifying (designed to be instructive or uplifting) and the entertaining (designed to amuse or please); and between that which is created to be excellent and that which is created to sell. Perhaps no program of cultural philanthropy could diminish that tension; but the Corporation's interwar grant-making certainly did not do so, and that limited the influence of what was achieved.

Of course, one study that initially derived from the Corporation's cultural interests did have enduring influence. That was Gunnar Myrdal's classic study of race relations in the United States, *An American Dilemma*. Plans for the study were shaped by the Corporation's interest in the Harlem Renaissance, even though the work that resulted said little about the arts or adult education. Seeking guidance about the best approaches to "Negro education," the Corporation sponsored one of the most important works of social science of the twentieth century. The study presented massive and varied data that might eventually lead to public policies to ensure racial integration. Although the origins of the Myrdal study in the history of its sponsoring agency have been obscure over the years, its significance as a model of applied public policy research has long been clear. The Myrdal study influenced public policies, directly, through its influence upon the 1954 *Brown v. Board of Education* decision, and, indirectly, through its slow and widespread influence upon the climate of opinion that made the *Brown* decision possible. Not as the study was initially envisioned, but as it turned out, *An American Dilemma* provided a model that the Corporation sought to emulate when, after the Second World War, its focus shifted again, this time to "strategic philanthropy."

CHAPTER FIVE

Mission vs. Market
Organizing the Education of Everyone

B EGINNING IN THE mid-1920s, cultural philanthropy returned
to the center of Carnegie Corporation grant-making. The Twenties were an innovative period in the history of American culture, the
era of the flapper, jazz, and youth revolt, of F. Scott Fitzgerald and
Zelda, and of Edna St. Vincent Millay and the Provincetown Players.
It was also a time of status quo, as seen in the Scopes Trial of 1925,
pitting fundamentalist Christianity against modern evolutionary science, and the bestseller *The Man Nobody Knows*, published the same
year, in which the advertising man Bruce Barton portrayed Jesus as a
businessman. The crusading energies of the first decades of the century
were less in evidence, if not completely dissipated, and few wanted to
hear about the poor in the urban slums or the "starving Armenians"
who had been made famous by Herbert Hoover's wartime relief work.[1]
Old realities persisted despite experiments among the young: the farm
lighted only with kerosene, the company shack built next to the open
pit mine, and for many citizens of a prosperous nation, hunger, poverty,
disease, and slums. The liberated "new woman" of the Twenties may
have inspired dreams and, later, historical stereotypes, but she coex-
isted with, and was probably outnumbered by, traditional housewives
likely to agree with the woman who wrote: "We crave adventure,
experimentation, drama, beauty; only we know that for ourselves they
cannot be bought save at the expense of our daily bread."[2]
   In response to popular interest in culture and to changes in definitions
of what culture was, the Carnegie Corporation provided funds to a

great variety of people, activities, and institutions within three loosely defined "program" areas: libraries, adult education, and the arts. So diverse as to seem almost random, Corporation grants supported the traditional, the maverick, and everything between. But amid the diversity, and across program areas, there was a common theme: the premise that leadership was urgently needed in cultural affairs. If culture were left to evolve willy-nilly without the guidance and criticism of educated connoisseurs, the crass, material self-interest of individual entrepreneurs would triumph over the public's need for sound information and true beauty, and the forces of the market would triumph over the ennobling mission of culture. Encouraging potential patrons and facilitating professional leadership were therefore the Corporation's dual goals. The challenge was to find ways to increase popular access to culture while also transferring responsibility for cultural conservation from the old-line patricians, who had once served as guardians of the genteel, to organizations and groups associated with the new professional scientific and engineering elites.

Frederick Paul Keppel as President of the Carnegie Corporation

As often as not, the Corporation's hopes for its cultural programs were not explicitly stated or fully and clearly explained. This was a reflection of the personality and style of Frederick Paul Keppel. Keppel was officially elected president in December 1922 but did not take office until the fall of 1923. First he had to fulfill commitments at the Russell Sage Foundation, where he had recently been appointed executive secretary of the New York Regional Survey and Plan. Remaining as the Corporation's chief executive until November 1941, he provided the stability and consistent leadership it needed. Charming, genial, energetic, and cultivated, he had a style and interests crucial to defining the Corporation's approach to cultural philanthropy throughout the interwar years.

Born on Staten Island in 1875, Keppel was the son of an art dealer who specialized in prints and engravings. He had grown up in a genteel, cultivated family of comfortable means. He attended the Yonkers public schools and, after a brief period working in the stock room of his father's business, he entered Columbia College and graduated in 1898. He was an excellent student, helped start a poetry magazine, and edited the college newspaper; he had been active in the fraternity

Psi Upsilon and rowed on the Columbia crew. After college, he worked briefly for Harper & Brothers, the publishers, and then, in 1900, began a long stint back at Columbia, where he served, first, as assistant secretary (1900–1902), then, as secretary (1902–10), and, finally, as dean of Columbia College (1910–17). Art, books, Latin, poetry—the stuff of a classical liberal education had loomed large in Keppel's experience. What is more, at least in him they had served the purpose assumed by traditional proponents of liberal culture: according to all accounts, Frederick P. Keppel was a man of character.[3]

Tall and rigorous, with a carefully trimmed mustache and a twinkle in his eye, Keppel was neither an earnest Victorian gentleman like Henry Pritchett nor a precise and tidy administrator like James R. Angell. He was much more gregarious than either and far more interested in people and their problems than in the discovery of a scientific calculus for social change. It was even claimed that he had "a genius for getting along with the rest of the human race" and that his office at the Carnegie Corporation was "the most informal and friendly in the business."[4] More consistently intelligent and all-embracing in his thought than incisive or profound, he tended to approach problems in a practical, ad hoc, intuitive fashion; he was as disinclined to offer elaborate and formally principled rationales for his actions as he was inclined to consider how they might affect the many individuals he knew. Respectful of human foibles while demanding hard work of himself and of those around him, "F.P.K.," as he was often called, ran the Carnegie Corporation more as a retail shop with many valued and welcome clients than as a scientific bureau involved in national affairs.[5]

During the First World War Keppel had served as third assistant secretary of war under Newton D. Baker. His chief responsibilities involved personnel issues, which kept him in close touch with Raymond Fosdick, who later became president of the Rockefeller Foundation. At the time, Fosdick was serving as chief of the Commissions on Training Camp Activities, which managed "a vast positive program" of recreation and education intended as an antidote to low morale and discipline problems; it ranged from moving pictures and Bible classes to courses on virtually every subject from bookkeeping to auto mechanics and French grammar.[6] According to Fosdick, these educational and recreational activities accounted for the closing of red-light districts, a reduction in the venereal disease rate, and a general buildup of the fighting forces.[7] Very different from the educational activities he had supervised at Columbia, Fosdick's program nevertheless kept Keppel, who was Fosdick's Washington liaison, engaged in educational administration of sorts.

Keppel would have liked to go to work for the Carnegie Corporation earlier than he did.[8] In fact, he had hoped to become president when he left the War Department in 1919; but, having been passed over in favor of Angell, he had gone instead to the American Red Cross, then, to the International Chamber of Commerce, and, finally, to the Russell Sage Foundation. The Regional Plan that he was to have directed at Russell Sage was in some ways a model for what he would try to do at the Corporation.[9] Calling upon the expertise of diverse professionals, among them architects, lawyers, social workers, and engineers, it provided data-rich forecasts of needs and resources for the New York metropolitan region, with recommendations for business, transportation, residential, recreational, and cultural development. Addressed to the various responsible government agencies, business concerns, and private citizen groups, it was, according to Roy Lubove's study of community planning, "eminently successful."[10] Many of its proposals were acted upon, and it helped stimulate county planning organizations throughout the region. With this close exposure to a model of progressive "good government" in action, as well as his previous experience, behind him, it was not difficult for Keppel to move on to the Carnegie Corporation.

The new chief executive's transition was eased by an already-agreed-upon mandate setting forth future directions for Carnegie philanthropy. Actively involved in the same Russell Sage-sponsored New York Regional Plan with which Keppel had been associated, Elihu Root had earlier participated in an effort to plan the development of Washington, D.C. This had led Root to equate good taste (as he defined it) with high character and moral integrity.[11] It placed him in close alliance with cultural custodians like the architects Charles F. McKim and Daniel H. Burnham (who was commissioned to build the headquarters for the NAS-NRC), the parks planner Frederick Law Olmsted, the sculptor Augustus Saint-Gaudens, and the painter and author F. D. Millet—all advocates of simple, classic designs and of education via exposure to tasteful and inspiring public art. Increasingly dismayed by the prevalence of buildings and public displays dominated by the bright and gaudy, the Victorian eclectic and gingerbread, Root came to believe that American culture had to be "elevated by a purer and nobler taste."[12] By the 1920s, his concern for popularizing neoclassical styles found its way into Carnegie Corporation policy documents. As early as 1922 it had been decided that the Corporation would assist "the fine arts and the general range of aesthetic interests,"[13] and become involved in "a movement for art education and art appreciation . . . to unite all the arts in the common endeavor to educate the public tastes and to train men and women who may interpret the arts to the body of the people."[14]

In addition, the Corporation's trustees had picked up on Henry Pritchett's concern about overpopulation in the colleges, and the memoranda that awaited Keppel urged that consideration be given to "the methods by which knowledge can be increased and its apprehension spread among the body of the people."[15] Efforts were also to be made, outside of schools and colleges as well as within, to promote "further . . . understanding of that deeper stratum of knowledge and feeling which involves philosophy, art, and the comprehension of human relations."[16] Finally, there was a wish to find some way to continue fostering the development of libraries. After all, as Elihu Root put it, that was the "Andrew Carnegie Tradition."[17]

With the direction set—the arts, adult education, and libraries were at the core of the Corporation's new program—Keppel began to talk, to listen, to hold informal meetings, and then to convene somewhat more formal conferences. Identifying and securing the cooperation of people who might lend status and authority was his first objective. For a man like Keppel, who was distinctly collegial in administrative style, a natural way to proceed was elite consensus-building, a first and necessary step to voluntary regulation through managerial cooperation. Keppel pursued a strategy that advocates of an "associative state" would have approved. Although disinclined to make public statements about politics, he demonstrated an astute understanding of the politics of knowledge as that politics was defined in the mid-1920s.

Organizing Cultural Leadership through Conferences and Associations

In the library field, the new Carnegie president found a ready ally for the development work he wished to undertake. Established in 1876 and dominated by well-educated, activist, ambitious men, the American Library Association was intended to elevate the status of the increasingly feminized field of librarianship.[18] It was much less representative of the people actually involved in library service than the numerous state and local library associations and commissions, whose traditional purpose was "to provide a little much needed training for untrained and too often uneducated persons actually in charge of small public libraries."[19] As was true of librarianship generally, these state and local organizations were dominated by women; the ALA, by contrast, was not. Between 1890 and 1923, for example, 393 women and 267 men held elected office in state library associations; 252 women and 117 men held elected office in local library associations; and 154 women and 121 men held elected office in library commissions. During this period, only one in four of the officers of the ALA were women.[20]

In Andrew Carnegie's day, the Carnegie Corporation had often sought advice and help from these state and local library groups, but during the war it had begun to turn to the ALA. The Corporation provided $320,000 to build army camp libraries, which in turn were operated by the ALA under the Commissions on Training Camp Activities. In his capacity as third assistant secretary of war, Keppel had gotten to know the ALA representatives, including Carl Milam, who served as the ALA's chief executive from 1920 until 1948. He had also had a chance to observe army camp libraries in use, describing them later as "havens of refuge . . . the only places in the camp where a man was reasonably free and reasonably secure from either ragtime or a prayer-meeting."[21] That Keppel should have turned to Carl Milam and the ALA to help the Corporation organize a postwar library program was therefore not surprising. The alliance presaged a general pattern of collaboration with professionally oriented managerial men that would promote the professionalization of culture.

In locating allies with whom the Corporation could work in developing adult education, Keppel had to begin by translating the trustees' rather vague recommendations into a clearer sense of the kinds of activities the Corporation might finance. Even though there was a long history in the United States of adult educational activities operated by organizations like the Chautauqua Institution, founded in 1874, formal programs of adult education during the prewar period tended to be equated with Americanization campaigns or other forms of remedial instruction to correct educational or cultural disadvantages.[22] The educational and recreational programs of the Commissions on Training Camp Activities had helped to break this mold, and Keppel certainly knew about them. But his early efforts to design a program of nonremedial adult education were influenced even more directly by *The Way Out*, a book about adult education in Great Britain.

The Way Out was a collection of essays, put together by representatives of the British Workers' Education Association, established by Albert Mansbridge in 1903.[23] Although not himself a university graduate, Mansbridge had mobilized an extraordinary group in support of his belief that "the root of the social problem is spiritual," and the answer educational.[24] At a time of growing trade union militancy, Mansbridge's interest in promoting cooperative reforms, in which all social classes would participate through joint worker-university sponsorship of nonvocational adult education, made sense to an entire generation of liberal Oxford scholars. Like the Workers' Education Association itself, the essays in *The Way Out* were learned but not arcane, rooted in traditional liberal values, and permeated with what J. F. C. Harrison, a historian of English adult education, has called "the unresolved conflict in workers' education."[25] The essays urged what was still at the time a radical experiment, especially in Great Britain—the offering of advanced study to working people. But it justified this with the conservative goal of social stability—the Fabian Socialist Beatrice Webb worried about an "aristocratic embrace."[26] Keppel found the essays in *The Way Out* helpful, seeing in the British movement a model for what the Carnegie Corporation might try to do.

With this preparation, Keppel called a conference in June 1924 to initiate a series of regional and national conferences. He invited the people he believed best able to advise him about adult education.[27] Invitations went to library leaders like Carl Milam of the American Library Association and John Cotton Dana of the Newark Library; to adult educators like Eduard C. Lindeman of the American Country Life Association, Everett Dean Martin of the People's Institute, Spencer Miller, Jr., of the Workers' Education Bureau, and C. R. Dooley from the personnel department of Standard Oil of New Jersey; to Charles Beard, the former Columbia historian who had helped found the New School for Social Research, the Workers' Education Bureau, and Ruskin College in England; to Alfred E. Cohn of the Rockefeller Institute; to James Earl Russell of Teachers College, Columbia University; and to a handful of others from agencies ranging from the YMCA to the Conference of Southern Mountain Workers and the publishing firm of Houghton Mifflin. This first gathering was followed by smaller meetings with a "local group" made up of the men Keppel most trusted: Beard, Cohn, Dana, Dooley, Lindeman, Martin, and Russell.[28] According to Keppel, the conference participants agreed on one point from the start: "Those whose only interest is to make money out of the leisure time of the American people are well organized, with ample capital and a long head-start. Those who see an opportunity for something better are, in general, unorganized, and very few of them have realized the need of working together."[29] Squaring off against commerce in favor of serious educational and cultural pursuits, the conference initiated an extended agenda-setting process that resulted in the formation of a new organization to assist the Corporation in adult education as the ALA did with libraries. This organization, the American Association for Adult Education (AAAE), was formally established in Cleveland, Ohio, on March 26, 1926.[30]

According to its constitution, the AAAE was "to promote the development and improvement of adult education in the United States and to cooperate with similar associations in other countries," by gathering and disseminating information, sponsoring studies, cooperating with community groups in the establishment of study groups "within and without regular educational institutions," and other similar means.[31] Open to anyone with "a direct and usually professional interest in adult education," the AAAE was governed by an executive board of which James Earl Russell of Teachers College, Columbia University, was first president.[32] The executive board was dominated by intellectuals and reformers, many of whom were university administrators and professors. Technically independent, the AAAE was, in fact, an adjunct of the Carnegie Corporation. Keppel's assistant, Morse A. Cartwright, became its chief executive officer, and its administrative expenses, which totaled $1,596,897 between 1926 and 1941, were borne by the Corporation. It was expected to recommend and administer Corporation grants in the field of adult education.[33]

Several points about the AAAE are particularly significant. First, at the time it was organized, public schoolteachers had already formed a national association to provide leadership for adult education: the National Education Association's Department of Adult Education. Having once been the only professional association centrally concerned with adult education, after 1926 the NEA group was distinctive only because its membership consisted of active practitioners of adult education—put otherwise, primarily female teachers of language and literacy. Beginning in 1926, the NEA group exhibited a new self-consciousness. According to adult educator Malcolm Knowles, the teachers' group, which had previously concerned itself only with the pedagogical problems of adult instruction, now began to express "coordinative ambitions."[34] The challenge it perceived in the AAAE was evident, first, in the formation, also in 1926, of a Commission on Coordination in Adult Education, and then in that Commission's claim "that education for adults is a desirable form of education extension under public auspices, and that the chief responsibility for the education of adults as well as children is public."[35] Note the emphasis on *public* as opposed to private responsibility for adult education. Along with gender, this represented a primary difference between the two groups. Not coincidentally, similar differences separated the ALA and the state and local library commissions.

The Corporation's decision not to rely upon the NEA's Department of Adult Education for advice and administrative help could have reflected Henry Pritchett's vehement opposition to the NEA.[36] But it may also have resulted from the advice of Viscount Haldane, a prominent leader of the British Workers' Education Association, to whom Keppel had sent Morse Cartwright for advice before launching the Corporation's adult education effort. Apparently Haldane had told Cartwright to beware of "special interest groups like the labor movement, the social workers movement, and the public schools"; he believed they "would attempt to swallow the adult education movement for the gain that might be in it for themselves."[37] In establishing the AAAE, Keppel was self-consciously trying to bring adult education to the attention of the mostly male university administrators and professors, whom he described as "our [educational] general staff."[38] The men he had in mind had once controlled the NEA, but did not by the 1920s; in 1935, they would reassert their leadership by establishing the small and elite Educational Policies Commission under the auspices of the NEA and its Department of Superintendence.[39] Keppel hoped that the AAAE might help gain the "guidance and control" that was needed for "this whole vast movement" to become associated with "our best educational traditions and leadership."[40]

If cooperation between the Carnegie Corporation and the ALA was suggestive of the kind of alliances Keppel wished to establish for the foundation, the founding of the AAAE further revealed his preferences. Keppel's choices suggest that he was seeking affiliation with what one might call the upper class of the educational profession—that is, college and university professors rather than public school teachers; men rather than women; school administrators rather than classroom teachers. Executive Director Morse A. Cartwright virtually acknowledged this when he described the AAAE as an organization in which, "fortunately, a rather large number of 'citizens interested in education,' as contrasted with professional educationalists, has been interested."[41] Intended to ensure leadership for the diverse lot of institutions the Corporation wished to join into an informal, alternative system of education, Keppel's effort revealed considerable insight in recognizing and tapping into the status systems that separated the powerful from the less powerful within the politics of knowledge. In an earlier generation, birth had ensured membership in the social elites from which

cultural custodians came, but now professional affiliations, if not formal professional credentials, were required. Keppel's preference for
alliances with groups dominated and controlled by men was evidence
of this transition. Men were more likely to hold professional status
than women.

While still engaged in the meetings that led to organization of the
AAAE, Keppel moved to identify advisers for the arts program he
hoped to initiate. He called an informal conference in the fall of 1924
to discuss a study he had commissioned Richard F. Bach of the Metropolitan Museum of Art to prepare on "The Place of the Arts in American
Life." The small group invited to this meeting was made up entirely of
men publicly prominent in the arts and relatively conservative in taste.
Among them was Royal Cortissoz, art critic for the *New York Tribune*
from 1891 until 1944; Frank Jewett Mather, art critic for the *Nation*
and director of the Princeton University Art Museum; Richard Aldrich,
former music critic for the *New York Times*; Royal B. Farnum, director
of art education for the state of Massachusetts and later educational
director of the Rhode Island School of Design in Providence; Paul J.
Sachs, a fine arts professor at Harvard University, who also directed the
Fogg Museum there and developed one of the country's first seminars in
museum administration; and Walter Sargent, an architect active in the
American Institute of Architects and in city planning.[42]

Like the advisers Keppel invited to the first conference on adult
education, these men represented a variety of institutions involved in
educating the public about the arts. Their views tended toward the
staid and traditional. It was telling, for example, that two of the nine,
Royal Cortissoz and Frank Jewett Mather, had been among the most
outspoken and hostile critics of the 1913 Armory Show, the landmark
exhibition that introduced Postimpressionism and other new, contemporary styles to New York. According to art historian Milton W.
Brown, Cortissoz was "the bellwether of the nay-sayers."[43] He found
modern art squalid and crude. In Brown's words, "He was just a little
frightened of these 'foolish terrorists' who wanted 'to turn the world
upside down' and whose art seemed to deny what he considered fundamental principles."[44] Cortissoz described Matthew Arnold as "the
critic whom I regard as my own spiritual ancestor," and concluded
after the Armory Show that Cézanne, van Gogh, Matisse, and Gauguin
"painted poorly."[45] Even a decade later, at the time he became an
adviser to the Carnegie Corporation, Cortissoz, warring against new
developments in American art, was calling for a return to the old
masters and to the Renaissance ideal of beauty pursued by such contem-

poraries as Paul Manship and George de Forest Brush. Perhaps even more than Cortissoz, Frank Jewett Mather was horrified by the Armory Show. The feeling it aroused, he claimed, was comparable to "one's feeling on first visiting a lunatic asylum."[46] He believed that the "isolated ecstatic state" represented by Postimpressionist painters would lead art "away from the classical conception of the picture as a composite, reflective, and intellectual statement." It was a "harbinger of universal anarchy."[47]

Having conferred with Mather, Cortissoz, and the other seven men, Keppel launched a program of grants administered more directly by the Carnegie Corporation than the grants for adult education and for libraries. Because Keppel rarely, if ever, explained his actions, the reasons were not recorded, although his personal interest in and familiarity with the arts certainly played a part, as did the existence of several organizations that could be readily counted upon for advice and assistance. Among these the American Federation of the Arts was most important. It was the single largest recipient of Carnegie dollars of all the arts organizations funded at this time, and its purpose was revealing of the Corporation's priorities.[48]

The Federation was an organization Elihu Root had helped found in 1909, one year after "The Eight," the forerunners of the Ashcan School, had shocked New York with "ugly," realistic art.[49] According to Root's speech to the Federation's first meeting, its purpose was "to afford an organization through which the general opinion of all Americans who are lovers of beauty in art and in nature may find expression and be made effective" through the encouragement of arts societies, art study in the public schools, and new and existing supervisory bodies that would ensure beauty in parks, public buildings, and private architecture.[50] However different in substantive focus, the Federation's purpose was not dissimilar from the purposes of the ALA and the AAAE. Furthermore, like those organizations, its ability to serve as an advocate for what Root had called "beauty in art and in nature" was greatly enhanced by the Carnegie Corporation's recognition and reliance.

If cultural leadership required a potential for asserting authoritative judgments and standards, it also necessitated the financial wherewithal to disseminate those judgments and standards and to advance them over and against those of commercial entrepreneurs. Apparently, in choosing to work with the American Federation of the Arts, the Corporation was not implicitly or explicitly choosing to work against or apart from alternative groups dominated by female champions of public

responsibility, as was the case in adult education and library development. That notwithstanding, in this field as in the others, its concern
was to nurture the leadership necessary to shape and guide public
taste, learning, and leisure. And the same concern was apparent as the
Corporation moved on, from the meetings and conferences where
alliances were formed and points of consensus identified, to the actual
awarding of funds. In this, educating the next generation of cultural
custodians, among whom professional credentials would be even more
important, was clearly the goal.

Organizing Cultural Leadership through Professional Education

In its grant-making, the Carnegie Corporation concentrated a large
proportion of its support for the arts on formal education programs at
the collegiate and graduate levels. Thus, between 1925 and 1931, it
awarded fellowships amounting to $239,000 to prospective college
arts teachers; fellowships were also given to students of archaeology,
music, architecture and planning, photography, and drama. Approximately two-thirds of the recipients were male; almost all used the grant
to study at Harvard with Paul J. Sachs (Radcliffe women were admitted
to the Harvard arts courses) or at Princeton with Frank Jewett
Mather.[51] Both Sachs and Mather viewed art as a branch of "high"
scholarship, and both were deeply interested in the development of
museums as integral parts of collegiate art instruction. Indeed, Sachs's
course in museum administration was designed to implement his belief
that "a museum worker must first and foremost be a broad, well-
trained scholar, a linguist, and then in due course, a specialist, a scholar
with wide bibliographical knowledge, a scholar with broad human
sympathies including a belief in popular education, a curator and
administrator taught to understand that in the twentieth century in
America a museum should be not only a treasure house but also an
educational institution, and last, but no means least, that he should be
a competent speaker and writer, as well as a man of the world with
bowing acquaintance to other fields."[52] The view Sachs taught fit
perfectly with the Carnegie Corporation's hopes for developing professional leadership in the arts.

The Corporation also provided significant sums to institutions to
initiate or improve advanced arts instruction. Thus, between 1924
and 1933, it provided endowment funds for fine or industrial arts

instruction to fourteen colleges. Yale received $150,000 for a professorship in the history of art; more typical grants of $50,000 went to institutions as varied as Vassar, Rochester, Milwaukee-Downer, and Tuskegee for development of their art departments.[53] "Art teaching sets" that included art history books, mounted photographs of architecture, sculpture, and painting, and collections of textiles were compiled, produced, and distributed, in 1926, to twenty colleges in the United States and Canada, and by 1941, to 302 colleges, secondary schools, and museums throughout the United States and the British Commonwealth. The works represented tended to be Western and traditional (as for example Egyptian and Greek architecture), although the American paintings did range from Thomas Eakins to Robert Henri.[54] In addition to the art sets, sets of music study materials were also developed and distributed.

The idea of using collections of reproductions as a form of museum extension education was not unique to the Carnegie Corporation. At about this time, the American Federation of the Arts was following up on experiments first undertaken by the Russell Sage Foundation and assembling color reproductions from the Metropolitan Museum of Art's collection in New York.[55] Closely in touch with both Russell Sage and the Metropolitan (Root and Pritchett were both trustees of the Metropolitan, and Keppel had many acquaintances there), the Corporation may well have derived the idea of art sets from this venture. Its efforts were distinctive in their focus on secondary schools, colleges, and universities, where one might most effectively reach the next generation of cultural leaders, not only the professionals who would actually direct the museums and teach and write about the art, but also the lay patrons and connoisseurs upon whom the professionals would need to depend for approval, attendance, and funds.

Because most arts organizations depended on private patronage, it was necessary to define leadership more broadly than with libraries, where, by the 1920s, traditions of public financing were well established and private patronage was less necessary. In the library field, therefore, the Corporation could focus its leadership concerns more narrowly than in the arts, concentrating almost exclusively on promoting professionalization. The Corporation's alliance with the ALA supported this focus, as did several studies undertaken before Keppel's appointment as president.

The first of these was *The American Public Library and the Diffusion of Knowledge*, written between 1921 and 1923 by Henry Pritchett's assistant, William S. Learned, and published in 1924. Learned developed a conception of the library as a "community intelligence service" that fit well with the Corporation's overall concern for mediating the public's spontaneous pursuit of knowledge, education, and culture. The library should be the place where people would turn "not only for 'polite' literature, but for every commercial and vocational field of information that it may prove practicable to enter."[56] The prescription accorded perfectly with the Corporation's wish to check the otherwise unrestrained forces of the market in culture. According to Learned's blueprint, the library was to be a place where "merchants will find . . . catalogues and trade lists; builders and plumbers, the technical books of their crafts; students, old or young, the orderly progress of books or materials in any important study; clergymen, the best works and periodicals dealing with religion; motorists, the latest road maps and touring guides; and artists, both technical works and comprehensive collections of pictures."[57] Library patrons would be assisted in their search for information and enlightenment by well-trained professional librarians. Given this prescription as well as Alvin Johnson's earlier study, the education of librarians had to be of urgent concern to the Corporation. Not coincidentally, a study of training for librarianship was also awaiting Keppel in 1923.

This study, *Training for Library Service*, had been written by Charles C. Williamson, an economist, who was at the time a reference librarian at the New York Public Library. To this day considered a landmark in library history, the study argued that the standards of librarian training should be raised by dividing librarians, according to education and ALA certification, into two grades, the "professional" and the "sub-professional or sub-clerical."[58] The professionals should attend one of the better library schools, which, Williamson maintained, should be encouraged to offer two years of postcollegiate instruction within a university setting. After graduation, their alumni should be ready for "positions requiring extensive and accurate book knowledge, skill in organization and administration, and expert technical knowledge in many special lines."[59] The subprofessionals, he continued, should be trained in the remaining undergraduate library schools; they needed only "instruction in cataloguing, in classification, in . . . record-keeping topics,—including filing, indexing, alphabeting,—and in typewriting."[60] Arguing against the then current belief that "the entire body of library workers, even down to the pages, should have a full library school training," Williamson hoped that segmentation might make the field more appealing to "college men and women as a career, not only because the professional type of work will be more attractive in itself, but also because it will make possible more adequate salaries." The wages of the subprofessionals might be further depressed by these reforms, he admitted, but the wages of the professionals would rise.[61]

What Williamson was really suggesting, of course, was that a new grade of librarian—male college graduates, with postgraduate librarianship training—be recruited to the field. As he certainly was aware, library work had not appealed to such people largely because it had been defined by gender-related behavioral expectations. As Dee Garrison's history of librarianship has shown, in this feminized occupation librarians were expected to serve rather than to prescribe for their clients; to define their work as predominantly routine rather than as principally intellectual—put otherwise, as more equivalent to housework than to scholarship; and to equate work potential not with competence to perform complex, often analytical tasks, but instead with personality—"the missionary spirit," "cultural strength," "breeding and background," "sense of literary values"—in short, with "all the amiable qualities which go to make a hostess."[62] Rather than attempting to change the culture of the profession as then constituted, Williamson's prescriptions were designed to foster a bifurcation not different from that which existed between (male) school administrators and (female) teachers, and between (male) doctors and (female) nurses.[63] It would be difficult to read the Williamson study without concluding that fostering hierarchical segmentation by gender was one of its goals.

The implications of the Williamson Report were apparent to contemporaries when it was published in 1923. In the introduction Williamson noted that he had been "obliged to limit the scope of his study to the so-called professional schools."[64] He meant that the Corporation had asked him to focus exclusively upon the fifteen then accredited training schools, and not to give equal attention to the many additional library schools, institutes, and classes that were also working for library progress. Had the Corporation wished to improve the education of all librarians without creating a new professional elite, the broader focus would have been necessary.[65] Williamson realized this, and so did others who read his report. For example, the vice-director of the Pratt Institute Library School, a woman, argued that it would be unwise to accept Williamson's suggestion that applicants to "professional" library schools be required to have earned a college degree. This would discriminate against the "women who have been unable to attend college but who have gained by reading, study and contacts all that college can give—culture, trained minds, broad outlook."[66]

Whether or not Keppel was aware of all the ramifications of the professionalizing strategy implicit in the Williamson report, the Ten-Year Program in Library Service he presented to the Corporation's board of trustees in March 1926 reflected it. The program included grants totaling $4,170,000: $1,440,000 for support of existing library schools, including library schools for blacks; $1,385,000 for the establishment of a new graduate school; and $1,345,000 for the ALA.[67] The bulk of the almost $3 million designated for education went to help improve the already better library schools. More important in some ways, Corporation funds defrayed the costs of a complicated new accrediting system set up by the ALA. This ranked schools according to course offerings and entrance requirements and assigned them the designation Type I, II, or III. As a side effect that may or may not have been anticipated and welcomed, this eclipsed the Association of American Library Schools (AALS), the existing library school credentialing agency, which had been established in 1915 by representatives from ten library schools, who wished to use accreditation as a carrot to encourage all schools to improve, rather than as a basis for drawing subtle, and in some cases limiting, lines of distinction between and among them. The AALS was controlled by women, as the ALA was not; indeed, 78 percent of its officers between 1915 and 1923 were women.[68] It was not insignificant, therefore, when, according to library historian Charles D. Churchwell, the AALS was "stripped . . . of the very activities that gave meaning and direction to its existence."[69] This occurred because the ALA, with Carnegie Corporation encouragement and financing, took over the AALS's credentialing function.

The Williamson, Learned, and Johnson reports, as well as the professionalizing strategy inherent in them, were mirrored in all aspects of the Corporation's Ten-Year Program and, at its end in 1936, in the clearly discernible outcomes of the program. The Graduate Library School at the University of Chicago that was started with Carnegie funds had been in operation for seven years. It had conferred sixteen master's degrees (five to men, eleven to women) and seventeen doctorates (twelve to men, five to women); it had begun to publish the *Library Quarterly*, a scholarly journal; and, following an initial period of administrative turmoil, it had been stabilized with a small but distinguished faculty that was developing a high reputation for research in "library science."[70] Despite obvious differences, the school's aspirations for librarian training were kindred to those held by Paul Sachs for his Harvard course in museum administration, and no less than the Sachs course, the Chicago Library School pleased Frederick Keppel.

Keppel was generally pleased with the library program. It had been the source for "marked progress . . . in virtually all phases of education for librarianship," he said.[71] But the Corporation's outside evaluator, Ralph Munn, director of the Carnegie Library of Pittsburgh, was less certain. He acknowledged and praised a "marked improvement" in library education, but bemoaned the fact that "current discussion of training deals so largely with the problems of advanced study that we are in danger of losing sight of the need to maintain and improve the basic first-year courses."[72] Less concerned with "leaders and statesmen" than with "the smaller public and college libraries, which after all are more typical and in the aggregate more important," Munn was critical of what he believed to have been an unwarranted and unwise emphasis on the production of "leaders and statesmen."[73] Whether his criticisms were valid, Munn was astute in discerning the Corporation's strategy for library development and, more generally, for cultural philanthropy of all kinds.

Safeguarding Culture through Excellence in Education

Hoping to strengthen the professional and advocacy organizations it thought most potentially influential, and to develop the informal communities of patrons and the scholars it thought necessary for cultural leadership, the Carnegie Corporation also approached the matter of enlightening public taste directly. Its logic was that taste could be improved by shaping the supply of educational and cultural services, programs, and materials and by granting funds to programs that would make "the best" in learning and culture more widely available. The assumption evident in this aspect of the Corporation's interwar cultural philanthropy was that the excellent, tasteful, beautiful, and edifying would be preferred to the mediocre, tawdry, crass, and merely selfishly useful and practical, if the former were more generally accessible. This premise was evident in all three of the Corporation's domains of interest.

In the library field, for example, there was a clear bias toward "the best" in the program of grants especially directed to college libraries. This program was organized in a fashion similar to the Ten-Year Program mentioned above. Relying as always on external advisory committees, the Corporation financed the development of book lists for college libraries and of standards for different types of college libraries. Of greater importance at a time of deep financial cuts in college library budgets caused by the Depression, and growing reliance on libraries caused by the introduction of more independent, research-oriented methods of instruction, were the Corporation's awards of funds for the purchase of books. Ranging from $25,000 to $1,500, book-purchase grants were awarded to 102 four-year colleges and 92 two-year colleges; there were also grants for other types of institutions, as for instance teachers colleges and colleges for blacks.[74] Although the book-purchase grants went to institutions as different as the University of Chicago and Bay City Junior College in Michigan, the colleges that received such funds had to be highly rated in terms of "performance and promise," and their location had to be judged "strategic" relative to other comparable institutions, so that their improvements might be widely copied.[75] As a result, as Neil A. Radford's detailed study of the Carnegie college library grants has shown, even if some colleges that were not well known, well funded, and prestigious were assisted, there was a "'Matthew effect' ('unto every one that hath shall be given, and he shall have abundance')" evident in the colleges selected.[76]

A similar bias toward "the best" was clear in the arts program, again with the presumption that efforts to create models of excellence could elevate taste more effectively than efforts to improve the average. Keppel's belief that "no amount of money can transform the second-rate into the first-rate" apparently dominated here as well.[77] Even though John Cotton Dana was included on the Corporation's list of advisers at this time, his conception of popular education in the arts was not widely adopted in Corporation-supported programs. Something of an eccentric, Dana was an innovative pioneer in both the library and museum fields. At the Newark Museum, which he established in conjunction with the Newark Library, he attempted to foster popular interest in culture and popular participation in cultural criticism by displaying everyday objects, including items such as those for sale in the local dime store. Dana believed the display of such objects would encourage greater and more constant aesthetic awareness and higher critical standards in all people.[78] However, despite acknowledgment of Dana and his point of view, the Corporation's goal in its grants to museums was to make available to more people the "fine arts," if not original Rembrandts then at least high-quality Rembrandt reproductions and imitations, as well as good examples of historical artifacts or scientific invention.[79] The point was not to illuminate "the arts in daily life" but, as Paul Marshall Rea, a Corporation museum consultant, explained in his study *The Museum and the Community* (1932), to encourage education through study and interpretation of a museum's own collection.[80] Attendance at museums should increase, where curators and administrators trained by Paul Sachs, Frank Jewett Mather, and other professional arts scholars could ensure that the public encounter "the best." Obviously, there could be no guarantee of such professional mediation in the dime store.

Finally, as the dispenser of the Corporation's grants in adult education, the AAAE revealed a similar preference. The range of activities supported was tremendous: the full list from 1926 until 1940 filled a twenty-eight page pamphlet.[81] But amid this diversity there was a consistent emphasis on programs that were advanced, in contrast to elementary, and liberal arts, in contrast to vocational or technical—"the best" in adult education as the Carnegie Corporation and therefore the AAAE defined it. One could see this pattern in three of the programs that received relatively large grants.

One of these was the Institute of Politics in Williamstown, Massachusetts, another pet of Elihu Root. "When foreign affairs are ruled by democracies," Root believed, "the danger of war will be in mistaken beliefs."[82] To counter this eventuality, the Institute was designed to bring together scholars and statesmen from around the world to present and listen to lectures and to participate in round-table discussions on general topics like world economic planning and specific questions like "The Foreign and Domestic Policy of the Kuomintang."[83] To reach more people, the Institute's deliberations were made available to U.S. newspapers and to the Associated Press and the United Press. "In this way it informs a world-wide public," it was claimed.[84] That may have been true, but as an experiment in adult education the Institute of Politics was best described as public education via the privately sponsored and privately organized education of leaders. Between 1924 and 1928, it received $75,000 from the Carnegie Corporation.

Another major recipient of Carnegie funds through the AAAE was the People's Institute in New York City. Founded in 1897 to permit immigrant wage-earners to hear famous lecturers and public figures, the People's Institute became something of a neighborhood center for a time and then, during the years of Carnegie Corporation grants amounting to $171,500, a place where "developing human excellence through adult education programs" was a major goal.[85] Offering at Cooper Union lectures and discussions for which, as Frederick Keppel once put it, "the reading of recondite works of psychology or philosophy is required," the People's Institute was the setting for an interesting experiment in humanist education.[86] The hope was that an understanding of the classics would serve as an antidote to commercialism, democ-

racy, humanitarianism, materialism, and utilitarianism in education.[87]
Everett Dean Martin, one of the participants in the Corporation's adult
education conferences, was the chief proponent of this idea; he was
assisted by a roster of lecturers that included philosophers Mortimer J.
Adler and Morris Raphael Cohen, sociologist Robert S. Lynd, historian
Allan Nevins, and the cultural critic Lewis Mumford. "Democracy is
all-powerful," Martin wrote in 1930, "but in precisely the measure
that it influences the values of civilization it tends to cheapen and
vulgarize them, as witness politics, the tabloid newspaper, the radio,
the motion picture, and popular music."[88] The question was, then, as
Morse Cartwright explained it, whether adult education at the People's
Institute could free people "from materialism, from bad taste in living,
in music, in drama, in recreation, and, most of all, from the utter
drabness of unfulfilled lives."[89]

The goal of the People's Institute experiment was explicitly linked to
elitist sentiments. Martin explained that the "aim [of adult education] is
not to provide a slight increase of information and a few noble sentiments
for the rank and file, but to select out of the undifferentiated mass those
who are naturally capable of becoming something more than automa-
tons"—in other words, those "worth educating."[90] The bias evident in
this statement was also evident in the participants in the People's Institute
program. In 1928, 43 percent of them were high school or college graduates, 62 percent were employed in industry or business, 17 percent in the
professions or government service, and 10 percent in unskilled labor;
only 11 percent were unemployed.[91] As with the Corporation's college
library grants, a "Matthew effect" was evident. Once again, too, the
elite emphasis indicated that, even with populists like Eduard Lindeman
listed as advisers—Lindeman, a contributor to the *New Republic*, was a
progressive social worker and writer who headed the Recreation Division of the Works Progress Administration—in actuality it was the proponents of liberal education and classical high culture who prevailed.
Lindeman was disillusioned by the Carnegie Corporation's adult education program, believing that the executive committee of the AAAE
"drifted toward Everett Dean Martin." David W. Stewart has argued in
his biography of Lindeman that Lindeman's "contributions were not
generally encouraged by the AAAE's first executive director," Morse A.
Cartwright.[92] A comparison to the preference for Paul Sachs's views over
John Cotton Dana's is inescapable.

In some ways very different from this early version of "Great Books"
discussion were the activities of the third group to receive large continuing grants ($140,250 between 1926 and 1940) from the Carnegie

Corporation: the Workers' Education Bureau of America. This was an organization that Charles Beard helped to found in 1921 "to collect and to disseminate information relative to efforts at education on any part of organized labor; to co-ordinate and assist in every possible manner the educational work now carried on by the organized Workers; and to stimulate the creation of additional enterprises in labor education throughout the United States."[93] As Beard envisioned it, the Association was to supplement the training offered in so-called union or labor colleges.[94] There, workers could learn practical skills such as those required in collective bargaining; or, as Frieda Miller of the Philadelphia Trade Union College once stated, they could take an economics course that "isn't a theoretical course. . . . [A course that would discuss] problems of our economic system today. How it is organized, what it does to people, whoever they are that participate in the economic processes; . . . what they need to do . . . that sort of economics."[95] By contrast, according to Beard, the Workers' Education Bureau was designed to encourage educational efforts to provide to workers the knowledge they needed to be citizens, knowledge about "foreign relations, domestic controversies, economic measures, and constitutional changes . . . those larger matters related to citizenship in this republic."[96] A primary means of providing this was book publication, and the Workers' Education Bureau supervised the writing, printing, and distribution of a "Workers' Bookshelf" that included H. L. McBain's *The Living Constitution* (1927); H. U. Faulkner's *Economic History of the United States* (1928); Stuart Chase's *The Tragedy of Waste* (1925); and George W. Wickersham's *World Court* (1927).[97] If some programs of labor education were fundamentally reformist, even radical, in purpose, as when they provided instruction in union organization, workers' education in both Great Britain and the United States tended instead to be liberal and learned. It was not surprising, therefore, that the Workers' Education Bureau really amounted to a working-class version of the Williamstown Institute of Politics. Once again, it represented the elite side of adult education.

Consistency amid a Changing Politics

One of several strains of consistency, an emphasis on liberal education for both workers and statesmen, was revealing of the origins of the Carnegie Corporation's interwar cultural philanthropy and of the leadership Keppel provided the foundation. Favoring elite conceptions of culture, Elihu Root and Henry Pritchett had hoped that, by identifying and educating leaders to set standards of taste and by exposing a wider public to "the best which has been thought and said in the world," the Corporation could help sustain social stability and common values. They had wished to moderate change and to adjust new immigrants to established "American" beliefs and behaviors, rather than to have American culture transformed through exchange between the established and the newly arrived. At the core of their conservative outlook was an allegiance to a world in decline.

Younger than Root by thirty years and younger than Pritchett by eighteen years, Keppel managed to develop programs that gratified these aging but still powerful trustees, yet at the same time interested younger men of his own generation. It was characteristic of Keppel that both the Institute of Politics, a project of interest to Root, and the Workers' Education Bureau, a project of interest to the historian Charles Beard, were part of the Corporation's adult education program. As was his wont, Pritchett—"a stormy petrel if ever there was one," Keppel later said—objected to grants to the Workers' Education Bureau, claiming that Beard was an embittered man and that his writings showed it; as was his own wont, Keppel soothed Pritchett as best he could.[98] Keppel was a diplomat of great skill. Few other people would have gathered a group of mostly older traditionalists for the first Carnegie Corporation arts conference and then presented them with an agenda featuring a report by Richard F. Bach, one of the Metropolitan Museum of Art's less traditional curators. But that was Keppel's style.

Tactful, tolerant, and by and large even-tempered, Keppel led the Carnegie Corporation in a style marked by determination and persistence of purpose. He insisted upon carrying through the programs to foster libraries, the arts, and adult education, even after the stock market crashed in 1929 and even in the years of extreme economic depression that followed, with the consequent social and political turmoil. Whether it would have been wiser to switch directions and devote all the Corporation's funds to emergency relief is moot. Keppel believed that it was the "responsibility" of foundations "to determine what *in the long run* represents the wisest use of the funds at their disposal," and, with that decided, to resist all calls to give up planned activities and attend only to immediate crises.[99] Having carefully designed the Corporation's cultural endeavors, he believed that it made sense to continue them until a reasonable period of experimentation had passed (usually ten years) or until, for some other reason, they reached an acceptable end.

Keppel's perseverence enabled some Corporation-backed innovations to survive long enough to find other public or private sponsors. This was the case with support for the library as "community intelligence center," an idea first developed by William S. Learned and subsequently promoted with Corporation funds. A later Corporation-sponsored study by the Social Science Research Council found that this idea had not been fully realized within the United States; nevertheless, after the Corporation's Ten-Year Program of Library Service had run out in the late 1930s, it was picked up by the federal government and by other foundations, notably the Rockefeller Foundation.[100] With continuing assistance from the American Library Association, it became the basis for the U.S. information centers that were widely established around the world.[101]

In other instances, Keppel's insistence upon continuing programs begun before the Great Depression failed to yield enduring results. This was true, for example, of the effort to organize an educational "general staff" for adult education.[102] Steadfast in its orientation, the AAAE never wavered from its emphasis on "learning, on the initiative of the individual, seriously and consecutively undertaken as a supplement to some primary occupation."[103] As AAAE chief executive Morse A. Cartwright put it in the Association's 1929–30 *Annual Report*, "only indirectly has the association attempted to reach 'the man in the street.'"[104] It was not surprising then that membership never climbed above 3,000, and that the Corporation always had to provide at least 90 percent of the AAAE's budget. Kept alive after Corporation funds were discontinued in 1941, first by institutional support provided by Teachers College, Columbia University, and then by Cleveland College in Ohio, in 1951 the AAAE was finally forced to merge with the NEA's Department of Adult Education to form the Adult Education Association of the United States. Although it was uncompromising in its mission, the AAAE had not been able to connect with the market for adult education that continued to flourish even during the Depression and the Second World War.[105]

In the end, then, the Corporation's interwar cultural philanthropy had a mixed and limited impact on the ecology of educational and cultural institutions in the United States. Despite the Corporation's efforts to nurture the leadership and the models of excellence that were presumed necessary to mediate the effects of commerce on culture, the organizations and causes it supported rarely survived without endowment funds from some source that could substitute for the market. Without such support, the books published by the Workers' Education

Bureau, to cite but one example, simply could not compete with the inexpensive and widely appealing Little Blue Books of Haldeman-Julius. This did not mean that the Corporation's activities had no effect. Its support for professional leadership and standards in the arts did contribute to movement in that direction. What is more, some of the fellowships and grants it awarded and some of the experiments it financed—for example, the adult discussions at the People's Institute—launched people into careers in which they continued to disseminate liberal education and high culture. Such outcomes are difficult, really impossible, to measure. Suffice it to say, therefore, that many books were published, exhibitions mounted, libraries improved, and lives changed; belief in trained expertise as a basis for "professional" judgments was enhanced. And yet, tensions between mission and market continued to be central to the development of American culture and education.

CHAPTER SIX

Public Policy and Sociology

Gunnar Myrdal's *An American Dilemma*

A T A C A R N E G I E   C O R P O R A T I O N board of trustees meeting on October 24, 1935, Newton D. Baker suggested that the executive committee "give consideration to the general questions of *negro education and negro problems* [*sic*], with particular reference to conditions in the Northern states."[1] The result, nine years later, was *An American Dilemma: The Negro Problem and Modern Democracy*, by the Swedish economist Gunnar Myrdal. The Corporation, initially wishing guidance about ways in which the problems of black Americans might be addressed through cultural philanthropy, received instead a two-volume treatise with lengthy and learned methodological notes and tremendous quantities of data that said little about practical questions of philanthropy but much about the shortcomings of American society.

None of the discernible outcomes of the Myrdal study bore direct relation to the Corporation's original intentions in commissioning the work. They were rather, to use Robert K. Merton's phrase, "the unanticipated consequences of purposive social action."[2] Largely defined by its author's interest in sociological concepts and theories developed by scholars at the University of Chicago, *An American Dilemma* had direct relevance for studies of social policy, culture, and race. In line with its author's Chicago orientation, it advanced a distinctive perspective on questions about race relations. Relationships between whites and blacks were presented as dependent upon an evolutionary process of mutual group accommodation; neither the African heritage nor the distinctive national identity of blacks as a people was featured. Relevant to the study of social policy, culture, and race, the study cost almost $300,000 and had a lasting impact on public opinion and public policy.[3]

Illustrating a disjunction between the expectations of a sponsor and the interests and aspirations of a scholar, *An American Dilemma* revealed some of the limitations of commissioned research. It also demonstrated the degree to which the social sciences were becoming an ever more necessary basis for persuasive, authoritative arguments on public questions. Myrdal's argument gained credence in many quarters because it was a work of sociology, but *An American Dilemma* was first and foremost an essay in moral judgment. "The Negro problem is not only America's greatest failure but also America's incomparably great opportunity for the future," Myrdal asserted. "America can demonstrate that justice, equality and cooperation are possible between white and colored people."[4]

The Origins of the Myrdal Study: "Negro Education"

At the outset, the decision to sponsor what Frederick P. Keppel later described as a "comprehensive study of the Negro in America" arose from a convergence of immediate concerns.[5] First, there was a matter of money. In the mid-1930s the Corporation was entering what Keppel hoped would be "a new and more forward-looking period."[6] Since his arrival at the foundation, most of its grant income had been devoted to the needs of the other Carnegie trusts, like the Carnegie Foundation for the Advancement of Teaching's pension obligations, to long-term commitments to institutions with which trustees were associated, like the American Law Institute, or to which monies had been promised before his appointment, like the Food Research Institute at Stanford; and also to the programs in library service, the arts, and adult education that Keppel had designed on the basis of general directives established before he assumed office. With most extant financial obligations met, there was likely to be $2.21 million available per year for new projects.[7]

Within this context, the question arose as to how, if at all, the Corporation might more actively participate in programs pertaining to race relations. Between 1911 and 1932 it had made grants amounting to more than $1.7 million for "Negro education." It had also regularly contributed to organizations ranging from the Commission on Inter-Racial Cooperation to the National Urban League and Carter G.

Woodson's Association for the Study of Negro Life and History.[8] It had financed a number of educational projects in British colonies in Africa, notably exchange programs for scholars and educators and the establishment of training schools for traveling Jeanes teachers, who, like their counterparts in the American South, offered supervision and curriculum materials designed to mesh school instruction with rural curriculum materials.[9] (The Jeanes teachers were named for Anna T. Jeanes, the Philadelphia philanthropist who created a fund in 1907 to finance this kind of extension education.) The question now was whether there was something new, different, distinctive, and more worthwhile that the Corporation might do.

Beginning in 1898, when Northern and Southern educational, religious, and philanthropical leaders first met at Capon Springs, Virginia, Northern philanthropists concerned with the education of blacks had coordinated their grant-making. They had based their programs on three assumptions; first, that the education of blacks was a Southern problem; second, that it could be handled most effectively if the cooperation of white Southerners were actively solicited; and third, that it would be advisable to view education in relation to regional economic development and within established patterns of relationship between black and white Americans. More education and more advanced education for whites, who would undertake the managerial and professional roles necessary for the further modernization of the South, become a primary goal, with plans to educate blacks following from this. As William H. Baldwin, Jr., president of the Long Island Railroad and a trustee of Tuskegee Institute, put it, Negroes were to be taught to "avoid social questions, leave politics alone; continue to be patient; live moral lives; live simply; learn to work . . . [and] know that it is a crime for any teacher, white or black, to educate the negro for positions which are not open to him."[10]

First developed at Capon Springs and at meetings of the Southern Education Board founded four years later, the consensus on philanthropic policy was confirmed and further elaborated by the Welsh-born sociologist Thomas Jesse Jones in *Negro Education: A Study of the Private and Higher Schools for Colored People in the United States* (1917). According to Jones, education should prepare Negroes to remain in rural areas of the South, in largely agricultural occupations. "The old rigid curriculum, with Latin four years, Greek two or three years, and mathematics two or three years," should be abandoned in almost all institutions.[11] According to the recommendations Jones provided for each and every one of the roughly 780 institutions considered, this was even advisable at a place like the Washington County Training School in Sandersville, Georgia, which had been "selected [by the state] as a central institution to provide more advanced training for the colored pupils of the county."[12] Even there it was not Latin or Greek or mathematics that mattered, but health, morals, service, and vocational training, especially in "the theory and practice of gardening," which, according to Jones, should be included in the education of "every colored pupil."[13]

Despite philanthropic concurrence, some people disagreed with Jones's views. One of these was W. E. B. Du Bois. Against his old rival Booker T. Washington, with whose views Jones was in essential agreement, Du Bois had long maintained, "If . . . the American people are sincerely anxious that the Negro shall put forth his best effort to help himself, they must see to it that he is not deprived of the freedom and power to strive."[14] It was clear to Du Bois, who had studied Latin, Greek, and mathematics and who held a doctorate from Harvard University, that unless industrial education were liberally conceived as a means "to strengthen the intellectual powers, fortify character, and facilitate the transmission from age to age of the stores of the world's knowledge," it would result in "blind leaders for the blind" and "men to be thought for, but not to think; to be led, but not to lead themselves."[15] He was not opposed to vocational education, but rather to the kind of limited or merely technical training that Washington and then Jones advocated. Du Bois's views had support in the black community, and indeed contributed to the protests at black colleges that occurred throughout the 1920s around the issues Du Bois defined as involving standards and white paternalism.[16] However, even though Du Bois's views were entirely compatible with the thinking of many progressive educators, they had little impact within white centers of power.[17]

Despite challenges from Du Bois and others, Jones remained highly influential among philanthropists, and his study served as "the Bible" at many foundations, including the General Education Board, the foundation that had the most money to give to "Negro education."[18] The vast and long-lived authority of the study began to crumble only when, as a result of the concerted efforts of black educators, the U.S. Bureau of Education agreed to publish a new survey. This made it prudent for the Phelps-Stokes Fund to reverse its initial refusal to provide funds for such a study. The result, Arthur Klein's *Survey of Negro Colleges and Universities*, was finally completed and published in 1929.[19] Within this context the Carnegie study was proposed.

The Corporation's Hopes: A New Approach to "Negro Education"

Newton D. Baker, who suggested the study of *"negro education and negro problems,"* was a lawyer. Secretary of war during the First World War, he was much admired by Frederick Keppel, who had served under him in the war department.[20] He was a liberal in politics but not on questions of race. Indeed, his suggestion of the study derived from premises that Du Bois would have abhorred and that, at least to some extent, Thomas Jesse Jones appreciated.[21]

Baker was skeptical of "special education" for blacks. As a prominent resident of Cleveland and its mayor from 1913 to 1916, he was convinced that, if the "Negro problem" had once been a Southern problem, by 1935 it had become a Northern problem as well—and a dangerously neglected one. Fearing that "in the past like neglect of like problems has resulted in such tragic episodes as the Springfield and East St. Louis riots [of 1908 and 1917]," he wanted the situation investigated and publicized as a national urban rather than an exclusively Southern problem.[22]

While "heartily in favor of better educational facilities for the Negroes," Baker had doubts nonetheless about the value of formal schooling as a means of promoting progress and good relations between the races.[23] Born in West Virginia to a loyal Confederate family with a long Southern lineage and educated in the South (and with four undergraduate years at Johns Hopkins University in the border state of Maryland), Baker shared the assumptions about race of many of his white contemporaries. Indeed, there were striking resemblances between his thinking and that of Ulrich Bonnell Phillips, the historian who argued that "the planters of the Old South . . . developed a fairly efficient body of laborers out of a horde of savages."[24] Baker's concurrence in this view was evident when, in December 1935, he wrote to Keppel:

I shall never be satisfied with American education until it has the wisdom of life as its primary objective. This defect is particularly distressing in our educational system as applied to Negroes, not at all because of any fault of theirs and really not much because of the fault of white people, but rather because of the extraordinary circumstances which led to our having so large a Negro population they need to be taught the wisdom of life more than the white children.

I think anybody who has read *Anthony Adverse* will share my feeling of unlimited amazement at the courage of the white people in this country who received the slaves from slave ships and undertook to make useful laborers of them. How many white civilizations could have dared to receive so many wild savages, who were practically uncaged animals, and spread them around over their farms in contact with their own families passes human comprehension. What has been done for the Negro in a hundred years is an unparalleled achievement and nothing but a theoretical democratic impatience can make us critical of it, though, of course, much more remains to be done.[25]

In another letter, one discussing problems of public housing in Cleveland, Baker wrote:

[C]olored people who came here a dozen years ago in response to a labor demand caused by the limitations put upon immigration . . . brought with them their habits, which were better adapted to cabin life in the palmetto swamps than they were to the sanitary and hygienic needs of congested life in an industrial city. The houses they took over had recently been vacated by a fairly sturdy lot of people who respected their houses and kept them in repair. After ten years of the new occupancy, they had to be torn down to keep them from falling down or crawling away. These same people now regard the new structures which the Government is building as especially designed for them, although the prices at which they are to be rented are quite beyond their economic capacity. The consequences I foresee are immense—pressure of a political kind to reduce rents, and racial conflicts between the tidy and the untidy, who will not live happily together in these socialized structures. My imagination has been able to conceive no plan by which peace and even a modest return can be secured in the administration of these properties.[26]

Baker also believed that there were "some biological questions involved" that had to be honestly faced in a "scientific spirit."[27] According to Daniel R. Beaver, "he had overcome the active racialism characteristic of his native state" by the time of World War I.[28] But his comments as late as the mid-1930s suggest that he still believed it worth testing the biological basis for racial differences. This added to his conviction that more than formal education was needed, if blacks were to learn all that was necessary to avoid "racial conflicts" between "the tidy and the untidy."[29] He was also aware that blacks were increasingly moving away from Southern farms, and this made it difficult for him to believe that "the theory and practice of gardening," for example, which Jones had urged, could be of much value. This concern increased his interest in the inquiry that became *An American Dilemma.*

Finally, Baker wanted to determine if there was a way in which "the Negro people can be made to work for their own education." Acknowledging that free public education was "the theory of the common school education in America," he still felt that "with an infant race like the black people in this country, education would mean more and be more helpful if its opportunity in some fashion could come in response to an aspiration and effort on their part."[30] How could this be encouraged and, more generally, how could "Negro education" be organized? Baker wanted that practical question of policy investigated.

For different reasons, Keppel also doubted the value of old approaches to "Negro education." Even though Jones insisted that literary studies had little, if any, value for blacks, Keppel was not convinced. Indeed, when he read a memorandum written in October 1934 by Robert M. Lester, secretary of the Corporation, in which Lester reported having told a group discussing library service for black schools and colleges that "the Corporation had been playing with the idea for some time of trying to find a way to help the negro liberal arts colleges of the type represented by Talladega, Wiley, Marshall, Paine, [and] Johnson C. Smith," Keppel scribbled in the margins "Memo" and "Details."[31] Although apparently unaware of the exploration Lester announced, he wanted it pursued.

Keppel admired the views of Alain L. Locke, a professor at Howard University who held a doctorate in philosophy from Harvard University, the first black American to receive a Rhodes Scholarship.[32] An important spokesman for the "New Negro" and the Harlem Renaissance, Locke ranked with Du Bois and the black historian Carter G. Woodson in calling attention to the rich cultural heritage of American blacks and attempting to foster a sense of cultural kinship among blacks around the world.[33] One of his important undertakings was editing a "Harlem Number" (March 1925) for the *Survey*, a journal devoted to progressive social reform. The issue came from the promotional efforts of Charles S. Johnson, the black sociologist who became president of Fisk University and who was at this time editor of the National Urban League's journal, *Opportunity*.[34] It outsold all previous issues of the *Survey* and in December 1925 was published in expanded form as *The New Negro*, a noted book still in print. It included fiction and poetry by Countee Cullen, James Weldon Johnson, Jean Toomer, Claude McKay, and Langston Hughes, among others, as well as articles by Robert R. Moton, E. Franklin Frazier, Arthur A. Schomburg, Du Bois, and many more.[35]

In the essays he contributed to this anthology, Locke argued: "for generations in the mind of America, the Negro has been more a formula than a human being—a something to be argued about, condemned or defended, to be 'kept down,' or 'in his place,' or 'helped up,' to be worried with or worried over, harassed or patronized, a social bogey or a social burden. The thinking Negro even has been induced to share this same general attitude. . . . Little true social or self-understanding has or could come from such a situation."[36] The situation was changing as a result of migration from country to city and from South to North, as well as growing race consciousness and solidarity. The "New Negro" was ready for "positive self-direction," Locke maintained; he was determined "to build the obstructions in the stream of his progress into an efficient dam of social energy and power" in order to realize American democratic ideals.[37] Viewing the arts as a key to social progress, Locke argued in *The New Negro* that painting, drama, music, and literature were media through which blacks could express and further develop their racial consciousness and whites, for their part, could gain a new view.[38]

Needless to say, Locke's views coincided with Keppel's. Finding Locke to be a man of "fertile mind," Keppel sought his company, and the two became sufficiently well acquainted for Locke to discuss his "plans and hopes" freely with the Corporation's president.[39] Such easy relations with Keppel, while not unusual for whites, were unusual for blacks. Unlike Du Bois, Locke was not considered a radical; and unlike Woodson, he was not temperamental and had not, as Woodson had, been a target of criticism from Thomas Jesse Jones, who had called him "a propagandist with a distinct antipathy to movements for racial cooperation."[40]

Keppel's interest in Locke was enhanced by Locke's willingness to participate in adult education programs supported by the Corporation. In 1927 Locke gave four lectures for the Adult Education Association of Cleveland, of which Newton Baker was president.[41] Locke's willingness to work with the American Association for Adult Education and its affiliates and to help promote a form of education disregarded or shunned by many other blacks was both encouraging and helpful to Keppel. The AAAE tended to promote liberal studies, in contrast to the more practical basic literary training and vocational education that was of primary interest to blacks.[42] In consequence, Locke became Keppel's and the AAAE's "official observer and advisor with reference to Negro adult education experiments."[43]

In that capacity, Locke served as a consultant on two experimental adult education projects that the Corporation supported at public libraries in Harlem and Atlanta between 1931 and 1934. These projects included courses and discussion about Afro-American culture. In Harlem the project centered in the study of the materials in the Schomburg Collection that the Corporation had purchased for the New York Public Library.[44] When Locke was asked to evaluate the two experiments, he supported grants for them with the argument that they demonstrated that "racially organized programs" provided "something very needed in the average Negro community,—a constructive, educative and non-propagandist channel for expression for their racial feelings and interests."[45] He recommended that the Harlem and Atlanta experiments be followed up, first, by "a campaign promoting more widespread interest in adult education projects for Negro groups and communities . . . in charge of a . . . young Negro man or woman"; and second, by the development of "popular, but accurate and systematic materials . . . in fields of Negro achievement, Negro cultural and historical backgrounds, the Negro problem both as related to the group itself and as correlated with general current social, political and economic problems."[46]

Despite Keppel's interest in adult education and respect for Locke, he drew back from the first of the two suggestions. According to Morse A. Cartwright, "he felt that the Negro adult education experiments were yet in such early stages that to propagandize for them at the present time might be dangerous."[47] One suspects, however, that more than this was involved in Keppel's response. Whether he personally agreed with the sentiment, Keppel was aware that most philanthropists still believed that organizations engaged in research on blacks or in educating them should be supervised, if not by whites alone, then at least by committees of mixed racial membership.[48] However unusual Woodson's reputation for unorthodox management and irascibility may have been, it was not unusual, though it was insulting, for the Social Science Research Council, which gave him $4,000 in 1928 for the Association for the Study of Negro Life and History, to insist that the project for which the grant was given be subjected to scrutiny by three white historians.[49] The Harlem and Atlanta experiments in adult education had proceeded under a similar arrangement, with the American Association for Adult Education, leadership and membership of which were almost entirely white, as the sponsor. Were the Corporation now to promote "racially organized" programs "in charge of a . . . young Negro man or woman," the hitherto prevailing pattern would have been broken.[50]

Because Locke was willing to accept a grant for his second proposal while renouncing the first, and was further willing to develop adult education materials under an arrangement that required, first, a detailed plan to be approved by the American Association for Adult Education, and thereafter, its agreement to any "major modification of the plan," a potentially difficult matter was resolved without overt conflict.[51] Acquiescing in a distrust of the capacity of blacks to conduct their affairs that was widespread among (white) foundation officers at this time, Keppel drew selectively from the advice Locke offered. He was unwilling to develop the Harlem and Atlanta experiments as Locke thought best, but he was willing to accept the belief that the experiments had been a "decided success"—a "most effective motivation for programs of adult study in Negro communities" and a great spur to "inter-racial interest and contact . . . even in a reactionary Southern community."[52] In Keppel's hopes for the Corporation's new study, Locke's views were also evident. From Keppel's perspective the study was intended to "get away from the point of view that 'education' and 'school institutions' can be the panacea," and to show the error of assuming that "the kind of education [i.e., vocational education] that we [whites] are none too well satisfied with for ourselves [can] be the prime salvation for the Negro."[53] As Keppel later reminded Gunnar Myrdal, he hoped that "out of this study can come a fundamental criticism of the way the work for Negro education has been proceeding," and that Locke should "not be left out of the picture."[54] Locke's views apparently held considerable appeal for the Corporation's president, even if he could not or did not always act in full support of them.

Planning a Study That Would Be "Objective"

To begin the planning necessary to carry out Baker's recommendation, Keppel sent his assistant John Russell to Cleveland in the spring of 1936 to consult with men and women Baker respected for their efforts to foster interracial cooperation. Preeminent among them was Russell Jelliffe, who with his wife, Rowena, had established an interracial social settlement in Cleveland's central ward in 1915.[55] The Jelliffes combined settlement work modeled on Hull House in Chicago—they had sought the advice of Jane Addams before moving to Cleveland—with cultural activities like those later advocated by Alain Locke. Beginning as the Playhouse Settlement, the name of the organization was soon changed to Karamu House (Karamu was a Swahili word meaning "a place of joyful meeting").[56] The Jelliffes believed that both African and American Negro culture were capable of arousing collective pride among blacks and new attitudes among whites. Plays with or about blacks were often produced at Karamu. Langston Hughes was writing such plays at Karamu when John Russell visited Cleveland in the spring of 1936.

Following Russell's visit, Keppel went to Cleveland in September

1936 "to talk this whole matter over" with Baker.[57] He was still not
sure how to carry out what he described as Baker's suggestion that
"the Corporation should consider the possibilities of usefulness with
the negroes, particularly the urban negroes."[58] The Corporation had
often explored the feasibility of new programs by developing and
supporting experimental projects like those which Locke had evaluated
in Harlem and Atlanta. Keppel's description, therefore, suggests that
it had not yet been determined that a formal investigation be commissioned in this instance. By October 1936 that decision had apparently
been made, and Keppel, following Newton Baker's advice, was actively
in search of a European to undertake the study.[59]

The choice of a "non-American" obviously enabled the Corporation
to sidestep an awkward choice between black and white American
scholars. Just as important, it provided a guarantee against unfavorable
comparisons with the Rosenwald Fund's study of race relations, which
had been completed in 1935 and was published in 1936. Entitled *Alien
Americans: A Study of Race Relations*, this study had been written by
Bertram Schrieke, a Dutch colonial administrator and scholar.[60] Were
the Corporation to commission an American-led study, it might seem
less objective.

Alien Americans, which has been described as "an 'American Dilemma'—*avant la lettre*," embodied many of the assumptions Baker
and Keppel wanted to avoid.[61] Although the study dealt with a number
of "alien" groups throughout the nation, it focused on racial problems
in the South. It argued that progress there would depend on a revitalized
agricultural economy in which "the new peasant"—"the new peasant"
was to be black—would play a vital role, "not [as] a serf," but as "a
hard-working stubborn character, proud of his freedom and independence on his self-owned land." *Alien Americans* also called for "special
attention" to "Negro interests" in education.[62] Except for the change
in name from "Negro" to "peasant," its educational prescriptions
echoed those of Thomas Jesse Jones. According to *Alien Americans*:
"Ancient ideals and slogans, such as 'A free college education for
everybody,' should be abandoned, whereas conscious endeavour
should be made to form a free peasant class. The school curriculum
should be based on and adapted to the rural needs, not framed after
an urban model. Here is a great task for the agricultural teachers under
the direction of the state departments. Since this planning cannot be
restricted to state lines, regular contact between men of vision in the
different states should be established. As in the past when new ideas
were introduced and new organizational forms had to be created,

philanthropic foundations might take the initiative and the lead."[63] Because Baker and Keppel were eager to displace this view, and because the Rosenwald Fund itself had sought an author who "had never visited the United States nor . . . met an American Negro . . . as a guarantee of unbiased opinion," the desire to seek a non-American author made sense.[64]

Keppel consulted many people in his search for a European author, his advisers on this matter ranging from Edward L. Thorndike, the Teachers College, Columbia University psychologist, who was a close friend and neighbor, to Melville Herskovits, the Northwestern University anthropologist, and Raymond Fosdick, president of the Rockefeller Foundation.[65] By July 1937, he had compiled a list of twenty-five candidates. It included prominent scholars such as Alfred Métraux, the Swiss anthropologist, and Bronislaw Malinowski, the Anglo-Polish anthropologist who was a professor at the London School of Economics; educators such as W. W. Vaughan, the former headmaster of Rugby, and William Rappard, a political scientist at the University of Geneva; and men experienced in colonial affairs, as for example Lord Hailey, a retired member of the Indian civil service and a former governor of the Punjab, who was the author of *An African Survey* (1938), which had been sponsored by the Carnegie Corporation, and Hendrick Mouw, a former Dutch administrator in the East Indies.[66] The last name added to Keppel's list was Karl Gunnar Myrdal. He had been nominated by Beardsley Ruml, James Angell's assistant during his brief term as president of the Corporation, and seconded by Lawrence K. Frank, Ruml's colleague at the Laura Spelman Rockefeller Memorial during the mid-1920s, when Ruml had made the Memorial a major force in the development of the social sciences.[67]

In 1937 Myrdal was thirty-nine years old. At the University of Stockholm he held the Lars Hierta professorship in political economy and financial science. He was also a member of the Swedish Senate. In 1929–30 he and his wife, Alva Myrdal, an expert in welfare policy, had been Rockefeller Foundation Fellows in the United States, and thereafter they had maintained close ties with representatives of the Rockefeller philanthropies, who frequently relied upon national advisers in making decisions about European fellowships and grants.[68] Ruml and Frank were therefore in a position to testify that Myrdal was "able, energetic, and competent in the social field, well-oriented psychologically . . . and would be good, if we could get him."[69] Reflecting trust among colleagues in philanthropy, the commendations from Ruml and Frank seem to have been decisive. Although the former

Chicago sociologist W. I. Thomas was also reported to know Myrdal well, there is no indication that Thomas's opinion was sought.[70]

On August 12, 1937, Myrdal was invited by Keppel to lead "a comprehensive Study of the Negro in the United States to be undertaken in a wholly objective and dispassionate way as a social phenomenon."[71] He initially refused but then reversed himself after a conversation with Ruml in Stockholm that gave his "temptation" to say yes "more of momentum."[72] On October 5, 1937, he cabled Keppel that he had "changed his mind."[73] Keppel was delighted. "We have our man for the general study of the Negro," he wrote to Newton Baker on November 15, 1937.[74] Also pleased, Baker replied, "I think a professor in Stockholm comes nearer filling the bill than any American can."[75] That was Baker's last comment on the study; he died a month later. But he had obviously shared Keppel's hope that Myrdal's competence and relative lack of familiarity with the United States would enable him to carry out an inquiry that could aspire to the apparent "objectivity" of the accounts of earlier foreign observers like Alexis de Tocqueville and Lord Bryce.

In light of this, it is important to note that Myrdal had denied the possibility of value-free social research some years before. In 1930, he had published *Vetenenskap och politik i nationalekonomien* (The political element in the development of economic theory), which contained an argument against the possibility of objectivity in the social sciences. According to Myrdal, a study should "always formulate its value premises explicitly in concrete terms and relate them to the actual valuations of social groups"; "in formulating the relevant attitudes . . . problems of social psychology should not be neglected."[76] The approach he advocated, further developed in "Das zweck-mittel-denken in der nationalökonomie" (Ends and means in political economy), written in 1933, was intended to make "political attitudes . . . alternative and simultaneous premises for science, without having previously been put through the workshop for objectivist theory."[77] He believed this approach would enhance the practical values of social research by illuminating the beliefs, attitudes, values, and perceptions so important in defining "real" situations and "objective" public problems.

Myrdal's published comments on problems of methodology in social research made it predictable that he would approach a study of "negro education and negro problems" in a less traditionally empirical and a more social psychological fashion than Keppel and Baker had anticipated. But his American sponsors were not aware of this. Having accepted appraisals of Myrdal offered by other philanthropists, Keppel had not sought information from Myrdal's professional colleagues, or secured translations or accounts of Myrdal's published works. Donald Young, a member of the staff and then president of the Social Science Research Council, said in 1967 that, in choosing a "non-American" author, the Corporation had substituted unknown for known biases.[78] Young was right. Reputation and connections were the primary bases for the selection of Myrdal.

Defining the Study

Keppel and Myrdal met in the spring of 1938. After he gave the Godkin Lectures on *Population, A Problem for Democracy* at Harvard, Myrdal traveled to New York. He and Keppel confirmed an agreement that, when Myrdal returned in the fall, he would be accompanied by his family and his Swedish associate, Richard Sterner, a skillful statistician and a political ally of the Myrdals. They also decided that Myrdal would spend the fall traveling and studying the existing literature on "the Negro problems," with which, according to Myrdal, he had no prior acquaintance whatsoever. Work on the study, for which Myrdal would have a staff, would then begin in the winter of 1939, with the manuscript to be delivered in 1941. According to Keppel's notes, previous Corporation grants for black education and interracial cooperation and pending applications, all of which were now awaiting the completion of the study, were then reviewed; a few suggestions were made to Myrdal, and Keppel asked if he would like "his men to go over all Carcorp and Rockefeller proposals."[79] If Myrdal was eager to begin an investigation that might contribute to the development of a new "practical political economy," Keppel was eager for guidance in grant-making.[80] Although it was probably not evident to either man, from the first there were discrepancies in aims.

Myrdal then returned to Sweden, leaving it to Keppel to plan the Southern tour that was to start the following fall. Keppel turned for help to Raymond Fosdick, his wartime acquaintance from the Commissions on Training Camp Activities, now president of the Rockefeller Foundation. Fosdick agreed to arrange for Jackson Davis, a Virginian who had been associated with the General Education Board since 1915 and was now its associate director, to be granted a temporary leave of absence so that he might accompany Myrdal and Richard Sterner on what turned out to be a two-month tour of the South.[81] Davis was a predictable choice as guide. He was a Southern liberal with ties to the Phelps-Stokes Fund, of which he became vice president in 1940 and president in 1946, as well as to the Carnegie Corporation, which had sponsored his trip to Africa in 1935. Davis was an expert on Southern and especially black education. It was Davis who had initiated the idea for the traveling "Jeanes teachers" that the Corporation helped to support in both Africa and the American South. His contacts with Southern public and private school officials were extensive.[82] The itinerary Davis arranged included schools and colleges for both blacks and whites in Virginia, North Carolina, South Carolina, Georgia, Alabama, Mississippi, and Louisiana, along with a number of plantations, tenant farmers' houses, and an occasional newspaper office, church, and textile mill. It was designed to provide a full and fair introduction to the institutions and general policies Keppel wanted appraised.

To pursue his own interests, Myrdal needed to explore the kinds of values and attitudes he deemed critical to a valid social analysis. As a result, when visiting Booker T. Washington High School in Birmingham, Alabama, he not only talked with students but also entertained them by singing Swedish folk songs. This upset his hosts, who expected blacks to entertain whites and not the reverse. When Jackson Davis yielded to the exhaustion of long days of travel, meetings, and talk, Myrdal and Sterner let him sleep while they visited "the joints and pubs . . . and the dance halls," where popular attitudes and the "actual situation" might be better appraised.[83] Davis was troubled by Myrdal's behavior, reporting to Lester, the Corporation secretary, that Myrdal did not seem to understand the seriousness of the black-white problem.[84] In fact, while ignorant of the etiquette of a caste society, which was respected by Jackson Davis, Myrdal was showing considerable insight. Unlike Davis, he recognized that the whites who denied discrimination in an Atlanta steelworkers' union were "lying."[85]

Although negative reports reached Keppel, he never wavered in his support for Myrdal. Rather, Myrdal said, Keppel gave him the courage to persevere. In the preface to the twentieth anniversary edition of *An American Dilemma* in 1962, Myrdal explained:

I was shocked and scared to the bones by all the evils I saw, and by the serious political implications of the problem which I could not fail to appreciate from the beginning. When I returned to New York I told Mr. Keppel of my deep worries. I should confess that I even suggested a retreat to him: that we should give up the purely scientific approach and instead deal with the problem as one of political compromise and expediency—a different type of inquiry, but one with which I had also had some experience. . . . I proposed that I should work with a three-man committee, composed of a Southern white, a Northern white, and a Negro, and I even proposed names for its membership. In such a group we could have taken considerations of political feasibility into account and worked out a basis for practical understanding, to which each could have subscribed. But if I was afraid, Keppel was not. Without a moment's hesitation, he told me that I was not going to have a committee to lean upon. The facts were before me. My job was simply to apply my professional tools to discover the truth for myself, without side glances toward what might be politically desirable or possible. And so this matter was settled.[86]

Keppel's support was also evident in his reaction to the sixty-three-page written report Myrdal submitted to him following the Southern journey. The report began with a troubling confession: "It is not to be denied that I have experienced greater *initial difficulties* in familiarizing myself with the subject matter of study than I had anticipated." Beyond that, he was not sure how to proceed, because of "the immense scope of the problem and its ramifications in the whole of American civilization. The American Negro as a social phenomenon is included in, and includes, all other American social, economic and political problems. I have, thus, to acquire a working knowledge of American history, geography, culture, political and institutional set-up [*sic*] before I can place the Negro in the right position in the national scheme."[87] Myrdal then allowed himself to engage in the sort of reflection on paper that would be a constant feature of his voluminous reports to the president of the Corporation. His freedom to express his unedited thoughts openly to Keppel had probably been of considerable help as he formulated his views. He wrote:

My chances of being able to produce a different type of result and, therefore, a valuable one, are, as I now see it, due not so much to my supposed freedom from preconceived and biased ideas about the American Negro, as to the fact that my approach to the problem of the American Negro must be *via* a fresh attempt to reach an understanding of American culture and civilization as a whole. I cannot be tempted to deal with the Negro while keeping the surrounding American society out of the picture as a self-evident and constant factor, which is more or less a fault of a great deal of the literature. I must state the problem of the Negro out of an observation of values and institutions prevalent in American society.[88]

From that beginning, the report went on to note, first, that in Myrdal's opinion the study should not be international—a possibility Keppel would have been interested in, owing to the Corporation's African programs; second, that it should not deal at length with questions of inborn differences between blacks and whites—a topic that, if not Keppel, certainly trustees like Frederick Osborn, an advocate of eugenics and demographic research, thought important; and third, since Myrdal had concluded that the African cultural heritage was "less preserved and less significant" than the cultural heritage of other groups, that this, too, was not to be emphasized—another interest of Keppel's as a result of his own association with Alain Locke.[89] According to Myrdal, the study would focus on the "actual situation," that is, on the ways in which contemporary attitudes, practices, and institutional arrangements would be likely either to promote "harmony" or to intensify "the several dilemmas confronting American culture because of the presence of the Negro."[90] Perhaps in the very act of writing Keppel, Myrdal formulated an attack on the problem that nine pages earlier he had despaired of. He then proceeded to discuss how he planned to carry out the necessary research, asking American scholars to undertake special studies on a variety of topics ranging from "discrimination" to "class and caste stratification within the Negro group" and "cultural achievements."[91]

Even though some of the special investigations Myrdal projected in January 1939 were to touch on matters relevant to Baker's and Keppel's initial questions, it could not have escaped Myrdal's sponsor that the project was already moving on a course different from what they had originally conceived. Myrdal's first report showed that he was not interested in providing guidance for grant-making. Little was said about education. Keppel had not previously indicated his awareness of the discrepancies between his and Myrdal's aims, but now he began to do so. After reading the report, he reiterated to Myrdal his hope that "out of this study could come a fundamental criticism of the way the work for Negro education had been proceeding."[92]

Besides revealing yet again what the Corporation, as represented by its president, wanted from its comprehensive study, Keppel's comment to Myrdal was characteristic of Keppel's interchange with Myrdal as an author and the director of the study. A suggestion rather than a directive, Keppel's comment was frank but respectful, in no way infringing upon Myrdal's scholarly freedom. Having already turned a deaf ear to criticism of Myrdal and of what by 1939 he admitted had been the "risky" idea of bringing him to the United States, Keppel continued to defend the inquiry. He never trespassed on Myrdal's right to control its direction, even as that direction continued to diverge from his own expectations.[93] Myrdal praised the strength and disciplined allegiance to scholarly values this showed, writing later: "As long as America has men like Keppel placed in responsible positions, periods of reaction and of intimidation of free scholars will pass, as they have done before. The trend toward ever greater fulfillment of the liberal ideals cannot be reversed, and America will remain a bastion of intellectual freedom and social progress."[94] Keppel later said that he had staked his reputation on this book.[95] His willingness to help by making suggestions, combined with his insistence upon regard for Myrdal's autonomy as scholar, were vital to the inquiry from beginning to end.

The work that followed the submission of Myrdal's initial statement of plans in January 1939 proceeded in two stages. The first—the research stage—involved having Myrdal's plans reviewed by fifty-one individuals. Some were black, others white. Some were Northern, others Southern. Some were scholars in sociology, anthropology, psychology, history, and other disciplines; others were educators, philanthropists, or leaders of interracial organizations. Some had established reputations as "radicals," as for example W. E. B. Du Bois; others, like Thomas Jesse Jones, were recognized "conservatives."[96] Whether or not this wide range of reactions actually affected Myrdal's thinking, it certainly informed the study's prospective audience that a major new inquiry was forthcoming.

A small week-long conference was called in Asbury Park, New Jersey, in April 1939. It was here that initial plans were finally revised and focused, as Myrdal engaged in intense conversations with Ralph J. Bunche, Charles S. Johnson, Guy B. Johnson, Richard Sterner, Dorothy S. Thomas, Thomas J. Woofter, Jr., Donald Young, and Charles Dollard. Except for Charles Dollard, Keppel's new assistant at the Carnegie Corporation, and Donald Young of the Social Science Research Council, all were scholars from universities where relevant lines of research were evolving that would, in one way or another, find their way into Myrdal's book. According to Myrdal's report to Keppel, the meeting was helpful in focusing his attention on problems of "status," on recent changes and tendencies toward change, and on the "dilemmas" associated with them. The consensus was that the emphasis should be on "race relations" and on "the *induced* changes (or the interferences) in the process of change and adjustment, represented by legislative programs, education work, interracial efforts, concerted actions by Negro groups, etc."[97] Increasingly clear as to the nature of the problems he would analyze, Myrdal returned to New York City, where he commissioned some forty research memoranda from scholars all over the country and continued to acquaint himself with secondary literature.[98] Whenever possible, he also took to the road, now usually accompanied by Richard Sterner and the black political scientist Ralph Bunche, whom Myrdal liked, respected, and found more helpful than Jackson Davis, even rather relishing the fact that they were "run out" of three Southern towns together.[99]

An American Dilemma, *a Study in the Mold of Chicago Sociology*

Before the research memoranda for *An American Dilemma* were ready for Myrdal's review, the first phase of the project was interrupted. Germany invaded Denmark and Norway in 1940, and Myrdal felt under obligation to return to Sweden, worried that if the Germans won the war he would become a political refugee. He left the United States in April. In his absence, Samuel Stouffer, a professor of sociology at the University of Chicago, served as Myrdal's liaison with the scholars who were writing research memoranda, making sure that their papers were completed. That was an important step forward, but the turn of events caused by the war must have greatly disheartened Keppel. Characteristically, he had respected Myrdal's decision to go home. And yet, with Myrdal in Europe and no certainty that he would return, the project was in danger of ending with nothing to show for the money and effort already expended. To preclude that, Stouffer was asked to serve as secretary of a committee consisting of Donald Young, president of the Social Science Research Council, Shelby Harrison, president of the Russell Sage Foundation, and William F. Ogburn, professor of sociology at the University of Chicago, which would review the research memoranda and arrange publication for at least some of them. Those published were Melville J. Herskovits's *The Myth of the Negro Past* (1941); Charles S. Johnson's *Patterns of Negro Segregation* (1943); Richard Sterner's *The Negro's Share* (1943); and a collection of investigations edited by Otto Klineberg, *Characteristics of the American Negro* (1944). But in March 1941 Myrdal decided that he could return to the United States to complete what he later described as his "war work."[100]

The second or drafting stage then began. Because Stouffer was convinced that "for his own sake Myrdal must keep his hands off the [research] manuscripts and spend his time on his own overview," and because, like Keppel, Charles Dollard was worried about Myrdal's "old weakness for expanding the scope of his project," it was arranged that he would not take up residence in Chicago but rather work in a college town.[101] Apparently, Myrdal's attraction to the University of Chicago and his inclination for a holistic, sociological study was of increasing concern to his sponsor. Having wanted a broad, general policy review, the Corporation was getting a complex scholarly inquiry that was taking significantly longer to complete than expected. However, once Myrdal was rusticated with Richard Sterner and a young University of Chicago graduate student in sociology by the name of

Arnold Rose, first, at Dartmouth College, and then, for most of a year, at Princeton, he did finally manage to digest the large amount of data and the many interpretations collected. Most of these were not fundamentally new, Myrdal's effort being to filter them through his newly acquired knowledge and opinions, and his better-established general point of view. The result was a manuscript that was indeed "comprehensive," mentioning the writings of a large number of scholars of varying perspectives. Yet, it was also selective in the emphasis it gave to the different perspectives in the works from which it drew.

Thus, some data that had been gathered by Melville J. Herskovits, the anthropologist of Northwestern University who had been asked to prepare a research memorandum, were included in the book. But since Myrdal had become convinced that Herskovits's "bias on the problem of African derivation of American Negro patterns is excessive," Herskovits's conviction of the importance of African survivals was deleted.[102] Instead, following the black sociologist E. Franklin Frazier, who was also asked to prepare a research memorandum, Myrdal presented the controversial argument that "*American Negro culture is not something independent of general American culture. It is a distorted development, or a pathological condition, of the general American culture.*"[103]

Similarly, while rejecting the basic themes of Ralph Bunche's critical interpretation of political ideologies, class conflicts, and class alliances, Myrdal did discuss Bunche's view of the National Association for the Advancement of Colored People and accepted his contention that the organization lacked widespread popular support.[104] Convinced that the study would be the most important of all those completed in the last twenty years—that it would be a policy-making document that would "influence procedures along interracial lines for certainly the next ten years and perhaps longer"—Walter White, executive director of the NAACP, was upset by this.[105] He thought it unfortunate that Myrdal had "leaned . . . heavily on the negative and academic judgments of Ralph."[106]

Not only in his discussion of the NAACP, but throughout the two volumes of *An American Dilemma*, Myrdal's interpretation was closer to the views of Bunche's generation, to which E. Franklin Frazier also belonged, than it was to the views of White, Du Bois, and other leaders of the preceding generation. Hence, as between the younger generation's emphasis on economic status and social class, and the older generation's emphasis on race, racial consciousness, and race solidarity, he tended to stress the former.[107]

Myrdal began sending out drafts of chapters for *An American Dilemma* in November 1941. "When writing this book, I have had in mind God and my scientific conscience and such intelligent and respectable readers as you, Mr. Keppel, Fred Osborn and colleagues like Louis Wirth and [E. Franklin] Frazier," he wrote Charles Dollard.[108] Whether Osborn (the Corporation trustee interested in eugenics and demography) reviewed the draft is unclear, but the four others did comment, Keppel's comments being particularly noteworthy here. Writing to Myrdal in July 1942, he said that the only point he wished to emphasize was that he agreed with Dollard on "the inherent dangers of overemphasizing the Woman-Negro analogy in Chapter 4."[109] Even though the analogy was apt and important and might better have been left where it was, Myrdal accepted Dollard and Keppel's suggestion, relegating "the parallel problem" to an appendix.[110] Keppel had already given up his hopes for a critical examination of "Negro education." In fact, the one chapter that dealt with education was written by Arnold Rose after Myrdal left the United States to return to his work in Sweden. Keppel had also given up any expectation that the study would result in immediate suggestions for grant-making. "As the book has developed," Myrdal told him, he had "more and more, been thinking of its long-range effects and not its immediate results and its effects on the study of the social problems generally and not only the Negro problem in America."[111] Keppel's suggestion concerning "the parallel problem" was a result of the tensions evident throughout the events surrounding the Corporation's study. Keppel believed in intellectual freedom, but, having courageously adhered to that belief, he had ended up as the sponsor of a study that was comprehensive, practical, and objective in Myrdal's sense and not in his own. With the prospective product, however admirable, already out of line with the purposes he had wished Myrdal's research to serve, all Keppel could do was to encourage the independent director he had chosen and commissioned to preserve the expected substantive focus on "the Negro problem."

To some extent, of course, that focus was realized in the book published by Harper & Brothers in 1944. But as Myrdal acknowledged both to Keppel and to Louis Wirth, *An American Dilemma* was not one book, but two.[112] For Keppel and the lay audience Keppel wanted it to reach, it was a study of the Negro; but for Myrdal and the scholarly audience he wished to address, it was also a sociological study in the tradition of the sociology developed at the University of Chicago.

Myrdal explicitly acknowledged his indebtedness to Chicago sociology in the introduction to *An American Dilemma*. Announcing that "our task in this inquiry is to ascertain social reality as it is," he explained that the study would present massive data about "who the Negro is, and how he fares. . . . But this is not all and, from our point of view, not even the most important part of social reality. We want to follow through W. I. Thomas's theme, namely, that when people define situations as real, they *are* real."[113] Thomas was one of the most important early sociologists at the University of Chicago and, as Lawrence K. Frank had indicated to Keppel in endorsing Myrdal, the two were close personal and professional friends. Between 1930 and 1936 Thomas frequently visited the Social Science Institute of the University of Stockholm, where Dorothy Swaine Thomas was doing research; Myrdal and his wife visited the Thomases when they were in the United States.[114]

Beyond explicitly referring to Thomas, Myrdal also explained one of the major trends he described in *An American Dilemma* by discussing how his approach diverged from that of Robert E. Park, a recently retired University of Chicago professor of sociology and one of the best-known and most influential scholars of race relations.[115] According to Myrdal, "social engineering"—meaning "the drawing of practical conclusions from the teaching of social sciences that 'human nature' is changeable and that human deficiencies and unhappiness are, in large degree, preventable"—would be more in demand after the war.[116] This projection derived, he maintained, from a willingness to acknowledge that "*biases in social science cannot be erased simply by 'keeping to the facts' and by refined methods of statistical treatment of the data.*" It also required discarding "*the entirely negative device of refusing to arrange its results for practical and political utilization.*"[117] Park had not done this, Myrdal asserted. Although Park was not a conservative, his writings exemplified "a systematic tendency to ignore practically all possibilities of modifying—by conscious effort—the social effects of natural forces." By implication, if not intent, they had perpetuated the "do-nothing" tendency of American social science, which, according to Myrdal, was also evident in the writing of W. I. Thomas and other scholars.[118] Yet while distancing himself from the "biases" he associated with the laissez-faire implications of Park's work, Myrdal also accepted and built upon Park's more general effort to turn socio-logical studies away from questions of racial difference and toward ones having to do with social class and relative group status. Park, a great and much-beloved teacher, had significantly influenced the views of E. Franklin Frazier and others of Frazier's generation, and Myrdal accepted many ideas from Frazier as well as from other students of Park and from Park himself.[119]

Finally, one should call attention to the influence of Louis Wirth, another important professor of sociology at the University of Chicago, who frequently consulted with Myrdal while he was working on *An American Dilemma* and who had nominated Arnold Rose to serve as one of Myrdal's assistants. Myrdal cited a letter from Wirth in support of the emphasis he placed on "valuations" in *An American Dilemma*.[120] Wirth believed that "the social scientist can make a contribution by making the values underlying social policy and human behavior explicit." This was what Myrdal attempted.[121] More important, Wirth viewed the study of consensus as "the central task of sociology."[122] He maintained that common understandings, expectations, and norms define sociology; he saw the formation and articulation of consensus as the key to democratic politics. It is not surprising, therefore, that Wirth was one of the four men Myrdal had in mind in writing *An American Dilemma*. By focusing on a consensus, the "American creed," and arguing that this consensus could and should become the actual basis for social practice in the United States, Myrdal built an argument compatible with Wirth's view of social dynamics. That is not to say that Myrdal directly derived his argument from Wirth; but there were significant reflections of Wirth's ideas in Myrdal's book.

Myrdal's close acquaintance with prominent University of Chicago sociologists and with their writings is easy to explain. The Chicago department of sociology was the premier center of sociology in the United States during the first half of the twentieth century, and group relations, including interracial relations, was an important subject of research there. Myrdal would have been likely to know this in any case, but his Rockefeller Foundation fellowship had enabled him to visit Chicago and become acquainted with the sociologists at the University. When asked to undertake the Carnegie study, he therefore recruited many of his closest collaborators from Chicago and oriented himself intellectually in reference to research done there.

Whether Frederick Keppel, who died in 1943, was aware that the Corporation's "comprehensive study" was a study in the mold of Chicago sociology is unknown. Before the book was completed, Dollard had told Myrdal that he and Keppel both liked "the idea of hanging the whole study on the peg which you describe as the American dilemma, i.e., the conflict between the average American's faith in the democratic creed and his tacit acceptance of social and legal measures designed to repress a large segment of the population marked off from the rest by the difference in color."[123] Later, Keppel privately expressed the belief that, even though *An American Dilemma* was sprawling and too long, it was essentially sound. He also predicted that it would "take its place with such untidy but nevertheless very important books as 'The Golden Bough' and 'The Education of Henry Adams.'"[124] But he never commented upon the study's relation to social science scholarship.

After *An American Dilemma* appeared, it was called "monumental" by W. E. B. Du Bois, and "a magnet to scholars" by historian Oscar Handlin.[125] It was cited in *Brown v. Board of Education*, the 1954 Supreme Court decision outlawing segregation in the public schools.[126] Entire books have been written about its reception and dissemination through reviews and discussion in the press.[127] Within the offices of the Carnegie Corporation, however, where it was initially intended to have its most direct effects, it seems by and large to have been ignored. Typically, in May 1947 the Corporation awarded $75,000 to the University of Chicago to help support training and research relevant to the improvement of race relations. Although the project was intended to help develop "new knowledge concerning the nature and effects of race prejudice" and to translate "existing knowledge into usable terms," neither *An American Dilemma* nor the concerns out of which it had sprung were mentioned.[128] Not until the 1960s did the Corporation proudly claim and build upon Myrdal's work. By then it was recognized, as Corporation secretary Sara L. Engelhardt stated later, in 1975, that "the Corporation's failure to follow up on the Myrdal study is perhaps the greatest missed opportunity in its history, one that can be regretted now in hindsight."[129] *An American Dilemma* may have been the most influential study ever commissioned with Carnegie funds, but because its author heeded the demands of scholarship and of his own conscience more than the immediate expectations of his sponsors, the study had its greatest immediate effects elsewhere.

III

〜━━‥━━〜

Strategic Philanthropy

A T T H E E N D of the Second World War, a new sense of urgency was evident in discussions of Carnegie Corporation policies and programs. The primary cause was the atom bomb. After Hiroshima and Nagasaki, another war was unimaginable. Convinced, as were many of their contemporaries, that the "present inter-Armageddon" would be "the last," the Corporation's trustees and officers recognized a need, not only to sustain the foundation's historic commitment to internationalism and peace, but to do so with even greater care and more deliberate planning.[1] Their considerations of what should be done were suffused with a sense of awesome responsibility that had not been evident before. Increasingly, too, these considerations were based upon recognition that the United States was engaged in "a cold war with the USSR" that was likely to be protracted.[2]

The problem was that sure knowledge of the conditions that would maintain world peace was as elusive in 1945 as it had been before and would remain thereafter. But it seemed reasonable to assume that the Corporation might contribute to efforts to build "a more ordered world," if it were, first, to attempt to foster a better understanding of international tensions, and then, to identify ways to communicate this knowledge to decision-makers in Washington and other national capitals, as well as to business and civic leaders all over the country and—most difficult of all, it was believed—to members of the public at large.[3] Beginning in 1946, therefore, many of the Corporation's activities were designed to be instrumental to these ends. "When a new project comes up, it will *not* be sufficient to know that a terribly competent man proposed it, or that it is a socially desirable project, or that it is feasible and well-formulated," John W. Gardner, a psychologist newly recruited to the Corporation's staff, argued in a memorandum contributed to the 1946 internal program review from which the Corporation's initial postwar priorities emerged. "We will want to know whether this project is relevant in terms of our basic strategy, whether it is a logical next step (or at least an indispensable step) toward the attainment of one or another of our objectives."[4]

The words "strategy" and "strategic" appear also to have been used outside the Corporation with unusual frequency and prominence at the time Gardner wrote this memorandum. President J. B. Conant of Harvard University argued in his 1946–47 president's report that "scientists who are directing their attention to the behavior of man as a social animal and are determined to assist in the development of American society toward our historic goals occupy a *strategic* post" (emphasis added).[5] Addressing the American Association for the Advancement of Science in the fall of 1948, Samuel A. Stouffer, the Chicago sociologist who had helped ensure completion of Gunnar Myrdal's study of race relations, claimed that "by developing limited theories, testable and tested empirically, by being modest about them and tentative, we can, I think, make a small but effective contribution toward an ultimate science of society whose engineering applications will help regulate the complex civilization wrought by physical science and technology."[6] The title of his speech was "Sociology and the Strategy of Social Science." Both Conant and Stouffer would loom large in postwar Corporation grant-making; to some extent, this was a result of the concern they shared with people at the foundation for more precise, deliberate, incremental, and hopefully effective planning for peace and progress. But talk of "strategy" was not unusual at the time, and especially when contrasted with post-First World War talk of "the new world of science," this small point of rhetoric is revealing.

Over the years, as the first shock of possible nuclear war waned a little, the precarious sense of responsibility once so much in evidence at the Corporation diminished, though it never disappeared entirely. The stress of events throughout the Cold War years and the 1960s did not allow that to happen, and the emphasis on *strategy* remained. If it had once been sufficient to justify a grant on its merits, it now became necessary, in addition, to demonstrate how that grant might fit within one of the Corporation's articulated and agreed-upon plans for reaching its long-range goals. By the 1970s, Corporation program officers were sometimes asked to try to restate their case for a new initiative, "this time treating it as a more unified strategy."[7] Furthermore, activities that might once have won support as ends in themselves were now sometimes thought of in strategic terms. Thus, when President Alan Pifer asked Corporation Secretary Sara L. Engelhardt in 1975 to prepare a review of grants to "the powerless," the resulting document included a section labeled: "Research as a Strategy."[8] Similarly a 1976 assessment of grants related "to the promotion of social justice" began with the reminder that "in 1972 the trustees and staff members reached a consensus on the proposal to use the legal system as one strategy."[9] Variously used, the term "strategy" and the general concept of planned, organized, deliberately constructed means to realize broadly stated ends had become a mainstay of Corporation grant-making.

Reflecting the world situation in the late 1940s, the Corporation's concern with strategy derived thereafter from the domestic situation in which the foundation found itself. Once a lone giant with resources sufficient to have a profound and direct influence on public policy, the Corporation underwent a slow shrinking of its power and resources relative to other institutions during these decades. This relative decline resulted from several developments: the establishment of new and sometimes larger private philanthropic foundations like the Ford Foundation; the creation by the federal government of public foundations, beginning with the National Science Foundation; and the passage of a variety of federal bills providing direct funds to universities, colleges, schools, libraries, and other institutions that had once been and perhaps continued to be among the Corporation's clients.

Within this thickening matrix of patronage agencies and authorities, the Corporation had to develop more carefully planned and often leveraged means to pursue its goals, if, as Vice President David Z. Robinson and Secretary Sara L. Engelhardt explained in 1980, its "relatively few dollars" were to "have any impact at all."[10] To oversimplify the point, the Corporation now needed to assume that its dollars could be matched and its goals either undermined, mitigated, redefined, or furthered by other agencies having both funds (often more funds) to give and ideas to go along with them. In consequence, a central goal of strategic philanthropy was to develop programs that might be followed or implemented by other organizations. This had the advantage of securing additional and sometimes more powerful backing for Corporation initiatives and of limiting the investment the Corporation needed to make. Thus, having financed the first university centers for foreign area study, the Corporation could leave their support and continued development to the Ford Foundation, as it transferred its attention to problems of education; or, having developed a conception of public television and a plan for its organization, it could call upon the federal government to implement the blueprint generated.

In addition to this increasingly competitive situation among grant-making bodies, the Corporation's steadily increasing concern with strategy derived as well from profound, if subtle, changes in patterns of public policy-making in the United States. Public policy-making, as a deliberate and self-conscious effort to define directions for public action, became an everyday adjunct of more and more spheres of common concern within more and more institutions after the Second World War. Earlier, policy-making had tended to focus on problems of geopolitics; one classic example was "The Inquiry," which during the First World War brought together diverse experts on international affairs, purposively and through scientific means to define intelligent policies for the United States to pursue at the peace table and, thereafter, in the peace that was meant to endure.[11] Now, policy-making became a necessary aspect of running a business, managing a nonprofit institution, or editing a newspaper. Requiring the formulation of strategies—some went so far as to equate policy-making with "strategizing"—policy-making within the Carnegie Corporation after the Second World War supported an emphasis on instrumental or strategic giving.

Four very different men presided over the Corporation during the four decades following the Second World War: Devereux C. Josephs, Charles Dollard, John W. Gardner, and Alan Pifer. In response to a changing national context, each pursued somewhat different goals. During the brief term of Josephs (1945–48), the Corporation's interest in international affairs was renewed and the professional staff increased in number and responsibilities. Formal staff reviews and discussion of grants and general foundation direction, apart from trustee meetings, began at this time. Internal administrative changes such as these derived from the president's unusual skill as an administrator and his keen sense of the importance of foundations. Foundation money, he once claimed, was "the venture capital of philanthropy."[12] Remaining an unusually active and well-informed member of the board of trustees even after he resigned the presidency to become chief executive of the New York Life Insurance Company, Josephs served as a persuasive and effective ally for his immediate successors, especially Charles Dollard, who relied heavily upon him as a supporter and interpreter to the trustees. Josephs remained active on the board until 1966.

Josephs was followed in the presidency by Charles Dollard, whose particular programmatic interest was the social sciences; by John W. Gardner, whose particular programmatic interest was education; and by Alan Pifer, whose particular programmatic interest was social justice. In pursuit of these interests, each man used a variety of strategies. Each of the chapters that follows focuses upon one of these: university reform, then leadership, and finally the commission. In all cases, however, despite differences in strategy, there was a tendency to assume that ideas and innovations generated with Carnegie funds could and would be passed on to governmental authorities. The earlier ecology of governing institutions, in which private centers of *governance* made it possible for the public institutions of the *government* to remain small and limited in function, had clearly changed. But that ecology was changing again by the end of Alan Pifer's presidency, and it was not clear how the new conservatism of the 1980s would force changes in the strategic philanthropy predominating at the Carnegie Corporation since 1945. That would remain to be seen after David A. Hamburg succeeded Alan Pifer as president in 1982.

CHAPTER SEVEN

Effective Expertise

New Designs for Social Research

IN THE SPRING of 1946, the Carnegie Corporation decided to make the further development of the social sciences a major new grant priority. As Charles Dollard explained in the decision, it derived from the conviction that "the disciplines concerned primarily with the behavior of human beings" were where the Corporation should "now look for light in the solution of problems which have been dramatized, though by no means produced, by the recent brilliant work of the nuclear physicists."[1] Having originally joined the Corporation's staff in 1938 as an assistant to Frederick P. Keppel, Dollard returned from military service at the end of 1945. During the presidency of Devereux C. Josephs (1945–48), he was promoted to the newly created position of vice president; then, after Josephs resigned, he was asked to succeed him as chief executive. Dollard's confidence in the great value the social sciences might have for world peace and human welfare was shared by most of his staff colleagues and by at least one trustee in addition to Josephs. This was Frederick Osborn, who had joined the Corporation's board in 1936. No less than Charles Dollard's, Frederick Osborn's enthusiasm was a result of personal experience and acquaintance. Both Dollard and Osborn had ties to scholars engaged in two distinctive approaches to social research: interdisciplinary research of the kind initially associated with personality and culture studies; and "hard" empirical survey research. These ties and their own personal knowledge disposed the Corporation to support projects intended to help join these approaches in order to make "studies of man" really "scientific."

In comparison to the previous support for the social sciences provided by the Rockefeller philanthropies, as well as the subsequent support for the "behavioral sciences" provided by the Ford Foundation, the Carnegie Corporation's overall outlay of funds was modest. But its grants helped to gain respect and notice for interdisciplinary behavioral approaches to social research, even before Ford Foundation grants made possible the university research inventories, the fellowships, the project funds, and the Center for Advanced Study in the Behavioral Sciences in Palo Alto, California, that, at least for a time, established the behavioral sciences as the most prestigious core disciplines of social inquiry. Corporation grants also facilitated transfer of interdisciplinary behavioral approaches to research and training programs having to do with the culture and social organization of different geographic areas, and social scientists working as "area study" specialists pioneered many concepts and methods that, in turn, proved useful to more disciplinary-oriented research in the social and behavioral sciences themselves.

As would be true from this time forward, the Corporation's postwar social science grants were designed to have a multiplier effect, being deliberately organized to influence the subsequent actions of other foundations and government agencies. They were often directed to trend-setting universities, particularly to Harvard, and to organizations connected to wide networks of scholars, notably the Social Science Research Council. In that way exemplifying the new strategic philanthropy that was coming into being, these grants also revealed the persistence of chance and personal connections as bases for philanthropic policies. Indeed, in few chapters of Carnegie Corporation history were coincidences of people and places more important than in the emergence, definition, and evolution of the foundation's social science and area studies programs.

John Dollard and Personality and Culture Studies

The story of the Corporation's new program in the social sciences must begin with one simple fact: Charles Dollard's older brother, John Dollard, was a social psychologist at the Yale University Institute for Human Relations. That Institute had been founded in 1929 to foster collaboration among scholars from all divisions of the Yale faculty, including its professional faculties of medicine and law. As James Rowland Angell had described it to E. E. Day, then of the Rockefeller

Foundation, it was intended "to make the study of human behavior in its individual and group relations one of the major objectives of the University's investigative and educational program."[2] Reporting its establishment to a 1928 meeting of the Association of American Universities, Angell stated that he hoped its research endeavors would facilitate the training of doctors, lawyers, ministers, biologists, psychologists, economists, sociologists, and students "in any other branches of learning," and promote the integration "into a single skill, technique, or profession, elements which heretofore have been separate and often wholly removed from one another, despite the fact that the human being whose interests and welfare are affected by them is a single individual."[3] Established with grants from the Rockefeller Foundation amounting to more than $6 million by 1949, the Institute was probably the first center for the collaborative, cross-disciplinary study of human behavior created in the United States.[4] The Institute for Research in Social Science at the University of North Carolina, organized by Howard W. Odum, had been founded in 1924, but its focus was on regional studies and not human behavior.[5]

Personality and culture studies, which arose from efforts to introduce psychological, psychiatric, and psychoanalytic concepts into anthropology and sociology (and vice versa), were a natural development at the Yale Institute. But their actual emergence at Yale was largely the result of the transfer of the anthropologist Edward Sapir in 1931 from the University of Chicago to a Sterling Professorship there. Sapir had been a student of Franz Boas at Columbia; following Boas, his early work had involved ethnographic descriptions of West Coast Indians as well as consideration of the methods and types of evidence, including grammar and word structures, that would allow ethnographers to study cultural change. Undertaken during the fifteen years Sapir spent as chief of the division of anthropology of the Canadian Geological Survey in Ottawa, his research changed in focus in 1925, when his first wife, who had been mentally and physically ill throughout most of their married life, died, and Sapir had eagerly accepted an invitation to join the still unified Department of Sociology and Anthropology at Chicago. Although he found congenial colleagues and a new wife to care for his three young children, Sapir still remained troubled by his first wife's death; seeking information that might help him understand her mental difficulties, which he feared were genetic and hence might be transmitted to their children, he had sought the advice of the psychiatrist Harry Stack Sullivan. The two men talked from morning until evening, and from then until Sapir's death in 1939 at the age of fifty-five, they remained intimate friends, mutually transforming colleagues, and constant allies in efforts to build collaboration between their respective fields.[6]

Becoming an interpreter from within for psychoanalytic psychiatry to the social sciences, Sapir wrote articles on topics like "Cultural Anthropology and Psychiatry," "The Emergence of the Concept of Personality in the Study of Cultures," and "The Contribution of Psychiatry to an Understanding of Behavior in Society."[7] He also helped gather a small but distinguished group of social scientists and psychologists (W. I. Thomas, Ernest Burgess, Robert E. Park, L. L. Thurstone, Floyd and Gordon Allport, Harold D. Lasswell, and Elton Mayo, among them) to meet with an even smaller but equally distinguished group of psychiatrists (William A. White, Harry Stack Sullivan, George M. Kline, and a few others) for two weekend colloquia in 1928 and 1929, where the conceptual bases for collaboration could be explored.[8] Having thus stimulated interest in exchange among at least some anthropologists, sociologists, and psychologists, Sapir presented the case for personality and culture studies to a wider audience in an address on "The Cultural Approach to the Study of Personality," delivered to the SSRC at its 1930 annual meeting in Hanover, New Hampshire.

The meeting to which Sapir spoke was the last of the renowned Hanover Conferences that the SSRC had hosted annually with Laura Spelman Rockefeller Memorial financing since 1925. As the anthropologist Robert Redfield explained in letters to his wife, the meeting brought together a fairly sizable group of "pedants and potentates"— "the executive secretaries of the big foundations" are all here, he informed her—for two weeks of lectures, seminars, and committee meetings, golf and tennis, and endless talk over "gin and ginger," the purpose being, formally and informally, to set priorities and policies for future social science research.[9] Although Sapir's lecture ran longer and elicited less immediate, formal, and recorded discussion than most given that year, his ideas apparently electrified the gathering.[10] Despite that, the American Psychiatric Association was not invited to join the other groups—the American Economic Association, the American Political Science Association, the American Sociological Association, the American Statistical Association, the American Psychological Association, the American Anthropological Association, and the American Historical Association—in electing delegates to the SSRC's board of directors, as Sullivan and Sapir had apparently hoped would be the case, even though the SSRC's board did state that "it is probable that the Council's interest will continue to run strongly in the direction of these inter-discipline inquiries."[11] A Committee on Personality and

Culture, "to encourage, coordinate, and extend research activities on the growth of the individual and his development through contact with social forces in various cultural settings," was then established in June 1931, and an international seminar on "the dependence on the individual's development upon the cultural system to which he is exposed" was planned for 1932–33 in cooperation with the Institute for Human Relations at Yale.[12] The seminar was to be led by Edward Sapir, who recruited a newly minted Ph.D. in sociology to assist him: Charles Dollard's brother John.

John Dollard was only thirty-two years old when Sapir tapped him. Sapir and Dollard had met at the University of Chicago when Dollard was a graduate student there. Dollard had written a dissertation in a tradition quite different from Sapir's; his thesis supervisor, the sociologist William F. Ogburn, was more interested in quantitative, large-scale, statistical analyses than in the qualitative, case-history studies in which Sapir was increasingly involved. But Dollard had also spent considerable time with Sapir, with whom he shared a growing interest in psychoanalytic thinking, and it was probably this common interest that attracted Sapir to Dollard when he was looking for help with the Yale seminar.[13]

Sapir's and Dollard's interest in psychoanalysis was not idiosyncratic at the University of Chicago at this time. With many others, even Ogburn participated in this. Ogburn did not agree with Sapir that psychoanalytic concepts could and should be transferred to and incorporated within social science, but he did believe that psychoanalytic concepts could tell social scientists "how to be less unscientific."[14] He thought psychoanalytic theory and indeed the experience of psychoanalysis, which he himself had undergone, could help people understand their "desires" and "the way our desires disguise themselves, how they originate, how they are conditioned, and the part they play in forming specific opinions."[15] As John Dollard himself recalled it, "analysis was up for discussion all the time" among Chicago students of his generation, and while still a graduate student he himself had "a piece of an analysis."[16] Thereafter he had also decided to use an SSRC postdoctoral fellowship to study psychoanalysis in Germany, where he was more fully analyzed by Hans Sachs, a disciple of Freud. Known to Sapir previously, and by 1932 armed with a more direct knowledge of Freudian psychoanalysis than most Americans had, John Dollard was a logical person to assist the older anthropologist in the seminar that was intended to give "significant impetus . . . to the scientific study of the causal factors of personality."[17]

After the 1932–33 seminar, relations between Dollard and Sapir may have become somewhat strained. Sapir is reported to have complained to Harry Stack Sullivan that Dollard was overly ambitious and competitive.[18] Yet according to Margaret Mead, Dollard was one of the scholars, in addition to Ruth Benedict and herself, who "profited" the most from Sapir's "speculations on personality and culture."[19] After participating in the seminar, Dollard was offered a continuing appointment at the Yale Institute for Human Relations, where he remained until 1969. His first book, *Criteria for the Life History* (1935), was called "a landmark in the study of personality and culture," and his next book, *Caste and Class in a Southern Town* (1937), further established him as an expert in the field.[20] Banned in Georgia and South Africa, the latter book argued that blacks and whites were frozen into a system structured by manifest and latent prejudice, in which whites gained from the invariably lower economic and social position in which blacks were forced to live. In addition to social pathological insights, it relied upon concepts of social class and social mobility that Dollard learned from W. Lloyd Warner, later well known for his "Yankee City" studies. He used these concepts, he explained subsequently, because association with "experimentalists" like Neal E. Miller, Carl I. Hovland, and Stouffer made him realize "how exceedingly blowzy our notions about personality were."[21] Thereafter, the joining of "soft," social-psychological, case-history-oriented social science and "hard," social-structural, statistically oriented social science became a central concern of John Dollard's long and distinguished career at Yale. Equally important here, pursuing cross-disciplinary studies of human behavior became a major interest of Charles Dollard's after he joined the Corporation's staff in February 1938.

Charles Dollard and Cross-Disciplinary Research

Siblings do not inevitably or invariably share interests, but John and Charles Dollard, who were born in rural Wisconsin to a father who was a railroad engineer and a mother who, according to John, was "very much reaching for higher things," appear to have done so. John was the oldest of the seven Dollard children. "I was sort of the banner-bearer," he recalled at the age of seventy-two; long before 1938 Charles, who was seven years younger, seems to have taken him as a standard and model.[22]

John Dollard was graduated from the University of Wisconsin in 1922, where Charles Dollard followed him, receiving an A.B. in English in 1928. After his graduation, John became a fund-raiser for the Wisconsin Memorial Union; after his graduation, Charles became assistant director of the Union. Having met the physicist Max Mason at Wisconsin, John Dollard moved with him to the University of Chicago when Mason became president. While serving as one of Mason's assistants, he met William F. Ogburn and began graduate work in sociology. His younger brother Charles did not move from the University of Wisconsin to Chicago, but he too shifted into university administration, becoming assistant dean of men at Wisconsin in 1936; also like John, he combined this with graduate work in sociology, though, unlike John, he never completed work for the doctorate.[23]

The understudy pattern evident in Charles Dollard's life up to 1938 ended to some extent in that year. When Charles Dollard met John Russell, who was then Frederick Keppel's assistant, and through Russell was offered a job as Keppel's second assistant, he gave up his studies to become an organizer and patron of scholars instead of a practicing, professional social scientist like John.[24] Even as a foundation staff member and officer, however, Charles Dollard followed his older brother's interests. Like John, Charles Dollard was concerned with race relations; in addition to serving as Keppel's immediate liaison to Gunnar Myrdal's "comprehensive study of the Negro," he later coauthored two studies with Donald Young.[25] And also like John, he was concerned with interdisciplinary studies of human behavior that would be "scientific in the best sense of the word." Described by John Gardner, who became president of Carnegie in 1955, as charming, witty, and sensitive in his relations with other people, Charles Dollard was described by others who knew him at the Corporation as overly critical of his colleagues and no less "ambitious" than Sapir had found John.[26] Whatever the cause—inordinate drive, or a tendency to depression from which John seems also to have suffered, or a reported difficulty in shouldering the ultimate responsibility for decisions (being number one and not number two)—Charles Dollard suffered a major nervous breakdown in the mid-1950s and in consequence left the Carnegie Corporation in 1955.[27] Before that happened, however, he had managed with considerable effectiveness to advance the cause of interdisciplinary, behavioral social research.

Charles Dollard did this initially by convincing Frederick Keppel that the Corporation should finance a postdoctoral fellowship program that would "enable a man who has his Ph.D. in his own field to do some really intensive work in one or two cognate fields"—an idea that came to Dollard from the anthropologist Ralph Linton and the psychologist Gordon Allport at the 1938 SSRC meeting in Buck Hill

Falls, Pennsylvania.[28] Having attended the meeting as a representative of the Corporation, Charles Dollard had returned to report to Keppel that "the most frequent, recurring topic of discussion concerned the necessity for 'cross-fertilizing' the various disciplines in the social sciences," and that the fellowship idea had been "the only specific solution" he had encountered.[29]

Keppel could not have been surprised by this. He had himself attended several of the SSRC's Hanover Conferences and, as a "potentate" who might make up for declining Rockefeller support, had been asked to address the 1930 conference on "Foundation Problems" two evenings before Sapir delivered his famous talk on "The Cultural Approach to Personality."[30] Keppel was certainly aware, therefore, that there was interest in "cross-fertilizing" the social sciences. But Keppel also knew, as Dollard would later discover, that the Corporation's board of trustees tended not to look with favor on the social sciences. Obviously speaking from his own experience, he had told the 1930 Hanover Conference that it was not at all certain that there would be "an increasing scale" of funding for social research during the next ten years. He pointed to "trustees" as one of the reasons for this. Speaking with considerable candor, he said:

I often envy my colleague, Dr. [John] Merriam, of the Carnegie Institution [whose brother, Charles Merriam, had been a founder of the SSRC and was present in Hanover in 1930], because when it comes to a profound question in geodetics, let us say, the trustees are perfectly willing to rely on the advice of the scientific hired man. But every trustee exercise[s] the God-given right to have views on economics and education.

They divide into two rather curious groups. There is the group that has become very, very propaganda-shy. They are afraid of new knowledge for fear it will be used in preachment. . . . Then there is another group that is all for propaganda. And between the two it is more than a little difficult to find an agreement particularly with regard to a large and a long program.

. . . The field of social science research [also] lacks the possibility of quick and spectacular results that interest and stimulate the trustees. . . . After insulin was discovered on a very small grant to the University of Toronto by the Carnegie Corporation its Trustees would take anything that medical research men offered them.[31]

In light of such trustee attitudes, which may have made it necessary *not* to evoke trustee comment on social research just as Myrdal's study was beginning, it was more surprising that Keppel acquiesced in Dollard's recommendation of cross-disciplinary fellowships than that he trimmed the initial proposal. Under his scrutiny, the originally modest plan for three annual two-year grants to be administered through a special SSRC committee became a program that would provide two annual one-year grants to be administered directly by the Corporation. The social scientists may have bemoaned Keppel's prudence, but the fellowships did enable three anthropologists—Clyde Kluckhohn, John Gillin, and David Mandelbaum—to immerse themselves in psychology, and enable three psychologists—Harry Harlowe, Robert Harris, and Lloyd Humphrey—to immerse themselves in anthropology.[32] What is more, regardless of the impact of the fellowships on the other five scholars, the fellowship Clyde Kluckhohn received proved vital to the advancement of the interests the Dollard brothers now shared. But that would be most evident after the Second World War.

Frederick Osborn and Survey Research

In the meantime, the increasing government demand for trained psychologists and, to a lesser extent, for anthropologists, brought an end to the cross-training fellowships and spurred the development of the more quantitative, empirical, "experimentalist" approach to social research that would also win Carnegie funds after the war.[33] Students of personality and culture studies also contributed to the war effort, in the process further developing and increasing the stature of their approach to the analysis of social problems. For example, research undertaken by the Foreign Morale Analysis Division of the Office of War Information—to which Clyde Kluckhohn, Ruth Benedict, Alexander H. Leighton, and others with training in cultural anthropology, psychiatry, and sociology were assigned—influenced the decision not to remove the Japanese emperor after Japan's surrender. Thereafter, as described by Leighton in *Human Relations in a Changing World* (1949), studies begun during the war established a research agenda that, with Corporation funding, Leighton for one would continue to pursue.[34] But during the war the Carnegie Corporation was most closely connected to the nerve center for "experimentalist" research that operated within the Information and Education Division of the War Department.

The director of the Information and Education Division was a Corporation trustee, Frederick Osborn. A wealthy, aristocratic New Yorker, Osborn had given up a successful business career just before the stock market crash of 1929 to devote himself entirely to the study of social problems. His particular interest at the time had been eugenics. Although his uncle, Henry Fairchild Osborn, head of the American Museum of Natural History in New York City, had been aligned with the racial determinism so widely popularized by his eugenicist friend Madison Grant, Frederick Osborn had managed through his uncle to meet a number of Columbia social scientists (including the anthropologist Margaret Mead) whose ideas had influenced him considerably. In consequence, as belief in the power and social significance of inherited racial traits lost popularity during the 1930s, Frederick Osborn had promoted a different, "new" eugenics that sought to study the relative power of "nature versus nurture."[35] Presented in scholarly monographs and a popular book, *Preface to Eugenics* (1940), Osborn's views helped to reform the American eugenics movement and were an important link between that movement and subsequent population research and birth control projects.[36]

An old friend of both President Franklin D. Roosevelt and Secretary of War Henry L. Stimson, Osborn was asked to chair the Joint Army and Navy Committee on Welfare and Recreation, from which the Information and Education Division emerged.[37] Thereafter he often relied upon his Carnegie Corporation connections for help. When he needed an assistant to get the Joint Committee and then the Information and Education Division started, he asked Harvard president James Bryant Conant for one of his assistants, Francis Keppel, the youngest of Frederick Keppel's five sons. And when he needed money to get the Information and Education Division started, he called Frederick Keppel, who dispatched $100,000 of Carnegie Corporation funds.[38] Thereafter, this towering, six foot-eight-inch patrician, who gained the rank of major general in the U.S. army, also called upon Charles Dollard, whose brother John served as a consultant to Osborn. Commissioned an army captain in 1942, Charles Dollard rose to the rank of lieutenant colonel before the war's end; his most important assignment was with the Research Branch of the Information and Education Division, of which be became chief in 1942 and deputy director of operations in 1944.

As the Second World War counterpart of the Commissions on Training Camp Activities that Raymond B. Fosdick had headed, the Information and Education Division served primarily to provide information to soldiers. In addition, through the Research Branch to which Charles Dollard was assigned, it undertook the unprecedented tasks of gathering information about what soldiers believed, wanted, and thought, and of communicating this to military and civilian policymakers in ways that might help them predict and prevent personnel and morale problems during the war and immediately thereafter. Its studies led to the point system used to organize postwar demobilization, and, by laying the basis for calculating the initial costs of the G.I. Bill, helped fundamentally and enduringly to change American higher education.

The Research Branch of the Information and Education Division was a significant pivot in the history of social research. If "aptitudes" became an important focal point of research after the First World War, "attitudes" achieved that distinction after the Second World War. If the further development of mental testing was the methodological outcome of the First World War, survey research that might identify and evaluate the options, preferences, and biases of large numbers of people was the equivalent for the Second World War.[39] The Research Branch's mixed roster of military and civilian personnel included some of the nation's most promising sociologists, psychologists, and statisticians. Its research director was Samuel Stouffer, the University of Chicago sociologist, who before the war had served as liaison to the scholars preparing research reviews for Gunnar Myrdal. Stouffer had completed his doctoral dissertation under the supervision of William F. Ogburn one year before John Dollard, and, according to Frederick Osborn, "was not only on the hard, factual side of sociology, but . . . had a keen sense of getting things done."[40]

The purpose of the Research Branch, as Stouffer later described it, was "to provide the Army command quickly and accurately with facts about the attitudes of soldiers which, along with other facts and inferences, might be helpful in policy formation." Stouffer felt that this aim limited the agency's immediate contribution to "science," which, he said, "seeks to set up conceptual models which have at least a limited generality, such that one can use the model to predict what will happen in a specified concrete situation."[41] But in forcing the Research Branch to serve an "engineering" function that, again in Stouffer's words, involved "the selection, among the conceptual models provided by science, of those which seem most applicable to the understanding or solution of a particular practical problem," it gave its personnel intense exposure to some of the most innovative models and techniques then available to social scientists.[42] "For me this was a continuation of my scientific education," Information and Education Division Director Frederick Osborn recalled in a memoir many years later, having earlier told Stouffer that his "association with you and the others will always seem to me the most interesting and rewarding part of my life."[43]

Osborn had been interested in the social sciences before the war. His wartime experience, which to some extent Charles Dollard had shared, led him to join Dollard in advocating that the further development of the social sciences should become a Corporation priority after the war. No less than Charles Dollard, he believed that "the study of man" could illuminate "those things which create tension" among people, and in so doing could advance the Corporation's concern with international cooperation and peace.[44]

Before the war, Osborn had been critical of the SSRC because he believed it was dominated by older men "around the age of 65 . . . who have the most personal charm and authority . . . [but] who tend more towards a philosophical approach" than toward the "hardboiled and critical attitude" of the "younger men, many of them highly trained and exceeding competent."[45] Writing to Frederick Keppel about the SSRC's 1938 annual meeting from which Charles Dollard had returned with the cross-training fellowship suggestion, Osborn had said: "There were exceptions to this rule; I should think Ogburn was one of the exceptions, but on the whole the discussion tended to be philosophical and historical, and I missed the crisp rather hardboiled approach which I have seen in meetings of the younger men."[46] Thus Osborn had already indicated a preference for "hard," quantitative methods. His leanings in this direction were now strengthened by the work of the Research Branch. Describing how the social scientists had gained acceptance from the military men, who at the start were none too inclined to accept scholarly advice, Osborn claimed that, "when confronted by a clear analysis of quantitative factual data which threw light on some aspect of a problem they were trying to solve, they gave our research people respectful attention, and used their data."[47] As he also conceded, "from these unique experiences in administration guided by research, I got some strong impressions of the factors which make for acceptance, by practical administrators, of the findings of social scientists."[48]

Applying these impressions in a memorandum entitled "Some Observations on 'Social Science' Grants" he prepared for discussion with Carnegie Corporation staff members, Osborn argued that "the enormous contribution of the Rockefeller Foundation to the Social Sciences in the past several years . . . may have greatly benefitted society, but they [sic] have done little to advance the social sciences." This was the case, he believed, because Rockefeller grants had gone primarily for "'research' by a 'social scientist' using subjective and intuitive processes, usually directed to the better understanding of a social problem but without the expectation of improving or testing social science techniques," and for "fellowships, or for a report on conditions, or to improve the conditions of cooperation (i.e. conferences, etc.)." In consequence, Osborn maintained, "the aim of the Carnegie Corporation in the social science field should be to advance our knowledge of man and his behavior by scientific, i.e., objective methods." If the Corporation could find the studies that might do this, he continued, "new studies will of themselves develop new personnel." In addition, Osborn explained that he favored psychology, anthropology, and sociology for Carnegie grants, because "these sciences have a common purpose in trying to find out about man and his behavior; they have a common and increasing interest in scientific methodology, which is now sufficiently advanced for their use; and they have a tendency, increasingly, to base their suggestions for solutions to practical problems on quantitative data which have practical value, rather than on their subjective judgments." By contrast, Osborn believed that economics, political science, and history "have less interest in the individual man; their interest in human behavior extends to the behavior of prices and goods; they make minimum use of scientific methodology, which is insufficiently advanced for their use; and their suggestions for the solution of practical problems tend to be based on their intuitive judgments rather than on their objective judgments."[49]

But Osborn was only one of fourteen trustees and, as his pro-natural sciences, anti-social sciences trustee colleague Vannevar Bush would bitterly observe later, the design of programs was already by this time becoming more of a staff than a trustee function, and one that was timidly fulfilled.[50] Even so, because he was something of an amateur expert on the social sciences, Osborn's support for grants in this domain was needed by the staff in winning the votes. Strongly seconded by former president Devereux Josephs, whose interest in the social sciences was greatly reassuring to the board, Osborn worked hard to advance "hardboiled" quantitative studies.[51] Conceivably this might have caused conflict between Osborn and Charles Dollard, since social research in a personality and culture mold, even though usually undertaken by anthropologists, psychologists, and sociologists, could be seen as "intuitive," "subjective," and maybe even, to quote John Dollard's view of concepts of personality circa 1932, "blowzy."[52] Yet conflict did not arise when the Corporation planned its immediate postwar social science grants. Once again, this was largely a result of coincidences having to do with people and places: first, Dollard's assignment to the Research Branch, which left him with a residue of convictions and personal connections similar to Osborn's; and second, the founding of the Department and Laboratory of Social Relations at Harvard.

The Harvard Department of Social Relations

Among the five scholars primarily responsible for establishing the Department of Social Relations at Harvard in 1946, one in particular was well known to the Carnegie philanthropists: Clyde Kluckhohn, one of the anthropologists who had received a cross-training fellowship before the war. A student of the Navaho, Kluckhohn had been a classmate of Charles Dollard's at the University of Wisconsin, and thereafter, with a common interest in psychoanalysis, he had become a close friend of John Dollard's as well. He had participated in the Sapir-Dollard seminar at Yale. Knowing of John Dollard's unusually full acquaintance with psychoanalysis, Kluckhohn had frequently discussed his interest in this field with him, and John Dollard had encouraged him to seek training. "We need some good solid observers in anthropology who have more than the Culture-Personality pattern that is current at the present time," John Dollard had written Kluckhohn in February 1939.[53] The following year, thanks to the Carnegie fellowship, Kluckhohn had moved to New York, where he became a member of Charles Dollard's "in-group," while engaging in systematic reading and "sustained but informal discussion" with Margaret Mead, Margaret E. Fries, and others among the increasing number of scholars interested in personality and culture studies.[54] He had also presented data he had collected on the Navaho to a seminar led by the Columbia University anthropologist Ralph Linton and the neo-Freudian psychoanalyst Abram Kardiner. The seminar, modeled on the Edward Sapir-John Dollard seminar at Yale, in turn became the model for a later one led by Kluckhohn and his colleagues Henry A. Murray and O. Hobart Mowrer at Harvard.[55]

As the establishment of the Kluckhohn-Murray-Mowrer seminar may suggest, Kluckhohn's Carnegie fellowship year led to fruitful intellectual exchange in Cambridge. Indeed, it provided additional grist for conversations already taking place among a small group of scholars who called themselves "the Levellers" in recognition of the many levels of analysis necessary for the study of human behavior.[56] This group included other notable Harvard scholars: the psychologists Murray and Gordon W. Allport, the social theorist Talcott Parsons, and the former Harvard English professor Bernard DeVoto. After Mowrer, a psychologist and learning theorist, moved to Harvard in May 1940—not coincidentally, Mowrer was recruited on Kluckhohn's suggestion from the Yale Institute for Human Relations—he too joined the group.[57] The Levellers became the founders of the Harvard Department of Social Relations.

According to Talcott Parsons, the department's first chairman, the Levellers "engaged in many informal discussions of substantive scientific problems . . . in the course of which the closeness of our interests became ever more obvious, so much so that our membership in different departments seemed increasingly anomalous."[58] Writing to Harvard's Arts and Sciences dean, Paul H. Buck, in the spring of 1943, the group therefore recommended "an organizational move in this direction."[59] Subsequently, in a letter suggesting that he might leave Harvard for Northwestern University if such a move were not made, Parsons again pressed the Levellers' suit. Having already informed Buck of the Northwestern offer, he said:

The offer from Northwestern has brought the whole complex situation here to a head in such a way as to *force* the crucial question of the future role at Harvard . . . of the *kind* of scientific work with which my own career has become identified. . . . Northwestern offers little if any financial advantage . . . [and] Harvard is still Harvard . . . [but] if I accept [the offer]—and quite frankly I am still giving it very serious consideration—a large element of my motivation would be a protest. It would be meant to force you to do some explaining as to why I HAD LEFT HARVARD. . . .

. . . History, Government and Economics have dominated the social sciences situation at Harvard for a generation. . . . Over against these stand the three weak departments. Psychology suffers greatly from its recent dependence on Philosophy. . . . Anthropology has often been regarded as a kind of exotic sideshow of the University. . . . Then the Sociology experiment was made and very badly bungled . . . [and] the thing has been allowed to stew in its own juice, and continue as one of the sorest spots in the faculty.

In the meantime a very big scientific development has been rapidly gathering force—what our group tried, however inadequately, to formulate as the growth of a "basic social science." I will stake my whole professional reputation on the statement that it is one of the really great movements of modern scientific thought, comparable for instance, to the development of Biology in the last third of the 19th Century. Like all really big pioneer movements it is not understood by the majority of the established high priests of social science. Like all such movements it lacks an adequate institutional frame work [*sic*] for developing its potentialities, and the development of such a framework is hindered by the vested interests of those already in the field. But like most such movements it is almost bound to come to its due in the end. . . .

This general situation is particularly pronounced here at Harvard, as I have outlined above. The essential question to me is whether Harvard is going to seize the opportunity to be a great leader in this movement or is going to move only as it is forced to do by the competition of other institutions. Which it is going to be seems to me will constitute a considerable factor in how far Harvard will, in the next generation, maintain a general position of leadership in the academic world or will depend for its position mainly on its wealth and past prestige.[60]

Parsons's letter obliquely alluded to what others reported more directly later. The Levellers were joined by common scholarly interests in the possibility of developing a "basic social science." In addition, they found common cause in antipathy to some of their senior colleagues, such "high priests of social science" as, in Parsons's case, Pitirim Sorokin, and, in Allport's and Murray's case, Edwin G. Boring.[61] Obviously aware of this, Buck responded by taking action on one of the steps Parsons had suggested: Parsons replaced Sorokin as chairman of the Department of Sociology.

In the spring of 1945, Buck also commissioned Parsons to visit and report on some of the principal existing models of cross-disciplinary research of interest to the Harvard clique of mostly younger maverick scholars. These models included the Institute for Human Relations at Yale, the Columbia Bureau of Applied Social Research, the North Carolina Institute for Research in Social Science, and some parts of the Bureau of Agricultural Economics. During the next academic year (1945–46), Parsons's survey was incorporated into a plan for a new "super department" developed by a faculty committee of which Parsons was chair. Thereafter, the plan was approved, first, by the Departments of Anthropology, Sociology, and Psychology, and, then, on January 29, 1945, by the full Harvard Arts and Sciences faculty. By that point, with dissenters like Sorokin braced for defeat (in fact, Sorokin refused to attend the January 29 meeting), the only disputed issue was the new department's name. Against the Parsons Committee recommendation of "Human Relations," "Social Relations" was chosen because the Harvard faculty did not want to be second to Yale.[62] Thereafter, Sorokin established his own Center for the Study of Altruism, for which he tried, but failed, to raise Carnegie funds. According to Charles Dollard, Edwin G. Boring had gone along with the plans for "a unified social science program," but, like Sorokin, remained "personally unhappy about the business" and feared that his research program would "have a hard time competing with the larger one."[63]

Although a shift in power from Sorokin and Boring to their younger colleagues was, in the first instance, a result of faculty and administration concurrence, it was facilitated by Carnegie Corporation sympathy with the Levellers' aspirations and plans. Remaining in close touch with developments that led to the establishment of the Department of Social Relations, Charles Dollard recommended Corporation support as one of the first items to be considered in connection with the new program in the social sciences announced in 1946.[64] In consequence, grants amounting to $335,000 were awarded to the new venture during its first ten years of existence. The sum was not inordinately large. Reflecting the concerns implicit in strategic philanthropy, the Corporation's grants were intended to provide significant assistance, while remaining small enough to ensure major financing by Harvard. As Charles Dollard explained, a key consideration in the Corporation's plans was "to commit Harvard so heavily to the Department of Social Relations enterprise as to cut off any line of retreat when foundation support comes to an end."[65]

Obviously hoping that the organization of a new department would foster acceptance of a "social relations" perspective at the nation's oldest and most prestigious university, the Corporation also tried to promote integration in more substantive, research-related ways. At the very start of the Department of Social Relations, Talcott Parsons had hoped to reconcile the different intellectual perspectives represented through a seminar to which all members would present their views of the best methods for the study of social relations. According to one then relatively junior member, the sociologist George C. Homans, the seminar that resulted was worthwhile as an educational device. Homans wrote in his autobiography that he had learned a great deal about rigorous statistical analyses from Samuel Stouffer. (Not coincidentally, Stouffer had transferred from the University of Chicago to Harvard via the Research Branch at the time when the Department of Social Relations was started.) But "the methods seminar did nothing to integrate the department methodologically," Homans said.[66]

As a result of this unsuccessful seminar, Parsons requested Carnegie funds in 1948 to help the department clarify the problems of social relations through the formulation of a common theoretical perspective. Undertaken in 1949–50, this endeavor involved all department members as well as two scholars from other institutions, Edward C. Tolman from the University of California and Edward A. Shils from the University of Chicago. Tolman and Shils joined the department's senior faculty in weekly meetings where concepts and basic theoretical premises were initially formulated; these were critically reviewed in subsequent weekly meetings of the junior scholars.[67] The result was *Toward a General Theory of Action,* informally referred to at Harvard as the "Yellow Book," which attempted to describe the fundamental categories of knowledge to be considered if "the convergence of anthropological studies of culture, the theory of learning, the psychoanalytic theory of personality, economic theory, and the study of modern social structure" were to serve as building blocks for a new, unified social science.[68]

Rich in ideas and diverse in perspective, *Toward a General Theory of Action* was controversial even within the Department of Social Relations at Harvard. Parsons believed that the Corporation-supported effort had been helpful as a means to "stimulate and focus our thinking in an area of fundamental concern to all of us."[69] But not all department members agreed. Homans maintained, for example, that this attempt at integration was no more successful than the earlier methods seminar. According to Homans, "Parsons himself laid the 'Yellow Book' before a meeting of the whole department . . . urging us all to read it and implying, though without quite saying as much, that it ought to be adopted as the official doctrine of the department to guide future teaching and research. . . . I spoke up and said in effect: 'There must be no implication that this document is to be taken as representing the official doctrine of the department, and no member shall be put under pressure to read it.' . . . A dreadful silence followed. . . . But finally Sam Stouffer . . . spoke up. . . . Somewhat reluctantly, he declared that the 'Yellow Book' ought not to be treated as departmental doctrine. There the matter dropped."[70] Himself eager to formulate a general social theory, Homans was transparent in his dislike of Parsons. For better or worse, he quashed the possibility of institutionalizing a common intellectual orientation to accompany the administrative unification of disciplines effected when the department was created. "General Theory" would henceforth be pursued by Talcott Parsons alone or in collaboration with other individual scholars.

In addition to financing work on *Toward a General Theory of Action,* the Carnegie Corporation helped support the department's research arm, the Laboratory of Social Relations. In contrast to most other foundation or government grants to the laboratory, these grants of approximately $275,000 between 1946 and 1956 made available "unrestricted pilot study funds" that could be used for any research deemed worthwhile by the laboratory's executive committee. They led to what Stouffer, who directed the laboratory, described as significant research findings on perception and motivation, emotions, learning, personality assessment, small-group behavior, attitudes, child training, language, values and the social system, and "role" as a social systems concept. Adding to the value of such findings, the availability of general funds was critical in helping younger scholars move on, after a Carnegie pilot study grant, to larger research projects supported by other foundations, federal agencies, or contract research institutes such as the newly established Rand Corporation. This was true for a number of younger scholars who later became prominent in the social or behavioral sciences, among them Robert Freed Bales, Jerome S. Bruner, Gardner Lindzey, Frederick Mosteller, Leo Postman, and E. Z. Vogt.[71]

Despite this, the laboratory was not a great success in developing or advancing a distinctive social relations research model. Insistently encouraging freedom of choice in research styles, methods, and questions, and tending to "back the individual, rather than the particular research problems," it never developed an official research program.[72] In a sense, therefore, its prime function was administering the Carnegie pilot study funds, and the funds indirectly secured through them. Perhaps because of this, the laboratory did not become what Edward Shils has called a "corporate intellectual reality," and neither did the department.[73] Unlike the Department of Sociology at the University of Chicago at the peak of its influence in the 1920s and 1930s, there was no "pervasive agreement underlying a wide diversity of substantive interests" among Harvard social relations scholars.[74] What is more, in contrast to such a highly influential contemporary center of social research as the Bureau of Applied Social Research at Columbia, headed by Paul Lazarsfeld, the Harvard Laboratory did not become a drill ground for graduate students.[75] However much it had inspired hope in Charles Dollard, the Harvard experiment did not become a national model. The department was disbanded in 1970.

A Strategic Relationship: Other Grants to Harvard

Although important within the Carnegie Corporation's postwar social science program, the Harvard Department and Laboratory of Social Relations were by no means the only beneficiaries of the foundation's aspirations or funds. Indeed, Harvard's prestige and the close personal ties that linked many Harvard administrators and faculty members to Corporation staff members placed the university in an unusual position—one that might even be called "strategic." In addition to grants to the Department and Laboratory of Social Relations, the Corporation awarded significant funds to other Harvard centers for work in and related to the social sciences.

In 1946, for example, it granted $300,000 to the Harvard Graduate School of Education to assist in the integration of the social sciences and education. Once again a source for attracting matching funds from the Harvard Corporation, the grant was used to move research as opposed to teacher training, and a social relations focus as opposed to a traditionally and exclusively educationist focus, to the core of the school's operations. Plans for these changes had originated in prewar conversations between President Conant, Parsons, Kluckhohn, and other faculty members later associated with the Department of Social Relations. Then, after the war, when Conant found himself unable to recruit a new education dean of established reputation, Parsons and his department colleagues strongly concurred in the wisdom of appointing Francis Keppel, recently returned to his university administrative position.

Keppel was respected by the social scientists because of his work for Frederick Osborn in the Research Branch. Appointed to promote the study of education from the perspective of social relations, and empowered with Carnegie dollars and other funds given to match them, he was able to recruit a number of prominent scholars of social relations to the Harvard education faculty, among them, Robert R. Sears, a social psychologist from the State University of Iowa who was president-elect of the American Psychological Association, and J. W. M. Whiting, an anthropologist trained in psychoanalysis by John Dollard and formerly affiliated with the Institute for Human Relations at Yale. Under Keppel's leadership, the Harvard Graduate School of Education moved toward a national standing rarely before achieved by an education faculty, and the model Keppel developed was emulated elsewhere. In fact, even though Harvard never became a national paradigm, education faculties having always varied greatly in organization, by the 1960s a behavioral social research emphasis was evident at other prominent institutions, including some departments at Teachers College, Columbia University, the largest graduate faculty of education in the United States.[76]

Another Corporation grant to Harvard inspired by hopes of diffusing a behavioral science approach to social research throughout the nation's leading university, supported the organization, establishment, and operation of the Russian Research Center. Founded in 1947, the Russian Research Center received $875,000 in Carnegie funds between 1947 and 1957. A product of the same set of personal ties that had already figured prominently in Carnegie social science giving, the new Harvard center evolved from difficulties Frederick Osborn faced in 1946–47 as the U.S. Representative to the United Nations Atomic Energy Commission. Osborn was charged with securing concurrence in the Baruch plan, which would have allowed the United States to turn over all atomic research information to international inspections of research and military facilities. A skillful negotiator, Osborn still found himself unable to persuade the Russians to agree to the on-site inspection requirement and was puzzled by the difficulties.[77] Aware that the Corporation had recently hired a psychologist by the name of John W. Gardner, Osborn appealed for help. Gardner agreed, although he apparently demurred from trying to fill "the role of psychological crystal gazer" and instead used the occasion to urge Corporation support of research about Russia.[78]

Gardner knew there was a dearth of Russian research, because he was surveying existing foreign area study programs in preparation for a new series of Corporation grants.[79] As part of its relatively lengthy postwar program review, the Corporation's staff had decided to make the promotion of "adult thinking in respect to foreign affairs and the recognition of our unavoidable international position" a focus of its activities. These activities were given a name, "Operation Flatbush"— apparently the Corporation's staff thought the typical person in need of education lived in the Flatbush neighborhood of Brooklyn—before they were defined.[80] However, once the decision to focus on adult education about international affairs had been made, the Corporation's staff sought the advice of prominent individuals like then Under Secretary of State Dean Acheson, convened any number of luncheons with bankers, businessmen, lawyers, and journalists at the exclusive all-male Century Club, and eventually decided that what was needed was the training of area studies specialists and the development of materials about important but often little-known areas of the world.[81] In combination with Frederick Osborn's immediate need for knowledge, plans made in connection with Operation Flatbush led the Corporation to finance the Russian Research Center at Harvard.

The magnet that made Harvard the university of choice for such a center was not expertise in Russian studies; had that been the criterion, the Corporation would probably have selected Columbia, as indeed the Rockefeller Foundation had done earlier. Rather it was a strong social relations faculty backed by a supportive administration that again drew the Corporation to Cambridge. The hope was "not only to stimulate a larger volume of research in the Russian field but to give impetus to studies which will make use of the best of modern social science methods in an attempt to understand some of the crucial problems of Russian behavior."[82] This would advance what Gardner called "the new approach to area study."[83] As he explained in a 1947 article for the *Yale Review,* this involved an emphasis on the social sciences and social psychology, rather than, as previously, on history and languages. Interdisciplinary rather than disciplinary inquiries were now central.

This "new" approach to area study was not entirely new. It derived from the thinking of many of the same social scientists who had participated with Edward Sapir, John Dollard, and others in the early development of personality and culture studies. It had begun to gain support during the war largely as a result of the Ethnogeographic Board, established in June 1942 by the SSRC, the NRC, the ACLS, and the Smithsonian Institution. The purpose of the Ethnogeographic Board was to provide information to government agencies about little-known but now strategically important places and people around the world. Its members early decided to rely upon "area" as opposed to "disciplinary" approaches in fulfilling their mission. This was because "Government agencies, particularly the military, operate in terms of areas, while universities, councils, and foundations are organized by disciplines." Of necessity, therefore, the Board had "to translate the discipline knowledge into the geographic categories used by the Government."[84]

After the war, with an increasing cadre of area specialists behind them, social scientists within the SSRC eagerly sought opportunities to continue developing the focus chosen by the Ethnogeographic Board. They saw an area studies orientation as a means "of bringing about cross-fertilization within the social sciences and of bridging the gaps between the social and the natural and humanistic disciplines . . . of working toward the fundamental totality of all knowledge. Here might lie means by which research in the social sciences could be made more cumulative and comprehensive."[85] In other words, they saw area studies as a means of realizing the same essential agenda that had earlier interested John Dollard and his network of colleagues, including those belonging to the Levellers.[86]

Since such studies would fit nicely with the Corporation's social science interests, Gardner made inquiries at Harvard about organizing the kinds of investigations into Russian behavior that Osborn needed. Kluckhohn was among the first people he contacted. In addition to his various ties to the Carnegie Corporation, Kluckhohn was a logical choice because he had helped pioneer the techniques used by social scientists in the Foreign Morale Analysis Division of the Office of War Information to analyze Japanese attitudes and opinions through the study of press reports, information from prisoners of war, and general descriptions of Japanese culture.[87] Later described by Margaret Mead and others as "the study of culture at a distance," these techniques had potential relevance to the analysis of Soviet behavior, since access to the U.S.S.R. was severely restricted.[88]

Kluckhohn, for his part, thought the idea of a research center important "from the point of view of scholarship and of the national interest."[89] He informed Gardner that he thought "the thing could be done well at Harvard. . . . It is the kind of undertaking to which people like Talcott Parsons could make a great contribution, even though not a Russian 'expert.'"[90] Doing field work on the Navaho in Ramah, New Mexico, in the summer of 1947, Kluckhohn promised to organize his

Harvard colleagues when he returned to Cambridge in the fall. He did, and within a few months the Corporation gave a grant of $100,000 to Harvard to organize the Russian Research Center. Thereafter, in 1948, funds amounting to $740,000 were dispatched in the largest single grant that had yet been made for area study research.[91]

Parsons remembered that when Kluckhohn was chosen as the first director of the Russian Research Center, the appointment "raised many eyebrows in academically conservative quarters because he lacked previous connection with study of Russia and Communism."[92] But the choice pleased the philanthropists at the Carnegie Corporation, who trusted Kluckhohn to develop this sensitive area of research. Like Stouffer at the Laboratory of Social Relations, Kluckhohn proved to be an effective administrator with a laissez-faire administrative style that allowed scholars great freedom to choose the topics they wished to investigate and the methods appropriate to them. The result was a long and impressive roster of scholars and studies. The center's early interview project with recent Russian émigrés was widely judged an exemplary success that proved "that scholars of different disciplines can work together fruitfully, learning a great deal from each other and about each other's methods in the process."[93]

Kluckhohn's laissez-faire administrative style had a negative side also, a somewhat ironic one. Even though the Russian Research Center was established to advance a behavioral sciences approach to area studies, it included among its earliest projects investigations into the Communist Party and the Soviet economy, both of which would have suited the agenda of a more traditionally constituted international studies center. According to Alex Inkeles, a colleague and friend of Kluckhohn's at the center, it was also noteworthy that by the time of Kluckhohn's resignation as director in 1954, the older disciplines and research methods of international study had displaced those the center was intended to encourage, especially anthropology, psychology, and sociology. "Almost everyone . . . agreed that the work done . . . in the more traditional disciplines [of economics, government, and history] is of the highest order," Inkeles stated. "Indeed in many ways [it is] magnificent. But it is not interdisciplinary, experimental, or methodologically innovative."[94]

Diffusing a Cross-Disciplinary, Behavioral Approach

The political scientist Robert A. Dahl once asked if the behavioral approach to social research that had become so prominent after the Second World War really represented "anything more than [a] mood."[95] It was an apt question that one could answer, as Dahl did, in various ways. The fate of the several programs the Corporation chose to assist at Harvard would tend to support the view that, yes, the "behavioral approach" was little more than a short-lived impulse to collaborate in the redesign of social research. Many of the centers and projects the Corporation invested in did not survive the generational conflicts, the postwar geopolitics, the personal loyalties, and the philanthropic encouragement that had given rise to them in the first place. Then again, even if centers of cross-disciplinary behavioral research like the Department and Laboratory of Social Relations did not gain permanence within the university's organizational structure, they did influence many people who helped spread behavioral social research elsewhere. What is more, even though Harvard occupied a special place within Carnegie Corporation philanthropy in the late 1940s and 1950s, it was hardly the only institution to receive the Foundation's funds; some of the other grants made at this time derived from and, in turn, nurtured more enduring change.

One such grant was the one for $40,500 that allowed Stouffer and a number of colleagues to sift the data gathered by the Research Branch of the Information and Education Division in search of their "scientific" significance. The immediate result was four volumes officially entitled *Studies in Social Psychology in World War II*, but generally known as *The American Soldier*, the main title of the first two volumes.[96] At the time these now well-known studies appeared, they evoked many, and many highly divergent, reactions. Indeed, when Harold D. Lasswell wrote to Stouffer "to join universal congratulations," Stouffer replied: "The congratulations are by no means universal, and the brickbats we've received are possibly more impressive than the bouquets. Therefore to get this word from you is a truly joyous event."[97]

Among the "brickbats" to which Stouffer referred was a review in the *New Republic* by Robert S. Lynd, best known to the public as the author, with his wife Helen Merrell Lynd, of the *Middletown* studies, and equally well known within social science circles for the argument he had made for a humane, explicitly ethical social science in *Knowledge for What? The Place of Social Science in American Culture* (1939). Entitling his review "The Science of Inhuman Relations," Lynd maintained that "these volumes depict science being used with great skill to sort out and to control men for purposes not of their own willing. It is a significant measure of the impotence of liberal democracy that it must increasingly use its social sciences not directly on democracy's own problems, but tangentially and indirectly . . . on such problems as how to gauge audience reaction so as to put together profitable synthetic radio programs and movies, or, as in the present case, . . . on how to turn frightened draftees into tough soldiers who will fight a war whose purpose they do not understand."[98] Joining Lynd in the "brickbat" category was a then relatively little-known sociologist by the name of Nathan Glazer, who reviewed *The American Soldier* for *Commentary*. *The American Soldier*, Glazer argued, was notable because "rarely was so little useful information about so large a question spread over so many pages." Why was this? According to Glazer, "because the aim was science, not understanding; the mechanical and formal confining of knowledge, not the increase of it."[99]

In contrast to these severely negative reviews, there were also the "bouquets." Stouffer mentioned several to Lasswell, including an auspicious review by Paul Lazarsfeld in the *Public Opinion Quarterly*. "The reviewer anticipates what is sure to become a favorite topic for Master's theses: 'The Contributions of *The American Soldier* to the Problem of . . . ,' " he remarked, before turning to a brief exposition of the contributions *The American Soldier* made to the study of primary groups and to concepts necessary to an understanding of "frame of reference," as for example the concept of "relative deprivation," and much more.[100] Far more than Lynd or Glazer, Lazarsfeld turned out to be the prophet. Indeed, his review could be cited as a "self-fulfilling prophesy" of the kind his Columbia colleague Robert K. Merton would later explicate.[101] Thanks in part to the interest of Lazarsfeld and Merton, *The American Soldier* became widely acknowledged as a "major model for its time of how social theory could be integrated with empirical quantitative investigations and analysis."[102]

Among the better known of the many monographs in a behavioral science mold supported by the Carnegie Corporation, *The American Soldier* was one example of a Corporation grant that had enduring results. Very different, but also important in terms of lasting diffusion, were the many scattered awards to programs and individuals variously engaged in social and psychological research with a behavioral focus. Breadth and variety are evident in projects as different as studies of resistance to technological change conducted by social anthropologists at Cornell University; studies of population conducted by mathematical demographers at Princeton University; and studies of group dynamics conducted at the National Education Association's national leadership training laboratory at Bethel, Maine. Significantly, too, at roughly the time the Corporation encouraged the organization of the Russian

Research Center at Harvard, it was also helping to define and finance Southeast Asian studies at Yale; Japanese studies at Michigan; Scandinavian studies at Wisconsin and Minnesota; Indian studies at Pennsylvania; Latin American studies at Vanderbilt, Tulane, North Carolina, and Texas; Near Eastern studies at Princeton; European studies at Columbia; and African studies at Northwestern. Furthermore, while investing in the Laboratory of Social Relations, it was also providing partial funding for the Institute for Social Research at Michigan. Even if the nature of the influence defies precise description, there can be no doubt that the broad distribution of these grants among institutions, across disciplines and domains of knowledge, and in support of both applied and theoretical research, helped demonstrate the wide relevance of interdisciplinary studies of human behavior.

One might note, too, that the Corporation helped to gain permanence for the behavioral approach to social research by supporting the SSRC. Long a center of sympathy for integrated behavioral study, the council was greatly strengthened by Corporation funds for administrative expenses, for specific projects and, most important, for fellowships, first in area studies and then in the social sciences. Corporation fellowship funds placed over $1.5 million for new research at the disposal of the SSRC. There were other fellowship programs then available to social scientists, as for example the Guggenheim Fellowships; but the Carnegie-SSRC awards were the most plentiful and the most significant in encouraging cross-disciplinary social research. They were kindred to the Rockefeller Foundation-NRC awards so important in the development of the natural sciences after the First World War.

Finally, as befitted a foundation that was becoming more and more deliberate in its efforts to ensure that its grants would yield a maximum return, the Carnegie Corporation served as a medium for interesting other supporting agencies in the approach to social study it had picked up from John Dollard and others and helped to establish at Harvard and elsewhere. It did this most crucially with the Ford Foundation, which was initially established in 1939 and then reorganized on a larger, national scale beginning in 1947.

The Ford Foundation's chief consultant in developing a new program was H. Rowan Gaither, Jr., a California lawyer and chairman of the Rand Corporation. Well-known to Charles Dollard, who served as a director of Rand, and to others at the Corporation, Gaither led a study group that produced a two-volume report, in 1949, from which Ford's initial program priorities emerged.[103] In developing the report, Gaither and his colleagues had the postwar program-planning memoranda written by the Carnegie Corporation staff at their disposal, and the influence of these was evident in the five program areas featured in the Gaither Report. These were the establishment of peace, the strengthening of democracy, the strengthening of the economy, education in a democratic society, and individual and human behavior.

Importantly, too, the Gaither Report was characterized throughout by an internationalist orientation. Comments on the urgent necessity "to avoid world war—without sacrificing our values and principles—and to press steadily toward the achievement of an enduring peace" were frequent.[104] Initially, this resulted in a large number of nonacademic projects, especially overseas development projects. By 1952, however, grants in support of area studies research and training and other academic projects had moved to center stage; the area study fellowships initially developed and financed by the Carnegie Corporation and administered by SSRC had now become a Ford Foundation program.[105] Not coincidentally, John Gardner served on the Board of Overseas Travel and Research that advised the philanthropists at Ford. In that capacity, he also tried to help the new foundation identify and become known to scholars engaged in area studies research. Typically, for example, he wrote to Clyde Kluckhohn (and others) to urge nominations of candidates for the area studies fellowships. His activities as an officer of the Carnegie Corporation had placed him in contact with many people who were likely to know of first-class candidates, and since the people at Ford feared that the Foundation's interests were still not well known, he had agreed to help in recruitment. As he explained to Kluckhohn, he was "doing this as a favor to the Ford Foundation."[106]

The Corporation's unofficial advisory role in the early years of Ford Foundation grant-making exemplified a long-standing practice of cooperation with other foundations. But this practice became even more frequent after the Second World War as well as more significant in terms of the Corporation's influence on public policy. Cooperation with other foundations enabled the Corporation to help set trends throughout the expanding world of philanthropic foundations. Equally important, it made it possible to limit the foundation's commitments to particular programs, and the resulting freedom to shift new problems and interests was critical to the policy design aspirations inherent in strategic philanthropy. However important grant-making remained at the Carnegie Corporation, institutional transfer of the kind so evident here became an important source for Corporation influence as strategic giving became ever more essential to its philanthropic style.

CHAPTER EIGHT

Leadership and Education

The New Men

T HE ELEMENTARY AND SECONDARY EDUCATION ACT of 1965 (ESEA) represented a turning point in the history of education in the United States. During the 1950s, public schools were caught in an unprecedented set of cross pressures arising from dramatically increasing student enrollments, teacher shortages, building inadequacies, curricular challenges, and political criticisms, in which educational philosophy was sometimes confused with patriotism and national loyalty. Although some of these problems might have been eased by federal funds, legislation providing general federal assistance for education was repeatedly blocked by battles over desegregation, aid to parochial schools, and fears of the creeping socialism assumed by some to be inherent in "big government." ESEA broke the political stalemate. Composed of five discrete sections, it provided aid to school districts with "educationally deprived children of low income families" (this included 94 percent of the nation's school districts in 1965); authorized money to the states to purchase educational materials and lend these to public and private schools; authorized funds to establish special supplementary educational centers and services; made money available for research and innovation; and provided assistance to strengthen state education departments.[1]

Linking unprecedented levels of federal funding to goals emanating from Washington, D.C., ESEA marked a shift in the initiation of educational policy from the state and local levels to the federal level.

Even though ESEA was far more flexible than earlier federal education aid bills, it remained both "directive and categorical."[2] It provided resources for specified educational purposes and, more generally, sought to foster equality of educational opportunity for students in rural Mississippi no less than students in urban Illinois or suburban Massachusetts.

Coincident with the new political arrangements ushered in by ESEA was a widely noted change in personnel. Writing in the *New York Times* in the summer of 1965, Fred M. Hechinger noted the appearance in Washington of "'new men' [who] were not education's Organization Men . . . the heads of the giant [education] associations or even of the state education departments."[3] Their leader, first as president of the Carnegie Corporation from 1955 to 1965, and then as U.S. Secretary of Health, Education, and Welfare after 1965, was John W. Gardner. As Hechinger recognized, Gardner had "hit on a way of combining foundation and government thinking on a huge, national scale." The changes in politics and personnel with which he was associated represented "fundamental changes verging on a coup d'état," Hechinger said.[4] A turning point in the history of public policy toward education, ESEA also marked the fruition of more than a decade of philanthropic activity at the Carnegie Corporation.

One element in this was collaboration with other foundations, especially the Ford Foundation and the Fund for the Advancement of Education, a spin-off of Ford established in 1951 to support educational innovations (in 1967, the Fund was reabsorbed by the Ford Foundation). At times, Ford and Carnegie planned educational initiatives together and shared their cost; at times, they financed distinct but compatible endeavors. Generally, Corporation grants were smaller, fewer in number, and more likely to involve research and the dissemination of ideas; Ford grants were more likely to support demonstration projects, and, earlier than was the case with the Carnegie Corporation, involved Ford with problems of urban education, especially those associated with race and delinquency. The differences between the foundations were not always clear and sharp, however, and their different but compatible programs had a mutually reinforcing effect, Ford's activism helping to pave the way for Corporation leadership in national discussions of education. One could see clear evidence of strategic philanthropy in the transfer to the federal government of the liberal educational agenda defined by the foundations.

John W. Gardner: From Psychology to Philanthropy

John William Gardner was fifty-two years old in 1965, when President Lyndon B. Johnson asked him to join the cabinet. After nineteen years at the Carnegie Corporation, he "had the job taped," he recalled.[5] He was ready for a change. As Secretary of HEW, he could pursue his long-standing interests in both leadership and education in new ways.

Gardner was a psychologist by training and the author of several books, including one entitled *Self-Renewal*. Having attended high school in Pacific Grove, California, he had been graduated from Stanford University in 1935, thereafter receiving the M.A. in psychology from Stanford and, in 1938, the Ph.D. from the University of California at Berkeley. His dissertation, entitled "On Levels of Aspiration," was a spin-off of work inspired by the Gestalt psychologist Kurt Lewin. After it was completed, Gardner had continued to investigate human motivation while also teaching psychology, first at Connecticut College for Women and then at Mount Holyoke College. He later remembered himself as being at that time "the most academic of academics—the kind of faculty member who never even bothers to attend faculty meetings. An inveterate reader and student."[6] Although that would change when he decided that he "had had enough of fine girls' colleges in sylvan glens," Gardner would continue to hold to his interest in the sources of human endeavor.[7]

After four years as a college professor, Gardner left Mount Holyoke to head the Latin American section of the Federal Communications Commission. When the United States entered the war, he joined the Marine Corps, eventually reaching the rank of captain. He was assigned to the Office of Strategic Sevices. Before the war, he had already begun to think that quantitative psychology of the kind he had studied was a "dead end." As early as 1940 he had written: "in narrowing the concept [of levels of aspiration] down to the point where it means something [quantitatively], we have narrowed it down to the point where it means nothing."[8] The war then provided him with additional reasons to look for a new line of work. "Our lives were overturned," he remembered. "We hated Hitler."[9] The result for Gardner was a greater awareness of the importance of politics and a wish to find a position that would allow greater and more direct involvement with public issues. Chance, in the form of a suggestion from fellow psychologist Henry Murray, one of the Harvard Levellers and a friend of Corporation president Devereux Josephs, led Gardner to Carnegie.

Established curiosities and "a profound interest in human motivation—an interest not just in institutions but in the people who create
or destroy the institutions, an interest in the things that move people,
the values they cherish, the symbols and myths they live by"—led him
to the concerns that now began to dominate his career.[10]

   In early 1946, when Gardner joined their ranks, the staff of the Carnegie Corporation was engaged in the program review that, among other
things, transformed Operation Flatbush into grants to develop foreign
area studies. Knowing very little about philanthropic foundations or
grant-making, the thirty-four-year-old psychologist was nevertheless
asked to contribute to the memoranda-writing and talk that the program
review involved. He told his new colleagues that he was doing so in the
spirit of Justice Oliver Wendell Holmes, who had once remarked: "No
man can go far if he never sets his foot down until he knows the sidewalk
is under it."[11] Modest though eager, Gardner was obviously already
skilled in the use of disarming wit; his prose was spare, direct, evocative.
That he had once thought of becoming a novelist makes sense: he was
interested in people and agile with words. The memoranda Gardner
wrote during his first years at Carnegie Corporation also revealed an
unusual capacity to break large problems into incremental questions,
and to apply the logic, if not the technical fine points, of the science
he had learned as a psychologist to the new tasks he now faced as a
philanthropist on the rise. To read his early program commentaries is to
encounter a powerful and earnest mind. The journalist Elizabeth Drew
would later describe him as "deeply unconventional. . . intense, restless,
impatient, . . . impulsive and uninhibited."[12] All these attributes were
evident earlier. A tall, good-looking man of large frame and often quizzi-
cal expression, Gardner quickly established himself as a major force
within the Corporation offices. Appointed to the staff in early 1946, he
was elected vice president in May 1949 and, owing to Charles Dollard's
poor health, became president in fact even before being officially elected
to the post in January 1955.

   Demonstrating a competence to lead, Gardner began at the same
time to advocate that the Corporation's staff generally, as a corporate
entity, assume a leadership role in formulating, first, the foundation's
own policies, and, increasingly over time, those of the nation. Thus, in
presenting his ideas for the postwar program, he argued that, regardless
of substantive emphasis, "one basic consideration" should remain
paramount in all that the Corporation did:

The Corporation should never forget that its most precious asset will be its
sense of direction. This means . . . we should continually discuss and re-discuss,

formulate and re-formulate our program until all of us have unshakably in mind the range and pattern of our objectives . . . When a new project comes up, it will *not* be sufficient to know that a terribly competent man proposed it, or that it is a socially desirable project, or that it is feasible and well-formulated. We will want to know whether this project is relevant in terms of our basic strategy, whether it is a logical next step (or at least an indispensable step) toward the attainment of one or another of our objectives. . . . The rest of the world is much too busy keeping its in-basket empty and its out-basket full to maintain any sense of direction. We must constitute our own board of strategy.[13]

What Gardner was recommending was a process of continuous, collaborative group reflection. He was also urging his colleagues to recognize that their own time, thought, knowledge, and experience constituted a resource at least as valuable as the Corporation's endowment. He was suggesting that, if they aspired to the role, they had the competence to frame their own program and priorities.

In advocating an active, self-reliant staff role, Gardner was breaking with Carnegie tradition. Heretofore, especially during Frederick Keppel's long presidency, external advisory groups had served as the primary consultants to the Corporation's president and trustees in making grant decisions. Now, owing to an enlarged staff, to Devereux Josephs's wish to institute more bureaucratic procedures, and to Gardner's aspirations, that began to change. Increasingly over the next twenty years, the Corporation's staff would follow Gardner's suggestion and constitute their own "board of strategy."[14] After Gardner's election as president, even the trustees played a less central role.[15] Although the wisdom of this atrophied board role would be questioned later, by 1955 decision-making was largely centralized within the foundation. With staff assistance, it was Gardner who formulated Corporation direction, it was Gardner who led.

Integral to this leadership role was Gardner's ability to educate. The line between leadership and education, especially what one might call "public education," was often imperceptible. Having early recognized the worth of the Corporation's nonmonetary resources, Gardner believed that these should be used for public benefit. In a 1953 memorandum reviewing previous grants for higher education and charting new directions, he stated: "The Carnegie Corporation because of its traditional position 'above the battle' can . . . make an important contribution in identifying and clarifying the major problems facing American . . . education."[16]

Soon after this statement had been made, the Corporation's principal medium of public information, its annual reports, began to appear in a new format. Beginning with the 1953 number, the pages and print were larger; the information about grants was more detailed; and the writing style was more informal and direct. Actually running the foundation during the winter of 1954, when the 1953 *Annual Report* was prepared (Charles Dollard was on sick leave), Gardner contributed the first of his subsequently well-known presidential essays. The following year, in the first annual report to appear while he was officially president, Gardner's essay assumed what would become a characteristic form. It had a distinct title—"A Time for Decision in Higher Education." It was not written as a report of the Corporation's activities for the year; that report followed in a separate section which now included photographs. Instead, Gardner's essay offered analysis and interpretation of a pressing public problem. Although his ideas about higher education would shape the Corporation's future grants program, they were presented here without reference to that. The essay was the kind that might have appeared in a general circulation magazine; indeed, beginning with the 1956 essay, "The Great Talent Hunt," which was reprinted in *Harper's Magazine,* a number were disseminated in precisely that fashion.

Other circumstances contributed to the Corporation's more popular style of public communication. Most important was the congressional investigation of foundations that began in the spring of 1952. Early reports about the views of Representative E. E. Cox of Georgia, who was chairing the investigating committee, had led the Corporation's staff to anticipate "an inquiry similar in character to those conducted by the McCarran Committee and the House Un-American Activities Committee."[17] In consequence the staff had worked nearly full-time from April until September in preparation for the committee's hearing, at which, in December 1952, Charles Dollard, Devereux Josephs, and trustee Russell Leffingwell testified. The final report of the Cox Committee was, in Charles Dollard's words, "a sober judgematic [*sic*] document which contains more praise than blame, and provides explicit support for the program the Corporation has been developing since the war."[18] But the investigation had shown, Dollard added, that "all foundations, including the Corporation, have done a relatively bad job of explaining their work to the public, including the Congress."[19] After the Cox Committee's probe, therefore, the Corporation decided to publish a quarterly report, the *Carnegie Quarterly,* and to redesign its annual reports and increase their circulation.

Directly affected by outside events like these, the changes introduced into the 1953 *Annual Report* augured a larger trend entirely compatible with and encouraged by John Gardner's views and interests. Gardner was keenly aware of the power of public opinion and of the degree to which public opinion would be shaped by public figures and public discourse. He was also sensitive to the fact that, relative to other funding agencies, the Corporation's financial resources were not vast. They were less than those of the Ford and Rockefeller Foundations, he often reminded the trustees, and "when the National Science Foundation moves into a field . . . it puts up funds on a scale which dwarfs anything the Corporation can do."[20] Convinced, in light of this, that the Corporation would need to "take infinite pains in husbanding our modest income and devoting it to precisely those projects which will have the most leverage in moving one or another field ahead," Gardner was delighted when he discovered that James Bryant Conant, former president of Harvard and now ambassador to the Federal Republic of Germany, might be available to lead a study of American high schools under Carnegie auspices.[21] Gardner, well aware of widespread concern over the state of America's schools and colleges, believed that Conant was just the person to provide the leadership necessary to focus this concern in constructive ways.

The Education of James B. Conant

Even before becoming president, Gardner had suggested to the Corporation's trustees that the foundation might "collaborate with leading educators in bringing to the informed layman a better understanding" of the problems of education.[22] Conant suited the role for several reasons. First, having served as president of Harvard from 1933 until 1953, he was a well-known and well-regarded educator. Before Conant's presidency, Frederick P. Keppel had observed that "Harvard's share of men of outstanding scholarly distinction had dropped rather than risen since the turn of the century. . . . Harvard is still *princeps,* but no longer *facile princeps.*"[23] But by the end of Conant's term, no such claims were heard. Conant had reinvigorated the university in a number of ways. He had established a national scholarship program to attract unusually able students from geographic areas and schools beyond Harvard's traditional recruitment base in the Northeast. Early in his administration, faculty personnel policies had been revised to ensure sixth-year tenure reviews involving external ad hoc review committees, in hopes of awarding permanencies only to the most outstanding scholars and to do so via fair, meritocratic procedures. With his encouragement, a faculty committee developed the widely admired "general education" curriculum adopted in October 1945. Reforms such as these had retrieved Harvard's preeminence and brought Conant wide acclaim.

A leading figure in higher education, Conant had also been prominently engaged in debates about the public schools. By profession, he was a chemist. He had been graduated from the academically elite Roxbury Latin School, and had taken both the B.A. degree (1914) and the Ph.D. (1916) in chemistry at Harvard. Thereafter, he had joined the Harvard faculty in organic chemistry, and had continued to teach there until his selection as president of Harvard in 1933. According to his own recollection, Conant's scientific background had not predisposed him to an interest in education. Indeed, at the time he became president of Harvard, he admittedly held many "prejudices against professors of education."[24] But the Harvard Graduate School of Education was facing difficulties in the 1930s. Conant's predecessor, A. Lawrence Lowell, had even compared the school to a "kitten that ought to be drowned."[25] Of necessity, therefore, the new president had concerned himself with the school as early as 1933, in the process learning a good deal about education and coming increasingly to see himself, and to be seen, as a lay expert about the public schools.

Conant's education in matters of professional education was somewhat unusual. His first tutor, to whom he was introduced by the University of Chicago president, Robert Maynard Hutchins, was Charles Hubbard Judd, a forceful advocate of educational research who had presided over the transformation of the University of Chicago School of Education after John Dewey's resignation as director in 1904. This had included changing the School of Education into a department. Judd believed that the training of prospective teachers, including their study of teaching methods, should be offered within the faculty of Arts and Sciences, educational research thereby becoming the singular purpose of the education faculty. A maverick among his professional peers, Judd was more concerned with developing "a science of education" and less concerned with immediately improving the practice of education than either James Earl Russell of Teachers College, Columbia University, or Ellwood Patterson Cubberley of Stanford University. More important here, he was totally at odds with Henry W. Holmes, the dean of the Harvard Graduate School of Education, who believed that improved teacher training was the most important ingredient in public school reform. With this in mind, Holmes had developed an Ed.M. sequence at Harvard with two years of full-time, post-B.A.,

preservice study. Judd had publicly criticized the effort. Whether Conant knew this or not, he found the Chicago model that Judd described
more appealing. It was less expensive than the Harvard Ed.M. curriculum, and it made obvious sense to a person who was not convinced
that courses in pedagogy taught by education professors had value.
They would not have made him a better teacher of chemistry, Conant
always said.[26]

Interested in having the Chicago model adopted by the Harvard
Graduate School of Education, Conant opened discussions with Dean
Holmes early in 1934. The programmatic result for Harvard was
approval in 1935 of the M.A.T. degree, designed as a joint degree of
the faculties of Arts and Sciences and Education, which required the
equivalent of a master's degree in a subject matter field as well as
in teaching methods and practice teaching. The result for Harvard's
president was a new educational adviser. Hoping for assistance in
his negotiations with Conant concerning the future of the School of
Education, Holmes had brought his younger colleague, Francis Trow
Spaulding, into the conversations; according to Conant, he and Spaulding "got on well together" from the start. "He was no 'yes-man,'"
Conant recalled. "He was a realist and quite ready to take the education
of the new president of Harvard as one of his assignments (though,
needless to say, this was never admitted openly)."[27] Whereas Holmes
was "affable," in Conant's eyes Spaulding "had the rare combination
of being approachable and open-minded without being in the least
uncertain as to his views. He liked an argument, but not for an argument's sake. . . . He had a disarming quality, and one could find oneself
heartily disagreeing with the man and still continue to like him and
even to admire his tenacity."[28] Almost in the fashion of Mozart and
Salieri, Spaulding quickly outshone Dean Holmes in Conant's eyes,
and in 1940 Spaulding replaced Holmes as dean of the Graduate School
of Education. The school was in desperate need of funds, and the shift
in leadership was virtually a condition for Conant's willingness to
allow continued operation with a deficit budget. Eager to save the
school he had served since 1920, Holmes resigned.[29]

Spaulding's appeal to Conant and influence upon him are not difficult to understand. The two men were three years apart in age. Both
were products of old New England families; both had been born and
raised in Massachusetts towns; and both were alumni of Harvard. Of
course, while Conant had worked as a chemist, Spaulding had studied
and then taught education. Unlike Henry Holmes, however, whose
interest in pedagogy excited Conant's admitted prejudices about educa-

tion, Spaulding was interested in educational administration and public policy, topics Conant appreciated. Apparently bright, competent, and widely admired by his peers, Spaulding was sufficiently close to him in background and interest to serve as his guide in educational affairs. If Judd began Conant's education in education, Spaulding continued it.

Although Conant claimed in his autobiography that Spaulding did not see "eye to eye with the leaders [of progressive education] at Teachers College," Spaulding's views were indisputably "progressive."[30] This was clear in *High School and Life,* a volume Spaulding prepared for the New York State Regents' Inquiry in 1938. He was concerned in the study with the academic offerings available to exceptionally able youngsters. "It seems fair to conclude," he stated, "that *the current program of secondary education is only partially successful in making the most of the abilities of exceptionally capable boys and girls.*"[31] Hence, there was a need for greater stimulation of academic ability. But increasing levels of academic achievement were not the sole focal point of Spaulding's attention, nor even the primary one. Rather, his underlying concern in *High School and Life* was the relationship between schooling and what he called "social competence," or "readiness for normal out-of-school living."[32] Great stress was placed on how the schools should foster the attitudes necessary for citizenship, the intelligent choice of vocation, and the pursuit of healthy sport and worthwhile recreation. *High School and Life* resembled the well-known NEA report, *Cardinal Principles of Secondary Education* (1918), a point Conant obliquely acknowledged when he observed that, to the extent Spaulding was a progressive, he was a progressive of the First World War variety. Spaulding's book was built around the belief that schools should serve many different purposes for many different people—in other words, that academic study should be part but not all of what schools offered individuals and society. To the extent that progressive educators, who varied greatly in point of view, shared a perspective, it was this broad conception of school purpose and clienteles.

Before he knew Spaulding, Conant had never thought about concepts like "social competence." If he had had to identify a model high school, it would likely have resembled his alma mater, the Roxbury Latin School. If he had had to describe the goals of schooling, he probably would have focused on preparing worthy applicants for colleges like Harvard. The fact that, in 1936 in New York State, twice as many students did not finish high school as finished, and further, that these students also needed instruction and educational guidance, simply had not occurred to him.[33] Under Spaulding's tutelage Conant began to consider data like these and to affirm in his speeches and writings that the high school should serve the needs of *all* students. Thus, with a nod to his own continuing education, he told a New York City audience in 1939 that

by tradition educators think of the channels which offer opportunity purely in intellectual terms. This is a great mistake. Talent is not synonymous with academic brilliance. No one attaches more importance to the development of the potential resources of intellectual ability in all economic levels than do I. I would do nothing to lower the standards of those institutions dedicated to this purpose. But this form of ability is only one aspect of the talents of mankind which can be useful to a nation. The skills of the artist and artisan are of equal significance for our national life. . . . The possibility of careers open to the *talented of all types* must be provided.[34]

Conant always acknowledged his intellectual debt to Spaulding, who died suddenly in 1950, at the age of fifty and at the peak of his career. Conant would say: "Spaulding . . . opened my eyes to what the free public school meant for the future of American society. If I have anyone to thank for starting me down the path which led in 1957 to my detailed study of American public schools, it is Francis Spaulding."[35] Spaulding had been particularly important in helping to broaden his conception of "talent," which proved crucial to the educational philosophy he would expound for the rest of his career.[36]

A concept of talent sufficient to encompass manual dexterity, leadership skills, and special intuitive qualities along with traditional academic competencies led Conant to believe that, if individuals differed in talent, they should also be expected to differ in vocation and in the educational programs, tracks, or streams that prepared them for those vocations. Recognizing that this belief would stand in tension with the egalitarian values of a democratic society, he concluded that the potential social and political problems resulting could be resolved if all youngsters were allowed freely to enter any and all streams of education, the placement depending entirely on individual competence. By 1940, he could summarize all this in graceful prose, advocating "a differentiation of labors with a corresponding differentiation in the types of education (but no ruling caste, no hereditary educational privileges, everyone to be 'as good as everyone else')."[37]

As Conant, assisted by Spaulding, spoke and wrote more and more frequently about education, organizations of educators began to seek his participation. None was more important to his growing prominence as a national educational statesman than the Educational Policies Commission (EPC). Established in 1935 with funds from the General Education Board, the EPC was meant to provide new and vigorous leadership for the professional education community and the public at large. Jointly sponsored by the NEA and the American Association of School Administrators (AASA), it consisted of fifteen elected members who convened twice a year to review, revise, and approve policy statements drafted by the executive secretary or some other educator. Elected to membership in 1941, Conant participated in EPC discussions that led in 1944 to publication of one of its best-known works, *Education for ALL American Youth*.

Intended to provide a blueprint for secondary education in the postwar world, *Education for ALL American Youth* endorsed three educational goals for all students: vocational efficiency, civic competence, and personal development. Recommending the provision of schooling through grade 14, it forecast college attendance for 15 to 20 percent of the nation's youth, and for the rest suggested courses in homemaking, mental hygiene, and "the world at work." To ensure wide choices among career options, the report stressed the importance of educational guidance, "the high art of helping boys and girls to plan their actions wisely, in the full light of all the facts that can be mustered about themselves and about the world in which they will work and live."[38] And "to help students grow in competence as citizens of the community and the nation; in understanding of economic processes and of their roles as producers and consumers; in cooperative living in family, school, and community; in appreciation of literature and the arts; and in the use of the English language," it recommended that all students enroll in a course called "Common Learnings" for fully one-third of their school time in grades 10, 11, and 12, and for one-sixth of that time in grades 13 and 14.[39] The course was intended to cut across traditional subject divisions in order to show the students the interrelatedness of the real-world problems they would find outside of school.

Endorsing *Education for ALL American Youth*, Conant also endorsed the so-called Harvard "Redbook," published only months after the EPC report. Entitled *General Education in a Free Society*, the Harvard report was concerned with simultaneously fostering curricular diversity and commonality at both the secondary and collegiate levels of education. It called attention to increases in school and college enrollments, to growing "atomization" in life and knowledge, and to the nation's continuing need for shared values and aspirations. It advocated "a scheme of relationship between subjects which shall be similar for all students yet capable of being differently carried out for different students . . . [with a] place for both special and general education: for those subjects which divide man from man according to their particular functions and for those which unite man and man in their common humanity and citizenship."[40] An unusually lucid and humane report, *General Education in a Free Society* recognized that the choice between encouraging high achievement among the most able and encouraging gains for all was an impossible one in a democratic society.

General Education in a Free Society gained wide and deserved acclaim among academics. According to Conant, however, professors of education did not join in the praise. He noted, for example, that "Spaulding was critical. Too much about our old friend Plato, he remarked."[41] Not only Spaulding but, in Conant's view, "those who looked to schools of education for guidance tended to consider the Harvard report as one more defense of the old liberal arts with only a change of name."[42] Beyond this divergence, there also seemed to be a clear difference in reaction to *Education for ALL American Youth*. Educationists hailed the report as "true gospel"; academics "either ignored or condemned" it.[43] Gaining experience in the politics of education as he increasingly assumed the role traditional to Harvard presidents of unofficial public school leader, Conant decided to use the occasion of the 1945–46 Sachs Lectures at Teachers College "to reconcile the two books."[44]

The lectures in which Conant sought to do this—in a sense, to show that both equality and excellence were necessary in public education—were not truly original, but they did reveal premises that would guide his pronouncements about education throughout the rest of his career. "I shall to a large degree be repeating the words of others," the Harvard president announced in opening the first of three talks. "In particular, the highly significant volume by Warner, Havighurst, and Loeb entitled *Who Shall be Educated?* has covered the same ground I shall cover and from a not dissimilar angle."[45] This acknowledgment was followed by a first lecture, "The Structure of American Society," which was derived quite directly from the Warner, Havighurst, and Loeb volume, and by two subsequent lectures, "General Education for American Democracy" and "Education beyond the High School," which were informed by the same study.

In "The Structure of American Society," Conant explained that one's educational philosophy must follow one's social philosophy. His social philosophy, he said, presumed that both generational social mobility and a deemphasis on social-class distinctions were central American goals. Asserting that "in our modern industralized society, national educational policy largely determines the future of our social structure," he went on to note an urgent need to promote equality of opportunity for each generation, in order to "restore a high degree of fluidity to our social and economic life." Fearing that "the social dynamite of this century" lay in the "latent struggle" between labor, on the one hand, and ownership and management, on the other, he looked to education as a means of "avoiding catastrophic political changes in times of severe economic dislocation."[46] He was suggesting that education could and should promote mobility, lest potentially opposing groups solidify over generations into hostile castes. Even though the educational philosophy he would elaborate from this basis included some elements of progressive thought, Conant's perspective was essentially conservative: educational reform was intended not to change but to preserve the existing social order.

The immediate source for Conant's views—Warner, Havighurst, and Loeb's *Who Shall be Educated?*— was conservative in the same sense. It equated social class with social status: "Class is present in a community when people are placed by the values of the group itself at general levels of inferiority and superiority and when the highly and lowly valued symbols are unevenly distributed among the several levels."[47] *Who Shall be Educated?* also portrayed education as one of the "elevators" that kept the American class system fluid and therefore different from a "caste" system.[48] Applauding this function, the study nevertheless concluded that educators "should try to adjust the educational system so that it produces a degree and kind of social mobility that is within the limits which will keep the society healthy and alive."[49]

Given this regulatory view of school purpose, the belief of Warner, Havighurst, and Loeb that expectations for mobility exceeded actual opportunities was significant. Because they shared the assumption commonly held in the 1930s and 1940s that economic growth was over and the frontier had closed forever, they called for efforts to move toward a more pyramid-like educational system in which upward movement would depend on student talent and educational guidance. They put the argument for a more stringent filtering of public school students—in *Notes on the State of Virginia* (1787), Thomas Jefferson had called this "raking the rubble"—as follows: "The American people, believing in a myth of unlimited social mobility, send their children to high school and college as speedways to place and power. If the educators attempt to regulate traffic, they are accused of being undemocratic, and they lose the confidence of the public. Yet there is clear evidence that our educational system is now permitting too many to use high school and college for the purpose of attaining unavailable professional and managerial positions, with resultant failure and frustration and loss of social solidarity."[50] Although Conant did not state it directly, he seems to have taken it upon himself to address the problem. Accepting the framework, data, and interpretations advanced by Warner, Havighurst, and Loeb, he used the Sachs Lectures to urge educators to act as social regulators, and to explain that this was not undemocratic.

Conant's reliance upon Warner, Havighurst, and Loeb's study suggests his affinity for a distinctive set of ideas—those of the so-called "Pareto Circle" at Harvard, a collection of scholars brought together by Leon J. Henderson, an old-line Bostonian and head of the Harvard Fatigue Laboratory. Both a chemist and a medical doctor, Henderson had done pioneering research on interactive exchanges between and among the different chemical elements that constitute human blood. Then, in 1926, encountering the writings of the Italian sociologist Vilfredo Pareto, he had concluded that Pareto's description of the social system was not different from his own description of interchange among the components of the blood. Promising a way to study social and human relations that might help to explain social change, Henderson's encounter with Pareto had had a profound effect upon his career and, through his wide and profound influence, upon American social science as a whole.[51]

Throughout the 1930s and early 1940s, Henderson devoted himself tirelessly to spreading Pareto's ideas, which were widely seen as a defense against the Marxist ideas then gaining some currency in the United States. Beginning in 1932, he offered a seminar on Pareto in the Harvard Sociology Department. Participating at various times were George C. Homans, Talcott Parsons, Crane Brinton, Charles P. Curtis, Joseph A. Schumpeter, Henry A. Murray, Clyde Kluckhohn, Robert K. Merton, and Elton Mayo. Henderson also introduced Paretan ideas into the old Saturday Club, founded in 1856 by Ralph Waldo Emerson, where notable men of Harvard lunched with notable men among their Boston neighbors. Having dreamed up the idea of the Harvard Society of Fellows, which enabled a select group of graduate students to pursue their studies with unusual freedom, and having served as chairman from its founding in 1933, Henderson also made the society a hub for discussion of Paretan ideas. As Barbara Heyl has noted in her study of the Pareto Circle, thanks to Henderson, "the concepts of social system and social equilibrium . . . enjoyed a special importance during the 1930's and early 1940's for a group of scholars at Harvard."[52]

Conant certainly knew of Henderson's interest in Pareto. Henderson's wife was Conant's wife's aunt. If they did not discuss Pareto at family gatherings, Conant may have heard Henderson talk at the Saturday Club or at the Society of Fellows. Whatever his contact with Paretan ideas through Henderson, Conant was certainly exposed to Pareto through the Warner, Havighurst, and Loeb study he accepted so entirely. Although Warner had moved to the University of Chicago by the time *Who Shall be Educated?* was published in 1944, he had served on the Harvard faculty between 1929 and 1936. Having studied with A. R. Radcliffe-Brown at the University of Sydney in Australia, at Harvard Warner had become a close colleague of the Australian-born industrial psychologist Elton Mayo. As an anthropological consultant to Mayo's famous Western Electric studies, Warner had been instrumental in demonstrating that interaction among workers was more important in production rates than the workers' physical environment. His contribution to the study had been praised not only by Mayo but also by Henderson. That *Who Shall be Educated?* embodied a Pareto Circle orientation was therefore not surprising. Warner had spent the early years of his career in close colleagueship with the leading members of this group, including Mayo; and, while Mayo's influence on Warner's work has been recognized, Henderson's influence was no less apparent. In *Who Shall be Educated?* Warner and his colleagues applied Paretan ideas to problems of educational policy. Albeit with greater remove from the original source, Conant followed suit after he and John Gardner agreed to a Carnegie Corporation-Conant collaboration in support of excellence and equality of opportunity in the public schools.

James B. Conant and the Carnegie Corporation: A Mutually Beneficial Partnership

In 1955, when John Gardner and Conant first discussed a partnership, American schools faced two potentially contradictory sets of challenges. The first had to do with increasing student enrollments, teacher shortages, and building and equipment inadequacies. In 1949–50, 28,492,000 students were enrolled in the nation's elementary and secondary schools; when schools opened their doors a decade later, the comparable figure was 40,857,000.[53] As the "war babies" began to fill the seats of first-grade classrooms, the capacity of public schools to deliver adequate educational services was strained to the limit. Quonset-hut schoolrooms and split-day sessions were a common, if unsatisfactory, response to the unprecedented demographic press of the postwar years.

The second set of challenges facing the schools was pedagogical and political. Amid the anxiety of the Cold War, the loyalty of teachers was often subjected to scrutiny and sometimes to testing through loyalty oaths offensive to many. Beyond that, the push toward multipurpose, differentiated schooling that was open, appealing, and of use to all—a schooling essential to many progressive educational endeavors—now came under heavy and increasing fire. If the Educational Policies Commission's 1944 report that Conant had endorsed, *Education for ALL American Youth*, reflected the concern for comprehensive schooling so typical of that era, the titles of some of the best-known educational commentaries of the early 1950s reflect the shift that occurred. Among the works published in 1953 and 1954 that exemplify the new emphasis upon high, rigorous, academically traditional standards were Albert Lynd's *Quackery in the Public Schools*, Arthur Bestor's *Educational Wastelands*, and Mortimer Smith's *The Diminished Mind*. Sometimes, too, the academic conservatism evident in works like these combined with politically reactionary sentiments to mobilize citizen groups against proponents of progressive educational ideals.

One of the most flagrant and widely known instances of such citizen action was the firing of Willard Goslin, the superintendent of schools in Pasadena, California, who was accused of association with William H. Kilpatrick and the "Columbia cult of progressive educators."[54] Discussed by Conant in the *New York Times Book Review*, such "venomous attacks" called for reaction: "Against government by intimidation all believers in democracy must be ready to stand."[55] John Gardner most certainly agreed. What is more, he believed that endless debate about progressivism was beside the point. The challenge was to find as many ways as possible to nurture the special talents of all children, including most especially the intellectually gifted.[56]

On this point, at least, the Corporation's president agreed with Admiral Hyman Rickover, a leading conservative critic of U.S. schooling. In contrast to Rickover, however, who urged the early, irreversible sorting of students, Gardner favored what he called "multiple chances."[57] Students should be organized by ability, he thought, the only alternative being a leveling down to mediocrity for all; but "the traditional democratic invitation to each individual to achieve the best that is in him requires that we provide each youngster with the particular kind of education which will benefit *him*. . . . The good society is not one that ignores individual differences but one that deals with them wisely and humanely."[58] Frequently seeking to articulate this position himself, Gardner still saw in Conant a possible spokesman for what was at the time an essentially middle-of-the-road, liberal position.

Conant, for his part, was ready for a new assignment. The possibility that the Corporation might finance Conant in the role of "minister without portfolio in the field of higher education" had actually been discussed before he left Harvard in 1953 to become U.S. High Commissioner and then ambassador to the Federal Republic of Germany.[59] Even before the Corporation had centered so many of its postwar social science and area studies grants at Harvard, Conant had served as an important Corporation consultant. He had been a member of the Committee on Scientific Aids to Learning, organized before the war by Frederick P. Keppel to recommend grants having to do with educational technology. This was the committee whose members recommended establishment of the Second World War National Defense Research Committee, or NDRC, of which Conant became chief, in which capacity he planned research leading to the invention and testing of the atom bomb. He had also played a leading part in the negotiations—initiated and facilitated by both the Carnegie Corporation and the Carnegie Foundation—that led to the establishment of the Educational Testing Service (ETS) of Princeton, New Jersey, in 1947. Services of this kind had placed the Corporation in Conant's debt, and early discussions of financing for his retirement activities reflected this.

Hoping that a study by Conant would, as he put it later, "command public confidence," Gardner wrote to the former Harvard president as soon as he heard that Conant might be interested in directing an educational survey.[60] Expressing enthusiasm at the prospect, he suggested teacher training as a topic. "No topic . . . is more in need of scrutiny," Gardner argued to Conant, "and if you were able to find the time to spend a couple of years on the problem, it would be a service to the country."[61] Explaining his preference for this topic, Gardner continued: "The subject has received abundant attention, but mostly of a controversial nature. There have been the bitter attacks of those who haven't the faintest idea what America has been trying to do in public education; and there has been a closing of ranks on the part of those who have a vested interest in the status quo. Meanwhile, the largest profession (and the lowest paid) bumbles along, doing better than anyone has a right to expect, but probably not nearly as well as it could."[62]

Also eager to ensure that the Corporation would be the primary financier and backer of whatever study Conant might undertake, Gardner succeeded in convincing Conant that his initial plan to "serve as a consultant to the Carnegie Corporation, and one or two other foundations, and the NEA," did not make sense, but failed to persuade him to focus on teacher education.[63] Even so, in December 1956 the Corporation voted $350,000 to support a two-year study by Conant of "the problems of the comprehensive high school," especially the problem of providing sufficient academic challenge for the gifted.[64] The following spring, Conant returned from Germany and settled in New York, where he recruited a staff of research assistants and opened an office. In the fall of 1957, he began to travel throughout the United States, investigating schools, conferring with educators and academics, and talking with professional and lay groups interested in education.

Conant vs. the Educational Establishment

The first of Conant's Carnegie-sponsored studies, *The American High School Today: A First Report to Interested Citizens*, appeared in 1959. The underlying message was that "American secondary education can be made satisfactory without any radical changes in the basic pattern."[65] To a known advocate of the comprehensive high school, this meant, first, that the comprehensive high school, defined as a school that could "provide a good general education for *all* the pupils as future citizens of a democracy, [and] . . . provide elective programs for the majority to develop useful skills, and educate adequately those with a talent for handling advanced academic subjects—particularly foreign languages and advanced mathematics," was more than a theoretical ideal.[66] Having personally visited fifty-five schools, mostly outside of large urban areas and in eighteen of the most heavily populated states, Conant reported finding eight that could be called comprehensive.[67] Yet on the basis of his school visits and those of his assistants, he was ready to warrant that the comprehensive high school could become the national norm. What was needed was change along the lines of the twenty-one specific reforms presented in his book, ranging from improvements in counseling systems to the establishment of an academic honors list, and the consolidation of small high schools in order to achieve school populations large enough to sustain the curricula diversity that comprehensiveness required.

Entirely compatible with his belief in common yet diversified schooling, *The American High School Today* was intended to help people, especially lay people, who were working to support and improve American public education. The audience Conant had in mind included not only individuals but also groups like the National Citizens Commission for the Public Schools. This organization had grown out of a suggestion Conant had made to the Educational Policies Commission in 1943, and had begun operation in May 1949 with primary financing from the Carnegie Corporation. By design, the Commission was made up of people who were not professional educators. It sought to encourage local citizens groups to work for the public school. It did this in the hope that the introduction of lay people into the politics of education could serve as a counterweight to the "80 per cent of the people called professors, teachers, superintendents of schools and so on" who did not know what "good education" was.[68]

At the time he wrote *The American High School Today*, Conant was worried that the positive reform efforts of groups like the National Citizens Commission was being undermined by contemporary educational debates. He shared Gardner's belief that much of the public talk was either ill-informed or defensive and wished to redirect it. "It would be my hope that in this report I could answer to some extent some of the unthinking and ill-informed critics of the American high school who yearn for the good old days of the orthodox curricula," he had explained to Gardner in December 1956.[69] "The sniping at the public schools by the type of critic I have in mind [he mentioned Admiral Rickover, in particular] results in a diminution of the taxpayers' support and tends to drive good people away from the teaching profession."[70]

Clear in his intentions for the study, Conant's report was purposefully styled to be moderate and nonalarmist in its findings. "My emphasis was on the positive side of my findings, and my view of the public high schools was perhaps overly optimistic," he confessed to Gardner in retrospect.[71] He had felt compelled to discuss his study earlier than might have been wise, he explained. Indeed, "if Sputnik had not loosed a torrent of uninformed and unintelligent criticism of the public schools, I should not have spoken so soon."[72] It was not that his findings, however prematurely reported, were flawed, but that with time and ripening, and within a less hysterical context, he might have more accurately and fully described his reservations about the schools, without having appeared to endorse the negative, narrow, and mistaken conception of schools that Conant associated with such critics as Admiral Rickover, Arthur Bestor, and Mortimer Smith.

Even before beginning the investigations that resulted in *The American High School Today,* Conant had told Gardner that his report might of necessity "be written in a lower key."[73] This would be required, he had indicated, if he found that few schools could offer the very best students (those with I.Q.'s of 115 or above) the kind of intense, demanding academic instruction one would find at Phillips Exeter Academy, while also serving all the rest. Given this, it seems likely that, even without Sputnik and the added reform pressure this placed on American schools, the Conant report would have been presented in a sunny hue. As political as it was genuinely exploratory in its purposes, Conant's study was intended to expose the more radical school critics as unnecessarily extremist and thus capture leadership of public debate for the moderates.

To get the report before the widest possible audience, a major dissemination campaign was launched. It was orchestrated by three "Joint Chiefs," representing the Educational Testing Service in Princeton, New Jersey, which administered Conant's grants; the National Citizens Commission for the Public Schools, which organized speaking tours for Conant; and the Carnegie Corporation. Meeting weekly to coordinate the continuing campaign, Conant's "Joint Chiefs" had 89,350 free copies of *The American High School Today* mailed to school boards, school administrators, governors, senators, congressmen, the NEA, and the press. Newspaper coverage and media interviews were arranged with, among others, Dave Garroway on NBC-TV and Edward R. Murrow on CBS-Radio. Released on January 28, 1959, the book was in a fourth printing by mid-March, with 17,000 clothbound copies and 196,000 paperback copies in print. According to the coordinator for the "Joint Chiefs," the Conant study had "done more to make the average man on the street conscious of the problems facing our high schools than perhaps any other publication of recent years."[74] Whether the publicist's claims of influence were correct, there is no doubt that the media campaign helped to make Conant's findings and recommendations, especially concerning the consolidation of small, local schools, matters of debate all over the United States.

While *The American High School Today* made its way into the national consciousness, the Carnegie Corporation's educational emissary remained troubled about the performance of the schools. More pessimistic in private than in public, Conant worried that the schools were "failing to make the necessary differentiation between what the academically talented students ought to study and what the others might well study." They had "become too soft," he feared.[75] What is more, as had been the case when the National Citizens Commission for the Public Schools was organized, educators, especially professors of education and superintendents, were failing to face the problem squarely. Increasingly with time, therefore, Conant came to agree with Gardner's initial view: teacher education was a topic that could offer a critical point of leverage in school reform. With a second Carnegie grant, this one for $300,000, Conant therefore set out upon the investigations that resulted in *The Education of American Teachers* in 1963. Having answered the conservative critics like Rickover, Bestor, and Smith, Conant found the way now clear for an appraisal of the profession itself.

One might note parenthetically that Conant's decision to study teacher education followed publication of several books by him in addition to *The American High School Today,* and that at least one of these, *Slums and Suburbs: A Commentary on Schools in Metropolitan Areas,* influenced his subsequent direction. As Conant himself described it, the book's reception was "mixed," and some aspects of the study were widely seen as "unfortunate."[76] At a time of deep concern over compliance with the *Brown v. Board of Education* decision outlawing separate schools for whites and blacks, it maintained that "the answer to improving Negro education in the large Northern cities is to spend more money and to upgrade Negro schools, many of which are in slums, rather than to effect token integration by transporting pupils across attendance lines. Fully integrated teaching staffs are a necessity as well."[77] Although *Slums and Suburbs* was more concerned with describing the "social dynamite" developing in the nation's cities as a result of the increasing numbers of unemployed urban youth dropping out of schools, public attention was riveted upon Conant's seeming endorsement of the concept of "separate but equal" schools.[78] Dismayed by this reaction to the book, Conant retreated from studies that could embroil him in such contentious social problems as desegregation.[79] By the 1960s, of course, increasing numbers of people believed that questions of educational policy could not be addressed effectively without consideration of the social problems underlying desegregation and equity. But to a reformer like J. B. Conant, who was not only convinced of the essential virtue and justice of American society, but who also, according to one review, was an "equable, unimaginative man" who had never known deep personal suffering, problems of desegregation could be diversionary.[80] They could make it more difficult to gain support for incremental school reforms, and might even place in doubt the wisdom of relying upon the public schools as ladders of mobility and regulators of opportunity.

Careful, as he had not been in writing *Slums and Suburbs,* to move ahead with the full knowledge of prominent educators, Conant began his study of teacher education by traveling widely and dispatching his assistants to institutions and localities he could not visit personally. In all, seventy-seven institutions in twenty-two states were visited, fifty-two by Conant himself. Extensive data on certification requirements for teachers were collected along with demographic information suggesting patterns of supply and demand. Thanks in large part to the knowledge of his assistants, Conant was also able to consider a good deal of historical material about teacher training and relationships between theory and practice in education. Despite all the data, however, the conclusions Conant reached were predictable.

Conant's recommendations in *The Education of American Teachers* would have been likely to win the approval of his tutor in education, Charles H. Judd. They bore considerable resemblance to the reforms Conant had advocated at Harvard in connection with the establishment of the M.A.T. degree. Although his suggestions ranged across a wide variety of issues bearing on the recruitment and licensing of teachers and the curriculum of teacher education, his most important recommendation had to do with streamlining certification requirements. Conant maintained that supervised apprentice teaching should be the only mandatory element in the training of all teachers and that competence to teach as well as the academic and professional prerequisites for this should be assessed by the colleges and universities. Claiming that "professors of education have not yet discovered or agreed upon a common body of knowledge that they all feel should be held by [all] school teachers," Conant stated that, "except for practice teaching and the special methods work combined with it, I see no rational basis for a state prescription of the time to be devoted to education courses."[81] The implication was clear: because there were no universally recognized principles of education, courses in education should not be mandated. Whether or not Conant was right, *The Education of American Teachers* was widely read as a frontal attack on the integrity of education as a science and a profession.

"It would be naive to predict that the author's recommendations for surgery in teacher education will be accepted as readily as was his prescription of vitamins for the high schools," Fred Hechinger observed in a review of *The Education of American Teachers* for the *New York Times.*[82] After all, Hechinger continued, what Conant had recommended "really amounts to a completely new start."[83] Stimulated by another massive dissemination campaign, the book circulated briskly.

"The president of McGraw-Hill, the publisher, has described the promotion results on this book as the best that his house has ever had on
any one book—and possibly the best that there has ever been on any
one book for any publishing house, barring the Kinsey Reports,"
Gardner was told in September 1963.[84] By October, 783,000 copies
were in circulation, 472,000 sold and 311,000 distributed as free
copies.[85] Commentators from outside circles of professional educators
tended to endorse the book, but as Hechinger had prophesied, educators, recognizing the full significance of the issues, were prone to
dissent.

This bifurcated reception had historical precedent. It was not different from the reception accorded Abraham Flexner's 1910 study of
medical education. Like Conant's appraisal of teacher education, that
survey evoked positive reactions among lay groups and dismayed and
angry reactions among professional groups. The Conant study dealt
with a "century-long battle between professors of education and those
in the liberal arts," and did so in such an antagonistic way that it was,
in the opinion of some, likely to hinder cooperation among them.
Similarly, the Flexner Report had supported reforms already under
way and had alienated many medical school reformers in the process.[86]
The Conant study represented a deliberate effort to wrest leadership
of educational affairs from the educational establishment, while the
Flexner Report had represented an effort to wrest leadership from old,
local medical practitioner elites. Within the history of the Carnegie
Foundation for the Advancement of Teaching, which had sponsored
the Flexner Report, the medical school survey marked a bold assertion
of power subsequently used to promote national professions and, more
generally, the organization of a nationally articulated society. Unlike
the Carnegie Foundation in 1910, however, the Carnegie Corporation
was already well known by the time the Conant teacher education
survey appeared in 1963. But, like the Flexner Report, *The Education
of American Teachers* asserted the claims of an outside force, the claims
of laymen like Conant, who were intelligent and informed about the
public schools and in a position to improve them simply because
they were not part of what Conant described as "the educational
establishment" that "guards the gates."[87]

At the time *The Education of American Teachers* appeared, Conant
was already becoming weary of his career as an educational critic. He
was tired of the controversy his studies had stirred and aware that his
most recent survey would upset many of his longtime friends and
acquaintances in organizations like the Educational Policies Commis-

sion. Deciding that he "needed a new project," he left the country in
the fall of 1963 to return to Germany, where he served for two years
as a Ford Foundation consultant to help the city of Berlin establish a
Pedagogical Center.[88]

Thus removed from the debate, Conant published the last of his
Carnegie-supported studies of education, *The Shaping of Educational
Policy*, in 1964. Its central argument was that, since educational planning was a state and local responsibility and "national" educational
planning was therefore impossible, what he called "nationwide" planning should be pursued instead.[89] This was urgently needed, Conant
explained, if the public schools, colleges, and universities were to meet
the challenges inherent in "the educational revolution" through which
the United States was passing.[90] It could be accomplished, Conant
noted, by forming an "Interstate Commission for Planning a Nationwide Educational Policy" to gather and disseminate the necessary
information.[91] Just as Conant's earlier suggestion had resulted, with
Carnegie Corporation financing, in the National Citizens Commission
for the Public Schools, so this suggestion would now lead to the formation of the Educational Commission of the States, again with initial
Carnegie Corporation money.

A rather bland presentation, or, as one commentator described it,
"a film with interesting images but no plot," *Shaping Educational
Policy* did not achieve wide acclaim.[92] A number of reviewers chided
Conant for yet again taking aim at "the educational establishment."
They were dismayed because he continued "to talk of America's educational 'establishment' but nowhere present[ed] evidence to suggest that
such an establishment exists."[93] Others contended that "inaccurate,
'quick and simple stories' of three or four states, cavalier disparagement
of the 'establishment,' and oversimplified 'how-to-do it' pamphlets for
mass consumption . . . are not very helpful and in the long run may
confuse more than shape educational policy."[94] Many of the points
raised by the critics were sound. Most important here, there is no
denying that Conant never really defined who did and did not belong
to the so-called "educational establishment." Obviously, he meant
those involved in teacher training. But who else? Unclear on that
point, Conant's use of the phrase was little more than an epithet.
Such complaints notwithstanding, *Shaping Educational Policy* was
significant because it repeated the antieducationist sentiments Conant
had long subscribed to, and combined these with a proposal for a new
noneducationist organization that could engage in educational policy-
making "nationwide."

Excellence and Equality:
Laying the Groundwork for ESEA

From his very first days at the Carnegie Corporation, John Gardner had revealed himself to be a brilliant strategist of public influence, and the Conant studies should be seen within that context. Eager to help improve all levels of U.S. education, Gardner met with Conant to discuss his studies, while also working with James A. Perkins, Corporation vice president from 1951 to 1963, and other staff members to help orchestrate the publicity, speaking engagements, and behind-the-scenes conferences that enabled Conant to capture center stage in the nation's educational debates and to hold on to that position throughout the early 1960s. At the same time Gardner also kept "interest in education stirring" through his own activities.[95]

Gardner was a member of a number of prestigious commissions and advisory groups. In 1960, for example, he served as chairman of the Rockefeller Brothers Fund Panel on Education and as chief draftsman of its report, *The Pursuit of Excellence: Education and the Future of America* (1961). Explicitly drawing upon Conant's studies, the report endorsed the idea of the comprehensive high school and rejected suggestions that separate academic and vocational schools could better meet the nation's educational requirements. More characteristic of Gardner, however, it emphasized the need to use the talent of each and every individual; expressed concern for ensuring the freedom necessary for creativity; and urged that democratic values not be allowed mistakenly to detract from the pursuit of excellence.[96]

The Rockefeller Brothers Fund report foreshadowed two books Gardner wrote at this time, *Excellence: Can We Be Equal and Excellent Too?* (1961) and *Self-Renewal: The Individual and the Innovative Society* (1964). Fitting squarely into an Emersonian tradition of concern about American culture, both books further developed Gardner's long-standing interest in fostering individualism and individual excellence "*in this society*, with all its beloved and exasperating clutter, with all its exciting and debilitating confusion of standards, with all the stubborn problems that won't be solved and the equally stubborn ones that might be."[97] Neither book went beyond, or indeed differed significantly from, Gardner's already articulated views on the role of education in mediating tensions between excellence and equality; rather, they reiterated his support for comprehensive schools, for individual guidance, multiple options, and multiple chances, and for ensuring that the most gifted be encouraged to realize the highest of which they were capable.

Well received and widely read, Gardner's books as well as his other writings for Corporation publications and for general circulation magazines stood in interesting counterpoint to Conant's. Although both men were essentially concerned with education, Conant's writings were more akin to technical papers than philosophic essays, while Gardner's were the reverse. Whereas Conant focused on administrative realities, the nuts and bolts of public schooling, Gardner tended to write of potential and aspiration, and of the necessity to maintain a balance between different and sometimes competing social goals. While Conant was relatively forthright in his criticisms of schools and school people, Gardner was inclined to use less direct, more muted tones. The two men said many of the same things. It was Gardner, though it could have been Conant, who entitled a chapter of *Excellence* "Education as a Sorting-Out Process," reiterating a phrase that had appeared in earlier works, including the Rockefeller Brothers Fund report.[98] But Gardner's concerns in the field of education were broader than Conant's and were presented in a far more evocative way.

The relationship of Gardner's and Conant's writings brings to mind a metaphor. It was as if, with Conant ably leading the armies of educational reform (assisted, of course, by the "Joint Chiefs" in charge of publicity), Gardner could hold himself in reserve to assume a stance more like that of a philosopher king. Gardner did not necessarily plan this division of labor. However unusual his skill in public affairs, the record does not indicate that kind of forethought. But there is no denying that his lay sermons on education reinforced Conant's position papers, and that the Corporation's collaboration with Conant set a special stage for the exposition of Gardner's views.

Gardner had long maintained that the Corporation should use at least three strategies to approach the improvement of education: direct comment on education, collaboration with lay leaders, and investment in a diverse range of new ideas and experiments. Along with Gardner's writings and the support the Corporation provided to Conant and to groups like the National Citizens Commission for the Public Schools, grant-making was therefore an important part of the Gardner-led, Corporation-financed educational reform effort. Looking back, Gardner said that, in directing funds to education, he and his colleagues had "ranged over every part of it," from higher and adult education to the special problems of women students, and to matters of importance to the elementary and secondary schools.[99] The Corporation's annual reports for the 1950s and 1960s suggest that, if anything, Gardner's recollection was an understatement. During those years, the Corporation financed an extraordinary catalogue of projects, ranging from the testing of liberal arts curricula for engineering students, to a study of the role of independent schools in teacher training, to experiments in teaching Far Eastern languages to American high school students, to the development (with the Ford Foundation) of the National Merit Scholarship program. Beyond that, grants went to scholars engaged in research that often began from fundamentally different orientations. Still, despite the variety, there were consistent themes as well as a number of grants that proved instrumental to changes in educational practice and the formulation of educational policy "nationwide."

Among these awards, the most important may have been the grants made in the early 1950s to support the development of a "new math" curriculum. Critical of the practical emphasis that had been central to the teaching of mathematics since the 1920s, the assumption having been that mathematics was important preparation for consumer activities, a group of mathematicians at the University of Illinois wished to change the emphasis schools placed on old concepts rather than on new discoveries. They believed there was too much stress on memorization and not enough on discovery. Students should be encouraged to think of mathematics as a living, developing field to which they could contribute new ideas, concepts, and procedures. The fundamental preoccupation of school math with drill rather than discovery had to be reversed.

To do this, professors from the Colleges of Education, Engineering, and Liberal Arts at the University of Illinois established a Committee on School Mathematics (UICSM) in 1952. Under the leadership of Max Beberman, the committee received funds from the Carnegie Corporation to develop textbooks and teacher manuals for a "new math" curriculum for grades 9 through 12. The goal, as Beberman explained it, was to develop the wherewithal necessary for "teaching meaningful and understandable mathematics."[100] This required clear language, he believed, since "it is easier to discover how to solve equations when you know what an equation and a variable are!"[101] Preceding the work of the better-known School Mathematics Study Group (SMSG) project—which, thanks in part to the wave of public hysteria that followed the launching of Sputnik in October 1957, won significant funds from the National Science Foundation—the work of the Illinois group helped lead the way to a thoroughgoing overhaul of the teaching of mathematics.[102] The Corporation further contributed to this by helping to finance the Commission on Mathematics of the College Entrance Examination Board and a variety of other projects that were designed to spread the "new math" into the junior high and elementary schools.[103]

As was true with so many projects assisted by Carnegie funds, the story of the so-called "new math" is significant in its own right. But in terms of the Corporation's interest in school reform, the Illinois mathematics project was important for three reasons: first, the curriculum was by design intended to foster the kinds of skills that would be necessary for further study and high-level performance, not for shopping at the A & P; second, university mathematicians played a critical role in its development and, despite collaboration, probably a more critical role than school mathematics teachers; and third, the project was expected to be "widely copied," as indeed it was.[104] Offering a formula for curriculum change that involved "new men," in this instance university professors of mathematics, in the promotion of academic excellence at the high school level, the Illinois mathematics project was criticized by some as overly demanding. It was better suited to the highly able students than to the average, it was claimed, and as a result it brought "into focus the key problem of twentieth-century democracy: how to educate men for leadership without dividing society into rigid classes of knowers and hewers."[105] While this was probably true, the Illinois venture nevertheless helped spark curriculum revision projects that eventually touched upon most traditional school subjects. New curricula in math, physics, chemistry, and biology were followed by new "social studies" and new curricula in foreign languages and the humanities.

The new curricula were widely disseminated partly because they won favor with educational reformers supported by the Ford Foundation. Beginning in September 1961, Ford initiated the Comprehensive School Improvement Program (CSIP) to concentrate discrete educational innovations within the same school system, thereby "bringing together a sufficient number of the new practices to create a critical mass—a chain reaction of change that would overcome the inertia of school systems and produce significantly different educational institutions."[106] In all, the CSIP involved more than $30 million spent at twenty-five different sites. Curriculum reform along the lines first pioneered in developing the new math was one of the many activities it made possible; it was most effectively instituted in suburban areas like Newton, Massachusetts, where the overall plans for change involved team teaching, university-school collaboration, and other practices that fit well with the curriculum development model involved.

Exemplifying the mutual reinforcement often evident between educational experiments financed by the Carnegie Corporation and translated into practice by Ford Foundation demonstration projects, the CSIP's support for new math and other new curricula was, in turn, enhanced by Carnegie grants for new studies of learning. Some of these had a major influence on the reform of educational policy and practice, none more significantly than the unrestricted funds the Corporation provided Jerome S. Bruner and George A. Miller in 1960 to establish and operate the Center for Cognitive Studies at Harvard. Carnegie grants to the center amounted to more than $1.25 million between 1960 and 1970. Widely seen as a mecca for scholars in the emerging field of cognitive science, the center encouraged research that confirmed and elaborated learning theories that had revolutionary implications for education. Howard Gardner dates the beginning of the "selling of cognition" to its establishment.[107]

Bruner and Miller were early participants in the postwar conferences and symposia from which cognitive studies appeared. The pioneers of this new science were trying to return psychology to the study of thinking and mind; to do this, they had first to break free of the behaviorist insistence upon studying only those properties that could be observed directly. Bruner's early research helped set the mold. With a number of colleagues at Harvard (Bruner joined the Harvard faculty in 1945), he had established that errors of perception—for example, miscalculating the size of a coin—derived from efforts to conform data to one's own "model of the universe." His subsequent work on "strategies" for problem-solving has frequently been cited to mark the beginning of the so-called "cognitive revolution."[108] A *Study of Thinking* (1956) called attention to all the complex cognitive processes that Bruner and his colleagues now thought more essential to an understanding of thinking than the connections previously associated with simple links between a "stimulus" and "response."[109]

Building on the work of the Swiss psychologist Jean Piaget, Bruner's work had clear relevance to efforts to organize different subject matters into school subjects accessible to exploration, comprehension, and mastery by young students.[110] Thanks to his acquaintance with several of the more prominent curriculum reformers, that relevance was recognized and mined. The connecting link was the physicist Jerrold Zacharias, an acquaintance of Bruner's who was involved in the Physical Science Study Committee; the connecting event was a study conference in September 1959 at Woods Hole, Massachusetts. Involving thirty-five men, the conference was organized by the National Academy of Sciences to bring together scientists, educators, and scholars interested in improving the teaching of elementary and secondary school science.[111] Asked to write the report of the conference, Bruner produced *The Process of Education* (1960). It quickly became known as "The Gospel According to St. Jerome."[112]

Simplifying complex theories of learning and thought, *The Process of Education* asserted that thinking was essentially the same for three-year-olds and Nobel Prize-winning scientists. Thinking involved mastering the structure of a subject: "discovery of regularities of previously unrecognized relations and similarities between ideas, with a resulting sense of self-confidence in one's abilities."[113] From that formulation, it was but a short step to defining the problem of curriculum design as involving little more than the description of the basic structures of an academic field. That point established, it followed that, given a sufficiently clear description, "any subject can be taught effectively in some intellectually honest form to any child at any stage of development."[114]

Bruner's report for the Woods Hole Conference of 1959 provided a psychological rationale for curriculum change along the lines favored by the new curriculum experts, many of whom were university scholars. These research-oriented professors tended to agree with Bruner's friend Zacharias, who, according to Bruner, wanted to "make physics teacher-proof."[115] As Bruner saw it, "Zach along with other reformers was convinced that the trouble with schools was the shoddy stuff they taught. The cure was to narrow the gap between knowledge locked up in the university library or the scholar's mind and the fare being taught in schools. . . . Never mind the oversimplification. It was extraordinarily energizing, and its generous view of educational possibilities seemed 'revolutionary' to all of us."[116] Bearing clear similarities to the assumptions inherent in the earlier Illinois experiments with "new math," Zacharias's views fit well with Bruner's report. Indeed, *The Process of Education* fueled an already keen interest in pushing schools toward greater "excellence," defined by Bruner as the achievement of each individual's "optimum intellectual development."[117]

Soon after the Woods Hole Conference, Bruner and his colleague George Miller received their first Carnegie Corporation grant. Describing John Gardner, who was responsible for the grant, as "our first Medici," Bruner believed in retrospect that the "first Carnegie grant made all the difference."[118] It enabled the Center for Cognitive Studies to become a place through which many of the most promising young scholars in psychology sought to pass. Before the Carnegie grant, Bruner was already on the ascendant among those concerned with education; the establishment of the center and the reputation it acquired brought him even greater prestige, which lent support to his view of the process of education.[119]

There were other psychologists in whom the Corporation invested at this time, whose work in one way or another had an influence on the kind of educational reform the Corporation favored. Perhaps none of these, not even Bruner, was more important than J. McVicker Hunt. Trained at Cornell and significantly influenced by John Dollard and others at the Yale Institute for Human Relations who were studying the relation of psychoanalytic theories to theories of learning, Hunt established that intelligence is an evolving quotient of ability that develops through interaction between one's environment and one's problem-solving capacities.[120] As presented in 1961 in *Intelligence and Experience,* Hunt's formulations demonstrated persuasively that two long-accepted maxims of educational policy and practice were wrong: first, the assumption that intelligence was established at birth; and second, the belief that intelligence develops at a predetermined rate.[121]

Hunt's findings were confirmed by longitudinal studies reported by Benjamin Bloom in *Stability and Change in Human Characteristics* (1964). Taken together, the so-called "environmentalism" of the two psychologists became what has been called "the *Zeitgeist*" of the day: "The importance of the early years in behavioral development seemed analogous to the importance of a foundation of a building: If the foundation is shaky, the structure is doomed. Seizing upon the promises of environmental theory, the public hailed the construction of a solid foundation for learning in preschool children as the solution to poverty and ignorance."[122] The door was now open to investigations of cultural and educational "disadvantage." If intelligence was developed through interaction with the environment, it followed that the nature of that environment could provide an "advantage" or a "disadvantage." Hunt explained the presumption: "The poor, be they black or white, typically do an inadequate job of teaching their children the abilities and motives needed to cope with schooling even though they love their children as much as any parents do."[123] In consequence, their children often grew up "disadvantaged"—"educationally disadvantaged" but not necessarily "culturally disadvantaged," as civil rights leaders like Kenneth B. Clark would have added.[124] That point established, it was logical to believe, as Hunt did, that education programs should give the children of the poor the teaching their parents did not provide.

Financed by a number of foundations, including the Carnegie Corporation, Hunt's findings, as confirmed by the findings of Bloom and others, helped to justify a wide range of early childhood education programs, including those financed by the federal government through Head Start. Once again, too, research sponsored by the Carnegie Corporation contributed to the educational policies and practices of the Ford Foundation's Comprehensive School Improvement Program. Having begun with a concentration of funds in "select" school districts like Newton, Massachusetts, the CSIP was redesigned in the wake of the civil rights protests of the early 1960s. New attention was given to school systems with large numbers of "disadvantaged" students, and early childhood education was featured. Subsequently, elements of the CSIP became important models for the planners of federal educational legislation. (This was also true of Ford's Great Cities-Gray Areas Program, which supported multifaceted community renewal and education programs in deteriorating "gray" zones between inner cities and suburbs.)[125] More important perhaps, the same research that had influenced the redesign of the Ford program facilitated passage of federal legislation. By explicating the concept of "disadvantage," Hunt, Bloom, and others helped to provide the political formula that finally, in 1965, made it possible to secure federal legislation assisting the nation's public elementary and secondary schools. If the Carnegie Corporation's grants to Max Beberman and others working to develop "new math" curricula and to Jerome Bruner helped change educational practice *nationwide,* its support to J. McVicker Hunt helped establish the need for a *national* educational policy.

Influenced by each of the three elements of Gardner's strategy, grant-making, direct comment on education, and support for lay involvement in educational affairs, this shift in federal educational policy derived from the convergence of many different factors. Studies of the origins of the Elementary and Secondary Education Act support Adam Yarmolinsky's contention that "successful new ideas seem to crop up all at once from a number of sources."[126] In fact, Norman C. Thomas has reported that "seven people including Abraham Ribicoff, Wilbur Cohen, Francis Keppel, Senator Wayne Morse, his aide Charles Lee, Representative John Dent, and Representative Roman Pucinski are credited with or claimed credit for tying aid to elementary and secondary education to the war on poverty in a manner that facilitated circumvention of the church-state issue."[127] Fitting well with conceptions of policy-making as a complex process that is rarely neat and rational, studies of the origins of ESEA also point out the significance of President Lyndon B. Johnson's secret task force on education, which was organized in 1964 with Carnegie Corporation president John Gardner as chairman.

The Gardner task force included thirteen prominent men. According to one participant, they were divided among "dreamers" and "practitioners"—the physicist Zacharias and the sociologist David Riesman fell into the first category, and school administrators like James E. Allen, New York State Commissioner of Education, fell into the second.[128] Bill Moyers, then special assistant to the president, who was responsible for putting the task force together, said later: "Although we started at Harvard, we were careful not to choose men only from the Establishment universities."[129] The group was dominated by Gardner and by Johnson's Commissioner of Education, Francis Keppel, the son of former Carnegie Corporation president Frederick P. Keppel, and the man Conant had chosen in 1948 to be dean of the Harvard Graduate School of Education. With Keppel using his keen interpersonal negotiating skills and Gardner using his great capacity to create consensus with evocative words, the two managed to unite the task force behind a report that called for direct federal assistance to education.

As would be true when the task force report, with some relatively minor modification, was written into the Elementary and Secondary Education Act of 1965, the report stressed the "education of the disadvantaged." Federal dollars were necessary, it maintained, to support a variety of services from preschool to work-training programs that were available to more affluent children but not to the "less fortunate children."[130] By tapping into the child benefit theory that allowed public monies to go to parochial schools without violating the Constitution, this argument made it possible to gain the acquiescence of the groups previously opposed to federal aid to education, especially representatives of Roman Catholic schools.[131] Personal diplomacy was also critical, notably the behind-the-scenes efforts of Francis Keppel, who cajoled, pressured, argued, and persuaded, in the process establishing and sustaining the coalition necessary for the passage of legislation. In a fashion not different from the mutual reinforcement Ford and Carnegie had earlier provided each other's educational reform efforts, the concepts embodied in Gardner's task force report enhanced Keppel's negotiating, while Keppel's negotiating fostered a political situation in which the task force's ideas could be translated into law.

Keppel had long recognized the value of ideas and hard data as supplements to personal lobbying in policy advocacy. With that in mind, he had proposed the creation of a national assessment of education soon after becoming Commissioner of Education in 1962. He was convinced that clearly formulated and reliable evidence was needed to strengthen arguments favoring the use of federal funds to foster more equal educational opportunity or the pursuit of other national goals.[132] The idea was a logical one for a man who had participated as closely as Keppel had in the work of the Research Branch of the Information and Education Division. As Frederick Osborn's assistant during the Second World War, Keppel had had ample opportunity to observe the credibility gained in arguing for a policy when one's position could be supported by the clear, precise, and hopefully numerical results of opinion polls and attitude surveys. He wanted similar data—educational equivalents to economic indicators like gross national product and national income—to use in reporting on the condition of education, which was his primary official responsibility as Commissioner of Education.[133]

Having sought advice from Ralph W. Tyler, a psychologist who was then director of the Center for Advanced Study in the Behavioral Sciences, Keppel had been assured that it would be possible to measure the "progress" of education—what was accomplished by different groups of students, in different regions of the country, in mastering different areas of knowledge and skill; achievement testing to measure the attainment of individual teachers, students, or schools was never the goal.[134] Thereafter, he had turned to the Carnegie Corporation for help in developing the project. The result was a Corporation-sponsored conference in September 1963 and another in December 1963; the formation in June 1964 of an advisory committee chaired by Tyler, called the Exploratory Committee on Assessing the Progress of Education ("exploratory" was dropped from the name in July 1968); and the assumption in June 1969 of responsibility for administering what became the National Assessment of Educational Progress (NAEP) by the Education Commission of the States, the organization suggested by Conant in 1964 and established with Carnegie funds. Beginning in the 1969–70 school year, tests in science, citizenship, writing, reading, math, social studies, and art, among other subjects, were administered to samples of children and young adults across the nation. Surrounded by controversy about technical questions of educational measurement, philosophical questions of educational purpose, and political questions of sponsorship and control, NAEP was a clear example of strategic philanthropy.[135] A project developed with a total of $2,432,900 in Carnegie funds became an undertaking involving a multimillion-dollar annual budget provided by the U.S. Office of Education throughout the 1970s. Although it did not go into operation until after ESEA was passed, it had been initiated earlier, and it helped begin the interplay among individuals—the "new men"—and between private institutions of governance and public agencies of the government that would also be evident in the formulation and implementation of ESEA.

The passage of ESEA marked a significant turning point in the history of education in the United States. Henceforth, there might be debate about the levels and categories of federal assistance, but not about the responsibility of the national government to further this domain of the national interest. Of course the people, events, ideas, and political brokering that made possible acceptance of this principle went well beyond the history of the Carnegie Corporation. Yet the Corporation in various ways had played a small, significant, and strategic part in paving the way for the 1965 act. Acknowledged by the invitation President Johnson extended to John Gardner to become Secretary of Health, Education, and Welfare—an invitation that was tendered shortly after ESEA was signed—Carnegie Corporation philanthropy had been an indispensable element in moving the "new men" described by Fred Hechinger onto the national stage.[136]

CHAPTER NINE

Steadfast Liberalism

Poverty, Protest, and Reform

"THE FACE OF POVERTY seems to stalk every aspect of American life. It thrives in the coal mines of Pennsylvania and on the Indian reservations of Arizona. It is black and white, rural and urban: it travels the empty road of shattered hopes from the deep South cotton fields to big city slums."[1] So began the October 1967 report of the Carnegie Corporation Task Force on the Disadvantaged. Appointed by Acting President Alan Pifer during the spring of 1967 and made up of five senior staff members, the task force recommended that "poverty become an explicit major focus of the Corporation's program."[2] As the authors of the report doubtless knew, their recommendations drew on external circumstances to justify a move toward the kind of program the Corporation's new president wished to develop.

1967 was a year of riots in Cleveland, Detroit, Newark, Boston, New Haven, and other cities. Two years earlier, the Watts neighborhood of Los Angeles had erupted in six days of violence that left six people dead, all of them black. Similar eruptions had continued through 1966 and 1967, leaving in their wake televised reports of arson, looting, and rampaging in the streets that were fast eroding middle-class liberal support for people living in poverty or denied decent housing, schooling, and jobs because of their race. 1967 was also a year of anti-Vietnam War marches and clashes with the police. Given the American public's growing disenchantment with the liberal agenda of Lyndon B. Johnson's War on Poverty, opposition to the war in Vietnam made it even less likely that the federal government would reaffirm its earlier commitment to eradicating the disease, hunger, illiteracy, unemployment, and want that remained facts of daily life for many people in a nation where there was also abundance of unparalleled dimensions.

In 1963 the continued existence of poverty amid plenty had helped mobilize the federal government to act, not only on immediate problems of economic sufficiency, but also on long-standing grievances arising from the systematic denial of civil rights to black Americans. Dwight Macdonald's *New Yorker* article "Our Invisible Poor" had caught the eye of Washington policymakers, who called it to President John F. Kennedy's attention. Contrasting John Kenneth Galbraith's *The Affluent Society* (1958) with Michael Harrington's *The Other America* (1962), Macdonald had used Harrington's data to show the inadequacy of Galbraith's argument. No longer could one believe that poverty in the United States was an anomaly existing only in isolated pockets of the country. Harrington had shown that "mass poverty exists": over forty million people lived below the poverty line. He also pointed out that "while only eleven per cent of our population is non-white, twenty-five per cent of our poor are."[3]

A great deal more than Harrington's argument, filtered through Macdonald's endorsement, stood behind the federal legislation of the 1960s. As Allen J. Matusow has contended, even though Harrington's work influenced Kennedy, "the government did not undertake a War on Poverty because Michael Harrington wrote a book. A constituency both aggrieved and vocal had first to demand it. In the spring of 1963 the civil rights movement took on mass dimensions, creating that constituency overnight."[4] It was at that time that Martin Luther King, Jr., led the March on Washington, best remembered for his "I Have a Dream" speech. But the Harrington-cum-Macdonald argument had provided the kind of focus that is often necessary to define a "problem" in terms that make it susceptible to public action.

Poverty: Alan Pifer's New Agenda

Within the Carnegie Corporation, the 1967 report of the Task Force on the Disadvantaged had very much the same effect that *The Other America* had had within the federal government. The report argued that poverty was too "deeply entrenched" to be susceptible to quick or easy remedy, and that the political factors militating against renewed federal action placed "a special burden on private financing."[5] The report was delivered at a time of transition. Appointed acting president in April 1965, when John Gardner became Secretary of Health, Education, and Welfare, Alan Pifer now became president in his own right after Gardner's resignation in August 1967 (until then, Gardner had been on a leave of absence).

As Pifer told an interviewer one week before the task force delivered its report, the topic most on his mind for the last two or three years had been the Corporation's program for the disadvantaged.[6] Actually, the Corporation had not had a distinct "program" for the disadvantaged in the mid-1960s, although since 1964 it had directed a large proportion of its grants to institutions educating blacks and other minority groups—23 percent of its appropriations in 1964, 15 percent in 1965, 19 percent in 1966, and 20 percent in 1967.[7] If the Corporation were now to develop a focus upon the problems of poverty, it would be building into its grant-making an emphasis that would be distinctive to its new president. Poverty was an area where, in Pifer's opinion, "John Gardner had missed the boat."[8] What is more, the focus on poverty recommended by the 1967 task force offered an orientation toward philanthropy that suited the style of the Corporation's new president uniquely well.

The son of an executive in a New England paper manufacturing company, Alan Pifer had attended Groton School, Harvard College, and Emmanuel College, Cambridge.[9] "That's a lot to live down, isn't it?" John Gardner had observed, when the two first met in 1953.[10] But Pifer's background, leavened by four years of service in the Second World War, during which he had been decorated for bravery in the Battle of the Bulge in Europe, seems to have been more empowering than burdensome. After completing his studies at Cambridge, he remained in England as the administrator of the newly established Fulbright exchange program between the United States and Great Britain, then came home and had the self-assurance to arrive at the Corporation's office looking for work without an appointment or an introduction. He obtained a place on the staff with a title and salary significantly below what he believed he deserved, but stayed on, assuming that he would soon receive a more appropriate status and paycheck. Most telling, perhaps, having heard of difficulties the Corporation had had with its board of trustees, he was now determined to develop a close, collaborative working relationship.

A keen advocate of strong professional staffs in foundation administration, Pifer knew that toward the end of Charles Dollard's presidency the trustees had tried to reassume considerable (Pifer thought excessive) power in initiating grants, and that John Gardner had worked hard to keep this from happening. He also knew that, however much its membership had changed over the years, traditionally the Corporation's board had been on the conservative side socially and politically. After his first speech to the trustees at a board meeting in 1959 in which he described grants to African universities, an older trustee had remarked: "I believe these fellows are just down out of the trees."[11] Pifer had been shocked. Despite that, however, even as acting president he had encouraged more active trustee participation in discussions of the foundation's program. "I felt that although life . . . would be easier for us if the board did not show too great an interest, this would prove to be a fundamental weakness," he commented in 1968.[12]

Beginning in 1970, Pifer also made the diversification of the Corporation's board of trustees a major goal. Until then, the trustees had all been white, Protestant, and male, with the exception of Mrs. Andrew Carnegie and her daughter (see appendix 1); by 1979, there were nearly as many women as men and several blacks, Hispanics, and Jews. Since most trustees still shared important social characteristics, including advanced educational credentials, professional careers, and middle- or upper-class status economically, the board actually remained quite homogeneous. But Pifer's steps toward diversity were significant for a foundation that had so long remained a WASP male preserve. They acknowledged a changing, more participatory politics across the nation and facilitated Pifer's efforts to win approval for some innovative, even risky, grants.

Integral to the personal assurance evident in Pifer's actions was a pronounced clarity of principle concerning what was fair, just, and democratic. One could see this in the Corporation's annual reports, for which Pifer, following Gardner's practice, wrote general introductory essays throughout his years as president. Perhaps less stunning in their literary craft than Gardner's essays had been, Pifer's were notable for moral earnestness and, at times, a didactic tone. Not at all ambiguous about what was right and wrong in the world, the essays bespoke the sure commitment of a lifelong liberal. They were grounded in traditional, middle-class, American values—in Gunnar Myrdal's "American creed," which Pifer frequently alluded to—and they took as given the value of private initiatives in policy-making.

In keeping with this, one of the most recurrent themes of Pifer's annual essays was foundation philanthropy. The Corporation's president believed that foundations were a "great social invention which has done . . . much for American life and, indeed, for mankind."[13] He was troubled by the 1960s investigations of foundations that were sponsored, first, by a committee led by Texas Congressman Wright Patman under the authority of the House Small Business Committee, and then by the House Ways and Means Committee, chaired by Arkansas Congressman Wilbur Mills. A strong advocate of accountability for foundations, Pifer was eager to ensure that these investigations did not proceed in an ill-informed and hostile atmosphere. With that in mind, he became one of the foundations' leading interpreters and defenders and often used his annual essays to advance their cause.

Pifer's essays called attention to the importance of pluralism in a democratic society and to the inextricable relationships he saw among pluralism, freedom, and private institutions. The essays frequently discussed the importance of accountability, which Pifer saw as the indispensable obverse of the freedom granted to private institutions. Over and over again, the essays also underscored the danger of ignorance and complacency to institutions and ideas vital to American society. Beginning in 1971, with "The Responsibility for Reform in Higher Education," his essays dealt in addition with the principles he believed essential to major Corporation initiatives—in this instance, those relevant to the Carnegie Commission on Higher Education. Whether the topic was working women, black Americans, children and youth, or Hispanics and bilingual education, Pifer made clear that his agenda at the Corporation was to further "four basic principles: the right to a job for anyone who needs to or wants to work; equal opportunity and fair rewards for everyone in all sectors of employment; development and utilization of the abilities of every citizen; and maximum flexibility for each person in the organization of his or her own pattern of life."[14] As he explained in 1973, in a personal reminiscence of twenty years at the Corporation, "the commitment to social justice . . . is a fundamental theme now running through all of the Corporation's programs. . . . I see no prospect of this slackening off, at any rate not while I am in a position to have some influence on the Corporation's sense of direction. My own belief in the right of every human being to enjoy equal opportunity, equal respect and equal justice before the law is a deeply held conviction, and I could no longer be at ease in an organization not firmly committed to seeking these ends in American life."[15] The Corporation's ninth president was a moral man whose belief in liberalism was strong and deep.

If principles and values as clear and certain as these naturally supported the personal assurance one could see in Pifer's behavior, they also reinforced a third characteristic that made the recommendations of the 1967 Task Force on the Disadvantaged congenial to him. This was his preference for an activist, problem-oriented approach to philanthropy. Although by 1968 Pifer confessed to a somewhat greater sense of caution than he had felt earlier, he still thought foundations should have "entrepreneurial qualities" and "not [be] afraid of publicity . . . [or] controversy."[16] He claimed that "one of the important aspects of foundation work . . . is . . . being able to combine money and ideas and organizational ability and working with outside groups (universities, private agencies and so on) in causing some things to happen that might not otherwise happen."[17] He was eager to involve the Corporation directly in policy-making and reform campaigns.

Less intellectual than John Gardner, Pifer was more of an activist. Unlike many of his Carnegie Corporation colleagues, he did not hold an advanced degree and had not worked in a university. Florence Anderson, who served as secretary of the Carnegie Corporation under both Gardner and Pifer, said that Gardner's more academic orientation led him to an interest in making a difference in the long run, whereas Pifer's more practical orientation led him to an interest in more immediate results. Gardner preferred to finance research, according to Anderson, and was content to leave the implementation of the research results to others; Pifer, by contrast, was eager to help translate research into programs that could provide tangible assistance to those in greatest need.[18] Confirming Anderson's observations, Pifer himself explained later that there had always been "a tension between [foundation] staff members who [were] interested in supporting social science research for the sake of research . . . and people like myself who were only interested in policy-oriented research."[19]

One might note parenthetically that Gardner may not have been quite as distant from activism as Pifer and other Corporation colleagues sometimes seem to have believed. During his last years at the Corporation, Gardner had apparently been interested in developing a new organization, to be called the "Committee on America's Future," that would "generate ideas for major studies of American life that needed doing and [that] would play a role in helping get these studies going."[20] The Corporation's trustees had not liked Gardner's suggestion. They believed the functions of the new committee would overlap with those of the Corporation itself; as a result, planning for a "Committee on America's Future" had not gone forward. But Gardner's idea exemplified the kind of active, engaged public role Pifer thought foundations should assume. During Pifer's first years as president, developing blueprints for federal action became a central Corporation strategy.[21]

A Carnegie Commission on Educational Television

When Pifer became acting president, the possibility of establishing a Carnegie commission to study the problems of educational television had already been raised with, and approved in principle by, the Corporation's board of trustees. The original proponents of the idea were Ralph Lowell, a Boston banker and chairman of the board of Boston station WGBH, and C. Scott Fletcher, former president of the Fund for Adult Education and, as of 1964, president of the Educational Television Stations division of the National Association of Educational Broadcasters. Both men were longtime supporters of educational television as a politically viable alternative to the lowbrow programs that had come to predominate on American television.

Advocates of educational television were aware that, despite Herbert Hoover's assurances to the contrary, the "possibility for service and for news and for entertainment and education" inherent in the television medium had been "drowned in advertising . . . chatter."[22] Dominated by commercial interests, American television was superficial, critics maintained—no better, as sociologist Edward Shils once put it, than "the childishness of the comic strips, the triviality of the press, the meanness of the luridly bound paperback."[23] Whether the inferior quality was a necessary attribute of all popular media of culture remained moot. It had been greatly troubling to some people that live theater and high-quality news reports like Edward R. Murrow's "See It Now" were taken from the air in the late 1950s in favor of quiz shows, situation comedies, and Westerns.[24]

But, along with critics, television had defenders, including, during the mid-1960s, the President and Vice President of the United States. Because Lady Bird Johnson continued to own radio and television stations in Texas even after her husband's election to the presidency, Lyndon Johnson preferred not to speak publicly on the subject. But Vice President Hubert Humphrey, who had once aligned himself with Newton Minow, the FCC chairman who described television as a "vast wasteland," did not feel called upon to exhibit such restraint. "I'm no snob, I like television," he announced. Likely reflecting the President's views, Humphrey maintained that television was "the greatest single achievement in communication that anybody or any area of the world has ever known."[25] Others were less extreme in their defense of the medium. Lee Loevinger, a controversial FCC commissioner who opposed increased government regulation, said that television was "the literature of the illiterate; the culture of the low-brow; the wealth of the poor; the privilege of the underprivileged; the exclusive club of the excluded masses . . . a golden goose that lays scrambled eggs."[26]

Within this context, it was perhaps not surprising that the federal agency charged with regulating the television industry, the Federal Communications Commission, seemed unwilling or unable to stand up to the commercial interests. Regulatory weakness reflected the history of television in the United States, where, thanks to physics and economics, television broadcasting had come of age dominated by three large commercial corporations—ABC, CBS, and NBC.[27] Powerful by virtue of the advertising markets they controlled, the networks had become even more powerful as television had become more important to electoral success and as, in reaction, elected officials had become more fearful of the networks' displeasure. Still, some public figures and some FCC commissioners were willing to face down the networks despite their power and influence. FCC Chairman E. William Henry had done this in 1963 when he tried to limit the time devoted to advertisements. But he had been defeated by industry pressure, congressional opposition, and a lack of agreement among members of the FCC. Unlike Henry, most people preferred to avoid confrontation.[28]

Owing to this, educational television easily became a matter of bipartisan, nonpolitical, "public" concern. Though opposed to increased regulation, the networks were not opposed to the development of alternative channels for instructional and cultural use. Alternative educational channels could satisfy demands for "excellence," without necessitating more public service or less popular (and less lucrative) entertainment on the commercial channels. To cultural liberals, who favored the popularization of culture so long as there was no diminution of traditional high standards, it was both impossible to cede the broadcast media in their entirety to the kitsch of "I Love Lucy" and "Gunsmoke," and impractical to try to strengthen the FCC. Cultural liberals were ambivalent at best on the merits of regulation, which could threaten liberties guaranteed under the Constitution. For all these reasons, educational television also made sense to them.

Taking the lead as the initial architects of educational television, cultural liberals believed that entertainment and education could and should coexist on the television spectrum. No one would want to watch educational television all the time, they maintained, and no one could "subsist and prosper on the standard commercial diet of gunpowder and pie."[29] As one advocate explained, "people who like to read enjoy Dostoevsky and detective stories; but people who read *only* detective stories remain blind to the depth of insight, the levels of taste, the glimpses of grandeur, that lend the greatest zest and interest to the career of being alive."[30]

Brokering funds from the Ford Foundation and its subsidiaries, the Fund for Adult Education and the Fund for the Advancement of Education, and then from the federal government (initially through the 1962 ETV Facilities Act), the champions of educational television helped launch more than one hundred stations by the mid-1960s. But the enterprise they built remained woefully underfinanced and technologically immature. In 1964, FCC Chairman E. William Henry went so far as to describe it as an "electronic Appalachia."[31] Established "as a means of eliminating cultural poverty—of making knowledge and enlightenment, culture and beauty, stimulation and controversy available to everyone who cares for them, and not merely to an elite," the educational stations had not even begun to realize their aspirations, he maintained.[32]

With this in mind, Ralph Lowell and Scott Fletcher set to work to organize a national commission "to investigate the financial structure that supports all aspects of educational television."[33] Because, as a senator, Lyndon Johnson had played an important role in facilitating passage of the 1962 ETV Facilities Act, Lowell and Fletcher hoped he would now agree to empanel a presidential commission. Owing to potential embarrassment from Lady Bird's ownership of broadcasting properties, however, Johnson had no wish to do so. He favored the commission idea, but wanted it established under private auspices. Already a trusted Johnson adviser, John Gardner was therefore asked if the Carnegie Corporation might support the investigation. Raising the question as "an unscheduled item" at an executive meeting of the Corporation's board of trustees on April 21, 1965, Gardner won unanimous approval for it.[34]

Thereafter, events moved quickly. In June 1965 Gardner reported to his Carnegie Corporation colleagues that the prospects for a commission were "shaping up pretty well. . . . The W[hite] H[ouse] has provided presidential endorsement and CC has the money."[35] Three months later, and a month after Gardner had become Secretary of HEW, it was decided that the Corporation would serve directly as sponsor for the study—"a new move for CC," staff member Arthur L. Singer observed.[36] Before the year was out, James R. Killian, chairman of the M.I.T. Corporation, had agreed to serve as chairman, with fourteen other prominent individuals on the commission. Selected by Corporation personnel, all had been informally approved by the White House. Although Alan Pifer remembered only one commissioner whose appointment was requested by the White House—J. C. Kellam, the manager of Lady Bird Johnson's television and radio stations—Leonard Marks, an old Johnson confidant, family attorney, and then director of the U.S. Information Service, remembered one other, Oveta Culp Hobby, chairman of the board of the Houston Post Company and a person Lyndon Johnson respected and trusted.[37]

Initially convened early in 1966, the commission held eight formal, full meetings, received testimony from 225 individuals or organizations, and visited ninety-two educational television stations in thirty-five states. By January 1967, its final report (in both hardcover and paperbound editions) was ready for release, with publicity and dissemination arranged by Tom Carskadon, a public relations consultant. The next month Johnson recommended passage of the Public Broadcasting Act of 1967 in his State of the Union Message. After congressional hearings, Johnson signed the act into law in November 1967.

The central conclusion of the Killian Commission was that public television—a term invented by the commission to describe programs "not economic for commercial sponsorship, . . . not designed for the classroom [or instructional television], and . . . directed at audiences ranging from the tens of thousands to the occasional tens of millions"—was an idea that was "ready for immediate action."[38] In consequence, of its twelve recommendations, the one that advocated "that Congress act promptly to authorize and to establish a federally chartered, nonprofit, nongovernmental corporation, to be known as the 'Corporation for Public Television,' " was the most important.[39] Although some of the commission's other recommendations were not translated into policy—most important, its proposal for a manufacturer's excise tax on television sets—this one was. The concept of a public television system supervised by an independent corporation was officially adopted within less than two years of its formulation.

Obviously, questions can be raised about the propriety and prudence of such close collaboration between the White House and the Carnegie Corporation, especially when the collaboration pertained to an issue of potential personal interest and gain to the President, and at a time when the Corporation's chief executive had just assumed high federal office. Queries also could be posed about the enduring value of concentrating on recommendations that were ready for "immediate action"— put otherwise, that already had support sufficient or nearly sufficient to become legislation—as opposed to studying more enduring, less actionable problems. Some of the enduring problems left aside by the Killian Commission could not be ignored by the Carnegie Commission on the Future of Public Broadcasting, chaired by William J. McGill, president of Columbia University, which was established in 1978 because "the invention [i.e., public broadcasting] did not work, or at least not very well."[40] Among these problems was that of how to popularize arts, news, and instructional materials without the appearance of "solemnity, complacency, narrowness of social frame, and political and intellectual timidity."[41] Overlooked earlier, in the Corporation's cultural programs of the 1920s and 1930s, this question could not be resolved by a commission, although it was inescapable if efforts to disseminate culture beyond the already cultivated were to be effective.

But if the shortcomings of the Carnegie Commission on Educational Television became evident with time, its accomplishments were immediately clear. The swift action of the commission, followed quickly by passage of federal legislation enacting its most essential recommendation, was a remarkable achievement. Few transfers from a foundation to the federal government, or from private design to public policy, could have more fully exemplified the strategic philanthropic style that the Carnegie Corporation first began to develop immediately after the Second World War and practiced with increasing pointedness thereafter.

Demonstrating the kind of public activism he believed in, Alan Pifer commended the members of the Killian Commission at a dinner in March 1967 where he described their work as one of the Corporation's "greatest achievements."[42] But he also noted that there was still "a considerable job to be done . . . in bringing to the masses of Americans an understanding that public television is for everyone, not just for those with refined aesthetic and intellectual tastes."[43] Foreshadowing his growing concern for greater access to the institutions of American society, that priority found its way onto the agenda of another Carnegie commission—the Carnegie Commission on Higher Education.

A Carnegie Commission on Higher Education

Just as the Carnegie Commission on Educational Television had initially coalesced around problems of finance, so did this new panel, although its scope broadened rapidly. Most important, just as the Carnegie Commission on Educational Television had embraced the goals of cultural liberals, in the process choosing to work toward better programming for television without fundamental changes in the structure of the communications industry, so in somewhat similar fashion would the Carnegie Commission on Higher Education work for an expansion but not a redesign of the essential structure of the American system of higher education.

Announced in January 1967, the Carnegie Commission on Higher Education was primarily financed by the Carnegie Corporation, although it was sponsored by the Carnegie Foundation for the Advancement of Teaching. Owing partly to miscalculations in the costs of pensioning and partly to a discrepancy in purpose, or more accurately, to Henry Pritchett's insistence upon carrying out educational surveys in addition to providing pensions, the CFAT had been virtually bankrupt since the 1920s.[44] Thereafter, as Alan Pifer explained in a 1971 memorandum, it was only because of periodic financial support from the Carnegie Corporation, and because its board of trustees was composed of prominent college and university presidents, that the CFAT had been successful.[45] By 1965, however, the Foundation's pension load had been reduced to the point where the CFAT could begin to meet its own commitments and begin repayment of Corporation loans, which over the years had amounted to $14.6 million, in addition to grants of $24.5 million. Because the trustees and officers of the Corporation wanted to help reestablish the CFAT as a viable foundation independent of the Corporation, they preferred that the loans to the CFAT actually *not* be repaid. In consequence, it was decided in 1965 that the Corporation would make annual grants to the Foundation in the approximate amount of Foundation repayments. This meant that the CFAT had approximately one million dollars a year to spend, which both the Corporation and the Foundation agreed should be used to support a multiyear, multivolume study of higher education.

According to a September 1966 memorandum prepared for Pifer, the mid-1960s were "a propitious time to launch a new and comprehensive study of the future financing of higher education."[46] This was because colleges and universities were facing a host of new pressures and expectations, ranging from "the development of a national belief that . . . all young people capable of benefitting by higher education [should] be persuaded to continue their education beyond the high school," to a reliance upon universities by all segments of society for new knowledge.[47] Convinced of this argument, the Foundation's trustees discussed the possibility of a study of higher education at their annual meeting in November 1966.[48] By December, planning for a study had proceeded to the point where Clark Kerr, president of the University of California, was approached as a possible chairman of the study commission. His subsequent firing by the California Board of Regents, which Pifer considered utterly unwarranted and peremptory, led to quick action to appoint the other fourteen members of the panel. A Carnegie commission to "study the future structure and financing of U.S. higher education" was announced to the press on January 24, 1967.[49]

Within the Corporation, major responsibility for working with the new commission was assigned to E. Alden Dunham, a program officer for higher education who also served as secretary of the CFAT. (To limit administrative expense for the CFAT, Corporation officers also served as Foundation officers throughout the 1950s, 1960s, and 1970s—in effect, the CFAT had been a wholly owned subsidiary.) Previously, Dunham had served as director of admissions at Princeton University and before that, from 1958 until 1962, as a staff assistant to J. B. Conant. A great admirer of Conant's, Dunham also became a great admirer of Kerr's. This was not at all surprising, since Kerr shared a basic similarity of view with the earlier Carnegie-supported educational statesman. Doubtless a result of a variety of factors, this similarity derived in part from Kerr's intellectual indebtedness to the writings of Joseph A. Schumpeter, who had participated in the same Pareto Circle at Harvard in the 1940s that had helped (indirectly, through W. Lloyd Warner's writings) to define Conant's point of view.[50] That aside, Dunham was additionally impressed that, "really for the first time in our national history," there would be a group "to set forth a blueprint of what higher education in the U.S. *should* look like ten to twenty years from now."[51]

In fulfilling its mission, the commission was profoundly influenced by the orientation and views of its chairman. In fact, the commission based its many reports on higher education on the conception of "the federal grant university" that Kerr had developed in his 1963 Godkin Lectures, *The Uses of the University*. Finding in increased federal aid to higher education the key to university development over the previous twenty years and for the foreseeable future, Kerr maintained that the challenge for the future involved finding ways through more deliberate planning to ensure greater balance among competing interests within the academy. Above all else, ways had to be found, he said, to achieve what President Kennedy had described as an "aristocracy of achievement arising out of democracy of opportunity."[52]

Beginning with this utilitarian conception of education, the Carnegie Commission on Higher Education ranged across a great variety of issues, but its most essential concern was evident in its first report. Having held its first meeting in June 1967, the commission released the report in December 1968 under the title *Quality and Equality: New Levels of Federal Responsibility for Higher Education.* Building on the Higher Education Act of 1965, the report recommended that federal aid to higher education be increased substantially in amount and distributed through opportunity grants to individuals. This would greatly increase access to higher education without forcing changes in the institutional organization of the system. *Quality and Equality* called for student aid sufficient "to remove effectively the financial barriers which now prevent many qualified students from entering or continuing higher education."[53] But it left to the institutions and state authorities to determine whether other barriers, those inherent in admission standards, curricula, and graduation requirements, for example, should or should not remain.

Presented by Kerr to congressmen and cabinet officials and widely distributed to journalists, the commission's proposal was frequently described in headlines such as "GI bill to educate [the] poor."[54] As Fred Hechinger noted in the *New York Times,* because the proposal for student aid would appeal to so many parents, it was politically "shrewd." It would be "difficult for Congress to ignore [it]," Hechinger said.[55] Revised in June 1970, *Quality and Equality* was widely acknowledged as the source for the Basic Educational Opportunity Grants that Congress authorized in 1972. It also provided the blueprint for the Fund for the Improvement of Postsecondary Education set up by Congress in the same year.

No less effective than the Killian Commission had been in shaping government action, the Kerr Commission was seen as a triumph by those within the Corporation most closely associated with it. Even before it finished its work, therefore, Pifer queried the CFAT's trustees concerning the merits of continuing the venture. "As the work of the Carnegie Commission on Higher Education has progressed," he explained, "it has become clear that this undertaking represents the only sustained, comprehensive attempt there has ever been in this country to place the entire field of higher education under review and to formulate a coherent set of policy recommendations for its development. Although the Commission's work is not yet completed . . . there is ample evidence that it has achieved a position of influence, is being listened to and is serving a highly important national purpose."[56] As a result, it was decided to continue the venture under slightly different arrangements, once all the Commission's reports were completed. Beginning in 1973, therefore, a Carnegie Council for Policy Studies in Higher Education was established. Its chairman was again

230 Strategic Philanthropy

Clark Kerr, now a member of the CFAT board; a majority of the council's members were also members of that board. Also, the CFAT obtained legal authorization to function as an operating as opposed to a grant-making foundation, and the Council would hopefully serve it as a transitional "operating arm." If the experiment were successful, the council's policy-making function could then be institutionalized within the Foundation, as in fact occurred in November 1979, when Ernest Boyer replaced Pifer as president and Kerr as, in a sense, executive director.

The commission and the council cost the two Carnegie trusts approximately $12 million in all. They published scores of monographs and reports that counted, measured, categorized, described, and evaluated virtually every aspect of the nation's roughly three thousand colleges and universities. Although some observers believed the commission was more effective than the council, together they had considerable influence, not only on governmental action at the federal level, but also on policies at virtually every level of the higher education system, from individual campuses to state authorities.[57] Most important, perhaps, and most difficult to demonstrate with certainty, they helped stabilize higher education during ten years of protest, expansion, and change. In part, they were able to do this because their recommendations generally suggested the preservation of traditional standards of institutional rank and quality along with greater access to the system. In other words, Harvard or Berkeley could and should preserve the qualities that made them "elite," while the overall "system" was to become more democratic through expansion at the lower levels.[58] The commission's and the council's reports were rooted in Kerr's belief in "aristocracy of achievement arising out of democracy of opportunity."[59] It was a formula for moderate, even moderating, change.

"Sesame Street": *An Experiment with Television for Children*

While the Carnegie commission and council were addressing access to higher education, other projects financed with Carnegie dollars were confronting other problems of educational access and equal opportunity. "Sesame Street" was one of these. It originated from the same studies of children and early learning that had provided the intellectual justification for so many of the federal government's antipoverty programs, including those financed through Title I of ESEA.

J. McVicker Hunt's book *Intelligence and Experience* (1961), dem-

onstrating that intelligence, as measured by the I.Q., was not determined at birth and fixed thereafter, had had revolutionary implications.
Along with studies of cognitive development in young children conducted by Jerome Bruner and others, it focused attention on the importance of early childhood experience and on the relationship between
such experience and subsequent educational competence and achievement. Restudying hundreds of studies of young children, Benjamin
Bloom had confirmed the direction of this work in *Stability and Change
in Human Characteristics* (1964), concluding that, by the age of school
entrance, children had developed most of the intelligence they would
have at maturity—50 percent by the age of four and an additional 30
percent by the age of eight.[60]

Having helped to support a good deal of basic research in cognitive
psychology during the 1950s and early 1960s, the Corporation also
financed many subsequent experiments with early childhood and preschool education. According to a review published in its 1969 *Annual
Report,* it did so because, "along with so many other private and public
agencies, the foundation [in 1965] was seeking ways in which it could
best contribute to the elimination or reduction of poverty and inequality of opportunity. It was an obvious step, therefore, to try to build on
what was already known."[61]

These experiments varied considerably in orientation. Some were
essentially behaviorist, as was certainly true of the "intellectual pressure cooker for children from the slums" operated by Carl Bereiter and
Siegfried Engelmann at the University of Illinois in Urbana.[62] Here,
four- and five-year-old children were drilled to recognize, describe, and
differentiate among letters, colors, numbers, and shapes. According to
Maya Pines, a freelance writer who prepared a book about early
learning experiments for the Corporation, the goal was to "do systematically, and artificially, what middle-class parents do naturally at
home"; though very controversial, it appeared to work.[63] According
to J. McVicker Hunt, children enrolled in the program "gained about
one year of psycholinguistic ability" in a three-month period.[64] Dramatic gains were also evident in children who participated in programs
with a more "progressive" orientation. One of these, directed by Omar
K. Moore at the University of Pittsburgh, encouraged children to use
individually programmed talking typewriters to learn to read, write,
and even compose poetry at their own speed. Enriched kindergarten
programs, such as those developed by Martin Deutsch for disadvantaged children in New York City, also appeared to have positive results,
although the gains were often less evident on standard tests.

As Lloyd Morrisett, who had supervised many of the Corporation's grants relevant to early childhood learning and development, explained in an editorial for *Science,* by the mid-1960s the overall conclusion to be drawn from all these experiments was unmistakable.[65] Preschool education made a significant difference in the capacities children needed to do well in school and, presumably, in life. Reinforcing Morrisett's claim, Susan S. Stodolsky and Gerald Lesser concluded in 1967 that "only a few hardy souls will now maintain that intelligence tests measure something innate, fixed, and pre-determined." The psychological studies of the 1950s had proven beyond serious doubt, they said, that "a child's score [on an intelligence test] may be thought of as an indication of the richness of the milieu in which he functions and the extent to which he has been able to profit from that milieu."[66] The question, then, was not *whether* early childhood education should be available to all, but *how* to provide it. In 1966, 94 percent of the three-year-olds, 81 percent of the four-year-olds, and 26 percent of the five-year-olds in the United States were not enrolled in any school; *Time* magazine estimated in that year that the costs of providing instruction to the nation's four-year-olds would be approximately $2.75 billion.[67]

Concerned about this problem, Morrisett apparently raised it at a dinner party at the home of Timothy and Joan Ganz Cooney in February or March of 1966. In response to a claim that "television was going to be the great educator of the future," Morrisett reportedly asked if it could be used to educate young children.[68] His query intrigued Joan Cooney, then a producer of documentaries for WNDT/Channel 13; by June, she was at work on a feasibility study for the Carnegie Corporation, the purpose of which was "to find out whether television, a medium that can reach more children than any other method presently available, can offer children a head start on their education, open their lives to a wide variety of experiences, and make learning interesting and inviting."[69] The Cooney feasibility study was presented to the Corporation in October 1966. Arguing that television was already very widely watched by young children of all socioeconomic groups, and watched for significant periods of time, it recommended that "television's potential for fostering the intellectual and cultural development of young children be fully tested and evaluated in the near future."[70] Two years later, the establishment of a Children's Television Workshop (CTW) was announced to the press.

During the intervening two years, approximately $8 million was raised to support the project. Of this, 48.8 percent came from federal sources, mostly the U.S. Office of Education, which provided 40.6

percent of the total. Once again, the Corporation had developed a plan in the implementation of which the federal government would be significantly involved.[71] This was because Lloyd Morrisett, Joan Cooney (who left WNDT/Channel 13 to become a consultant to the Carnegie Corporation in May 1967), and Barbara Finberg, a Corporation program officer who was beginning to concentrate on early childhood education, had gone to Washington in June 1967, to see Harold Howe II, the U.S. Commissioner of Education. Well acquainted with many people at the Carnegie Corporation, including Morrisett, Howe had quickly become interested in the idea of a children's series. "Let's do it," Cooney remembered him saying at the end of their meeting.[72] Thereafter Howe became one of the project's most effective proponents. According to Finberg, "Howe took upon himself the job of spokesman and convener and negotiator."[73] Thanks to his endorsement and advocacy and to the persistence of Morrisett, Cooney, and Finberg, CTW began with a mix of public and private funds, both coming from different sources, including, in the private category, the Ford Foundation, which had initially denied Morrisett's request for assistance.

Before the formal announcement of the launching of CTW, Cooney was also selected as its executive director. Cooney's background was in documentary television production, not in children's programming. Her only formal training in education was at the undergraduate level: she had majored in education at the University of Arizona, from which she had been graduated in 1951. Furthermore, as a woman, she would not necessarily have been considered for the position. "It was not always assumed that she would be the project director," Finberg remembered. "The idea evolved as Joan did the feasibility study and . . . [as] it became more evident that she understood and had the vision of what the program could be, better than anyone else."[74] Cooney herself believed that she got the top place on the staff of the new show by winning the confidence of Lloyd Morrisett, who had dreamed up the idea of the show and been central in its development and organization as an institution, and who would become chairman of CTW's future board of trustees. "I didn't know exactly what my role was going to be in the early days," she said in 1972. "There was nothing in my record to indicate that I should be head of any project funded to the tune of $8 million. But Lloyd Morrisett had worked with me so long and so closely that he had no doubts."[75]

According to virtually all the people who joined the "Sesame Street" team, the choice of Cooney was critical. Gerald Lesser, for example, who was the Bigelow Professor of Education and Developmental Psychology at Harvard, and who became chairman of CTW's ten-member Board of Advisors, had had many previous requests to serve as a consultant to children's television programs, most of which had involved little more than lending his name and title. This had made him skeptical, when first approached by Cooney. "But Joan's request was different. She was serious," Lesser recalled. Combined with respect for Morrisett, whom he already knew, the impression Cooney made convinced Lesser that "it seemed worth a try."[76] His decision was significant because, according to Cooney, it was Lesser who made the difficult marriage between academics and television people so essential to "Sesame Street" work.[77]

The experience of David Connell, the former executive producer of "Captain Kangaroo," who became the first executive producer of "Sesame Street," was not different. Having survived more than ten years of the unrelenting grind of daily television production, he had moved on to a happy life as an independent film producer. He was making considerable money and enjoying himself, and was not eager to give it all up when Cooney approached him. But, like so many others, he was charmed by her and therefore agreed to help.[78] Attributing much of her idealism to having learned as a young woman "that if right thinking people don't get into mass communications the other kind will," Cooney apparently combined deep social commitments with unusual competence and charisma.[79] A near perfect complement to the earnest and laconic Morrisett, Cooney's more personable manner enabled her to recruit and effectively lead the many talented, independent people who got "Sesame Street" on the air.

Announced at a March 1968 press conference, "Sesame Street" was first broadcast on November 10, 1969. The long delay was intended to allow careful prebroadcast planning, a highly uncommon feature of children's television. In its second week the show was turned on in almost two million homes nationwide, according to Nielsen ratings; furthermore, since those ratings did not include households with annual incomes of less than $3,000, and planning for "Sesame Street" included special efforts to reach poor urban households, the Nielsen numbers were low.[80] According to a Louis Harris audience survey conducted for the Corporation for Public Broadcasting, "Sesame Street" was viewed in 47 percent of all households with children under six in 1970 and by 56 percent in 1972.[81] Projected from the first as an experiment—Martin Mayer described it "the largest educational experiment ever"—"Sesame Street" obtained ratings much larger than initially expected by the program's planners.[82]

Despite this success, it was not the ratings that were of primary interest to the teams of evaluators employed to study CTW's first program. To them, the question was: Did children learn? Led by Edward L. Palmer, an internal research team asked this question in a variety of formative evaluation studies designed to enhance the program's instructional effectiveness. Using a machine called a "distractor," they sought to determine which segments of the program held the attention of viewers and which did not. Under the leadership of Samuel Ball of the Educational Testing Service in Princeton, N.J., the external evaluation team asked:

1. Do 3- through 5-year-old children who view *Sesame Street* at home or in classrooms learn more than comparable children who do not view the show?
2. Of those children who watch the show, what characterizes the children who learn most and least from the show?
3. Is the show effective among various subgroups of 3- through 5-year-old children—for example, boys and girls, lower and middle class children, heavy and light viewers, high and low achieving children.
4. Inasmuch as *Sesame Street* adopted a magazine-style format, what elements in the show seemed to be most effective in terms of attention holding and amount learned?[83]

The answers to these questions filled a 373-page monograph. Generally, they indicated that "Sesame Street" was effective as a medium of preschool instruction. More specifically, the ETS evaluation team found that:

—Children who watched the most learned the most. . . .
—The skills that received the most time and attention on the program itself were, with rare exceptions, the skills that were best learned. . . .
—The program did not require formal adult supervision in order for children to learn in the areas the program covered. . . .
—Children learned more the more they watched [regardless of] . . . age, sex, geographic location, socioeconomic status (SES), mental age (intelligence), and whether children watched at home or at school.[84]

These findings, especially the last, suggested to the ETS team that while "Sesame Street" could be helpful to all children, under certain conditions it could help overcome educational disadvantages. Even though educationally disadvantaged children might rank lower on pretest measures than advantaged children, if they watched the program more often than advantaged children, they would gain more. Hence, the differences between the two groups might diminish by the time they enrolled in school.

Of course, as the ETS evaluators were careful to suggest, "Sesame Street" did not teach all the attitudes, values, and skills necessary to adequate performance in first grade. Although its prebroadcast development had involved a complicated and unusual collaboration among educators, psychologists, television producers, writers, musicians, puppeteers, public relations people, and fund-raisers, many of its key elements derived from Joan Cooney's first feasibility study for the Carnegie Corporation, which had drawn heavily upon research previously funded by the Corporation. Recalling the study, Cooney told an interviewer in 1972:

What I did for the study was go around the country seeing all the important cognitive psychologists. Carnegie gave me the initial list of the psychologists they wanted me to see. I expanded it to some extent, but I operated primarily from their list. I had no bias when I began. . . . I felt keenly the needs of the disadvantaged child. I was a very big supporter of [Martin] Deutsch. . . . I didn't think then, and I don't think now, that the total child should be ignored in order to develop his brain. But I felt his brain had been ignored, always, by the traditionists in favor of his emotional and physical development. I was terribly interested in disadvantaged children learning to read in school, and getting them enough of a start early on.[85]

In light of Cooney's views and the cognitive slant of many Carnegie-funded psychological studies, it was not surprising that "Sesame Street" also had a cognitive orientation. Although somewhat modified and elaborated in meetings of the educational advisers, writers, and producer, the program's "minimum educational aims" did not diverge significantly from the ones Cooney had initially derived from a list of skills developed by Carl Bereiter and Siegfried Engelmann in *Teaching Disadvantaged Children in Preschool*.[86] Although Jack Gould of the *New York Times* reported after CTW's first press conference that the organization wished "to avoid the blackboard" in order first to nuture children's "latent curiosity to learn," according to Morrisett, "From the beginning our emphasis was on cognitive goals. The basic emphasis. The affective goals were not those the project was formed around."[87]

The "Sesame Street" emphasis on cognitive achievement was criticized by some. The educational commentator John Holt claimed, for example, that the program was too much like school. "The program asks, 'How can we get children ready to learn what the schools are going to teach them?', instead of 'How can we help them learn what the schools may *never* teach them?'"[88] But the more telling criticisms had to do with the program's capacity to help some children catch up with their so-called "advantaged" peers. A controversial secondary analysis of the ETS evaluation of "Sesame Street" led by Thomas D. Cook and sponsored by the Russell Sage Foundation concluded that, contrary to the ETS claims, the program was, if anything, "increasing achievement gaps [between advantaged and disadvantaged children] in those domains where it effectively teaches."[89] The finding was not surprising, since Louis Harris and his associates had discovered that more white than black households tuned in to the show, and that there was a direct correlation between education levels and frequency of viewing (the more educated the household, the more "Sesame Street" was watched); futhermore, viewing was a necessary condition for gains.[90] However, according to CTW's Edward L. Palmer, the goal of narrowing the gap between advantaged and disadvantaged was dropped between initial planning for the program and actual broadcasting. The consensus had been, Palmer stated, "that a television series available to all children could not be expected to serve as a vehicle for 'compensatory education.' "[91] In consequence, Palmer (and others at CTW) believed the criticism advanced by Cook was misguided. They felt evaluations had to be concerned with correlations between goals and outcomes, if they were to be at all valid.

Whether Palmer's criticism of Cook's criticisms was sound—after all, whatever the goals shared among the program's initial production force, the ETS evaluators had claimed that "in terms of attainments, *Sesame Street* helped to close the gap between advantaged and disadvantaged children"—the Cook evaluation only confirmed what the inventors of "Sesame Street" had known from the very beginning.[92] As Lloyd Morrisett observed in 1974: "*Sesame Street* is not 'the answer' to early education problems or to deficiencies in children's television programming. It is one effort and a more successful one than we originally dreamed, to use television to benefit children's development."[93] He was aware, as were Joan Cooney and the people at the Carnegie Corporation, that "the real answer to problems of early education is for the total culture of childhood, including television as an important element, to work in harmony with the family and later the school. The environment in which children live needs to foster constructive cognitive and emotional growth from birth onwards."[94] But how to do that? The problem had to be investigated, if the Corporation were to pursue its interests in fostering equal opportunity and in lessening poverty and disadvantage, and the strategy used was again a Carnegie panel. This one was called the Carnegie Council on Children.

All Our Children: *The Report of Another Carnegie Council*

The possibility of organizing an advisory group to study what Morrisett had termed "the culture of childhood" was first discussed within the Corporation during the summer of 1970. Having read a study of child-rearing in the U.S.S.R. and the United States by Urie Bronfenbrenner and having spent part of the summer in the Soviet Union, Alan Pifer had become newly concerned about the education of American children. His reaction is not difficult to understand. It would have been hard to read Bronfenbrenner's study and not be troubled. A Cornell University psychologist and one of the architects of Head Start, Bronfenbrenner had found that, in comparison with the Soviet Union, American society was segregated not only by race and class but also by age. From this he had concluded that, "if the institutions of our society continue to remove parents, other adults, and older youth from active participation in the lives of children . . . *we can anticipate increased alienation, indifference, antagonism, and violence on the part of the younger generation in all segments of our society— middle-class children as well as the disadvantaged.*"[95] Combined with this dire prophecy was the suggestion that changes would be needed in the classroom, school, family, neighborhood, and larger community, to address the existing impoverishment caused by age segregation.

Compelling in presentation and argument, and apparently confirmed by what Pifer observed in the Soviet Union, Urie Bronfenbrenner's study led Pifer to write a memorandum to Barbara Finberg and David Z. Robinson, who became vice president of the Carnegie Corporation in the summer of 1970, telling them of his concern that too much was being asked of the schools. "While education," he began, "has been construed rather narrowly to mean what takes place in schools, the schools, paradoxically, have been expected to discharge a wide range of responsibilities having to do with a variety of aspects of child development not traditionally considered part of education." What was needed, therefore, was more attention to all aspects of child development and to the ways in which a variety of institutions might provide help and support to children. Said Pifer: "Part of the great significance of *Sesame Street* is that it did break out of the narrow and confining bounds of the school and look more broadly to what else might readily be available to influence child development constructively."[96]

In addition to this initial observation, the Corporation's president placed two additional thoughts before Finberg and Robinson: first, "that the breakdown of the American family as a basic educational institution . . . may now have reached such an advanced stage as to make it most unlikely that the family will ever be able to reassume its former educational role"; and second, that, in the face of family decline, society would have to assume "primary responsibility for socialization of the young." From this diagnosis, Pifer moved on to suggest a commission including both specialists and "broad gauged laymen" to prepare a status report on U.S. children; develop a taxonomy of objectives for bringing up children, "given the realities of today's world"; describe how these objectives *could* be met "irrespective of present conventions, myths, prejudices, institutions, etc."; and make proposals for more immediately possible but eventually complementary reforms.[97] Seven years and approximately $2.7 million later, the final report of the Carnegie Council on Children appeared. Entitled *All Our Children: The American Family under Pressure*, it developed an agenda for public policy that followed logically from Pifer's original mandate. Aspects of that agenda could be interpreted as being at odds with the Corporation's liberal charter and tradition. The Carnegie Council on Children represented movement by the Corporation to a broader conception of liberal reform than it had tended to accept earlier.

After proposing the idea of a commission and securing trustee concurrence, Pifer turned the responsibility for its development over to Barbara Finberg. A 1949 graduate of Stanford University who had joined the Corporation's staff in a part-time editorial position in 1959, Finberg had developed considerable expertise in the domain of early childhood education. After familiarizing herself with the recommendations of other advisory groups focusing on the problems of children, she presented the panel idea to her staff colleagues in January 1971. Thereafter, while continuing to engage the full Corporation staff in discussion, she began to consult people outside the Corporation; by January 1972 with Pifer's full concurrence she was ready to ask Kenneth Keniston to investigate the feasibility of a panel on children. Following the pattern of "Sesame Street," the study that led to the Carnegie Council on Children was to be carried out by someone who, just as Cooney had not been an expert in children's television, was not an expert on young children.

Kenneth Keniston was a professor of psychiatry at the Yale University School of Medicine who was well known for several books on adolescent development, notably *Young Radicals: Notes on Committed Youth* (1968) and *The Uncommitted: Alienated Youth in American Society* (1965). Born in 1930 in Chicago, Illinois, and educated at

Harvard and at Bailliol College, Oxford, where he had studied first as a
Rhodes Scholar and then as a candidate for a Ph.D. (1956), Keniston had
taught at Harvard before moving to Yale in 1962. (Before the council
finished its work, Keniston moved again to M.I.T.) In 1969, when the
Carnegie Commission on Higher Education had been criticized for not
being representative (most of the original members were white, middle-
class, middle-aged, and male), Keniston had been asked to join the panel
to represent student views. A man of impressive credentials, whose competence in a panel situation was known to the Corporation through the
Kerr Commission, Keniston could use his colleagues at Yale as a sound-
ing board to test the children's commission idea.

To do this, Keniston met biweekly with a seminar examining what
questions about children a panel might address. At the same time,
Finberg began to develop a list of possible commission members. The
group that resulted was purposefully small—eleven people in all, including Keniston. Moreover, unlike both the Carnegie Commission
on Higher Education and the Carnegie Commission on Educational
Television, it was diverse—both male and female; black, white, and
Hispanic; geographically spread throughout the country; and in terms
of professions, heavily academic (six held university faculty appointments), though law, medicine, and the League of Women Voters were
represented. The name had been changed from "Carnegie Commission" to "Carnegie Council on Children" to take account of Keniston's
belief that the term *commission* "conjures up images of Eisenhower,
Kerner, Scranton, etc., and requires a lengthy discussion of what this
group will not be."[98] The panel held its first meeting in Wellfleet,
Massachusetts, in September 1972. Thereafter its seven-member staff,
led by Keniston, now on leave from his regular duties at Yale, set to
work gathering data and drafting material for subsequent council
discussions.

After its first seven months in operation, Keniston reported to the
Carnegie Corporation that the council had agreed its essential task was
to show the interrelationship between and among distinct problems
affecting children. He also noted: "Large areas of consensus have
emerged in the Council's discussions so far: e.g., the conviction that
America's 'child-centeredness' is largely mythical when it comes to
effective action to help 'other people's' children; a willingness to consider the need for basic changes in American society if it is truly to
nurture the next generations; a firm rejection of a romantic view of the
American past. Areas of disagreement have also begun to be debated:
e.g., whether poverty-related problems affecting children would best

be solved through income redistribution, direct provision of services, or job creation; whether market mechanisms are adequate for the provision of services to children; what are the limits of legitimate public intervention in the lives of individual families, and so on."[99] After this, the council continued to meet six to eight times a year, usually for three days, in a variety of locations around the nation, each meeting focusing upon a different set of issues, with different guests in attendance. The staff was also increased in order to undertake a variety of background research studies on topics as diverse as how families and children are affected by television, why people decide to have children, and how schools have been shaped by social and political forces.[100]

Not all went smoothly during the three years of the council's operations. In 1973 at least one staff member objected to "the ostentatiousness of our meetings' life-style." To discuss poverty at elegant restaurants and resorts was "hypocritical," it was charged.[101] The next year, Florence Anderson, who as Corporation secretary was responsible for reviewing projects before continuing installments on grants were paid, told Finberg that she was worried about the organization of what seemed to be an ever-increasing staff: "Who is in charge here? . . . I need more information."[102] Subsequently, tension arose concerning whether staff members were to think of themselves as independent scholars or as assistants to the members of the council.[103] Despite all this, the council's main report was ready for publication early in 1977.

"In the United States," it asserted at the outset, "when we look at children and plan policies and programs in their behalf, we usually neglect . . . the social and economic influences that define and limit the range of choices parents of every social level can make for their offspring."[104] *All Our Children* then went on to puncture the myths that had sustained such myopic vision—especially the myth of the self-sufficient family—and to suggest policies that would help discount the forces working against parental choice. Beginning with an analysis of changes in the family, of "the stacked deck" facing poor and nonwhite families and those with handicapped children (the council estimated these to be a quarter to a third of all American families), and of the often destructive influence of technology (food additives no less than television) on American children, *All Our Children* presented a variety of recommendations, including a full-employment policy and income supports, expanded and better integrated social services for families, and increased health and legal services for children. The report's final chapter, "Converting Commitment into Politics," ended with a statement labeled "A Vision of the Possible":

. . . The society we imagine would be one that put children first. . . .

The society we want would be one where no parent able to work suffered the stigma and degradation of not being able to provide for his or her family.

It would be a society where being a parent would be seen as an honorable calling, a form of work as worthy of public support as the defense of the nation or the construction of superhighways.

It would be a society where every child would have a chance . . . limited only by ability and aspirations.

It would be a society where more children survived to adulthood, and where more adults enjoyed more robust physical vitality.

It would be a society where parents had available to them the kinds of help they needed and where they had a powerful voice in every institution affecting them and their children.

It would be a society where present excessive inequalities of income, power, and dignity were much reduced.

It would be a society where the rights of parents and children were more adequately represented in the courts and throughout the land.

It would be, in short, a society that took seriously and had translated into its basic outlooks and policies today's rhetoric that claims children to be our "most precious natural resource" and calls families "the building blocks of our society." Such a nation would, we believe, be a better society for all Americans, which is precisely as it must be if we are to do a better job for all our children.[105]

Predictably, perhaps, there was considerable media coverage of the report. Having early decided that dissemination and publicity were critical to the venture, the council (with help from the Corporation) had concentrated a great deal of time, effort, and money on plans for reaching different audiences. This was considered necessary because, as Peter O. Almond, one of the council's associate directors, explained, "children aren't considered 'hot topics' for the media," unless the story is associated with scandal.[106] Be that as it may, with a full-time staff working on dissemination, *All Our Children* did win comments, which tended to be predictable. According to Almond, experts in children's policy tended to find the study too visionary and not sufficiently illuminating concerning next steps. Thus Edward Zigler, the administrator of Head Start, noted: "The Carnegie Council on Children has performed a service by lending its name and weight to the call for a more just economic system in the interest of families and especially of children. . . . [But] I would have welcomed a bit less vision . . . and more concrete proposals on how to go about the difficult task of making even a piece of that vision a reality."[107] Other commentators who were not so eager for blueprints tended either to like the report because it was compassionate and humane, or to dislike it for political or ideological reasons.[108] Thus, conservatives tended to see the report as a simplistic endorsement of the "failed" policies of the 1960s, while radicals tended to believe that the council's call for more services for families was an implicit endorsement of professions and professionalism, which they thought had helped cause the family's disintegration in the first place.[109]

In 1979, when the council's other report, *Small Futures: Children, Inequality and the Limits of Liberal Reform* by Richard deLone, appeared, reviews were again split along political lines.[110] In a brief and selective argument, deLone tried to buttress the council's recommendations by demonstrating the historical failure of American social and educational policies to promote equality. Writing in the *New York Times*, Diane Ravitch attacked the book, claiming that it revealed deLone's "faith in the virtue of the omnicompetent state" and would "undermine political support for the social-welfare programs that it attacks."[111] Writing in the *Nation*, Philip Green defended deLone— "he manages to put a proper emphasis on the pains and costs of inequality"—and noted that he "has been subjected to the complete arsenal of criticism that *The New York Times* can bring to bear on an author who steps outside the bound of approved moderate discourse. In his case, the heavy guns are triggered by Albert Shanker, Fred Hechinger, and Diane Ravitch."[112]

Controversy could serve to educate public sentiment about the nation's need to consider the nature and adequacy of its commitment to children. Furthermore, since the council's association with the Carnegie Corporation was widely recognized, controversy was likely to help announce the aspiration that Barbara Finberg had once described as "the Corporation's interest in providing leadership toward the development of a greater sense of responsibility and more socially responsible programs for children in the U.S."[113] For these reasons, and because "it made a persuasive case for the collective responsibility of citizens toward all children," which was what he had wanted in the first place, Alan Pifer judged the council worthwhile.[114] But the council followed a line of argument that went well beyond the liberal reformism of the earlier Carnegie panels and, indeed, of the Corporation's traditional commitment to social improvement through education, and its perspective was controversial inside as well as outside the Corporation.

Some of the recommendations of the Keniston group—for example, those concerning more widely available and better integrated social services for children and families—were of a piece with the moderate reformism of other Carnegie groups. Thus, to urge more social services for the poor was not different from urging greater access to colleges and universities organized within the established institutional system, as the two groups led by Clark Kerr had done.[115] And yet, while noteworthy, similarities such as these were actually less revealing than the willingness of the Keniston group to go further than the other groups in emphasizing the central importance of economic change. Without a more equal distribution of economic resources, Keniston and his colleagues had decided, children would remain in peril. Education alone could not offer equality, even equality of opportunity. This was a valid and important observation that was often overlooked in discussions of education. But it was a somewhat startling and really quite radical position for a panel sponsored by the Carnegie Corporation to take. It was only twenty years since J. B. Conant, with Corporation support, had argued that, with some relatively modest reforms, schooling could offer all American youngsters an equal start in life. And now the Corporation was associated with the work of a group that was implicitly suggesting that Conant had been wrong.

Liberal Commitments Challenged: The Influence of Christopher Jencks

The Corporation's willingness to lend the Carnegie name to reports that called for economic as well as educational reform was, in part, a result of criticisms of educational policies and practices that began to appear in the mid-1960s. Most important among these, in terms of thinking within the Carnegie Corporation, were the studies carried out at the Harvard Center for Educational Policy Research by Christopher Jencks, David Cohen, Marshall Smith, Stephan Michelson, and their associates.

Established in 1968, the center was an outgrowth of a Corporation-financed seminar on James S. Coleman's monumental study for the U.S. Office of Education entitled *Equality of Educational Opportunity* (1966).[116] As Jencks had told Alan Pifer, the seminar left "a number of us [wanting] to pursue the lines of inquiry Coleman suggested."[117] The Coleman study had indicated that so-called educational "inputs" such as facilities and numbers of teachers were not directly and causatively related to educational "outputs," that is, to measurable student achievement. As Charles E. Silberman observed in *Fortune,* the report had shattered many basic assumptions about education—the "pillars of current educational policy."[118] Coleman himself was surprised by his findings, having expected that differences in achievement between black and white students would correlate with differences in the schools they attended.[119] Surprising and indeed greatly dismaying to many, running against the conventional wisdom, and filled with data worthy of reanalysis, the Coleman study was quickly and widely seen as a rich source for significant new investigations. The Harvard Center for Educational Policy Research was designed to foster research along the lines of inquiry the Coleman Report had opened up. In addition, as explained by Fritz Mosher, a psychologist trained by Jerome Bruner at Harvard and, since 1964, a member of the Corporation's staff whose special responsibility was elementary and secondary education, the new Harvard Center was intended "as a device to harness (and keep at Harvard) Sandy Jencks' interest in making explicit, and influencing, the understandings upon which educational policy decisions are made in this country."[120]

Jencks, a sociologist educated at Harvard with a year at the London School of Economics, had begun his career on the staff of the *New Republic* and had then moved on to become a fellow at the Institute for Policy Studies in Washington, D.C. He had also served as a consultant to a variety of government agencies and private policy-making organizations. In 1959 he had joined with David Riesman, many of whose studies, beginning with *The Lonely Crowd* (1950), had been financed by the Corporation, in a Carnegie-supported study of American higher education that was published in 1966 under the title *The Academic Revolution*. The year before that book appeared, Jencks had been appointed to the faculty of the Harvard Graduate School of Education.

Recognized from the first as significant, over the years the questions Jencks and his colleagues at the Harvard Center were asking continued to impress Fritz Mosher and others at the Corporation. These questions, it was believed, were essential to educational policy and to what the Corporation itself had done, was doing, and should do with its grants in education. Jencks and his associates were dealing with "fundamental questions about the role of schools," Mosher noted in December 1970. "The talent and accomplishment of this group set them apart from anything else now available, and entitle them to first priority in our consideration," he maintained.[121] Between 1968 and 1973, therefore, the center received nearly $700,000 in direct support from the Corporation. *Inequality: A Reassessment of the Effects of Family and Schooling in America* (1972), by Jencks and six colleagues, was the best known and most controversial study to result.

The book was announced at a press briefing arranged by Basic Books, Jencks's publisher. "I want to begin with a general observation, namely that this study is certain to be misinterpreted," Jencks announced. He then summarized what he believed to be the book's most important conclusions:

(1) Educational opportunity is very unequally distributed in the United States.
    . . .
(2) Nonetheless, inequality in educational opportunity is not responsible for most of the inequality in educational results that we see all around us. . . .
(3) While variations in school quality do not account for inequality in the outcomes of education, it does not follow that genetic inequality is really responsible for inequality in outcomes. . . .
(4) Whatever their origins, differences in the outcomes of schooling have surprisingly little effect on an individual's prospects for adult economic success. . . .
(5) Unfortunately, while we can say that the outcomes of schooling do not explain much of the variation in men's incomes, we cannot say what *does* explain these variations. . . .
(6) All this means that equalizing opportunity, and especially equalizing educational opportunity, will not do much to equalize the results of economic competition.

Even though the book was not "an attempt to discredit the schools," Jencks then explained, it would likely be read as such. And even though the book argued that "a greater degree of economic equality than we now have in America" can be achieved, it was also likely to be read as an argument asserting the inevitability of inequality.[122]

Jencks's predictions came true. *Inequality* most certainly was seen as an attack on schooling. The noted psychologist Kenneth B. Clark described the book as nothing "but another attack on school reform under the guise of research"—flawed research at that.[123] Thomas Pettigrew, also a social psychologist, criticized the book, questioning, among other points, Jencks's acceptance of "the current right-wing theme that the liberal reforms of the 1960s failed." Along with that, however, Pettigrew noted that "if Jencks's interpretations can be challenged, their vulgarization by the mass media can hardly be taken seriously. With little regard for the text, many stories simply twisted the major thrust to maintain that 'Harvard Proves Schools Fail.'"[124]

But was the press really to blame? Philip W. Jackson of the University of Chicago did not think so. He believed that popular readings of *Inequality* reflected the fact that Jencks had dealt at length with what schools could *not* do in terms of promoting equality, and had not balanced that discussion "with an equally thoughtful account of what the genuine contribution of schooling might be."[125] *Inequality* did not indicate until the end of the last chapter, and then only briefly, that its purpose in criticizing schooling as a means for promoting equality was to suggest the advantages of income redistribution as a strategy for reaching that goal.[126] And that too encouraged misinterpretation. Finally, as James S. Coleman observed, Jencks's interest in arguing for income equalization and in showing the differences between equality of opportunity and equality of results (as measured by income) did not fit well with his coauthors' studies of education. If the findings of those studies, which did pertain to "the determinants and effects of educational attainment and achievement," had been published in a separate book, Coleman believed, that book "would not have been as newsworthy or attention getting, but it would have stood the test of deeper scrutiny."[127]

Coleman may have been right. The economist Lester C. Thurow also thought *Inequality* was two books in one.[128] Regardless, Jencks had wanted to write the arresting, controversial book he had produced. Even though he was not at all sanguine that the book would actually have much influence on public policy, he avowed that hope in reflecting on the book after its release. Jencks believed that the school reforms of the 1960s had been sold to the public on the basis of overinflated promises, and that this had made "other social reforms" (presumably income policies), which might have been more effective in promoting equality, more difficult to justify. *"Inequality,"* Jencks said, "was an attempt to change the terms of public debate about how to deal with poverty and inequality."[129]

However one might assess its general success in fulfilling this objective, *Inequality* had a discernible effect upon Carnegie Corporation debates. As Fritz Mosher recalled in 1977, even if some and perhaps even all members of the staff rejected Jencks's conclusions, "the debate and discussion clarified our thinking."[130] After *Inequality*, the Corporation continued and indeed increased its support for schooling. In fact, a renewal of a program of grants to elementary and secondary education was announced in its 1972 *Annual Report*. But the Corporation's program was now based on different assumptions. It accepted the call for a moderation in educational rhetoric and expectations that *Inequality* had presented and was built around a new concern for equity and effective schooling.

This concern was also compatible with the arguments advanced by Ronald Edmonds and others in a Corporation-financed symposium entitled "A Black Response to Christopher Jencks's *Inequality* and Certain Other Issues." Edmonds's piece was published, along with others, in a special 1973 issue of the *Harvard Educational Review* devoted to the Jencks study. Later well known for his work with "instructionally effective schools," Edmonds pointed out that, whatever Jencks's motives may have been, if his work were read as an argument for letting the schools "off the hook," it would do poor people and black people a tremendous disservice.[131] Schooling was vital for all children, Edmonds reminded his readers; schools needed to be held accountable for what all their students did and did not learn. Accordingly, accountability became a central goal of the Corporation's more modestly described, perhaps chastened objectives in this domain.

Liberal Commitments Redefined: The Influence of Marian Wright Edelman

Edmonds's message was a familiar one to Mosher and his Corporation colleagues. Informed by Jencks and "A Black Response to Christopher Jencks," the Corporation's program in elementary and secondary education, and the thinking of the Corporation's staff on all matters, was also informed by involvement with a variety of legal rights and legal advocacy groups. Support for organizations like the NAACP Legal Defense Fund and the Mexican-American Legal Defense and Educational Fund had increased after the 1967 report of the Task Force on the Disadvantaged. This was part of a general movement among foundations toward increased financing of civil rights organizations.[132] The Corporation learned much from this involvement, especially from Marian Wright Edelman, the founder in 1968 of an organization called the Washington Research Project (WRP). Edelman enjoyed unusual respect within the Corporation and played an unusual role. Convinced that "the deaths of Whitney Young and Martin Luther King left a void in black leadership in America, and focused attention, as perhaps never before, on the rising young leaders who will take over the movement in the coming decade," Corporation staff members agreed with people who thought that "without question, one center of action will be Marian Wright Edelman."[133] As a result, they invested a great deal of money in projects with which she was involved (more than $3.2 million between 1970 and 1982), asked her to serve on the Carnegie Council on Children, and generally listened with care to what she thought.

A native of Bennettsville, South Carolina, who had been educated at Spelman College, the University of Geneva, and the Yale University Law School, Edelman was the first black woman admitted to the bar in Mississippi, where she had spent five years (1963–67) running the NAACP Legal Defense Fund office. "There was never a time in the South when I didn't hate segregation, and there was never any question that I was going to do something to change it," Edelman told an interviewer in 1975.[134] Working as a legal advocate in Mississippi at a time of growing disillusionment and anger among blacks and increasing and increasingly violent resistance to desegregation among whites, Edelman had realized that far more than the case-by-case enforcement of individual rights was needed to address the problems of hunger, disease, inadequate education, and unemployment that faced black and poor people in Mississippi. This realization caused Martin Luther King, Jr., and others to concur in the idea that a group of poor people should go to Washington to stage a sit-in at HEW.[135] The idea led in the spring of 1968 to the Poor People's Campaign, which in Edelman's words was designed to bring "to Washington hundreds of community people to make demands on federal agencies."[136]

At the time of the campaign, Edelman had been living in Washington, D.C., where she was attempting "to develop concepts and plans for more effective representation of civil rights and policy concerns in Washington policymaking" on a Field Foundation fellowship.[137] Already troubled about "the divergence between the needs and aspirations of poor and minority communities and federal policy," and about significant gaps between legal statutes and their enforcement, she spent April, May, June, and part of July of 1968 "preparing papers for the poor people to present to federal agencies and negotiating with these federal agencies for concessions on the poor people's demands."[138] She was working in an office rented with Field Foundation funds, when along with a partner and a secretary she founded the Washington Research Project. Having established, through the Poor People's Campaign, "the principle that federal agencies should take into consideration the views of the poor in policymaking," the WRP subsequently established ties with Clark College in Atlanta, so that black students could be trained in advocacy work.[139] By 1970, the staff of WRP had been increased and funds had been raised from a number of foundations, including the Carnegie Corporation, which helped finance WRP efforts to monitor compliance with federal educational policies.

In April 1971, Edelman moved to Boston. Still actively involved in WRP, she also became affiliated with the Harvard Center for Law and

Education. The center, supported by the Office of Economic Opportunity and sponsored jointly by the Law School and the Graduate School of Education, was involved in research and litigation concerning desegregation, the enforcement of Title I of ESEA, student rights, tuition vouchers, and school finance. It was distinct from but overlapped with the Center for Educational Policy Research founded by Christopher Jencks and others.

Edelman was asked to become director in the fall of 1971, a post she expected to fill without lessening her involvement in WRP. She told Eli Evans, the Corporation program officer responsible for grants to WRP: "I see great potential in the Center in developing new issues in the education area which WRP does not have the resources to do. Child advocacy is going to be a big thing over the next ten years, and someone must begin to define the nature of such advocacy and design ways in which it can be most effective, to map out with care the status of children in this society and those aspects which are most readily changeable. . . . I would like to see the Center in fact become a Children's Defense Fund of sorts, breaking new ground in this whole area."[140] By November, in a report of the activities of WRP during 1971, Edelman had a proposal for a Children's Defense Fund ready for discussion. "Children," she stated, "are the unrecognized, neglected and mistreated minority in America, much as the poor were prior to their 'discovery' by [Michael] Harrington."[141] Poor children, and especially poor children who "suffer disabilities of color and minority status, bilingualism and migrancy, and also handicapped children, institutionalized children, children without parents," she continued, were especially in need of advocacy efforts. Beyond that, "the rights of children are a natural expansion and refinement of the 1960s movement for civil rights and social justice. In the 1970s, children's rights may well provide the most promising vehicle for addressing broader problems of poverty and race in this country. . . . There is much that we do not know about what is best for children—about their learning processes, for example, or about what constitutes a good education. . . . But there is much we do know about what is harmful to children which we must correct now. CDF is concerned with establishing a floor of decency for every child."[142] First and foremost, it would work to enforce the right of children to go to school.

A year later, as a previously approved Carnegie grant to WRP was nearing its end, Edelman presented a formal proposal. Shepherded through the Corporation's internal review processes by Barbara Finberg, the project won initial support at the level of $200,000 for a period of three years. According to Finberg, "CC support of the CDF would make explicit what has been an unspoken but ever present tenet of CC's interest in education, the right of every child to an education."[143] Ensuring that a child's right to an education was in no way abridged or violated was to be a central purpose of CDF.

The pragmatism inherent in this aim was characteristic of Edelman, who was impatient with theories and intent upon "establishing principles with remedies which will mean something in the lives of people."[144] She was certainly aware of Jencks's position on the limits of educational reform, having been at Harvard at the time *Inequality* was being written. No less than Jencks, she also believed there were basic inequalities in the United States that were unfortunately sustained by myths and misdirected public debate. Realizing, however, that it was necessary to try "to break down . . . problems . . . into manageable pieces for public education and action," she was able to see value in the enforcement of every child's right to schooling.[145] Among other things, enforcement of this right could serve as an immediate "action" strategy for establishing a variety of other rights for children, for poor families, and for all people who suffered from discrimination or deprivation of any kind. Combined with efforts at "public education"—ventures like the Carnegie Council on Children—it might eventually advance the larger sense of social responsibility that was necessary before more direct approaches to problems of equality, including income solutions, could receive serious consideration.

Within the Corporation, Edelman's sense of strategy made sense, especially amid the "radical pessimism" triggered by the Coleman report and reinforced thereafter by the Jencks study and other works of educational criticism.[146] As Fritz Mosher and Vivien Stewart argued subsequently, even if schooling could not solve all the problems of poverty, it could and should be relied upon as a kind of "fail-safe system" to teach all children the basic, minimal skills of reading, writing, and arithmetic.[147] Mosher's and Stewart's logic was not different from Edelman's, and the Corporation's grants within its elementary and secondary program—to advocacy groups, to lawyers working on problems of equal financing, to psychologists developing new tests, and to any number of other projects variously pertaining to equity and effective schooling—were entirely compatible with its grant to the Children's Defense Fund. More important, a logic pointing to the strategic value of equal and effective schooling was necessary to the Corporation's continued operation. After all, even if the limits of schooling and of education generally as means for advancing equality and social justice were clearer by the time Alan Pifer retired from the Corporation's presidency in 1982 than they had been when he assumed office in 1965, these traditional instruments of liberal reform were still required strategies for the Carnegie Corporation. For better or worse, they remained essential to its mandate to promote the "advancement and diffusion of knowledge and understanding among the people of the United States."

CONCLUSION

American Dilemmas

I N T H E E N D, what can be said about an organization that had
given away more than half a billion dollars by 1982 and spent more
than $36 million doing so? As the sponsor of innumerable books,
research projects, art exhibits, television programs, individual study
tours and fellowships, and institutional experiments and innovations,
the Carnegie Corporation had had a large and incalculable effect on
the lives of many people in the United States and throughout the world.
Its funds had often made a significant difference in a scholarly career,
in the development of a field of knowledge, or in the life of a college,
research institution, or library. Frequently, the impact of a grant went
well beyond the people or projects directly involved and the immediate
purposes for which that grant was intended. Frequently, too, those
purposes were different for the Corporation (and for different people
associated with the Corporation) and for the "grantees" and the people
professionally and personally associated with them. The metaphor of
a lawn party attended by many different people for many different
reasons, which has been aptly applied to suggest the complexity of
policy-making, captured a quality common in all forms of purposive
social action, including foundation philanthropy.[1]

Some Carnegie Corporation grants involved small amounts of
money and yielded large returns; others involved large amounts of
money and yielded small or even no returns. But there was little necessary or invariant relation between the size of a grant and its associated
outcomes, whatever those might be. Indeed, there was no simple calculus by which to analyze what the Carnegie Corporation had attempted

and achieved, let alone to explain the myriad relationships between goals and outcomes. Still, over the years, a number of persistent dilemmas ran through the Corporation's history, indicative of difficult problems facing the United States.

First, there was the matter of expertise, which the Corporation had variously but continuously sought to foster. That expertise, defined simply as special, advanced knowledge, was necessary in a large modern society was indisputable. Clearly, therefore, in directing money to the investigations from which expertise might appear, the Corporation had performed a vital public function. The value of the dollars it had spent helping to establish and sustain the nation's infrastructure of universities, libraries, independent research institutes, scholarly councils, and media of professional and scholarly communication was readily apparent; it could be measured most easily in a host of inventions in medicine, economics, museum administration, and other areas of knowledge-related professional concern. In addition, many grants had encouraged high skill and new knowledge in less immediately useful domains of scholarship and culture—expertise in photography or Chinese poetry, for example—and these had merit beyond practical, technological gain.

Granted, then, that expertise was vital and that the Corporation's willingness to invest in its development was publicly beneficial, questions remained about the difficulties expertise and its nurturance presented in a democratic society. Increasing as demand for high-level knowledge and skill increased, expertise was the phenomenon at issue in the politics of knowledge. Having always existed in one form or another, the politics of knowledge as a politics concerning the nature and uses of expertise had intensified in the early twentieth century as a result of population growth, advances in engineering and science, the extension of education, and most important here, tensions between expertise and democracy. Expertise could stand in opposition to universal and equal participation in public affairs; it could provide a basis for claims to superordinate rights. And yet, despite this, it was necessary to modern life.

Viewing the United States as an experiment in democratic self-government, Alexis de Tocqueville had commented as early as 1840 upon a pervasive American distrust of unusual learning and learnedness: "Not only is confidence in the superior attainments of certain individuals weakened among democratic nations, but the general notion of the intellectual superiority which any man whatsoever may acquire in relation to the rest of the community is soon overshadowed."[2] Within fifty years, the implications of increasing expertise for democracy had become a frequent theme in writings about American education and politics. Some commentators saw expertise as a means to make democracy more efficient and less fractious. One of the best known of these was Harvard president Charles W. Eliot, who called for a "confidence in experts, and [a] willingness to employ them and abide by their decisions." He believed that, "in any democracy which is to thrive, this respect and confidence must be felt strongly by the majority of the population."[3] Implying a deference and trust fundamentally different from the autonomy and independence of mind and judgment once thought necessary for citizenship in a democratic society, Eliot's formulation had veered toward suggesting a delegation of inalienable rights.

Not for Eliot but for others, a potential for conflict between expertise and democracy was of great concern. This had been true for John Dewey, who had revered science and expected it to promote progress in many spheres of social life, but who had also feared the potentially illiberal consequences of an overreliance on experts. He had made this clear in a review of Walter Lippmann's *Public Opinion* for the *New Republic* in 1922. Generously praising Lippmann's pioneering analysis of the problems attending accurate news reporting, Dewey had demurred from Lippmann's solution to these problems. He did not approve Lippmann's suggestion of a disinterested, highly trained intelligence service, consisting of experts who would interpret events for the executives and public administrators.[4]

Mr. Lippmann has thrown into clearer relief than any other writer the fundamental difficulty of democracy. But the difficulty is so fundamental that it can be met, it seems to me, only by a solution more fundamental than he has dared to give. When necessity drives, invention and accomplishment may amazingly respond. Democracy demands a more thoroughgoing education than the education of officials, administrators and directors of industry. Because this fundamental general education is at once so necessary and so difficult of achievement, the enterprise of democracy is so challenging. To sidetrack it to the task of enlightenment of administrators and executives is to miss something of its range and its challenge.[5]

In his short review, Dewey had not explicated the full logic of his criticism, but his meaning was clear: democracy required education and information for all citizens sufficient to enable them to participate meaningfully in decisions that would affect them. There could not be two grades of citizens, two tracks of education, two levels of participation in public affairs. Expertise had to be balanced with effective, universal education, in order to preserve the participation essential to a democratic way of life.

In a sense, the issue Dewey had raised by dissenting from Lippmann's

Public Opinion had little direct relation to Carnegie Corporation phi-lanthropy. One might note parenthetically, however, that Lippmann, but not Dewey, was considered for membership on the Corporation's board of trustees. This made sense, for after Andrew Carnegie's death a perspective more like Lippmann's than Dewey's had been built into the Corporation's purposes and policies.

A preference for efficiency over participation—in a sense, for exper-tise over democracy—was most pronounced in the early 1920s, when the Corporation, acting on the assumptions of scientific philanthropy, joined with other foundations, notably the Commonwealth Fund and the Laura Spelman Rockefeller Memorial Fund, to establish or endow centers of scientific expertise and to finance their work. The National Research Council of the National Academy of Sciences, the National Bureau of Economic Research, and the American Law Institute, were all intended to convene different bodies of experts, to consider and investigate important public problems, and to present the results to appropriate administrative bodies and in some instances to the public at large. The Corporation's concurrence in the aspirations of scientists, economists, and lawyers eager to consolidate positions of leadership and privilege had strengthened a streamlined, hierarchical model of policy-making in the United States.

Subsequently, while continuing to invest large sums in the develop-ment of specialized, expert knowledge, the Corporation had also sought to disseminate knowledge more generally. Here it had tried to advance Dewey's corrective to Lippmann's expert intelligence elite. Andrew Carnegie's library "planting" may be said to have begun this effort, which continued intermittently down through the grants of the 1970s promoting more equal and effective public schooling. Momen-tarily leaving aside the question of whether those efforts were effective, the significance of education to this first dilemma revealed by the Carnegie Corporation's history should be clear. Expertise is necessary in a modern society; but efforts to nurture expertise without correlated efforts to promote education will erode the basis for democracy. Educa-tion is therefore the only way out of an impossible choice between unacceptable alternatives—on the one hand, expertise; on the other, democracy.

Some though not all Corporation trustees, officers, and grantees had been concerned with the problem of reconciling the unusual power implicit in expertise with the necessity for equal voice and vote inherent in democracy. Their efforts had indicated that, while it was all well and good to insist on effective, equal, universal education, the associated difficulties were immense and involved another basic dilemma facing the United States.

Most Corporation investments in education had facilitated the development of new programs or new materials or the training of new personnel for schools, colleges, and universities. On several occasions, however, the Corporation had tried to increase access to education by enhancing the educational potential of noninstructional cultural institutions and media. Its grants during the 1930s for libraries, adult education, and the arts, and its advocacy, beginning in the late 1960s, of educational and then public television were examples. Undertaken for a variety of reasons, these initiatives might have encouraged the elaboration of a more universally effective educational system, one that would include but go beyond the instruction of the young in schools and colleges—an educational system that would offer more education to more people with more varied curricula, pedagogies, patterns of organization, institutional support, and correlated opportunities to work or simultaneously engage in other activities. Such an enlarged, comprehensive system of education was needed in the United States as early as the 1930s and certainly by the late 1960s, to ensure that the general citizenry was not disenfranchised wholly or in some domains as an inevitable consequence of advancing knowledge and technological innovation. Alone, schools, colleges, and universities, no matter how effective, could not do this. Needed or not, neither the 1930s programs nor those of the 1960s promoting extended education through cultural activities had been fully successful; neither had been able enduringly to change the ecology of culture and education in the United States.[6]

The shortcomings of the Corporation's cultural initiatives could be explained in part by a failure to surmount the tension between mission and market that is commonly present in institutions of education and culture in the United States. Equally in the case of a college seeking to maintain high academic standards, a publishing firm seeking to produce high-quality works, and a television station seeking to offer educational or public affairs programs, an institution's purposes or offerings—its mission—must appeal to a clientele that can support its operation—a market; otherwise, it cannot survive. To the extent that an institution can operate with endowment funds or other nonmarket subsidies, it can define its mission according to its own or other nonmarket standards; to the extent that it is dependent upon one or more markets, it will have to define its mission to suit the standards of those markets. In the case of the Carnegie Corporation's cultural ventures, full success had been elusive because the purposes and curricula offered had been neither sufficiently popular nor sufficiently popularized through powerful pedagogies to ensure paying audiences.

That this was so is significant. High culture is expensive. Its direct production costs are often substantial, and it usually appeals to already well-educated audiences, which means that it also carries heavy indirect costs.[7] After all, if graduates of liberal arts colleges are more likely to go to museums and attend the theater or opera, as many studies have indicated, then it seems reasonable to argue that the costs of college attendance might well be conceived as indirect costs associated with the marketing of high culture. One need not even go that far, however; the point is that excellence in culture, like excellence in education, is costly in a variety of ways.

Partly as a result of economics, high culture has also tended to be the culture of the elite. Not surprisingly, therefore, when the Carnegie Corporation became involved in efforts to disseminate high culture more widely, it inevitably attempted to popularize the cultural standards of elite groups. During the 1930s it hoped to expose everyone to the kinds of "Great Books" discussions it had supported at the People's Institute in New York City. But not all people wanted such education, especially if they had not already had much formal schooling. Even with a subsidy to lower its price, high culture had not become popular. Later Alan Pifer noted the same phenomenon when he confessed to the Carnegie Commission on Educational Television that relatively few Americans were interested in what public television might provide.

As a result of inescapable tensions between mission and market, then, the Carnegie Corporation had faced another dilemma. It could abandon the aspiration to enlarge education through efforts to popularize culture, or it could acknowledge that the task was more difficult than previously realized and in need of new and different strategies. To choose the second alternative, the Corporation would need to give up old, fixed definitions of culture—culture in Matthew Arnold's sense of the term—and acknowledge in its grant-making the degree to which standards for all institutions of culture and education, whether schools, theaters, or television stations, were derived from the different "taste cultures" of different social classes and groups.[8] Correlations between taste and social class had been clear, if unstated and unrecognized, in the Corporation's cultural philanthropy, which tended to mirror the "high" taste culture of its largely upper-class and, until 1970, almost exclusively WASP and male board of trustees. Puritan plain style of the kind Elihu Root had wanted incorporated into public art was not a popular style, which is why Root wanted it disseminated in the first place, hoping it would be instructive.

During the 1970s, the Corporation's board had been diversified, opening new possibilities to overcome the unfortunately constraining impact of a narrowly based, socially and culturally homogeneous board. However necessary, greater social and cultural diversity among the Corporation's trustees was still only a first step. Developing initiatives that might succeed in interesting more people in cultural affairs would need not only broader definitions of culture—of excellence, art, literary merit, and the like—but also a new process for arriving at those. Without changes in the substance of culture to accompany changes in audience, the mission-market dynamic would again undermine whatever was tried. Access to culture, like access to schooling, is not merely a matter of entry or admission; curriculum, pedagogy, and all aspects of the experience need to be meshed with the experience of the participants, if their interest is to be retained. Established processes for setting curricula, choosing art works, selecting scripts, and evaluating and criticizing these, also need to be reformed so as to take fuller account of both sponsor and audience values and tastes. More difficult still as a result of historical traditions tending to the contrary, all these changes would need to be undertaken and understood in ways that made sure they would not be read as signs of decline or dilution. Too often in the past, as David Cohen and Barbara Neufeld have observed, "advances for equality have been accompanied by the gradual debasement of . . . education. This debasement lies partly in the eyes of beholders who have difficulty believing that an equal institution can be excellent, and partly in the dilution of academic standards by educators and communities who cannot believe that excellent and demanding education is possible for most students."[9] Excellence for everyone must still be excellent. There is no reason why educational differences need to be assigned "hierarchical ranks."[10] Our long-established tendency to do this could be changed.

Obviously, these problems are easier to state than to resolve; to repeat, they are extraordinarily difficult to address in actual programs. Difficulties notwithstanding, the alternative—abandoning efforts to broaden education through broadened participation in culture—is not an acceptable option in a society where more education is needed for many reasons, not least, to make sure that increasing expertise does not result in decreasing democracy. What is more, it could not be an acceptable choice for a foundation chartered as the Carnegie Corporation is to advance and diffuse knowledge and understanding.

The first two dilemmas pervading the history of the Carnegie Corporation related to a third having to do with modes of influence. What was one to make of the Corporation's increasing concern after the Second World War with finding ways to shape the public agenda? Had the emphasis on strategy that began to emerge in the late 1940s become over time a search for influence in which means were confused with ends? To what extent were the agendas advanced by the Carnegie Commission on Educational Television or the Carnegie Commission on Higher Education premised upon knowledge of what would and would not be acceptable to the U.S. Congress? The point is not to suggest that influence apart from the soundness of the recommendations advanced had been the goal. Not at all. Rather, it is to wonder about the consequences of directly seeking evident impact.

The Corporation's logic for moving toward a more strategic style of philanthropy, and later for relying heavily on commissions to explore new directions for public policy, was indisputable. There was no question that after the Second World War the number of organizations attempting to influence public policy increased greatly, as did the size of public and private foundations. Within this context, it may well have made sense to develop means to generate and announce policy recommendations in authoritative ways, thereby helping the Corporation to pass its initiatives along to others in a stronger position to implement them. But, as Paul E. Peterson concluded in 1983, soon after serving as rapporteur for the Twentieth Century Fund Task Force on Federal Elementary and Secondary Education Policy, "Commissions are more appropriate for dramatizing an issue, resolving political differences, and reassuring the public that questions are being thoughtfully considered" than for "fact-finding, rigorous analysis, and policy development."[11] After engaging in policy-making at many levels and in many roles, Senator Daniel P. Moynihan was also convinced that, "when radical change takes place . . . it comes through knowledge, not slogans, not simply enthusiasm, but through the impact of knowledge."[12] In pursuing a reasonable strategy for maximizing its potential to influence the public agenda, it seems possible, therefore, that the Corporation had at the same time limited its long-term influence. Certainly, its investments in psychological studies of learning and development in young children, such as its grants to Jerome S. Bruner and J. McVicker Hunt, had fed into very large, even revolutionary, changes in policy. But then again, those grants had been stunning triumphs, and there were many grants for basic research that had been made to no avail. Nevertheless, by the 1970s, it seemed that the

Corporation's emphasis upon strategic giving had caused it to favor investments in immediate blueprints for reform more than, but not to the full exclusion of, fundamental research.

The question of whether surer, immediate impact or less certain, long-range influence was a more appropriate goal was, of course, inseparable from questions of philanthropic purpose. In 1911, when Andrew Carnegie founded the Carnegie Corporation, he had hoped that the foundation would finance and organize new institutions to increase opportunities for education, self-improvement, and exposure to culture. These institutions would, in turn, discover "genius" in the few and develop individual self-discipline and a capacity for cooperative social interaction in the many. From Carnegie's perspective, this was how the Corporation would contribute to governance. He saw education as potentially diminishing the necessity for government regulation. He defined governance as many nineteenth-century working-men did, as individual self-control and freely given cooperation. A result of education, governance would facilitate "anarchy with a schoolmaster."[13]

The trustees who had defined the Corporation, and their successors on the board and staff, had not fully subscribed to Carnegie's views of governance, philanthropy, and purposes for the Carnegie Corporation. They had hoped that the Corporation could contribute to governance more directly—in the 1920s, by helping to establish new institutes of expert, scientific research; in the 1950s, by redefining the knowledge government officials and diplomats could call upon in their negotiations with other countries; and in the 1960s, by informing government action quite directly, through public advocacy of the kind J. B. Conant or later the various Carnegie commissions had engaged in. If it had once been sufficient or even desirable simply to award funds to worthy seekers, that was increasingly seen as mere "scatteration," a practice looked down upon in foundation circles as amateur. Increasingly over the years, therefore, the Carnegie Corporation had shifted, not completely or officially, but in emphasis and spirit, from acting as a philanthropic bank—an organization primarily engaged in grant-making—to serving as a philanthropic center for policy analysis—an operating agency. Growing administrative costs, increasingly complex staff discussions and grant reviews, and, of course, all the premises inherent in strategic philanthropy, were evidence of the change.

There was no question as to the legitimacy of the direction in which the Corporation had moved; it was a direction that many foundations pursued. But the trend was problematic in terms of its consequences for American politics and education, and it framed the dilemma of influence. More and more frequently, important and controversial public questions were debated within Carnegie commissions or the Carnegie Corporation itself. Often these debates proceeded in collaboration with other organizations of policy analysis with which the Corporation had relationships. Ultimately, position papers or legislative proposals might result, which the public media could report and public agencies or even the electorate accept, reject, or ignore. Regardless of the wisdom of the policies generated, the process could have a foreshortening effect on American politics and education.

One example might make the point. There had been nineteen members of the Carnegie Commission on Higher Education; adding staff, Corporation and CFAT observers, and perhaps some consultants, about forty or fifty men and women had the opportunity directly to hear and join in the commission's debates. One matter that had been carefully investigated and fully discussed was whether federal aid to higher education should be distributed directly to students or initially to institutions, which would then distribute funds to students. To understand the question, which had important implications for higher education and future federal aid formulas, instruction and study had been required. Some reports describing the pros and cons of the alternatives appeared in the press. But those who played a role in formulating the commission's recommendation had been offered, not only an unusual chance to participate in politics, but, even more valuable, an unusual educational experience.

There are of course instances when commissions are invaluable in policy-making. Obviously, too, Greek city-state or New England town-meeting models of democracy, in which all questions are debated and decided by all citizens, could not be fully or directly applied in a society as large and complex as the United States. Still, wide and direct conversation, open advocacy, frank disagreement, and negotiations about pressing issues that affect all people must remain the ideal. They are the essence of democracy and of democratic education. Indeed, as Amy Gutmann has noted in studying education: "the most distinctive feature of a democratic theory of education is that it makes a democratic virtue out of our inevitable disagreement over educational problems. The democratic virtue, too simply stated, is that we can publicly debate educational problems in a way much more likely to increase our understanding of education and each other than if we were to leave the management of schools, as Kant suggests, 'to depend entirely upon the judgment of the most enlightened experts.' "[14] Gutmann's point pertains to many public matters in addition to education and certainly to those of concern to the Carnegie Corporation.

Whether commissions can stimulate public study and discussion of public issues is not certain, nor is how they might do so clear; but that such study and debate can have value is indisputable. Beyond theoretical arguments, voting patterns since the Second World War make this clear. Approximately 50 percent of those eligible to vote do so.[15] This wide failure to exercise the most elementary democratic right is a result of many things, including an impoverished public political life; it cannot be separated from a slow, steady migration of policy-making and the attendant study and debates from open, often local arenas such as neighborhood schools and community centers to places where policy professionals gather—places like the Brookings Institution, the Russian Research Center at Harvard, and the Carnegie Corporation. This is not to romanticize a small-town past by featuring its seemingly simple, human scale and overlooking its constraining features, including the tyrannies of local majorities opposed to equality and civil rights. But it should be noted that immediately efficient strategies for influence may not be the same as more enduring, demanding educational ones.[16]

One final point is important. The dilemmas revealed by the history of the Carnegie Corporation were not unique to one foundation. Other foundations have participated in the politics of knowledge and, like the Corporation, have tended to be more successful in developing expertise than in fostering effective, universal popular education. Other organizations, including the National Endowment for the Humanities and other public agencies, have wrestled with the problems of popularizing culture, and have also done so with less than full success. And other foundations, think tanks, and professional associations have taken advantage of immediate opportunities to advance one or another reform, sometimes in the process giving insufficient attention to the associated long-range, unanticipated, and even undesirable consequences of their actions and achievements. That the dilemmas revealed in the history of the Carnegie Corporation were so widely shared made them more urgent; it also suggests yet again the importance of this foundation in the governance of the United States.

Notes

Appendices

Bibliographic Essay

Index

Notes

INTRODUCTION
The Politics of Knowledge

1. I have derived this term from David Michael Grossman, "Professors and Public Service, 1885–1925: A Chapter in the Professionalization of the Social Sciences" (Ph.D. diss., Washington University, 1973), 111.
2. Quoted in Clarence H. Cramer, *Newton D. Baker: A Biography* (Cleveland: World Press, 1961), 63.
3. *The Autobiography of Andrew Carnegie*, ed. John C. Van Dyke (Garden City, N.Y.: Doubleday, Doran, 1933), 327.
4. Carnegie Corporation (hereafter CC), *Annual Report* (1982), 3 and 11.

CHAPTER ONE
Liberal Commitments

1. Quoted in Joseph Frazier Wall, *Andrew Carnegie* (New York: Oxford University Press, 1970), 884.
2. Henry S. Pritchett, "Fields of Activity Open to the Carnegie Corporation," Trustee Memorandum, 15 April 1916, Corp. Files.
3. Andrew Carnegie to Trustees of Carnegie Corporation, 10 November 1911, in *Forty Years of Carnegie Giving: A Summary of the Benefactions of Andrew Carnegie and of the Work of the Philanthropic Trusts Which He Created*, comp. Robert M. Lester (New York: Charles Scribner's Sons, 1941), 166.
4. Reproduced in Wall, *Carnegie*, 224–25.

5. Andrew Carnegie, *Triumphant Democracy* (1885; Garden City, N.Y.: Doubleday, Doran, 1935), dedication.
6. Burton J. Hendrick, *The Life of Andrew Carnegie*, 2 vols. (Garden City, N.Y.: Doubleday, Doran, 1932), I: 264–65.
7. Quoted in Wall, *Carnegie*, 442.
8. Ibid., 445.
9. Andrew Carnegie, *The Gospel of Wealth* (1884; Garden City, N.Y.: Doubleday, Doran, 1933), Part I: 16.
10. Ibid., Part I: 13, 14, 15, 3.
11. Andrew Carnegie, *An American Four-in-Hand in Britain* (1883; Garden City, N.Y.: Doubleday, Doran, 1933), 279.
12. Quoted in Burton J. Hendrick and Daniel Henderson, *Louise Whitfield Carnegie: The Life of Mrs. Andrew Carnegie* (New York: Hastings House, 1950), 138.
13. Wall, *Carnegie*, 108.
14. Quoted in ibid., 821. For the numbers of libraries see Florence Anderson, *Carnegie Corporation Library Program, 1911–1961* (New York: Carnegie Corporation of New York, 1963).
15. Reproduced in George S. Bobinski, *Carnegie Libraries: Their History and Impact on American Public Library Development* (Chicago: American Library Association, 1969), 205.
16. Quoted in Wall, *Carnegie*, 819.
17. Quoted in ibid., 425.
18. Matthew Arnold, *Culture and Anarchy*, ed. J. Dover Wilson (1869; Cambridge: University Press, 1960), 6.
19. Ibid., 70.
20. Ibid.
21. For Arnold's views see Raymond Williams, *Culture and Society: 1780–1950* (1958; New York: Columbia University Press, 1983), chap. 6; Bruce A. Kimball, "Matthew Arnold, Thomas Huxley, and Liberal Education: A Centennial Retrospective," *Teachers College Record* 86 (Spring 1985): 475–87.
22. Andrew Carnegie to Andrew D. White, 4 and 12 December 1904; Andrew Carnegie Papers, Library of Congress, Washington, D.C. (hereafter AC Papers); "Cornell," in *Miscellaneous Writings of Andrew Carnegie*, edited by Burton J. Hendrick, (Garden City, N.Y.: Doubleday, Doran, 1933), I: 257.
23. Arnold, *Culture and Anarchy*, 22.
24. Quoted in Simon Goodenough, *The Greatest Good Fortune: Andrew Carnegie's Gift for Today* (Edinburgh: MacDonald, 1985), 177.
25. Andrew Carnegie, "White and Black in the South" [1904], in *Miscellaneous Writings*, II: 82.
26. Andrew Carnegie, "The Negro in America" [1907], in *Miscellaneous Writings*, II: 119.

27. This and all other aggregate grant totals given in this chapter are from Goodenough, *The Greatest Good Fortune.*
28. See Barry D. Karl and Stanley N. Katz, "Foundations and Ruling Class Elites," *Daedalus* 116 (Winter 1987): 1–40.
29. Andrew Carnegie to Trustees of the Endowment, 14 December 1910, in *Forty Years of Carnegie Giving,* 161–62.
30. Andrew Carnegie to Charles W. Eliot, 31 December 1904, AC Papers.
31. Andrew Carnegie to Henry S. Pritchett, 14 December, 1905, AC Papers.
32. Bobinski, *Carnegie Libraries,* 107.
33. Quoted in Wall, *Carnegie,* 895.
34. Quoted in ibid., 823.
35. Ibid., 796.
36. Quoted in ibid., 822.
37. Mark Sullivan, *Our Times: The United States, 1900–1925,* 6 vols. (New York: Charles Scribner's Sons, 1933), IV: 140.
38. Pritchett, "Fields of Activity Open to the Carnegie Corporation," p. 2, Corp. Files.
39. Henry S. Pritchett to Andrew Carnegie, 16 November 1905, CFAT Files.
40. Henry S. Pritchett to Frederick P. Keppel, 4 January 1935, Corp. Files.
41. Hendrick, *Carnegie,* II: 352.
42. Charter of Incorporation, in *Forty Years of Carnegie Giving,* 170–71. The charter was modeled on that of the Carnegie Institution of Washington. See John L. Cadwalader to Elihu Root, 6 January 1911, Elihu Root Papers, Library of Congress, Washington, D.C. (hereafter Root Papers).
43. Quoted in Bobinski, *Carnegie Libraries,* 43.
44. Quoted in ibid., 104–105.
45. Quoted in ibid., 90.
46. Quoted in ibid., 91.
47. Quoted in ibid., 103.
48. Quoted in ibid., 162.
49. *Autobiography of Andrew Carnegie* (Garden City, N.Y.: Doubleday, Doran, 1933), 359.
50. Alvin Johnson, *Pioneer's Progress* (New York: Viking, 1952), 236.
51. Abraham Flexner, *Medical Education in the United States and Canada,* CFAT Bulletin No. 4 (1910).
52. Johnson, *Pioneer's Progress,* 239.
53. Alvin S. Johnson, "A Report to Carnegie Corporation of New York on the Policy of Donations to Free Public Libraries," 18 November 1915, Corp. Files. While there is no way to confirm the supposition, the introduction to this report reads sufficiently like Pritchett's writing style to warrant the hypothesis that it was he who did the editing.
54. Ibid., 5, 7, and 12.
55. Ibid., 18, and generally chap. 6.
56. Johnson, *Pioneer's Progress,* 238.
57. Ibid., 239.

PART I
Scientific Philanthropy: Introduction

1. Ellis W. Hawley, *The Great War and the Search for a Modern Order: A History of the American People and Their Institutions, 1917–1933* (New York: St. Martin's, 1979); Craig Lloyd, *Aggressive Introvert: Herbert Hoover and Public Relations Management* (Columbus: Ohio State University Press, 1972); and Joan Huff Wilson, *Herbert Hoover: Forgotten Progressive* (Boston: Little, Brown, 1975).
2. Stephen Skowronek, *Building a New American State: The Expansion of National Administrative Capacities, 1877–1920* (Cambridge: Cambridge University Press, 1982), 165.
3. James Rowland Angell, "The Organization of Research," *Scientific Monthly* 11 (July 1920): 27.
4. Robert M. Yerkes, ed., *The New World of Science: Its Development during the War* (New York: Century, 1920).

CHAPTER TWO
A Clearinghouse of American Science: The National Research Council

1. George Ellery Hale, "Introduction," in *The New World of Science: Its Development during the War,* ed. Robert M. Yerkes (New York: Century, 1920), vii.
2. Ibid., xiii.
3. George Ellery Hale, "Plan for the Promotion of Scientific and Industrial Research by the National Academy of Sciences and the National Research Council," n.d. (presented to the Board of Trustees of the Carnegie Corporation on 7 November 1917), p. 6, Corp. Files.
4. Frederick H. Seares, "George Ellery Hale: The Scientist Afield," *Isis* 30 (May 1939): 244.
5. Nathan Reingold, "The Case of the Disappearing Laboratory," *American Quarterly* 29 (Spring 1977): 82.
6. George Ellery Hale to Elihu Root, 10 March 1913, George Ellery Hale Papers, The Observatories of the Carnegie Institution of Washington, Pasadena, California (hereafter Hale Papers).
7. James McKeen Cattell, "The Origin and Distribution of Scientific Men," *Science* 66 (25 November 1927): 514; and Michael M. Sokal, "*Science* and James McKeen Cattell, 1894 to 1945," *Science* 209 (July 1980): 49 (for the membership numbers).
8. Hamilton Cravens, "American Science Comes of Age: An Institutional Perspective, 1850–1930," *American Studies* 17 (Spring–Fall 1976): 49–70.
9. Daniel J. Kevles, *The Physicists: The History of a Scientific Community in Modern America* (New York: Alfred A. Knopf, 1978), 96–98.

10. Stanley M. Guralnick, "The American Scientist in Higher Education, 1820–1910," in *The Sciences in the American Context: New Perspectives,* ed. Nathan Reingold (Washington, D.C.: Smithsonian Institution Press, 1979), 99–141.

11. Kevles, *The Physicists,* 96.

12. Frederick W. True, *A History of the First Half Century of the National Academy of Sciences, 1863–1913* (Washington, D.C.: National Academy of Sciences, 1913), 352.

13. A. Hunter Dupree, "The National Academy of Sciences and the American Definition of Science," in *The Organization of Knowledge in Modern America, 1860–1920,* ed. Alexandra Oleson and John Voss (Baltimore: Johns Hopkins University Press, 1979), 342–63.

14. George Ellery Hale to Charles D. Walcott, 25 January 1908, quoted in *The Legacy of George Ellery Hale: Evolution of Astronomy and Scientific Institutions in Pictures and Documents,* ed. Helen Wright, John W. Warnow, and Charles Weiner (Cambridge, Mass.: MIT Press, 1972), 72.

15. George Ellery Hale, "National Academies and the Progress of Research" [1914], reprinted in *The Legacy of Hale,* ed. Wright, Warnow, and Weiner, 180.

16. Ibid., 181.

17. Ibid., 188 and 177.

18. Ibid., 177.

19. Ronald C. Tobey, *The American Ideology of National Science, 1919–1930* (Pittsburgh: University of Pittsburgh Press, 1971), 27.

20. Ibid., 29.

21. Andrew Carnegie to George Ellery Hale, 11 May 1914, and Henry S. Pritchett to George Ellery Hale, 7 May 1914, Corp. Files.

22. Quoted in Helen Wright, *Explorer of the Universe: A Biography of George Ellery Hale* (New York: E. P. Dutton, 1966), 159.

23. Ibid., 173.

24. Andrew Carnegie to Robert S. Woodward, 19 January 1911, in *Forty Years of Carnegie Giving: A Summary of the Benefactions of Andrew Carnegie and of the Work of the Philanthropic Trusts Which He Created,* comp. Robert M. Lester (New York: Charles Scribner's Sons, 1941), 131.

25. Quoted in Joseph Frazier Wall, *Andrew Carnegie* (New York: Oxford University Press, 1970), 862.

26. Quoted in Wright, *Explorer of the Universe,* 310.

27. Quoted in ibid., 309.

28. *Dictionary of American Biography,* s.v. "Cattell, James McKeen"; Sokal, "*Science* and James McKeen Cattell," *Science,* 43–52.

29. Michael M. Sokal, "The Origins of the Psychological Corporation," *Journal of the History of the Behavioral Sciences* 17 (January 1981): 54–67.

30. James McKeen Cattell, "The Organization of Scientific Men," in *James McKeen Cattell: Man of Science,* ed. A. T. Poffenberger, 2 vols. (Lancaster, Penn.: Science Press, 1947), II: 362.

31. Ibid., 365 and 367.

32. Ibid., 368.
33. Ibid., 366.
34. James McKeen Cattell to Andrew Carnegie, 21 November 1914, Andrew Carnegie Papers, Library of Congress, Washington, D.C. (hereafter AC Papers).
35. James McKeen Cattell to William N. Frew, 28 November 1914, Carnegie Papers.
36. Robert H. Kargon, ed., *The Maturing of American Science: A Portrait of Science in Public Life Drawn from the Presidential Addresses of the American Association for the Advancement of Science, 1920–1970,* (Washington, D.C.: AAAS, 1974), 1–29.
37. Carol W. Gruber, *Mars and Minerva: World War I and the Uses of the Higher Learning in America* (Baton Rouge: Louisiana State University Press, 1975), 187–212.
38. Quoted in Matthew Josephson, *Edison: A Biography* (New York: McGraw-Hill, 1959), 447.
39. Lloyd N. Scott, *Naval Consulting Board of the United States* (Washington, D.C.: Government Printing Office, 1920), 10.
40. Kevles, *The Physicists,* chap. 8.
41. National Academy of Sciences, *Annual Report* (1916), 32.
42. Cattell, "The Organization of Scientific Men," II: 365.
43. R. A. Millikan, "The New Opportunity in Science," *Science* 50 (September 1919): 286. See also Robert H. Kargon, *The Rise of Robert Millikan: Portrait of a Life in American Science* (Ithaca: Cornell University Press, 1982), chap. 4.
44. Kargon, ed., *The Maturing of American Science,* 5–6.
45. Quoted in Kevles, *The Physicists,* 112.
46. National Academy of Sciences, *Annual Report* (1917), 55–57; National Academy of Sciences, *Annual Report* (1918), 26; and A. Hunter Dupree, *Science in the Federal Government: A History of Policies and Activities,* (1957; Baltimore: Johns Hopkins University Press, 1985), 311–12.
47. Both letters are quoted in Kargon, ed., *The Maturing of American Science,* 6–7. See also Nathan Reingold, "National Aspirations and Local Purposes," *Transactions of the Kansas Academy of Science* 71 (Fall 1968): 235–46.
48. Trustee Resolution, 28 March 1919, Corp. Files.
49. Elihu Root to George Ellery Hale, 20 May 1913, Hale Papers.
50. Henry S. Pritchett to George Ellery Hale, 3 February 1913, Hale Papers.
51. The characterization of Pritchett was James Breasted's; it is quoted in Wright, *Explorer of the Universe,* 311.
52. Quoted in Tobey, *The American Ideology of National Science,* 24.
53. *Dictionary of American Biography,* s.v. "Root, Elihu."
54. Philip C. Jessup, *Elihu Root,* 2 vols. (New York: Dodd, Mead, 1938), I: 278–79.
55. Charles W. Toth, "Elihu Root," in *An Uncertain Tradition: American*

Secretaries of State in the Twentieth Century, ed. Norman A. Graebner (New York: McGraw Hill, 1961), 40–58; David Healy, *U.S. Expansionism: The Imperialist Urge in the 1890s* (Madison: University of Wisconsin Press, 1970), chap. 8 ("Elihu Root: A World of Order and Progress").

56. Elihu Root, "Invisible Government: Speech on the Short Ballot Amendment, August 30, 1915," in *Addresses on Government and Citizenship by Elihu Root,* ed. Robert Bacon and James Brown Scott (Cambridge, Mass.: Harvard University Press, 1916), 191–200.

57. Martin J. Schiesl, *The Politics of Efficiency: Municipal Administration and Reform in America, 1800–1920* (Berkeley: University of California Press, 1977), 2. See also Samuel P. Hays, "The Politics of Reform in Municipal Government in the Progressive Era," *Pacific Northwest Quarterly* 55 (October 1964): 157–69.

58. Jessup, *Root,* I: 278.

59. Root, "Invisible Government," 206.

60. Ibid.

61. Jessup, *Root,* II: 185.

62. Alvin Johnson, *Pioneer's Progress: An Autobiography* (New York: Viking Press, 1952), 239.

63. Millikan, "The New Opportunity in Science," 297.

64. *Elihu Root. President of The Century Association. 1918–1927. Addresses Made in His Honor. At the Club House. April 27, 1937* (New York: printed for the Club, 1937), 52.

65. *The Autobiography of Robert A. Millikan* (New York: Prentice-Hall, 1950), 132.

66. Root's views are best traced through his speeches. In addition to *Addresses on Government and Citizenship* (n. 56), see *Miscellaneous Addresses by Elihu Root,* ed. Robert Bacon and James Brown Scott (Cambridge, Mass.: Harvard University Press, 1917), and *Men and Policies, Addresses by Elihu Root,* ed. Robert Bacon and James Brown Scott (Cambridge, Mass.: Harvard University Press, 1925).

67. Millikan, "The New Opportunity in Science," 297.

68. Louise Whitfield Carnegie to Elihu Root, 29 August 1932, Elihu Root Papers, Library of Congress, Washington, D.C. (hereafter Root Papers).

69. James Bertram to Elihu Root, 14 December 1908, Root Papers.

70. Elihu Root, "Andrew Carnegie: Address at a Memorial Meeting . . . April 25, 1920," in *Men and Policies,* 49.

71. Hale, "Plan" [1917], p. 8, Corp. Files.

72. Dupree, *Science in the Federal Government,* 327.

73. "Organization and Work of the National Research Council under Peace Conditions," n.d. [1919], pp. 6 and 7, Corp. Files.

74. Elihu Root, "The Need for Organization in Scientific Research," *Bulletin of the National Research Council* 1 (October 1919–February 1921): 9.

75. H. E. Howe, "The Organization of Scientific and Industrial Research at Home and Abroad," in ibid., 21–43.

76. Quoted in Kevles, *The Physicists,* 152, n. 1.
77. Quoted in Daniel J. Kevles, "George Ellery Hale, The First World War, and the Advancement of Science in America," *Isis* 59 (Winter 1968): 433.
78. "Press Release from the National Research Council . . . January 26, 1920," copy in Corp. Files. See also *A History of the National Research Council, 1919–1933,* Reprint and Circular Series No. 106 (Washington, D.C.: National Research Council, 1933), chap. 1.
79. Cattell, "The Organization of Scientific Men," II: 371.
80. Reingold, "The Case of the Disappearing Laboratory," 79–101.
81. Kevles, "George Ellery Hale," 436.

CHAPTER THREE
Propaganda or Research?
Creating an Institute of Economics

1. Irving Fisher, "Economists in Public Service," *American Economic Review* 9 supp. (March 1919): 5.
2. Ibid., 20 and 5.
3. Quoted in David M. Grossman, "American Foundations and the Support of Economic Research, 1913–1929," *Minerva* 20 (Spring/Summer 1982): 61.
4. Ibid.
5. Ibid.
6. Wesley Clair Mitchell to Lucy Sprague, 18 October 1911, quoted in Lucy Sprague Mitchell, *Two Lives: The Story of Wesley Clair Mitchell and Myself* (New York: Simon and Schuster, 1953), 187. On Mitchell's view generally see Arthur F. Burns, ed., *Wesley Clair Mitchell: The Economic Scientist* (New York: National Bureau of Economic Research, 1952).
7. Quoted in Grossman, "American Foundations and the Support of Economic Research," 67.
8. Quoted in ibid., 68.
9. Quoted in Mitchell, *Two Lives,* 291.
10. Quoted in Grossman, "American Foundations and the Support of Economic Research," 63.
11. Graham Adams, Jr., *Age of Industrial Violence, 1910–1915: The Activities and Findings of the United States Commission on Industrial Relations* (New York: Columbia University Press, 1966), chap. 7.
12. Henry S. Pritchett, "Fields of Activity Open to the Carnegie Corporation," n.d. [1916], p. 6, Corp. Files.
13. Ibid.
14. Adams, *Age of Industrial Violence,* 220–22.
15. Henry S. Pritchett to Elihu Root, 31 July 1916, Corp. Files.
16. Elihu Root to Henry S. Pritchett, n.d. [August 1916], Corp. Files.
17. Pritchett, "Fields of Activity," p. 2.

18. Quoted in Adams, *Age of Industrial Violence*, 25.

19. Allen F. Davis, "The Campaign for the Industrial Relations Commission, 1911–1913," *Mid-America* 45 (October 1963): 211–28; *Biographical Dictionary of American Business Leaders*, s.v., "Rorty, Malcolm Churchill."

20. Quoted in Herbert Heaton, *A Scholar in Action: Edwin F. Gay* (Cambridge, Mass.: Harvard University Press, 1952), 93.

21. M. C. Rorty, *Some Problems in Current Economics* (New York: A. W. Shaw, 1922), 7.

22. Wesley C. Mitchell, "Statistics and Government," in *The Backward Art of Spending Money and Other Essays* (New York: McGraw-Hill, 1937), 49–50. See also David W. Eakins, "The Origins of Corporate Liberal Policy Research, 1916–1922: The Political-Economic Expert and the Decline of Public Debate," in *Building the Organizational Society: Essays on Associational Activities in Modern America*, ed. Jerry Israel (New York: Free Press, 1972), chap. 10.

23. Quoted in Mitchell, *Two Lives*, 351. See also Robert L. Church, "Economists as Experts: The Rise of an Academic Profession in the United States, 1870–1920," in *The University in Society*, vol. 2, *Europe, Scotland, and the United States from the 16th to the 20th Century*, ed. Lawrence Stone, 2 vols. (Princeton: Princeton University Press, 1974), II: chap. 12.

24. Mitchell, "Statistics and Government," 47.

25. Mitchell, *Two Lives*, 302.

26. Wesley C. Mitchell, "The National Bureau's First Quarter-Century," *25th Annual Report* (May 1945), 11–40; Oswald W. Knauth to Beardsley Ruml, 2 December 1920, Corp. Files.

27. *Dictionary of American Biography*, s.v. "Angell, James Rowland"; W. S. Hunter, "James Rowland Angell, 1869–1949," in National Academy of Sciences, *Biographical Memoirs* (Washington, D.C.: NAS, 1951), II: 190–208.

28. "James Rowland Angell," *A History of Psychology in Autobiography*, ed. Carl Murchison (1936; reprint ed.: New York: Russell & Russell, 1961), III: 18.

29. Henry S. Pritchett, "The Administration of the Carnegie Corporation," draft memorandum, n.d. [1918], p. 5, Corp. Files.

30. "James Rowland Angell," in *A History of Psychology in Autobiography*, III: 1.

31. James Rowland Angell, "The Organization of Research," *Scientific Monthly* 11 (July 1920): 25–39; and Angell, "The National Research Council," in *The New World of Science: Its Development during the War*, ed. Robert M. Yerkes (New York: Century, 1920), 417–38.

32. [James R. Angell], "Proposals with Reference to General Policy: A Memorandum submitted by the President to the Board of Trustees of the Carnegie Corporation," n.d. [9 May 1921], p. 8, Corp. Files.

33. Ibid.

34. Max Farrand to James R. Angell, 8 November 1920, Corp. Files.
35. Oswald W. Knauth to Beardsley Ruml, 2 December 1920, Corp. Files.
36. Ibid.
37. Memorandum "To W[alter] A J[essup] from EG," 5 March 1942, Corp. Files, details Corporation grants from 2 May 1921 until 5 March 1941.
38. [James R. Angell,] "The Functions of a Giving Corporation," n.d. [1921], p. 4.
39. James R. Angell to Henry S. Pritchett, 30 June 1921, and Henry S. Pritchett to James R. Angell, 5 July 1921, Corp. Files.
40. James R. Angell to Beardsley Ruml, Beardsley Ruml Papers, Joseph Regenstein Library, University of Chicago, Chicago, Illinois.
41. James R. Angell to Henry S. Pritchett, 30 June 1921, Corp. Files.
42. Herbert Hoover to Henry S. Pritchett, 18 November 1921, Corp. Files.
43. Ellis W. Hawley, "Herbert Hoover, the Commerce Secretariat, and the Vision of an 'Associative State,' 1921–1928," *Journal of American History* 61 (June 1974): 117; chart of "The Recent Trends of Employment" prepared by the Division of Statistics of the Russell Sage Foundation," in Mary Van Kleeck, "Unemployment Ended?" *Survey* 48 (June 1922): 388.
44. Carolyn Grin, "The Unemployment Conference of 1921: An Experiment in National Cooperative Planning," *Mid-America* 55 (April 1973): 83–107.
45. Record of Interview, James R. Angell and Edwin Gay, 15 December 1920, Corp. Files.
46. Oswald W. Knauth to W. S. Learned, 13 June 1922, Corp. Files.
47. Ibid.
48. Edward E. Hunt to Henry S. Pritchett, 29 December 1921, Corp. Files.
49. Guy Alchon, *The Invisible Hand of Planning: Capitalism, Social Science, and the State in the 1920s* (Princeton: Princeton University Press, 1985), 83.
50. James R. Angell to Henry S. Pritchett, 22 May 1920, Corp. Files.
51. Herbert Hoover to Henry S. Pritchett, 18 November 1921, Corp. Files.
52. Edwin Gay to Herbert Hoover, 22 October 1921, quoted in Alchon, *The Invisible Hand of Planning*, 83.
53. E. E. Hunt to Owen D. Young, 13 February 1922, quoted in Alchon, *The Invisible Hand of Planning*, 86.
54. Vernon Kellogg to Ray Lyman Wilbur, 21 January 1921; James R. Angell, "Plan for the Establishment of a Research Institute to Study in Its Widest Bearings the Problems of Production, Distribution and Consumption of Food Stuffs," n.d.; and "The Food Research Institute, Stanford University, 1922–1923: Foundation, Organization, General Policies, Research Work in Progress, Publications, February 1, 1923," Stanford University Archives, Palo Alto, California. A copy of the press release announcing the establishment of the Institute, and various news clippings, are in the Food Research Institute Collection, Hoover Institution Archives, Palo Alto, California.
55. Charles B. Saunders, Jr., *The Brookings Institution: A Fifty Year History* (Washington, D.C.: Brookings, 1966); Donald R. Critchlow, *The Brook-*

ings Institution, 1916–1952: Expertise and Public Interest in a Democratic Society (DeKalb: Northern Illinois University Press, 1984).

56. "Institute of Economics. Letter and Accompanying Memorandum Relative to the Establishment of an Institute of Economics. Carnegie Corporation of New York. 1922," p. 1, Corp. Files.

57. Henry S. Pritchett, "Memorandum to the Trustees of the Carnegie Corporation," n.d. [1922], p. 3.

58. Ernest Barbour O'Byrne, "The Research Institutes of Stanford University" (Ph.D. diss., Stanford University, 1951), 31. See also Joseph S. Davis, "The Bending of the Twig," in *Dedication Addresses, April 6, 1970*, Food Research Institute, Stanford University, 15–19.

59. Mitchell, "The National Bureau's First Quarter-Century," 12.

60. The social composition of the social settlements is discussed in detail in Allen F. Davis, *Spearheads for Reform: The Social Settlements and the Progressive Movement, 1890–1914* (1967; New Brunswick: Rutgers University Press, 1984), chap. 2.

61. Joan Jacobs Brumberg and Nancy Tomes, "Women in the Professions: A Research Agenda for American Historians," *Reviews in American History,* 10 (June 1982): 275–96.

62. Mary Jo Deegan, *Jane Addams and the Men of the Chicago School, 1892–1918* (New Brunswick, N.J.: Transaction, 1988); and Ellen Condliffe Lagemann, "The Challenge of Jane Addams: A Research Note," *History of Higher Education Annual 6* (1986): 51–61.

63. Pritchett, "Administration of the Carnegie Corporation," p. 2.

64. Trustee Resolution, 21 May 1921, quoted in General Policy Summary, prepared for W[alter] A J[essup] by R[obert] M L[ester], Corp. Files.

65. CC, *Annual Report* (1924), 7; To W[alter] A J[essup] from R[obert] M L[ester], "Corporation Policy as to Propaganda and Pressure Groups," 5 January 1942, Corp. Files.

66. Richard T. Ely to Frederick P. Keppel, 21 December 1929, Corp. Files.

67. A. E. Taylor to Ray Lyman Wilbur, 15 May 1923, Food Research Institute Papers, Stanford University Archives.

68. Angell to Ruml, 4 December 1921, Ruml Papers, Chicago.

69. Quoted in Alva Johnston, "Beardsley Ruml: The National Idea Man—III," *New Yorker* 20 (24 February 1945): 33.

70. Raymond B. Fosdick, *The Story of the Rockefeller Foundation* (New York: Harper & Brothers, 1952), 199.

CHAPTER FOUR

Conceptualists vs. Realists: An Institute to Restate The Law

1. The American Law Institute, *Proceedings,* 1 (1923): 4.

2. Ibid., Part I: "Report of the Committee on the Establishment of a Perma-

nent Organization for the Improvement of the Law Proposing the Establishment of the American Law Institute"; and George W. Wickersham, James Byrne, John Millburn, and Harlan Stone to Henry S. Pritchett, 20 May 1922, and Press Release, 29 April 1923, Corp. Files.

3. John W. Salmond, "The Literature of Law," *Columbia Law Review* 22 (March 1922): 198.

4. Quoted in Laura Kalman, *Legal Realism at Yale, 1927–1960* (Chapel Hill: University of North Carolina Press, 1986), 17.

5. Crystal Eastman, *Work-Accidents and the Law* (New York: Charities Publication Committee, 1910), 119–24, 152.

6. Reginald Heber Smith, *Justice and the Poor*, CFAT Bulletin No. 13 (1919), p. 15.

7. Quoted in Gerald Lawrence Fetner, "Council to the Situation: The Lawyer as Social Engineer, 1900–1945" (Ph.D. diss., Brown University, 1973), 50.

8. Quoted in Robert H. Wiebe, "The House of Morgan and the Executive, 1905–1913," *American Historical Review* 65 (October 1959): 53.

9. Press Release, 29 April 1923, Corp. Files.

10. Elihu Root, "The Restatement of the Substantive Law," in *Men and Policies: Addresses by Elihu Root*, ed. Robert Bacon and James Brown Scott (Cambridge, Mass.: Harvard University Press, 1925), 160.

11. Quoted in Richard Sloane, "American Law Institute at 60," *New York Law Journal*, 17 April 1984, 4.

12. Ibid.

13. William Draper Lewis, " 'How We Did It': History of the American Law Institute and the First Restatement of the Law," in *Restatement in the Courts* (permanent ed.; St. Paul, Minn.: American Law Institute, 1945), 1; and Robert Stevens, *Law School: Legal Education in America from the 1850s to the 1980s* (Chapel Hill: University of North Carolina Press, 1983), 96.

14. Wesley Newcomb Hohfeld, "A Vital School of Jurisprudence and Law: Have American Universities Awakened to the Enlarged Opportunities and Responsibilities of the Present Day?" AALS, *Proceedings* 14 (December 1914): 79.

15. Ibid., 136.

16. Joseph H. Beale, "The Necessity for a Study of Legal System," AALS, *Proceedings* 14 (December 1914): 33–34.

17. Ibid., 33–34, 44.

18. Eugene A. Gilmore, "Some Criticisms of Legal Education," AALS, *Proceedings* 18 (December 1920): 154.

19. Ibid.

20. Herbert Croly, *The Promise of American Life* (1909; New York: E. P. Dutton, 1963), 136 and 137.

21. Woodrow Wilson, "The Lawyer and the Community," in *Report of the 33rd Annual Meeting of the ABA* (1910), 425, 428, 430.

22. Edward Stevens Robinson, *Law and the Lawyers* (New York: Macmillan, 1937), 4.
23. Elihu Root, "Some Duties of American Lawyers to American Law," *Yale Law Journal* 14 (December 1904): 73.
24. William Draper Lewis, "Legal Education and the Failure of the Bar to Perform Its Public Duties," *Transactions of the ABA* (1906), 35 and 48.
25. Gilmore, "Some Criticisms of Legal Education," 147.
26. Jerold S. Auerbach, *Unequal Justice: Lawyers and Social Change in Modern America* (New York: Oxford University Press, 1976), is the best general source on this.
27. William V. Rowe, "Legal Clinics and Better Trained Lawyers—a Necessity," *Illinois Law Review* 11 (April 1917): 602–3.
28. Harlan F. Stone, *Law and Its Administration* (New York: Columbia University Press, 1915), 178.
29. Quoted in Stevens, *Law School,* 99.
30. George W. Wickersham quoted in "Failure of Law Office to Give Adequate Training," *ABA Journal* 8 (March 1922): 149.
31. Ellen Condliffe Lagemann, *Private Power for the Public Good: A History of the Carnegie Foundation for the Advancement of Teaching* (Middletown, Conn.: Wesleyan University Press, 1983), 59–74.
32. The letter is reproduced in Alfred Zantzinger Reed, *Training for the Public Profession of the Law,* CFAT Bulletin No. 15 (1921), xviii.
33. Quoted in Auerbach, *Unequal Justice,* 125.
34. All this is described in fuller detail in Lagemann, *Private Power for the Public Good,* 75–84, and in Stevens, *Law School,* chap. 7.
35. Elihu Root, [Remarks to] New York Bar Association in *Proceedings of the Thirty-Ninth Annual Meeting* (1916), 479.
36. Henry S. Pritchett, "Fields of Activity Open to the Carnegie Corporation," 15 April 1916, p. 2, Corp. Files.
37. Carnegie Institution of Washington, *Year Book No. 20* (1921), 6.
38. Hamilton Cravens, *The Triumph of Evolution: American Scientists and the Heredity-Environment Controversy, 1900–1941* (Philadelphia: University of Pennsylvania Press, 1978), 54.
39. Richard W. Leopold, *Elihu Root and the Conservative Tradition* (Boston: Little, Brown, 1954), 171.
40. *Dictionary of American Biography,* s.v. "Merriam, John Campbell."
41. American Law Institute, *Proceedings* 1 (1923): 4.
42. Ibid., 41.
43. Ibid., 56 and 55 for the quote, and 48–53 for a description of the process.
44. Lewis, "How We Did It," 5–7.
45. Elihu Root, "The Origin of the Restatement of the Law," *Oklahoma State Bar Journal* 3 (February 1933): 309.
46. Remarks by William Draper Lewis in "A Symposium Held at the 33rd Meeting of the AALS, 'What Would Law Teachers Like to See the Institute Do?' " in *American Law School Review* 8 (December 1935): 511.

47. Christopher Columbus Langdell as quoted in Arthur E. Sutherland, *The Law at Harvard* (Cambridge, Mass.: Harvard University Press, 1967), 175.

48. James Barr Ames as quoted in Calvin Woodard, "The Limits of Legal Realism: An Historical Perspective," *Virginia Law Review* 54 (May 1968): 716.

49. Lewis, "How We Did It," 8, and "What Would Law Teachers Like," 511.

50. Lewis, "How We Did It," 7–9.

51. Henry Steele Commager, *The American Mind: An Interpretation of American Thought and Character since the 1880s* (New Haven: Yale University Press, 1950), 381–90.

52. For a discussion of similarities between professionalization in the social sciences and in the law see John Henry Schlegel, "Between the Harvard Founders and the American Legal Realists: The Professionalization of the American Law Professor," *Journal of Legal Education* 35 (September 1985): 311–25.

53. Henry S. Pritchett to William Draper Lewis, 5 January 1923, Corp. Files.

54. Lewis, "How We Did It," 12.

55. Ibid., 10 and 20.

56. Ibid., 19.

57. Stevens, *Law School*, chap. 8; John Henry Schlegel, "American Legal Realism and Empirical Social Science: From the Yale Experience," *Buffalo Law Review* 28 (Summer 1979): 459–586; and "American Legal Realism and Empirical Social Science: The Singular Case of Underhill Moore," *Buffalo Law Review* 29 (Spring 1980): 195–323.

58. Herman Oliphant, "The Problems of Logical Methods, from the Lawyer's Point of View," *Proceedings of the Academy of Political Science* 10 (July 1923): 324.

59. Ibid.

60. Ibid., 325. See also Herman Oliphant, "A Return to Stare Decisis," *American Law School Review* 6 (March 1928): 215–31.

61. For the background to this see G. Edward White, "From Sociological Jurisprudence to Realism: Jurisprudence and Social Change in Early Twentieth-Century America," *Virginia Law Review* 58 (September 1972): 999–1028.

62. *Dictionary of American Biography*, s.v. "Oliphant, Herman."

63. Remarks by Hessel E. Yntema in "What Would Law Teachers Like to See the Institute Do?" 505.

64. Ibid.

65. This comment was made in a slightly revised version of the remarks cited above that appears in *Michigan Law Review* 34 (February 1936): 472. For similarly critical commentaries see Joseph W. Bingham, "The American Law Institute vs. The Supreme Court In the Matter of Haddock v. Haddock," *Cornell Law Quarterly* 21 (April 1936): 393–435; William W. Cook, "Legal Research: Statement of American Law Institute Is Greatest

Problem Facing the Bar Today. . . ." in *American Bar Association Journal*
13 (May 1927): 281–85; and Mitchell Franklin, "The Historic Function of
the American Law Institute: Restatement as Transitional to Codification,"
Harvard Law Review 47 (June 1933–34): 1367–94.

66. Charles E. Clark, "The Restatement of the Law of Contract," *Yale Law
Journal* 42 (March 1933): 646.

67. Ibid., 656, 664, 654.

68. For Lewis's reply see his remarks to the symposium on "What Would
Teachers Like to See the Institute Do?" 510–14. The Wickersham response
was sent in draft form to Frederick P. Keppel, president of the Carnegie
Corporation, on 21 September; see Corp. Files. A published version
appeared as "Address of President Wickersham," *ABA Journal,* June
1933, 327–29, 337.

69. The quotes are from the Wickersham manuscript sent to Keppel.

70. Benjamin N. Cardozo to F. P. Keppel, 2 January 1930, Corp. Files.

71. Edward A. Purcell, Jr., *The Crisis of Democratic Theory: Scientific Naturalism & the Problem of Value* (Lexington: University Press of Kentucky,
1973), 159–78; and Bruce A. Ackerman, "*Law and the Modern Mind,*
by Jerome Frank," *Daedalus* 103 (Winter 1973): 119–30.

72. George W. Wickersham, *The Changing Order* (New York: G. P. Putnam,
1914), and *Dictionary of American Biography,* s.v. "Wickersham, George
Woodward."

73. Wickersham quoted in "Failure of the Law Office to Give Adequate Legal
Training," *ABA Journal,* 149.

74. Root, "The Restatement of the Substantive Law," 161.

75. Preface to Christopher Columbus Langdell, ed., *A Selection of Cases of
the Law of Contracts* (Boston: Little Brown, 1871), as quoted in Woodard,
"The Limits of Legal Realism: An Historical Perspective," 342–43.

76. Elihu Root, [Remarks to] New York Bar Association in *Proceedings of
the Thirty-Ninth Annual Meeting* (1916), 479.

77. For Russell Leffingwell's views of the ALI, see his letters to Frederick P.
Keppel under the following dates, all in Corp Files: 7, 13, and 28 January
and 3 November 1930; 2 February 1931; 28 December 1934; 21 December 1938.

78. Elihu Root, "Foreword," *Justice and the Poor,* ix.

79. Ibid., ix–x.

80. Norris Darrell and Paul A. Wolkin, "American Law Institute," *New York
State Bar Journal* 52 (February 1980): 99–143: Herbert F. Goodrich and
Paul A. Wolkin, *The Story of the American Law Institute, 1923–1961*
(St. Paul, Minn.: American Law Institute Publishers, 1961); and Herbert
Wechsler, "Restatements and Legal Change: Problems of Policy in the
Restatement Work of the American Law Institute," *Saint Louis University
Law Journal* 13 (Winter 1968): 185–94. Interestingly, Wechsler was direc-
tor of the ALI when he wrote the last article cited above, which was at
least in part written "because our work in the Restatements, and some

things I have said about that work, have recently been attacked" (p. 187). Even though the ALI had changed, in the late 1960s it continued to be a source of controversy within the legal profession.

81. William Twining, *Karl Llewellyn and the Realist Movement* (London: Weidenfeld and Nicolson, 1973). For one of Llewellyn's important statements of realist philosophy, see his article "A Realistic Jurisprudence—the Next Step," *Columbia Law Review* 30 (April 1930): 431–65.

PART II
Cultural Philanthropy: Introduction

1. Charles W. Eliot, "The Function of Education in Democratic Society: An Address [1897]," in Charles William Eliot, *Educational Reform: Essays and Addresses* (1898; New York: Arno Press, 1969), 412.
2. CFAT, *Annual Report* (1921–22), 101.
3. Frederick P. Keppel, "Education for Adults," in *Education for Adults and Other Essays* (New York: Columbia University Press, 1926), 9–15.
4. Colin B. Burke, "The Expansion of American Higher Education," in *The Transformation of Higher Learning, 1860–1930: Expansion, Diversification, Social Opening, and Professionalization in England, Germany, Russia, and the United States*, ed. Konrad H. Jarausch (Chicago: University of Chicago Press, 1983), 117.
5. Stuart McConnell, "E. Haldeman-Julius and the Little Blue Bookworms: The Bridging of Cultural Styles, 1919–1951," in *Prospects: An Annual of American Cultural Studies*, ed. Jack Salzman (New York: Cambridge University Press, 1987), II: 59.
6. Joan Shelley Rubin, "Self, Culture, and Self-Culture in Modern America: The Early History of the Book-of-the-Month Club," *Journal of American History* 71 (March 1985): 783.
7. Charles C. Alexander, *Here the Country Lies: Nationalism and the Arts in Twentieth—Century America* (Bloomington: Indiana University Press, 1980), 7–8.
8. Quoted in Rubin, "Early History of the Book-of-the-Month Club," 787.
9. Quoted in McConnell, "E. Haldeman-Julius," 68.

CHAPTER FIVE
Mission vs. Market:
Organizing the Education of Everyone

1. Loren Baritz, ed., *The Culture of the Twenties* (Indianapolis: Bobbs-Merrill, 1970).
2. Paul A. Carter, *Another Part of the Twenties* (New York: Columbia University Press, 1977), 163.

3. *Dictionary of American Biography*, s.v. "Keppel, Frederick Paul"; and David Keppel, *F.P.K.* (Washington, D.C.: privately printed, 1950).

4. Ralph Hayes, "Keppel's Job Is to Pour Oil on Troubled Waters," *The American Magazine* 99 (June 1925), 176; and John M. Russell, "Inside FPK," in *Appreciations of Frederick Paul Keppel by Some of His Friends* (New York: Columbia University Press, 1951), 75.

5. Henry James, "President of the Carnegie Corporation," in *Appreciations of Frederick Paul Keppel by Some of His Friends,* 58–61.

6. Raymond B. Fosdick, "The War and Navy Departments Commissions on Training Camp Activities," in American Academy of Political and Social Science, *Annals* 79 (September 1918): 131; and "The Training Camp Becomes a University," *Literary Digest* 56 (16 February 1918): 54–56.

7. Fosdick, "The War and Navy Departments Commissions on Training Camp Activities," 142.

8. Nicholas Murray Butler to Frederick P. Keppel, 12 February 1919, and 18 April [1919], Frederick P. Keppel Papers, Rare Book and Manuscript Library, Columbia University, New York City (hereafter Keppel Papers).

9. John M. Glenn, Lilian Brandt, and F. Emerson Andrews, *Russell Sage Foundation, 1907–1946,* 2 vols. (New York: Russell Sage Foundation, 1947), II: 440–42.

10. Roy Lubove, *Community Planning in the 1920s: The Contribution of the Regional Planning Association of America* (Pittsburgh: University of Pittsburgh, 1963), 117.

11. Philip C. Jessup, *Elihu Root,* 2 vols. (New York: Dood, Mead, 1938), I: 280 and 282.

12. Ibid., 281.

13. [James R. Angell], "Proposals with Reference to General Policy," [9 May 1921], Corp. Files.

14. [Henry S. Pritchett], "A Policy for the Carnegie Corporation," [1922], Corp. Files.

15. Ibid.

16. John A. Poynton, S. H. Church, and John C. Merriam, "To the Carnegie Corporation of New York," 15 November 1922, Corp. Files.

17. CC, *Annual Report* (1940), 12.

18. Dee Garrison, *Apostles of Culture: The Public Librarian and American Society, 1876–1920* (New York: Free Press, 1979), 173, indicates that some 66% of librarians were female by 1878; 78%, by 1919; and 90%, by 1920.

19. Charles C. Williamson, *Training for Library Service: A Report Prepared for the Carnegie Corporation of New York* (Boston: D. B. Updike, 1923), 110–11.

20. Margaret Ann Corwin, "An Investigation of Female Leadership in Regional, State, and Local Library Associations, 1876–1923," *Library Quarterly* 44 (April 1974): 137 and 139.

21. Frederick P. Keppel, "Library Service for the Army," *Library Journal* 44 (August 1919): 502.

22. C. Hartley Grattan, *In Quest of Knowledge—A Historical Perspective on Adult Education* (New York: Association Press, 1955), 219.
23. Oliver Stanley, ed., *The Way Out: Essays on the Meaning and Purpose of Adult Education by Members of the British Institute of Adult Education* (London: Oxford University Press, 1923).
24. W.E.A., *Education Year Book* (1918), 325.
25. J. F. C. Harrison, *Learning and Living, 1790–1960: A Study in the History of the English Adult Education Movement* (London: Routledge and Kegan Paul, 1961), 264.
26. Ibid., 268.
27. CC, "Preliminary Draft, Minutes of Conference on Adult Education," 18 June 1924, Corp. Files.
28. Frederick P. Keppel, "[Memorandum] To The Members of the Adult Education Conference," 19 December 1924, Corp. Files.
29. CC, *Annual Report* (1926), 19–20.
30. All the conferences are discussed in detail in Amy Deborah Rose, "Toward the Organization of Knowledge: Professional Adult Education in the 1920s" (Ed.D. diss., Teachers College, Columbia University, 1979), chaps. 5, 6, and 7.
31. CC, "Digest of Proceedings of National Conference on Adult Education and First Meetings of the American Association of Adult Education," 26 March 1926, Corp. Files.
32. American Association of Adult Education, *Annual Report* (1926), 13–15.
33. Carnegie Corporation Office Memorandum, series II, no. 10, "Tentative Program, 8 December 1924."
34. Malcolm Knowles, *A History of the Adult Education Movement in the United States* (Huntington, N.Y.: Robert E. Krieger, 1977), 211.
35. National Education Association, *Proceedings* (1927), 332.
36. Ellen Condliffe Lagemann, *Private Power for the Public Good: A History of the Carnegie Foundation for the Advancement of Teaching* (Middletown: Wesleyan University Press, 1983), 187–89.
37. Interview with Morse A. Cartwright, Oral History of the Carnegie Corporation, Oral History Research Office, Columbia University, New York (hereafter OHCC), p. 132.
38. Frederick P. Keppel, "Education for Adults," in *Education for Adults and Other Essays* (New York: Columbia University Press, 1926), 15.
39. This was the group that David B. Tyack and Elisabeth Hansot have called the "educational trust" in *Managers of Virtue: Public School Leadership in America, 1820–1980* (New York: Basic Books, 1982).
40. Keppel, "Education for Adults," 15.
41. Morse Adams Cartwright, *Ten Years of Adult Education: A Report on a Decade of Progress in the American Movement* (New York: Macmillan, 1935), 24–25. Ronald James Hilton claims, in "The Short Happy Life of a Learning Society: Adult Education in America, 1930–1939" (Ph.D.

diss., Syracuse University, 1981), 270, that contemporaries saw the AAAE as "elitist."

42. The advisers are listed in Brenda Jubin, *Program in the Arts, 1911–1967,* Carnegie Corporation Review Series #40 (1968), 5.

43. Milton W. Brown, *The Story of the Armory Show* (New York: Joseph H. Hirshhorn Fund, 1963), 131.

44. Ibid.

45. Ibid., 131–32 and, for the quote, *Dictionary of American Biography,* s.v. "Cortissoz, Royal."

46. Quoted in Brown, *The Story of the Armory Show,* 136.

47. Quoted in ibid., 133 and 139.

48. Frederick P. Keppel and Robert M. Lester, *Review of Grants in the Arts, 1911–1933,* Carnegie Corporation Review Series #14 (1933), 15. Jubin, *Program in the Arts, 1911–1967,* accounts for all grants, although the years used do not coincide exactly with the interwar arts program. However, according to Jubin, $517,750 was awarded to the American Federation of the Arts between 1913 and 1953, whereas the American Association of Museums received $291,450 between 1929 and 1948, and the College Arts Association $122,700 between 1926 and 1941. Among the other organizations receiving large amounts were the American Council of Learned Societies, which received $155,750 between 1928 and 1942, and the American Institute of Architects, which received $227,400 between 1924 and 1939.

49. Joshua C. Taylor, *The Fine Arts in America* (Chicago: University of Chicago Press, 1979), 155–56.

50. "Proceedings of the Convention at Which the American Federation of Arts Was Formed, Held at Washington, D.C., May 11th, 12th, and 13th, 1909" (Washington, D.C.: Press of Byron S. Adams, 1909), 9.

51. Jubin, *Program in the Arts, 1911–1967,* 5–6, 60–68.

52. Quoted in Karl E. Meyer, *The Art Museum: Power, Money, Ethics. A Twentieth Century Fund Report* (New York: William Morrow, 1979), 40.

53. Keppel and Lester, *Review of Grants in the Arts, 1911–1933,* 8–9, 28.

54. Jubin, *Program in the Arts, 1911–1967,* 7–9, 79–115; Florence Anderson, "Memorandum on the Use of Art and Music Study Material" (New York: Carnegie Corporation, 1941); and the "Carnegie Art Reference Set for Colleges" (New York: Rudolph Lesch Fine Arts, 1939), Introduction. Florence Anderson claimed that the art sets were "a consolation prize" for institutions that would not otherwise have received support from the Corporation (Interview with Florence Anderson, OHCC, p. 168).

55. Glenn, Brandt, and Andrews, *Russell Sage Foundation, 1907–1946,* II: 370–71.

56. William S. Learned, *The American Public Library and the Diffusion of Knowledge* (New York: Harcourt, Brace, 1924), 12.

57. Ibid.

58. Charles C. Williamson, *Training for Library Service: A Report Prepared for the Carnegie Corporation of New York* (Boston: D. B. Updike, 1923), 4.

59. Ibid., 7.

60. Ibid.

61. Ibid., 8, 9.

62. Garrison, *Apostles of Culture,* 191.

63. Joan Jacobs Brumberg and Nancy Tomes, "Women in the Professions: A Research Agenda for American Historians," *Reviews in American History* 10 (June 1982): 275–96.

64. Williamson, *Training for Library Service,* Introduction.

65. Sarah K. Vann, *The Williamson Reports: A Study* (Metuchen, N.J.: Scarecrow Press, 1971), supports these points and contrasts a first draft of the report originally submitted in 1921 with the one published in 1923, the major difference being in the detail provided about particular schools.

66. "The Williamson Report: Comments from the Library Schools," *Library Journal* 48 (1923): 901–2. See also "The Williamson Reports—II: Comments from Librarians," *Library Journal* 48 (1923): 999–1005.

67. CC, *Annual Report* (1926), 9–11; "The Carnegie Corporation Program in Library Service," *Library Journal* 51 (1926): 527–28.

68. Corwin, "An Investigation of Female Leadership in Regional, State, and Local Library Associations, 1876–1923," 137.

69. Charles D. Churchwell, *The Shaping of American Library Education* (Chicago: American Library Association, 1975), 68.

70. John Richardson, Jr., *The Spirit of Inquiry: The Graduate Library School at Chicago, 1921–1951* (Chicago: American Library Association, 1982).

71. Quoted in Ralph Munn, *Conditions and Trends in Education for Librarianship* (New York: Carnegie Corporation of New York, 1936), vi.

72. Ibid., 22 and 16.

73. Ibid., 11.

74. Neil A. Radford, *The Carnegie Corporation and the Development of American College Libraries, 1928–1941* (Chicago: American Library Association, 1984), 42–44, 50, 66–68, 73, and passim.

75. Ibid., 191.

76. Ibid.

77. CC, *Annual Report* (1933), 14.

78. Edward P. Alexander, *Museum Masters: Their Museums and Their Influence* (Nashville, Tenn.: American Association for State and Local History, 1983), chap. 13.

79. "Proceedings of the Informal Conference on the Arts Held under the Auspices of the Carnegie Corporation of New York, 16–17 December 1941," pp. 16–21, Corp. Files.

80. Paul Marshall Rea, *The Museum and the Community, with a Chapter on the Library and the Community* (Lancaster, Pa.: Science Press, 1932).

81. AAAE, "The Fifteen-Year Record" (1940), Corp. Files.

82. Quoted in Harry Augustus Garfield, *Lost Visions* (privately printed, 1944), "Appendix," by Arthur Howland Buffington, 253. Garfield was president of Williams College when the Institute was founded in 1921.

83. Institute of Politics, *Proceedings* (1928).

84. Garfield, *Lost Visions*, 251.

85. Robert Bruce Fisher, "The People's Institute of New York City, 1897–1934: Culture, Progressive Democracy, and the People" (Ph.D. diss., New York University, 1974), 354–55.

86. Frederick Paul Keppel, "The Adult Education Movement," *Current History* 27 (January 1926): 514.

87. Fisher, "The People's Institute," 366–67.

88. Everett Dean Martin, *Liberty* (New York: W. W. Norton, 1930), 97–98.

89. Quoted in Fisher, "The People's Institute," 372–73.

90. Everett Dean Martin, *The Meaning of a Liberal Education* (New York: W. W. Norton, 1926), 317.

91. Fisher, "The People's Institute," 391.

92. David W. Stewart, *Adult Learning in America: Eduard Lindeman and His Agenda for Lifelong Education* (Malabar, Fla.: Robert E. Krieger, 1987), 90–91.

93. *Workers' Education in the United States: Report of Proceedings, Second National Conference, 1922* (New York: Workers' Education Bureau, 1922), appendix. Beard's role as a founder is discussed in George S. Counts, "Charles Beard, the Public Man," in *Charles A. Beard: An Appraisal*, ed. Howard K. Beale (Lexington: University of Kentucky Press, 1954), 241.

94. *Workers' Education . . . Proceedings, 1922*, 96.

95. Ibid., 36.

96. Ibid., 96.

97. Report of the Workers' Education Bureau Press, Inc., 1925–1933, and Report, 1932–1933, Corp. Files.

98. Frederick Keppel to Geoffrey Parsons, 14 November 1939, Keppel Papers; Henry S. Pritchett to Elihu Root, 13 January 1926, Corp. Files.

99. CC, *Annual Report* (1933), 13.

100. Robert D. Leigh, *The Public Library in the United States: The General Report of the Public Library Inquiry of the Social Science Research Council* (New York: Columbia University Press, 1950).

101. Gary E. Kraske, *Missionaries of the Book: The American Library Profession and the Origins of United States Cultural Diplomacy* (Westport, Conn.: Greenwood Press, 1985); Doris Cruger Dale, ed., *Carl H. Milam and the United Nations' Library* (Metuchen, N.J.: Scarecrow Press, 1976); and Frank A. Ninovich, *The Diplomacy of Ideas: U.S. Foreign Policy and Cultural Relations, 1938–1950* (Cambridge: Cambridge University Press, 1981).

102. Keppel, "Education for Adults," 15.
103. Ibid., 11.
104. American Association for Adult Education, *Annual Report* (1929–30), 19.
105. Knowles, *A History of Adult Education in the United States*, 197–220.

CHAPTER SIX
Public Policy and Sociology:
Gunnar Myrdal's *An American Dilemma*

1. Carnegie Corporation, Trustee Minutes, 24 October 1935, Corp. Files.
2. Robert K. Merton, "The Unanticipated Consequences of Purposive Social Action," *American Sociological Review* 1 (1936): 894–904.
3. David W. Southern, *Gunnar Myrdal and Black-White Relations: The Use and Abuse of* An American Dilemma, *1944–1969* (Baton Rouge: Louisiana State University Press, 1987).
4. Gunnar Myrdal with Richard Sterner and Arnold Rose, *An American Dilemma: The Negro Problem and Modern Democracy*, 2 vols. (New York: Harper & Brothers, 1944). There are many editions of *An American Dilemma*; I shall refer to the one-volume edition published in 1944. The quote is from p. 1021.
5. Frederick P. Keppel, "Foreword," *An American Dilemma*, vi.
6. [Frederick P. Keppel], "The Carnegie Corporation: Finances, Program, Control and Administration" [Memorandum for the Trustees, September 1934], Newton D. Baker Papers, Division of Manuscripts, Library of Congress, Washington, D.C. (hereafter Baker Papers).
7. Ibid.
8. Frederick P. Keppel to Thomas Jesse Jones, 12 July 1932, Corp. Files, provides the amount of grants; the institutions receiving funds can be traced through the *Annual Reports*.
9. These are described in detail in Richard David Heyman, "The Role of Carnegie Corporation in African Education, 1925–1960" (Ed.D. diss., Teachers College, Columbia University, 1969), and Edward Henry Berman, "Education in Africa and America: A History of the Phelps-Stokes Fund, 1911–1945 (Ed.D. diss., Teachers College, Columbia University, 1969).
10. Quoted in Louis R. Harlan, *Separate and Unequal: Public School Campaigns and Racism in the Southern Seaboard States, 1901–1915* (Chapel Hill: University of North Carolina Press, 1968), 78.
11. *Negro Education: A Study of the Private and Higher Schools for Colored People in the United States*. Prepared in Cooperation with the Phelps-Stokes Fund under the Direction of Thomas Jesse Jones. Department of the Interior, Bureau of Education, Bulletin 1916, No. 38 [vol. I] and no. 39 [vol. II] (1917; reprint ed., New York: Negro University Press, 1969), I: 42.

12. Ibid., II: 245–46.
13. Ibid., I: 97.
14. W. E. B. Du Bois. "The Training of Negroes for Social Power (1903)," *Outlook* 75 (October 1903): 409.
15. Ibid., 410. See also W. E. B. Du Bois, *The Souls of Black Folks* (1903; reprint, New York: Dodd, Mead, 1979), chaps. 3 and 4.
16. Raymond Wolters, *The New Negro on Campus: Black College Rebellions of the 1920s* (Princeton: Princeton University Press, 1975), especially chap. 2.
17. Dan S. Green and Edwin D. Driver, *W. E. B. Du Bois on Sociology and the Black Community* (Chicago: University of Chicago Press, 1978), 31, 39–48; and Elliot Rudwick, "W. E. B. Du Bois as Sociologist," in James E. Blackwell and Morris Janowitz, *Black Sociologists: Historical and Contemporary Perspectives* (Chicago: University of Chicago Press, 1974), 41–50.
18. Anson Phelps Stokes, "Address," in "Memoriam, Thomas Jesse Jones, 1873–1950" (New York: Phelps-Stokes Fund, 1950), 15.
19. Arthur J. Klein, *Survey of Negro Colleges and Universities,* Department of the Interior, Bureau of Education, Bulletin 1928, No. 7 (Washington, D.C.: Government Printing Office, 1929).
20. Frederick P. Keppel, "Newton D. Baker," *Foreign Affairs* 16 (April 1938): 503–14.
21. Newton D. Baker to F. P. Keppel, 23 December 1935, Newton D. Baker Papers.
22. Newton D. Baker to F. P. Keppel, 22 April 1936, Baker Papers.
23. Baker to Keppel, 23 December 1935.
24. Ulrich Bonnell Phillips, "The Plantation as a Civilizing Factor," *Sewanee Review* 12 (July 1904): 258–67.
25. Baker to Keppel, 23 December 1935.
26. Newton D. Baker to Robert M. Lester, 26 December 1934, Baker Papers.
27. Baker to Keppel, 23 December 1935.
28. Daniel R. Beaver, *Newton D. Baker and the American War Effort, 1917–1919* (Lincoln: University of Nebraska Press, 1966), 224.
29. Baker to Keppel, 23 December 1935.
30. Ibid.
31. Memorandum of Conversation, R[obert] M L[ester] and Milam, Favrot, and S. L. Smith, 19 October 1934, Corp. Files.
32. *Dictionary of American Negro Biography,* s.v. "Locke, Alain Leroy."
33. Nathan Irvin Huggins, *Harlem Renaissance* (New York: Oxford University Press, 1971), 56–60 and passim.
34. Patrick Joseph Gilpin, "Charles S. Johnson: An Intellectual Biography," 2 vols. (Ph.D. diss., Vanderbilt University, 1973), I: 33–39.
35. Alain Locke, ed., *The New Negro* (1925; reprinted, New York: Atheneum, 1968).
36. Ibid., 3–4.

37. Ibid., 8 and 12.
38. Ibid., 199–213, 254–67.
39. F. P. Keppel to Alain Locke, 13 December 1938; Alain Locke to F. P. Keppel, 1 June 1928; F. P. Keppel to Alain Locke, 2 June 1928; and Notes of Meeting, Alain Locke and F. P. Keppel, Sunday, 2 June 1928, all in Alain L. Locke Papers, Manuscript Division, Moorland-Spingarn Research Center, Howard University, Washington, D.C. (hereafter Locke Papers).
40. *Dictionary of American Negro Biography*, s.v. "Woodson, Carter Goodwin," 666.
41. Mildred Chadsey to Alain L. Locke, 2 November 1927, and Catherine Nock to Alain L. Locke, 23 January 1928, Locke Papers.
42. Charlotte R. Morgan, "Finding a Way Out: Adult Education in Harlem during the Great Depression," *Afro-Americans in New York Life and History* 8 (January 1984): 17–29.
43. Morse A. Cartwright to William H. Cooper, 15 February 1937, Locke Papers.
44. L. Hollingsworth Wood to David Mannes, 10 February 1937, L. Hollingsworth Wood Papers, Schomburg Center for Research in Black Culture, New York Public Library, 515 Lenox Avenue, New York City.
45. Alain Locke, Report of Negro Adult Education Projects, 15 March 1934, Locke Papers.
46. [Alain Locke], Final Memorandum: New Projects in Adult Education for Negro Groups, 15 April 1934, Locke Papers.
47. Morse A. Cartwright to Alain Locke, 21 June 1934, Locke Papers.
48. John H. Stanfield, *Philanthropy and Jim Crow in American Social Science* (Westport, Conn.: Greenwood Press, 1985).
49. *Dictionary of American Negro Biography*, s.v. "Woodson, Carter Goodwin," 666.
50. Alain Locke, Report of Negro Adult Education Projects, 15 March 1934, and Final Memorandum: New Projects in Adult Education for Negro Groups, 15 April 1934, Locke Papers.
51. Associates in Negro Folk Education, Memorandum of Organization, n.d. [February 1935], Locke Papers.
52. Alain Locke, Report of Negro Adult Education Projects, 15 March 1934, Locke Papers.
53. Summary, J. Th. Moll to H. Mouw, enclosed in J. Th. Moll to F. P. Keppel, 2 November 1936, and F. P. Keppel in J. H. Huizinga, 1 February 1937, Corp. Files.
54. [Gunnar Myrdal, Notes of] Conference with Dr. [*sic*] Keppel, Sunday, 12 March 1939, Corp. Files.
55. Newton D. Baker to John M. Russell, 24 March 1936, Baker Papers.
56. Arna Bontemps and Jack Conroy, *Anyplace But Here* (New York: Hill and Wang, 1945), 280. See also John Selby, *Beyond Civil Rights* (Cleveland: World Publishing, 1966).
57. F. P. Keppel to Newton D. Baker, 21 September 1936, Baker Papers.

58. Ibid.
59. "To Whom It May Concern," Memorandum 2 July 1942, Corp. Files; Interview with Gunnar Myrdal," Oral History of the Carnegie Corporation, Oral History Research Office, Columbia University, New York (hereafter OHCC), p. 6.
60. Bertram Schrieke, *Alien Americans: A Study of Race Relations* (New York: Viking, 1936).
61. *International Encyclopedia of the Social Sciences,* s.v. "Schrieke, Bertram," XIV: 64.
62. Schrieke, *Alien Americans,* 193 and 191.
63. Ibid., 191.
64. Ibid., vii.
65. Negro Study—Personnel Suggestions—Through 15 July 1937, Corp. Files.
66. Ibid.
67. Ibid.; Lawrence K. Frank to F. P. Keppel, 13 July 1937, Corp. Files. See also Martin Bulmer and Joan Bulmer, "Philanthropy and Social Science in the 1920s: Beardsley Ruml and the Laura Spelman Rockefeller Memorial, 1922–1929," *Minerva* 19 (Autumn 1981): 347–407.
68. *International Encyclopedia of the Social Sciences,* Biographical Supplement, s.v. "Myrdal, Gunnar." Allan C. Carlson, "The Role of Alva and Gunnar Myrdal in the Development of a Social Democratic Response to Europe's Population Crisis, 1928–1938" (Ph.D. diss., Ohio University, 1978).
69. Lawrence K. Frank to F. P. Keppel, 13 July 1937, Corp. Files.
70. Ibid.
71. F. P. Keppel to Gunnar Myrdal, 12 August 1937, Corp. Files.
72. Gunnar Myrdal to F. P. Keppel, n.d. [received 11 September 1937]; and Gunnar Myrdal to F. P. Keppel, 7 October 1937, Corp. Files.
73. Cable, Gunnar Myrdal to F. P. Keppel, 5 October 1937, Corp. Files.
74. F. P. Keppel to Newton D. Baker, 15 November 1937, Baker Papers.
75. Newton D. Baker to F. P. Keppel, 23 November 1937, Baker Papers.
76. Gunnar Myrdal, *Vetenenskap och politik i nationalekonomien* (*The political element in the development of economic theory*), translated from the German by Paul Streeten (Cambridge, Mass.: Harvard University Press, 1961), 204.
77. Gunnar Myrdal, "Das zweck-mittel-denken in der nationalökonomie" ("Ends and means in political economy"), in Paul Streeten, ed., *Value in Social Theory: A Selection of Essays on Methodology by Gunnar Myrdal* (London: Routledge & Kegan Paul, 1958), 230.
78. Interview with Donald Young, OHCC, p. 38.
79. F. P. Keppel, Memorandum of Notes for Discussion with Myrdal, 11 May 1938, Corp. Files.
80. The quote is from Myrdal, "Das zweck-mittel-denken in der nationalökonomie," 230.
81. F. P. Keppel to Raymond B. Fosdick, 8 June 1938, Corp. Files.

82. *National Cyclopedia of American Biography,* s.v. "Davis, Jackson."
83. Interview with Gunnar Myrdal, OHCC, pp. 24–26.
84. Record of Interview R[obert] M L[ester] and Jackson Davis, 14 November 1938, Corp. Files.
85. Interview with Gunnar Myrdal, OHCC, p. 25.
86. Gunnar Myrdal, "Author's Preface to the Twentieth Anniversary Edition," *An American Dilemma* (New York: Harper & Row, 1962), xxv–xxvi.
87. Gunnar Myrdal to F. P. Keppel, 28 January 1939, p. 4.
88. Ibid., 8.
89. Ibid., 10–11.
90. Ibid., 10.
91. Ibid., 13–19.
92. [Gunnar Myrdal, Notes of] Conference with Dr. [*sic*] Keppel, Sunday, 12 March 1939, Corp. Files.
93. F. P. Keppel to Howard W. Odum, 27 May 1939, Corp. Files. On Keppel's defense of the study, see Interview with Gunnar Myrdal, OHCC, pp. 32, 80–81.
94. Myrdal, "Author's Preface to the Twentieth Anniversary Edition," *An American Dilemma,* xxvi.
95. F. P. Keppel to Gunnar Myrdal, 2 September 1942, Corp. Files.
96. The names of the individuals are listed in Myrdal, *An American Dilemma.*
97. Gunnar Myrdal to F. P. Keppel, 26 April 1939, Corp. Files.
98. The memoranda and their authors are listed in Myrdal, *An American Dilemma.*
99. *Current Biography,* s.v. "Bunche, Ralph J(ohnson)." See also Record of Interview C[harles] D[ollard], Mr. Myrdal and Mr. Sterner, 20 November 1939, Corp. Files.
100. Interview with Gunnar Myrdal, OHCC, p. 87.
101. Memorandum to Dr. [*sic*] Keppel from C[harles] D[ollard] and Samuel A. Stouffer, 28 February 1941, Corp. Files.
102. Record of Interview C[harles] D[ollard] and Mr. Myrdal, 7 March 1939, Corp. Files; Interview with Gunnar Myrdal, OHCC, pp. 57–58.
103. Myrdal, *An American Dilemma,* 928.
104. Ibid., 831–36.
105. Memorandum to Mr. [Walter] White from Mr. [Roy] Wilkins, 21 October 1939, Corp. Files.
106. Walter White to Gunnar Myrdal, 29 July 1942, Corp. Files.
107. This generational difference is discussed in detail in James O. Young, *Black Writers of the Thirties* (Baton Rouge: Louisiana State University Press, 1973). As it pertains to the Myrdal study it is also featured in Walter A. Jackson, "The Making of a Social Science Classic: Gunnar Myrdal's *An American Dilemma,*" *Perspectives in American History,* n.s. 2 (1985): 221–67.
108. Gunnar Myrdal to Charles Dollard, 22 June 1942, Corp. Files.

109. F. P. Keppel to Gunnar Myrdal, 13 July 1942; and Charles Dollard to Gunnar Myrdal, 28 November 1941 and 10 July 1942, Corp. Files.

110. Joan Acker, "Women and Social Stratification: A Case of Intellectual Sexism," *American Journal of Sociology* 78 (January 1973): 936–45.

111. Gunnar Myrdal to F. P. Keppel, 22 June 1942, Corp. Files.

112. Gunnar Myrdal to F. P. Keppel, 2 September 1942; Gunnar Myrdal to Louis Wirth, 2 July 1942, Corp. Files.

113. Myrdal, *An American Dilemma*, xlix.

114. Bulmer, *The Chicago School of Sociology*, chap. 4; Morris Janowitz, ed., *Social Behavior and Personality: Contributions of W. I. Thomas to Theory and Social Research* (New York: Social Science Research Council, 1951).

115. Fred H. Matthews, *Quest for an American Sociology: Robert E. Park and the Chicago School* (Montreal: McGill-Queens University Press, 1977); and R. Fred Wacker, *Ethnicity, Pluralism, and Race: Race Relations Theory in America before Myrdal* (Westport, Conn.: Greenwood Press, 1983).

116. Myrdal, *An American Dilemma*, 1023.

117. Ibid., 1041.

118. Ibid., 1050.

119. G. Franklin Edwards, *E. Franklin Frazier on Race Relations* (Chicago: University of Chicago Press, 1968); Matthews, *Quest for an American Sociology;* and Wacker, *Ethnicity, Pluralism, and Race.*

120. Myrdal, *An American Dilemma*, 1063–64.

121. Louis Wirth, "On Making Values Explicit," in Albert J. Reiss, *Louis Wirth on Cities and Social Life* (Chicago, University of Chicago Press, 1964), 157.

122. Reiss, "Introduction," in ibid., xviii.

123. Charles Dollard to Gunnar Myrdal, 28 November 1941, Corp. Files.

124. F. P. Keppel Confidential Memorandum to Walter A. Jessup, 27 July 1942, Corp. Files.

125. E. B. Reuter and W. E. B. Du Bois, "Myrdal's *An American Dilemma*: Two Reviews," *Phylon* 5 (1944): 121; and Oscar Handlin, "Review of the Twentieth Anniversary Edition of *An American Dilemma*," *New York Times Book Review*, 21 April 1963, p. 1.

126. *Brown v. Board of Education*, 347 U.S. 483 (1954).

127. Southern, *Gunnar Myrdal and Black-White Relations: The Use and Abuse of* An American Dilemma, 1944–1969.

128. Carnegie Corporation, Trustee Agenda, 15 May 1947, p. 22, Corp. Files.

129. [Sara L. Engelhardt], "Carnegie Corporation and the Powerless: The Past Ten Years in Perspective," Memorandum to Executive Staff, 22 January 1975, p. 27, Corp. Files.

PART III
Strategic Philanthropy: Introduction

1. "A Program on International Relations," Trustee Agenda, 20 November 1945, Corp. Files.
2. [Pendleton Herring with the help of Charles Dollard and John W. Gardner], "The Conduct of Cold War," 8 July 1947, Corp. Files.
3. [Charles Dollard], "The Social Sciences," Trustees Agenda, 16 May 1946, Corp. Files.
4. "A Program for Carnegie Corporation, To: Mr. Josephs, From: Mr. Gardner," 3 July 1946, p. 1, Corp. Files.
5. "Report of the President of Harvard College . . . for 1946–47," *Register of Harvard University* 46 (1949): 20.
6. Samuel A. Stouffer, "Sociology and the Strategy of Social Science," in *Social Research to Test Ideas: Selected Writings of Samuel A. Stouffer* (New York: Free Press, 1962), 10.
7. Memorandum to Staff, from F[ritz] M[osher] and R. B., "Elementary and Secondary Education Revisited—Strategically," 10 April 1972, p. 1, Corp. Files.
8. S[ara] L E[ngelhardt], "Carnegie Corporation and the Powerless: The Past Ten Years in Perspective," 22 January 1975, p. 16, Corp. Files.
9. [Memorandum] to Trustees, [From: Eli Evans,] "For Discussion: Carnegie Corporation and Litigation: A Four Year Assessment," 1 June 1976, Corp. Files.
10. Sara L. Engelhardt and David Z. Robinson, "Carnegie Corporation's Program: Where We Are and How We Got There," 11 March 1980, p. 22, Corp. Files.
11. Lawrence Gelfand, *The Inquiry* (New Haven: Yale University Press, 1963).
12. "Interview with Devereux Josephs," Oral History of the Carnegie Corporation, Oral History Research Office, Columbia University, New York, p. 43.

CHAPTER SEVEN
Effective Expertise:
New Designs for Social Research

1. [Charles Dollard], "The Social Sciences," Corp. Files.
2. James R. Angell to E. E. Day (Memorandum on the Institute for Human Behavior), 20 December 1928, in the Laura Spelman Rockefeller Memorial Collection, Series 3.6, Box 79, Folder 826, Rockefeller Archive Center, North Tarrytown, N.Y.
3. James R. Angell, "The Yale Institute for Human Relations," Association of American Universities, *Proceedings* (1929), 51.

4. Mark A. May, "A Retrospective View of the Institute for Human Relations at Yale," *Behavior Sciences Notes: HRAF Quarterly Bulletin* 6 (1971): 141–72.

5. Guy Benton Johnson and Guion Griffis Johnson, *Research in Service to Society: The First Fifty Years of the Institute for Research in Social Science at the University of North Carolina* (Chapel Hill: University of North Carolina Press, 1980); and Wilson Gee, *Social Science Research Organizations in American Universities and Colleges* (New York: Appleton-Century, 1934).

6. *International Encyclopedia of the Social Sciences*, s.v. "Sapir, Edward"; Harry Stack Sullivan, "Edward Sapir, Ph.D., Sc.D.," *Psychiatry* 2 (February 1939): 159; and Helen Swick Perry, *Psychiatrist of America: The Life of Harry Stack Sullivan* (Cambridge, Mass.: Harvard University Press, 1982), chap. 28.

7. The first two articles are among the essays in Edward Sapir, *Culture, Language, and Personality: Selected Essays*, ed. David G. Mandelbaum (Berkeley: University of California Press, 1949); the third article appeared in *American Journal of Sociology* 42 (1937): 862–70.

8. American Psychiatric Association, Committee on Relations with the Social Sciences, *Proceedings: First Colloquium on Personality Investigation*, 1–2 December 1928; American Psychiatric Association, Committee on Relations of Psychiatry and the Social Science Research Council, *Proceedings: Second Colloquium on Personality Investigation*, 29–30 November 1929.

9. "50th Anniversary of the 1930 Hanover Conference: The Letters of Robert Redfield . . . ," *Items* 34 (1980): 35–37.

10. Social Science Research Council, Hanover Conference [Transcript]: Sunday Evening Session, 31 August 1930, "The Cultural Approach to the Study of Personality," Dr. Edward Sapir, pp. 72–99. Social Science Research Council Files, 605 Third Avenue, New York City.

11. Social Science Research Council, *Annual Report* (1929–30), 19; and Perry, *Harry Stack Sullivan*, 265–77.

12. Social Science Research Council, *Annual Report* (1930–31), 27–28.

13. "Interview with John Dollard," Department of Sociology Interviews, 1972, Box 1, Folder 7, Department of Special Collections, The Joseph Regenstein Library, University of Chicago, Chicago, Illinois.

14. William F. Ogburn, "Bias, Psychoanalysis, and the Subjective in Relation to the Social Sciences" (1922), in *William F. Ogburn on Culture and Social Change*, ed. Otis Dudley Duncan (Chicago: University of Chicago Press, 1964), 301.

15. Ibid.

16. "Interview with John Dollard," pp. 2 and 12.

17. Social Science Research Council, *Annual Report* (1930–31), 28.

18. Perry, *Harry Stack Sullivan*, 366.

19. Margaret Mead, *An Anthropologist at Work: The Writings of Ruth Benedict* (Boston: Houghton, Mifflin, 1959), 209.

Notes to Pages 158–161

20. Quoted in *International Encyclopedia of the Social Sciences,* s.v. "Dollard, John."

21. John Dollard, "Preface—1949," *Caste and Class in a Southern Town* (1937; New York: Harper & Brothers, 1949), xi–xii.

22. "Interview with John Dollard," p. 6.

23. *Current Biography 1948,* s.v. "Dollard, Charles."

24. "Interview with John Russell," Oral History of the Carnegie Corporation, Oral History Research Office, Columbia University, New York (hereafter OHCC), pp. 127–33.

25. The two studies were undertaken for the Research Branch of the Information and Education Division of the War Department, and were entitled "Command of Negro Troops" and "Leadership and the Negro Soldier." They were discussed in Charles Dollard and Donald Young, "In the Armed Forces," an article that appeared in *Survey Graphic* 36 (1947): 66–68, 111–19, a special edition devoted to the problem of "Segregation."

26. "Interview with John W. Gardner," OHCC, p. 6. Cf. "Interview with Frederick Osborn," OHCC, pp. 45–50, and "Interview with John Russell," OHCC, p. 137.

27. "Interview with Frederick Osborn," OHCC, pp. 38–41, and "Interview with Francis Keppel," OHCC, p. 52. "Interview with John Dollard" hints that John Dollard suffered from depressions. In explaining his early interest in psychoanalysis, John Dollard said: "I was just dirty sick. I was very neurotic" (p. 13). Doubtless from concern for Charles Dollard, most of his Corporation colleagues refused to discuss his mental illness in their oral histories.

28. "CD and Annual Meeting of Social Science Research Council, Buck Hill Falls, Pa., 13–15 September 1938," Corp. Files.

29. Ibid.

30. The title for Keppel's talk as printed in the SSRC conference transcript was different from the original title suggested by Permanent Secretary Robert S. Lynd, which was "The Social Science of Spending Foundation Money during the Next Decade" (Robert S. Lynd to Frederick P. Keppel, 6 August 1930, Corp. Files), although the actual talk dealt generally with the topic Lynd had suggested. See Social Science Research Council, Hanover Conference [Transcript]: Friday Evening Session, 29 August 1930, pp. 1–28, SSRC Files.

31. Keppel speech transcript, p. 4.

32. Records of Interviews, FPK and Ralph Linton, 19 December 1938; CD and Ralph Linton, 7 January 1939; CD and FPK, 10 January 1939; CD and Ralph Linton, 4 February 1939, Corp. Files. The names of the candidates considered and selected for the fellowships can be traced through correspondence pertaining to "Interdisciplinary Fellowship," Corp. Files.

33. Charles Dollard to Ralph Linton [and identical letter to Donald Young], 3 March 1942, Corp. Files.

34. Alexander H. Leighton, *Human Relations in a Changing World: Observations on the Uses of the Social Sciences* (New York: E. P. Dutton, 1949).

35. Frederick Osborn, *Voyage to a New World, 1889–1979: A Personal Narrative* (from recordings by Joan Annet Osborn) (Garrison, N.Y.: privately printed, 1979); obituary, *New York Times,* 7 January 1981.

36. Among Osborn's writings on the subject were: (with Frank Lorimer) *Dynamics of Population: Social and Biological Significance of Changing Birth Rates in the United States* (New York: Macmillan, 1934); *Preface to Eugenics* (New York: Harper & Brothers, 1940); "American Educational Policy: Significance of Differential Reproduction for American Educational Policy," *Social Forces* 14 (October 1935–May 1936): 23–32; "Development of a Eugenic Philosophy," *American Sociological Review* 2 (June 1937): 389–97; and *The Future of Human Heredity: An Introduction to Eugenics in Modern Society* (New York: Weybright and Talley, 1969).

37. Osborn, *Voyage to a New World,* chap. 5; Jack Edward Pulwers, "The Information and Education Program of the Armed Forces: An Administrative and Social History (1940–1945)," (Ph.D. diss., Catholic University of America, 1983), 325–46.

38. Author's interview with Francis Keppel, 10 June 1986, Cambridge Mass. The grant to Osborn's Joint Committee is mentioned in CC, *Annual Report* (1942), 53.

39. Dorwin Cartwright, "Social Psychology in the United States during the Second World War," *Human Relations* 1 (1947): 333–52.

40. Osborn, *Voyage to a New World,* 96: *International Encyclopedia of the Social Sciences,* s.v. "Stouffer, Samuel A."

41. Samuel A. Stouffer, Edward A. Suchman, Leland C. DeVinney, Shirley A. Star, and Robin M. Williams, Jr., *The American Soldier: Adjustment during Army Life,* vol. 1 of *Studies in Social Psychology in World War II* (Princeton: Princeton University Press, 1949), 6.

42. Ibid.

43. Osborn, *Voyage to a New World,* 99; Frederick Osborn to Samuel Stouffer, 12 September 1948, Samuel A. Stouffer Papers, Harvard University Archives, Nathan M. Pusey Library, Harvard University, Cambridge, Mass.

44. Record of Interview, D[evereux] C J[osephs] and Frederick Osborn, 13 May 1947, Corp. Files.

45. Frederick Osborn to Frederick P. Keppel, 16 September 1938, Corp. Files.

46. Ibid. See also Frederick Osborn, "To What Extent Is a Science of Man Possible?" *Scientific Monthly* (November 1939): 452–59.

47. Frederick Osborn, "The Present Status of Social Science," [Speech for the] Milbank Dinner, 20 October 1946, pp. 13 and 15, Corp. Files.

48. Ibid.

49. [Frederick Osborn], "Some Observations on 'Social Science' Grants," February 1947, p. 3, Corp. Files.

50. "Interview with Vannevar Bush," OHCC, p. 54 and passim.

51. "Interview with Devereux C. Josephs," OHCC, pp. 64–66; and CC, *Annual Report* (1946), 26–28.

52. John Dollard, "Preface—1949," *Caste and Class in a Southern Town*, p. xi.

53. John Dollard to Clyde Kluckhohn, 12 February 1939, Clyde Kluckhohn Papers, Harvard University Archives, Nathan M. Pusey Library, Cambridge, Mass. Hereafter Kluckhohn Papers.

54. Charles Dollard to Clyde Kluckhohn, 3 March 1939; Clyde Kluckhohn, "Preliminary Report to Professor Linton on Fellowship for Training in Psychology," 14 January 1940, Corp. Files.

55. [Ralph Linton], "Preliminary Report to Carnegie Foundation on Fellowships for Cross-Disciplinary Training in Anthropology and Psychology," n.d. [1940], Corp. Files; Oral History of Abram Kardiner, 1965, Oral History Collection of Columbia University, pp. 292, 298, 321; and Clyde Kluckhohn, "The Influence of Psychiatry on Anthropology in America during the Past One Hundred Years," in *One Hundred Years of American Psychiatry* (New York: Columbia University Press, 1944), p. 611, including n. 92.

56. Talcott Parsons, "Clyde Kluckhohn and the Integration of Social Science," in *Culture and Life: Essays in Memory of Clyde Kluckhohn*, ed. Walter W. Taylor, John L. Fischer, and Evon Z. Vogt (Carbondale: Southern Illinois University Press, 1973), 32.

57. Arthur G. Powell, *The Uncertain Profession: Harvard and the Search for Educational Authority* (Cambridge, Mass.: Harvard University Press, 1980), 217.

58. "Report of the Chairman on the First Decade: 1946–1956," in *Department and Laboratory of Social Relations, Harvard University, the First Decade, 1946–56*, p. 12, in Department of Social Relations Papers, Harvard University Archives, Nathan M. Pusey Library, Harvard University, Cambridge, Mass. Hereafter Departmental Papers.

59. Ibid.

60. Talcott Parsons to Dean Paul H. Buck, 3 April 1944, Talcott Parsons Papers, Harvard University Archives, Nathan M. Pusey Library, Harvard University, Cambridge Mass. Hereafter Parsons Papers.

61. "O. Hobart Mowrer," in *A History of Psychology in Autobiography*, ed. Gardner Lindzey (Worcester: Clark University Press, 1952), IV: 339; "Gordon W. Allport," in *A History of Psychology in Autobiography*, ed. Edwin G. Boring and Gardner Lindzey (New York: Appleton-Century-Croft, 1967), V: 17–18. See also Talcott Parsons to Pitirim A. Sorokin, 19 June 1941, and Pitirim A. Sorokin to Talcott Parsons, 24 June 1941, and Talcott Parsons to Dean Paul Buck, 19 June 1944, Parsons Papers.

62. "Report of the Chairman on the First Decade . . ." pp. 14–16, Departmental Papers. Parsons's account of the shift in chairmanship of the

Department of Sociology, which is the basis for my discussions, does not agree with Sorokin's in his autobiography, *A Long Journey: The Autobiography of Pitirim A. Sorokin* (New Haven: College and University Press, 1963), 251. Sorokin claimed he wanted to give up the chairmanship and forced J. B. Conant to replace him. Despite that, his autobiography does make clear his antipathy to the new department. He believed it had resulted in "the drowning of sociology in an eclectic mass of the odds and ends of these [other] disciplines"; it had grown in "staff, budget, research funds, and self-advertising," but had not "produced as many distinguished sociologists" (p. 251). See also Pitirim A. Sorokin, *Fads and Foibles in Modern Sociology and Related Sciences* (Chicago: Henry Regnery, 1956).

63. Pitirim A. Sorokin to Charles Dollard, 3 November 1950, and Dollard to Sorokin, 10 November 1951; Record of Interview, CD and Edwin G. Boring, 10 January 1946, Cambridge, Mass., Corp. Files.
64. CC, *Annual Report* (1947), 32.
65. Record of Interview, CD and Stouffer, 26 September 1946, Corp. Files.
66. George Casper Homans, *Coming to My Senses: The Autobiography of a Sociologist* (New Brunswick: Transaction Books, 1984), 301.
67. CC, *Annual Report* (1949), 23; "Report of the Chairman on the First Decade . . . ," pp. 33–34, Departmental Papers.
68. Talcott Parsons and Edward A. Shils, eds., *Toward a General Theory of Action* (Cambridge, Mass.: Harvard University Press, 1951), 3–4. Also listed on the title page were Edward C. Tolman, Gordon W. Allport, Clyde Kluckhohn, Henry A. Murray, Robert R. Sears, Richard C. Sheldon, and Samuel A. Stouffer.
69. "Report of the Chairman on the First Decade . . . ," p. 34, Departmental Papers.
70. Homans, *Coming to My Senses,* 303.
71. [Samuel A. Stouffer], "The Laboratory of Social Relations" in *Department and Laboratory of Social Relations, Harvard University, The First Decade, 1946–56,* pp. 80–127, Departmental Papers.
72. Ibid, p. 82.
73. Edward Shils, "Tradition, Ecology, and Institution in the History of Sociology," in *The Calling of Sociology and Other Essays on the Pursuit of Learning* (Chicago: University of Chicago Press, 1980), 224.
74. Ibid., 225.
75. Ibid., 219.
76. Powell, *The Uncertain Profession,* chap. 9.
77. Osborn, *Voyage to a New World,* 111–20.
78. Record of Interview, "CD and Frederick Osborn—Lunch at the Century," 30 September 1947, Corp. Files.
79. "Interview with John W. Gardner," OHCC, pp. 28–50.
80. Record of Interview, "D[evereux] C J[osephs] and Arthur Page (at 195 Broadway)," 2 November 1945, Corp. Files.
81. Devereux C. Josephs to Dean G. Acheson, 17 September 1945; Devereux

C. Josephs to Sumner Welles, 17 October 1945; [Memorandum] "To the Century Group, from Beardsley Ruml," 18 February 1946, p. 6, Corp. Files.

82. "Interview with Gardner," OHCC, pp. 37–39; and "Research Program on Russia, Harvard University," 15 October 1947, Corp. Files.

83. John W. Gardner, "Are We Doing Our Homework in Foreign Affairs?" *Yale Review* 27 (1947): 406.

84. Wendell Clark Bennett, "The Ethnogeographic Board," *Smithsonian Miscellaneous Collections* 107 (April 1947): 3.

85. Robert B. Hall, *Area Studies: With Special Reference to Their Implications for Research in Social Sciences* (New York: SSRC, 1947), 2.

86. Julian Steward, *Area Research: Theory and Practice* (New York: SSRC, 1950), 80 ff.

87. [John W. Gardner], "Russian Studies," 14 July 1947, Corp. Files; and Alex Inkeles, "Clyde Kluckhohn's Contribution to Studies of Russia and the Soviet Union," in *Culture and Life*, ed. Taylor, Fischer, and Vogt, 65.

88. Margaret Mead, "Anthropological Contributions to National Policies during and Immediately after World War II," in *The Uses of Anthropology*, ed. Walter Goldschmidt (Washington, D.C.: American Anthropological Association, 1970), 145–57; Margaret Mead and Rhoda Métraux, *The Study of Culture at a Distance* (Chicago: University of Chicago Press, 1953).

89. Clyde Kluckhohn to John Gardner, 23 July 1947, Kluckhohn Papers.

90. Clyde Kluckhohn to John Gardner, 14 September 1947, Kluckhohn Papers.

91. Robert A. McCaughey, *International Studies and Academic Enterprise: A Chapter in the Enclosure of American Learning* (New York: Columbia University Press, 1984), 134.

92. Parsons, "Clyde Kluckhohn and . . . Social Science," in *Culture and Life*, ed. Taylor, Fischer, and Vogt, 35.

93. Philip E. Mosley, "The Growth of Russian Studies," in *American Research on Russia*, ed. Harold H. Fisher (Bloomington: Indiana University Press, 1959), 14. See also Russian Research Center, Harvard University, "Five Year Report and Current Projects," May 1953, Russian Research Center Papers, Harvard University Archives, Nathan M. Pusey Library, Harvard University, Cambridge, Mass.; and Clyde Kluckhohn, "Russian Research at Harvard," *World Politics* 1 (January 1949): 266–71.

94. Inkeles, "Clyde Kluckhohn . . . and the Soviet Union," in *Culture and Life*, ed. Taylor, Fischer, and Vogt, 61.

95. Robert A. Dahl, "The Behavioral Approach in Political Science: Epitaph for a Monument to a Successful Protest," *American Political Science Review* 55 (December 1961): 766.

96. *Studies in Social Psychology in World War II*, vol. 1, Samuel A. Stouffer et al., *The American Soldier: Adjustment during Army Life* (Princeton:

Princeton University Press, 1949); vol. 2, Samuel A. Stouffer et al., *The American Soldier: Combat and Its Aftermath* (Princeton: Princeton University Press, 1949); vol. 3, Carl I. Hovland et al., *Experiments in Mass Communication* (Princeton: Princeton University Press, 1949); and vol. 4, Samuel A. Stouffer et al., *Measurement and Prediction* (Princeton: Princeton University Press, 1950).

97. Harold D. Lasswell to Samuel Stouffer, 23 September 1949, and Samuel Stouffer to Harold D. Lasswell, 27 September 1949, Stouffer Papers.

98. Robert S. Lynd, "The Science of Inhuman Relations," *New Republic* 121 (August 1949): 22–25.

99. Nathan Glazer, " 'The American Soldier' as Science: Can Sociology Fulfill Its Ambitions?" *Commentary* 7 (November 1949): 496.

100. Paul F. Lazarsfeld, *"The American Soldier*—An Expository Review," *Public Opinion Quarterly* 13 (1949): 383 and 386.

101. Robert K. Merton, *Social Theory and Social Structure,* enlarged ed. (New York: Free Press, 1968), chap. 13.

102. *International Encyclopedia of the Social Sciences,* s.v. "Sociology," p. 11. One example of Lazarsfeld and Merton's interest was the symposium reported in *Continuities in Social Research: Studies in the Scope and Method of 'The American Soldier,'* ed. Robert K. Merton and Paul F. Lazarsfeld (Glencoe, Ill.: Free Press, 1950).

103. "Study for the Ford Foundation, Informational Bulletin No. 2," January 1949, p. 25, is a reprinted version of an untitled memorandum written by Charles Dollard on 2 August 1946, Corp. Files.

104. *Report of the Study for the Ford Foundation on Policy and Program, November 1949,* 2 vols. (Detroit: Ford Foundation, 1949), I: 25.

105. McCaughey, *International Studies and Academic Enterprise,* 144–155.

106. John W. Gardner to Clyde Kluckhohn, 7 April 1952, Kluckhohn Papers.

CHAPTER EIGHT

Leadership and Education: The New Men

1. There is a good synopsis of ESEA, Public Law 89-10, in Eugene Eidenberg and Roy D. Morey, *An Act of Congress: The Legislative Process and the Making of Education Policy* (New York: W. W. Norton, 1969), 247–48.

2. Stephen K. Bailey and Edith K. Mosher, *ESEA: The Office of Education Administers a Law* (Syracuse: Syracuse University Press, 1968), 3.

3. Fred M. Hechinger, "Education: White House Conference Points Up New U.S. Role," *New York Times,* 25 July 1965, 9E.

4. Ibid.

5. Author's interview with John W. Gardner, 3 February 1986, Washington, D.C.

6. Elizabeth Drew, "Reporter at Large: Conversation with a Citizen [John W. Gardner]," *New Yorker* 49 (23 July 1973): 45.

7. Ibid.
8. John W. Gardner, "The Use of the Term 'Levels of Aspiration,'" *Psychological Review* 47 (January 1940): 67.
9. Author's interview with John W. Gardner, 3 February 1986.
10. Drew, "Reporter at Large," 45.
11. To: Mr. Josephs, From: Mr. Gardner, "A Program for Carnegie Corporation," 3 July 1946, Corp. Files.
12. Drew, "Reporter at Large," 35.
13. Gardner, "A Program for Carnegie Corporation," 3 July 1946, Corp. Files.
14. Ibid.
15. "Interview with Frederick Osborn," Oral History of the Carnegie Corporation, Oral History Research Office, Columbia University, New York (hereafter OHCC), p. 129.
16. Carnegie Corporation, Trustee Agenda, "Postwar Program in Education," 17 November 1953, pp. 27–28, Corp. Files.
17. Carnegie Corporation, Trustee Agenda, "The Congressional Investigation," 15 January 1953, p. 8, Corp. Files.
18. Ibid., p. 10.
19. Ibid., p. 12.
20. John W. Gardner, "CC Board Meeting Presentation," 19 November 1958, p. 10, Corp. Files.
21. Ibid.
22. Carnegie Corporation, Trustee Agenda, "Postwar Program in Education," 17 November 1953, p. 28, Corp. Files.
23. Frederick P. Keppel, "President Lowell and His Influence," in *Philanthropy and Learning with Other Papers* (New York: Columbia University Press, 1936), 116–17.
24. James B. Conant, *My Several Lives: Memoirs of a Social Inventor* (New York: Harper & Row, 1970), 180.
25. Stephen Louis Preskill, "Raking from the Rubbish: Charles W. Eliot, James B. Conant and the Public Schools" (Ph.D. diss., University of Illinois at Urbana-Champaign, 1984), 165.
26. Charles DeWayne Biebel, "Politics, Pedagogues and Statesmanship: James B. Conant and the Public School, 1933–1948" (Ph.D. diss., University of Wisconsin, 1971), 78–79.
27. Conant, *My Several Lives*, 187.
28. Ibid., 188.
29. The best general source for the history of the Graduate School of Education is Arthur G. Powell, *The Uncertain Profession: Harvard and the Search for Educational Authority* (Cambridge, Mass.: Harvard University Press, 1980).
30. Conant, *My Several Lives*, 188.
31. Francis T. Spaulding, *High School and Life. The Regents' Inquiry* (New York: McGraw-Hill, 1938), 114.

32. Ibid., 4.
33. Ibid., 75.
34. James B. Conant, "A Free Classless Society: Ideal or Illusion," *Harvard Alumni Bulletin* 17 November 1939, 248.
35. James Bryant Conant, "An Autobiographical Fragment," in *Leaders in American Education: The 70th Yearbook of the National Society for the Study of Education*, Part II, ed. Robert J. Havighurst (Chicago: University of Chicago Press, 1971), 119.
36. Ibid., 120.
37. James Bryant Conant, "Education for a Classless Society: The Jeffersonian Tradition," *Atlantic Monthly* 165 (May 1940): 594.
38. Educational Policies Commission, *Education for ALL American Youth* (Washington, D.C.: NEA and AASA, 1944), 40.
39. Conant, "Autobiographical Fragment," 123.
40. *General Education in a Free Society* (Cambridge, Mass.: Harvard University Press, 1945), 32.
41. Conant, "Autobiographical Fragment," 124.
42. Ibid.
43. Ibid.
44. Ibid., 125.
45. James Bryant Conant, *Public Education and the Structure of American Society*, The Julius and Rosa Sachs Lectures, November 14, 15, and 16, 1945 (New York: Bureau of Publications, Teachers College, Columbia University, 1946), 2.
46. Ibid., 3–4.
47. W. Lloyd Warner, Robert J. Havighurst, and Martin B. Loeb, *Who Shall be Educated? The Challenge of Unequal Opportunities* (New York: Harper & Brothers, 1944), 19.
48. Ibid., 36, 120–23.
49. Ibid., 158.
50. Ibid.
51. Benjamin Barber, "L. J. Henderson: An Introduction," in *L. J. Henderson on the Social System* (Chicago: University of Chicago Press, 1970), 1–53.
52. Barbara S. Heyl, "The Harvard 'Pareto Circle,'" *Journal of the History of the Behavioral Sciences* 4 (October 1968): 316.
53. Lawrence A. Cremin, *American Education: The Metropolitan Experience, 1876–1980* (New York: Harper & Row, 1988), 545.
54. James B. Conant "The Superintendent Was the Target," *New York Times Book Review*, 29 April 1951, 7:1.
55. Ibid., 7:27.
56. John W. Gardner, *Excellence: Can We Be Equal and Excellent Too?* (New York: Harper & Brothers, 1961), especially chap. 12.
57. Ibid., 69.
58. Ibid., 75.

59. Record of Interview, J[ohn] G[ardner] and D. C. Josephs, 30 September 1955, Corp. Files.
60. John W. Gardner, "Foreword," in James B. Conant, *The American High School Today: A First Report to Interested Citizens* (New York: McGraw-Hill, 1959), ix.
61. John W. Gardner to James B. Conant, 14 November 1955, Corp. Files.
62. Ibid.
63. James B. Conant to John W. Gardner, 24 August 1956, Corp. Files.
64. CC, *Annual Report* (1957), 34.
65. Conant, *American High School Today*, 96.
66. Ibid., 15.
67. Ibid., 22.
68. David B. Dreiman, *How to Get Better Schools: A Tested Program* (New York: Harper & Brothers, 1956), 71.
69. "Memorandum Prepared by James B. Conant for Mr. John Gardner. Subject: Proposed Study of Certain Problems Connected with the American Comprehensive High School," 21 December 1956, Corp. Files.
70. Ibid.
71. "Confidential Supplement to J. B. Conant's THE AMERICAN HIGH SCHOOL TODAY . . . 12 January 1959," enclosed with James B. Conant to John W. Gardner, 19 January 1959, Corp. Files.
72. Ibid.
73. "Confidential Memorandum Prepared by James B. Conant for Mr. John Gardner . . . Subject: Proposed Study of Certain Problems Connected with the American Comprehensive High School," 21 December 1956, Corp. Files.
74. Mary B. Ford, "Report on the Dissemination Campaign of THE AMERICAN HIGH SCHOOL TODAY . . . 25 March 1959, Part II, p. 1, Corp. Files.
75. "Confidential Supplement . . . 12 January 1959," Corp. Files.
76. Conant, *My Several Lives*, 623; and Christopher Jencks, "Academic Haves and Have Nots," *New Republic*, 13 November 1961, 34.
77. James B. Conant, *Slums and Suburbs: A Commentary on Schools in Metropolitan Areas* (New York: McGraw-Hill, 1961), 146.
78. Ibid., 2.
79. Conant, "Autobiographical Fragment," 138.
80. Maxine Greene, "Conant and the Perilous Profession," *Journal of Higher Education* 35 (February 1964): 108.
81. James Bryant Conant, *The Education of American Teachers* (New York: McGraw-Hill, 1963), 141 and 142.
82. *New York Times Book Review*, 15 September 1963, 7:53.
83. Ibid.
84. Memorandum to J[ohn] G[ardner], from M[argaret] E M[ahoney], "Dissemination of James B. Conant's *The Education of American Teachers,*" 20 September 1963, Corp. Files.

85. Fragment of a letter to Miss Margaret Mahoney, 7 October 1963, p. 2, Corp. Files.
86. Lindley J. Stiles, "Dr. Conant and His Critics," *Teachers College Record* 65 (May 1964): 712.
87. Conant, *The Education of American Teachers*, 15, and chap. 2 passim.
88. Conant, *My Several Lives*, 624.
89. James Bryant Conant, *Shaping Educational Policy* (New York: McGraw-Hill, 1964), 110.
90. Ibid., 2–8.
91. Ibid., 123.
92. James E. McClellan, *Toward an Effective Critique of American Education* (Philadelphia: J. B. Lippincott, 1968), 61.
93. Paul Nash, "Conant's Shaping Educational Policy," *Boston University Graduate Journal* 15 (1966–67): 35.
94. Richard Wynn, "An Inept Lesson in Educational Policy Making," *Phi Delta Kappan* 46 (February 1965): 256.
95. Author's interview with John W. Gardner, 3 February 1986.
96. Rockefeller Panel Reports, *Prospects for America* (Garden City, N.Y.: Doubleday, 1961), Report V, 337–87.
97. Gardner, *Excellence*, xiii.
98. *Prospects for America*, 369.
99. Author's interview with John W. Gardner, 3 February 1986.
100. Max Beberman, *An Emerging Program of Secondary School Mathematics* (Cambridge, Mass.: Harvard University Press, 1958), 4.
101. Ibid.
102. William Wooton, *The Making of a Curriculum* (New Haven: Yale University Press, 1965).
103. Frederick H. Jackson, "The Private Foundations," in *Modern Viewpoints in the Curriculum: National Conference on Curriculum Experimentation, September 25–28, 1961*, ed. Paul C. Rosenbloom (New York: McGraw-Hill, 1964), 211–16. Jackson was a Corporation program officer.
104. Carnegie Corporation, Trustee Executive Committee Agenda, 14 June 1956, Corp. Files.
105. Benjamin DeMott, "The Math Wars," *American Scholar* 31 (Spring 1962): 310.
106. *A Foundation Goes to School: The Ford Foundation Comprehensive School Improvement Program, 1960–1970* (New York: Ford Foundation, 1972), 9. See also Paul Woodring, *Investment in Innovation: An Historical Appraisal of the Fund for the Advancement of Education* (Boston: Little, Brown, 1970).
107. Howard Gardner, *The Mind's New Science: A History of the Cognitive Revolution* (New York: Basic Books, 1985), 32.
108. *Current Biography Yearbook* (1984), s.v. "Bruner, Jerome (Seymour)."
109. Jerome S. Bruner, Jacqueline J. Goodnow, and George A. Austin, *A Study of Thinking* (New York: John Wiley, 1956).

110. Bruner's indebtedness to Piaget, whom he described as the founder of modern developmental psychology, was acknowledged in the dedication of *Studies in Cognitive Growth: A Collaboration at the Center for Cognitive Studies,* ed. Jerome Bruner et al. (New York: John Wiley, 1966).

111. Jerome S. Bruner, *In Search of Mind: Essays in Autobiography* (New York: Harper & Row, 1983), 177–86. Jerome S. Bruner, *The Process of Education* (Cambridge, Mass.: Harvard University Press, 1960), v–xvi, describes the conference and lists the participants.

112. Andrew T. Weil, "Harvard's Bruner and His Yeasty Ideas," *Harper's Magazine* 229 (December 1964): 82.

113. Bruner, *The Process of Education,* 20.

114. Ibid., 33.

115. Bruner, *In Search of Mind,* 179.

116. Ibid., 179–80.

117. Bruner, *The Process of Education,* 9.

118. Bruner, *In Search of Mind,* 125–26.

119. Gardner, *The Mind's New Science,* 32.

120. *International Encyclopedia of the Social Sciences,* s.v. "Hunt, J. Mc-Vicker."

121. J. McVicker Hunt, *Intelligence and Experience* (New York: Ronald, 1961).

122. Edward Zigler and Karen Anderson, "An Idea Whose Time Had Come: The Intellectual and Policy Climate," in *Project Head Start: A Legacy of the War on Poverty,* ed. Edward Zigler and Jeanette Valentine (New York: Free Press, 1979), 7–8.

123. J. McVicker Hunt, *The Challenge of Incompetence and Poverty: Papers on the Role of Early Education* (Urbana: University of Illinois Press, 1969), vii–viii.

124. Kenneth B. Clark, "Cultural Deprivation Theories: Their Social and Psychological Implications," in *The Educationally Deprived: The Potential for Change,* ed. Kenneth B. Clark et al. (New York: Metropolitan Applied Research Center, 1972), 11.

125. *A Foundation Goes to School,* 11, 36. See also Peter Marris and Martin Rein, *Dilemmas of Social Reform: Poverty and Community Action in the United States,* 2nd ed. (Chicago: University of Chicago Press, 1973).

126. Adam Yarmolinsky, "Ideas into Programs," *Public Interest* 2 (Winter 1966): 73.

127. Norman C. Thomas, "Policy Formulation for Education: The Johnson Administration," *Educational Researcher* 2 (May 1973): 4–5.

128. William B. Cannon, the task force's executive secretary, as quoted in Hugh Davis Graham, *The Uncertain Triumph: Federal Education Policy in the Kennedy and Johnson Years* (Chapel Hill: University of North Carolina Press, 1984), 62. The task force members are listed on p. 64.

129. Quoted in William E. Leuchtenberg, "The Genesis of the Great Society,"

The Reporter 34 (21 April 1966): 37. This article was the first published report of the task force.

130. "Report of the President's Task Force on Education." 14 November 1964, p. 6.

131. James L. Sundquist, *Politics and Policy: The Eisenhower, Kennedy, and Johnson Years* (Washington, D.C.: Brookings Institution, 1968), 210–12.

132. William Greenbaum with Michael S. Garet and Ellen R. Solomon, *Measuring Educational Progress: A Study of the National Assessment* (New York: McGraw-Hill, 1977), 8–12.

133. Author's Interview with Francis Keppel, 10 June 1986, Cambridge, Massachusetts.

134. Ralph W. Tyler, "Education: Curriculum Development and Evaluation: An Interview Conducted by Malca Chall in 1985, 1986, 1987," Regional Oral History Office, Bancroft Library, University of California, Berkeley, California, pp. 294–97.

135. Harold C. Hand, "National Assessment Viewed as the Camel's Nose," *Phi Delta Kappan* 47 (September 1965): 8–13; and Martin T. Katzman and Ronald S. Rosen, "The Science and Politics of National Educational Assessment," *Teachers College Record* 71 (May 1970): 571–86.

136. Hechinger, *New York Times*, 25 July 1965, 9E.

CHAPTER NINE
Steadfast Liberalism:
Poverty, Protest, and Reform

1. "How Can Carnegie Corporation Attack Poverty? A Report from the Task Force on the Disadvantaged [Stephen E. Stackpole, Margaret E. Mahoney, Frederic A. Mosher, Barbara D. Finberg, and Eli Evans]," 16 October 1967, p. 1, Corp. Files.

2. Ibid., 9.

3. Dwight Macdonald, "Our Invisible Poor," *New Yorker*, 19 January 1963, 84.

4. Allen J. Matusow, *The Unraveling of America: A History of Liberalism in the 1960s* (New York: Harper & Row, 1984), 119.

5. "How Can Carnegie Corporation Attack Poverty?" 1 and 3.

6. "Interview with Alan Pifer," Oral History of the Carnegie Corporation, Oral History Research Office, Columbia University, New York (hereafter OHCC), p. 171.

7. "How Can Carnegie Corporation Attack Poverty?" Appendix A.

8. "Interview with Pifer," OHCC, p. 168.

9. *Current Biography*, 1969, s.v. "Pifer, Alan (Jay Parrish)."

10. "Interview with Pifer," OHCC, p. 3.

11. Ibid., p. 107.

12. Ibid., p. 109.
13. Alan Pifer, "Foundations at the Service of the Public," CC, *Annual Report* (1968), 14.
14. Alan Pifer, "Working Women: Toward a New Society," CC, *Annual Report* (1976), 12.
15. Alan Pifer, "Twenty Years in Retrospect: A Personal View," CC, *Annual Report* (1973), 7–8.
16. "Interview with Pifer," OHCC, p. 214.
17. Ibid., p. 36.
18. "Interview with Florence Anderson," OHCC, pp. 622–25.
19. Alan Pifer to the author, 28 June 1988.
20. "Interview with Pifer," OHCC, p. 177.
21. Alan Pifer himself discussed this as a possible role for foundations in "The Foundation in the Year 2000," Occasional Papers: no. 1 (New York: Foundation Library Center, 1968).
22. Quoted in Daniel J. Czitrom, *Media and the American Mind from Morse to McLuhan* (Chapel Hill: University of North Carolina Press, 1982), 76.
23. Edward Shils, "Daydreams and Nightmares: Reflections on the Criticism of Mass Culture," in *Intellectuals and the Powers and Other Essays* (Chicago: University of Chicago Press, 1972), 248.
24. Erik Barnouw, *Tube of Plenty: The Evolution of American Television* (New York: Oxford University Press, 1975).
25. Quoted in James L. Baughman, *Television's Guardians: The FCC and the Politics of Programming, 1958–1967* (Knoxville: University of Tennessee Press, 1985), 142.
26. Quoted in Elizabeth Brenner Drew, "Is the FCC Dead?" *Atlantic Monthly* 220 (July 1967): 32.
27. Stanley M. Besen, Thomas G. Krattenmaker, A. Richard Metzger, Jr., and John R. Woodbury, *Misregulating Television: Network Dominance and the FCC* (Chicago: University of Chicago Press, 1984), 5.
28. Erwin G. Krasnow and Lawrence D. Longley, *The Politics of Broadcast Regulation*, 2nd ed. (New York: St. Martin's Press, 1978), chap. 7.
29. John Walker Powell, *Channels of Learning: The Story of Educational Television* (Washington, D.C.: Public Affairs Press, 1962), 118.
30. Ibid.
31. Quoted in John D. Burke, "The Public Broadcasting Act of 1967: Part I: Historical Origins and the Carnegie Commission," *Educational Broadcasting Review* 6 (April 1972): 114.
32. Ibid.
33. Ibid., 112.
34. F[lorence] A[nderson]'s Informal Notes on Executive Committee Meeting, 21 April 1965, Corp. Files.
35. F[lorence] A[nderson]'s Informal Notes on EXCCM Meeting, 16 June 1965, Corp. Files.

36. Carnegie Corporation, Staff Meeting Minutes, 22 September 1965, Corp. Files.
37. "Interview with Alan Pifer," OHCC, pp. 243–44; Burke, "The Public Broadcasting Act: Part I," 118.
38. *Public Television: A Program for Action. The Report and Recommendations of the Carnegie Commission on Educational Television* (New York: Harper & Row, 1967), 3.
39. Ibid., 5.
40. *A Public Trust: The Report of the Carnegie Commission on the Future of Public Broadcasting* (New York: Bantam, 1979), 11.
41. Benjamin DeMott, "The Trouble with Public Television," *Atlantic Monthly* 243 (February 1979): 47.
42. "Remarks by Alan Pifer. Dinner for Carnegie Commission on Educational Television," 15 March 1967, Corp. Files.
43. Ibid. This was still the problem of public television, according to a former Carnegie Corporation vice president, Lloyd N. Morrisett, in "Rx for Public Television," in *The Future of Public Television,* ed. Douglass Cater and Michael J. Nyhan (New York: Praeger, 1976), 163.
44. For more detail see Ellen Condliffe Lagemann, *Private Power for the Public Good: A History of the Carnegie Foundation for the Advancement of Teaching* (Middletown, Conn.: Wesleyan University Press, 1983).
45. [Alan Pifer], "Future of The Carnegie Foundation for the Advancement of Teaching," 5 April 1971, Corp. Files.
46. John J. Corson to Alan Pifer, "A Proposal for the Study of Financing of Higher Education under the Auspices of the Carnegie Foundation for the Advancement of Training [*sic*]," September 1966, CFAT Archive, Princeton, N.J.
47. Ibid.
48. Ibid.; F[lorence] A[nderson]'s Informal Notes on CFAT Board Meeting 11/16/66, CFAT Archive, Princeton.
49. CFAT press release, 24 January 1967, CFAT Archive.
50. Kerr mentioned Schumpeter's influence in an interview with the author, 28 July 1980, Berkeley, Calif.
51. E. A[lden] D[unham] Memorandum re A[lan] P[ifer]'s Opening Remarks to the Commission on the Future of Higher Education, 31 May 1967, Corp. Files.
52. Quoted in Clark Kerr, *The Uses of the University* (Cambridge, Mass.: Harvard University Press, 1963), 75.
53. Carnegie Commission on Higher Education, *Quality and Equality; New Levels of Federal Responsibility for Higher Education* (Hightstown, N.J.: McGraw-Hill, 1968), 17.
54. *Business Week,* 14 December 1968, 39.
55. Fred Hechinger, "Education: For Equality of Opportunity," *New York Times,* 15 December 1968, 9E.
56. Pifer, "Future of the Carnegie Foundation . . ." 5 April 1971, Corp. Files.

57. Lagemann, *Private Power for the Public Good*, 145–50.
58. Martin Trow, "The Democratization of Higher Education in America," *Archives Européennes de Sociologie* 3 (1962): 231–62, explains the differences between the terms "elite" and "mass" higher education as used by the commission.
59. Kerr, *The Uses of the University*, 75.
60. Benjamin S. Bloom, *Stability and Change in Human Characteristics* (New York: John Wiley, 1964), 88.
61. CC, *Annual Report* (1969), 21.
62. Maya Pines, *Revolution in Learning: The Years from Birth to Six* (New York: Harper & Row, 1966), 50.
63. Ibid., 53.
64. Ibid., 65.
65. Lloyd N. Morrisett, "Pre-School Education," *Science* 153 (9 September 1966): 1.
66. Susan S. Stodolsky and Gerald Lesser, "Learning Patterns in the Disadvantaged," *Harvard Education Review* 37 (Fall 1967): 548.
67. These numbers are given in [Joan Ganz Cooney and Linda Gottlieb,] "Television for Preschool Children: A Proposal," 19 February 1968, Corp. Files.
68. Richard M. Polsky, "The Children's Television Workshop: 1966–1968" (Ed.D. diss., Teachers College, Columbia University, 1973), 9.
69. Memorandum to Alan Pifer and Lloyd Morrisett from Barbara Finberg, 2 June 1966, Corp. Files.
70. Joan Ganz Cooney, "The Potential Uses of Television in Preschool Education: A Report to Carnegie Corporation of New York," October 1966, p. 7, Corp. Files.
71. Polsky, "The Children's Television Workshop," p. 131, has a table indicating the sources of funds for the prebroadcast period and the first year on the air.
72. Ibid., 61.
73. Quoted in ibid., 101.
74. Quoted in ibid., 112.
75. Quoted in ibid., 113.
76. Gerald S. Lesser, *Children and Television: Lessons from Sesame Street* (New York: Random House, 1974), 5 and 7.
77. Joan Ganz Cooney, "Foreword," *Children and Television*, xvii–xviii.
78. Ibid., 37.
79. *Current Biography* (1970), s.v. "Cooney, Joan Ganz," p. 97.
80. Ibid., 99.
81. Quoted in Thomas D. Cook et al., *"Sesame Street" Revisited* (New York: Russell Sage Foundation, 1975), 293.
82. Martin Mayer, *About Television* (New York: Harper & Row, 1972), 133.
83. Samuel Ball et al. *The First Year of Sesame Street: An Evaluation* (Princeton, N.J.: Educational Testing Service, 1970), 6.

84. Samuel Ball and Gerry Ann Bogartz, *A Summary of the Major Findings in "The First Year of Sesame Street: An Evaluation"* (Princeton: Educational Testing Service, 1970), 3–5.

85. Quoted in Polsky, "The Children's Television Workshop," 22.

86. Ibid., 41.

87. Jack Gould, "Aquaman vs. The Alphabet," *New York Times,* 24 March 1968, D29; and Polsky, "The Children's Television Workshop," 43.

88. John Holt, "Big Bird, Meet Dick and Jane: A Critique of *Sesame Street,*" *Atlantic Monthly* 227 (May 1971): 72.

89. Cook et al., *"Sesame Street" Revisited,* 20.

90. Ibid., 295, and chap. 8 generally.

91. Edward L. Palmer, *Television and America's Children: A Crisis of Neglect* (New York: Oxford University Press, 1988), 98.

92. Ball, *The First Year,* 357–58.

93. Morrisett, "Introduction," *Children and Television,* xxvi.

94. Ibid.

95. Urie Bronfenbrenner, *Two Worlds of Childhood: U.S. and U.S.S.R.* (New York: Russell Sage Foundation, 1970), 117.

96. Alan Pifer to B[arbara] F[inberg] and D[avid] Z R[obinson], Memorandum re Carnegie Commission on Children, 20 August 1970, Corp. Files.

97. Ibid.

98. Kenneth Keniston to Barbara Finberg, 17 April 1972, Corp. Files.

99. [Kenneth Keniston], "Interim Report [Carnegie Council on Children]," 10 April 1973, Corp. Files.

100. "Interim Report," 22 April 1974.

101. Mark Gerson to Barbara Finberg, 13 March 1973, Corp. Files.

102. F[lorence] A[nderson], Memorandum to B[arbara] Finberg, DZR, FLJ, 3 November 1974, Corp. Files.

103. Carnegie Corporation, Staff Meeting Minutes, 8 May 1975, Corp. Files.

104. Kenneth Keniston and the Carnegie Council on Children, *All Our Children: The American Family under Pressure* (New York: Harcourt Brace Jovanovich, 1977), xiii.

105. Ibid., 220–21.

106. Peter O. Almond, "What We Were Up Against: Media Views of Parents and Children," in *Child Abuse: An Agenda for Action,* ed. George Gerbner, Catherine J. Ross, and Edward Zigler (New York: Oxford University Press, 1980), chap. 13.

107. Quoted in ibid., 226.

108. Examples of positive reviews are Carll Tucker, "The Citizens Who Need Us Most," *Saturday Review,* 15 October 1977, 56, and Henry Mayer, "All Our Children," *New York Times Book Review,* 11 September 1977, 22.

109. *Time,* 19 September 1977, 118; and Christopher Lasch, "The Siege of the Family," *New York Review of Books,* 24 November 1977, 15–17.

110. Richard deLone, *Small Futures: Children, Inequality, and the Limits of*

Liberal Reform (New York: Harcourt Brace Jovanovich, 1979). The other books published as "Background Studies" for the council's work were: Alison Clarke-Stewart, *Child Care in the Family: A Review of Research and Some Propositions for Policy* (New York: Academic Press, 1977); John U. Ogbu, *Minority Education and Caste: The American System in Cross-Cultural Perspective* (New York: Academic Press, 1978); and John Gliedman and William Roth, *The Unexpected Minority: Handicapped Children in America* (New York: Harcourt Brace Jovanovich, 1980).

111. Diane Ravitch, "Liberal Reforms and Radical Visions," *New York Times Book Review,* 16 September 1979, 3.

112. Philip Green, *Nation,* 15 December 1979, 629–31.

113. B[arbara] F[inberg], Memorandum re "CC and children," to A[lan] P[ifer], D[avid] Z R[obinson], 10 August 1971, Corp. Files.

114. CC, *Annual Report* (1981), 11.

115. W. Norton Grubb and Marvin Lazerson, *Broken Promises: How Americans Fail Their Children* (New York: Basic Books, 1982), suggests the "liberal" character of the report.

116. The papers that resulted from the seminar were published in Frederick Mosteller and Daniel P. Moynihan, eds., *On Equality of Educational Opportunity: Papers Deriving from the Harvard University Faculty Seminar on the Coleman Report* (New York: Random House, 1972).

117. Christopher Jencks to Alan Pifer, 12 March 1968, Corp. Files.

118. Charles E. Silberman, "A Devasting Report on U.S. Education," *Fortune* 76 (August 1967): 18.

119. Thomas F. Pettigrew and Daniel P. Moynihan, Memorandum to Theodore Sizer, 15 September 1966, Corp. Files.

120. F[ritz] M[osher], Memorandum to A[lan] P[ifer] and L[loyd] M[orrisett] on Harvard University: Graduate School of Education Center for Educational Policy Research—Research on the Effects and Effectiveness of Schools, 10 October 1968, Corp. Files.

121. F[ritz] M[osher], Memorandum to A[lan] P[ifer] and D[avid] Z R[obinson] re Harvard University—Harvard Graduate School of Education: Center for Educational Policy Research, 14 December 1970, Corp. Files.

122. "Statement by Christopher Jencks Regarding *Inequality* . . . At the Press Briefing Held at the Waldorf Astoria on September 7, 1972," Corp. Files.

123. Kenneth B. Clark and Lawrence Plotkin, "As I See It," in *Christopher Jencks in Perspective* (Arlington, Va.: American Association of School Administrators, 1973), 34.

124. Thomas E. Pettigrew, "The Advantages of a Harvard Education," *Psychology Today* 6 (April 1973): 12 and 13.

125. Philip W. Jackson, "After Apple-Picking," *Harvard Educational Review* 43 (February 1973): 16.

126. Christopher Jencks et al., *Inequality: A Reassessment of the Effect of Family and Schooling in America* (New York: Basic Books, 1972), 261.

127. James S. Coleman, "Review Symposium: *Inequality* . . ." *American Journal of Sociology* 78 (May 1973): 1526.

128. Lester C. Thurow, "Proving the Absence of Positive Associations," *Harvard Educational Review* 43 (February 1973): 70.
129. Christopher Jencks, "Inequality in Retrospect," in ibid., 104.
130. CC, Staff Meeting Minutes, 24 May 1977, p. 4.
131. Ronald Edmonds et al., "A Black Response to Christopher Jencks's *Inequality* and Certain Other Issues," *Harvard Educational Review* 43 (February 1973): 41.
132. This is discussed in detail, with varying interpretations of increased grants, in J. Craig Jenkins and Craig M. Eckert, "Channel Black Insurgency: Elite Patronage and Professional Social Movement Organization in the Development of the Black Movement," *American Sociological Review* 51 (December 1986): 812–29; and David J. Garrow, "Philanthropy and the Civil Rights Movement," Center for the Study of Philanthropy, Graduate School and University Center, City University of New York, October 1987.
133. Memorandum to D[avid] Z R[obinson] and A[lan] P[ifer] from E[li] E[vans] re Washington Research Project, 15 April 1971, Corp. Files.
134. Margie Casady, "Impatience with Small Talk: A Sketch of Marian Wright Edelman," *Psychology Today* 9 (June 1975): 60.
135. Adam Fairclough, *To Redeem the Soul of America: The Southern Christian Leadership Conference and Martin Luther King, Jr.* (Athens: University of Georgia Press, 1987), 358.
136. "Proposal of the Washington Research Project of the Southern Center for Studies in Public Policy—1971–1972," enclosed with letter from Marian Wright Edelman to Eli Evans, 11 September 1970, p. 2, Corp. Files.
137. Ibid., p. 1.
138. Ibid., p. 1, 2.
139. Ibid., p. 3.
140. Marian Wright Edelman to Eli Evans, 15 September 1971, p. 3, Corp. Files.
141. [Marian Wright Edelman], Proposal to Establish a Children's Defense Fund, attached to Memorandum to Eli Evans and Florence Anderson, 23 November 1971, Corp. Files.
142. Ibid., 2, 4–5.
143. B[arbara] F[inberg] to A[lan] P[ifer] and D[avid] Z R[obinson] re Washington Research Project: for support of Children's Defense Fund, $600,000, 2 November 1972, Corp. Files.
144. Marian Wright Edelman, "On Mounting Effective Child Advocacy," *Proceedings of the, American Philosophical Society* 119 (December 1975): 473.
145. Ibid.
146. Draft Memo to A[lan] P[ifer], D[avid] Z R[obinson], from B[arbara] F[inberg] and F[ritz] M[osher], "Possible Extensions of CC's Educational Program," n.d. [1970], Corp. Files.

147. Fritz Mosher and Vivien Stewart, "Program in Elementary and Secondary Education," 1977, Corp. Files.

CONCLUSION

American Dilemmas

1. Eleanor Farrar, John E. DeSanctis, and David Cohen, "Views from Below: Implementation Research in Education," *Teachers College Record* 82 (Fall 1980): 77–100.
2. Alexis de Tocqueville, *Democracy in America*, ed. Phillips Bradley (1835, 1840; 2 vols.; New York: Alfred A. Knopf, 1945), II: 259.
3. Charles W. Eliot, "The Function of Education in a Democratic Society [1897]," in Charles William Eliot, *Educational Reform: Essays and Addresses* (1898; reprint ed.: New York: Arno Press, 1969), 408, 409, and 412.
4. Walter Lippmann, *Public Opinion* (New York: Harcourt, Brace, 1922).
5. John Dewey, "Review of *Public Opinion* by Walter Lippmann," *New Republic* 30 (May 1922), 288.
6. The best description of what a changed ecology might look like is Lawrence A. Cremin, *Public Education* (New York: Basic Books, 1976).
7. Dick Netzer, *The Subsidized Muse: Public Support for the Arts in the United States*, A Twentieth Century Fund Study (Cambridge: Cambridge University Press, 1978).
8. Herbert Gans, *Popular Culture and High Culture: An Analysis and Evaluation of Taste* (New York: Basic Books, 1974). See also Lawrence W. Levine, *High Brow and Low Brow: The Emergence of Cultural Hierarchy in America* (Cambridge, Mass.: Harvard University Press, 1988).
9. David K. Cohen and Barbara Neufeld, "The Failure of High Schools and the Progress of Education," *Daedalus* 110 (Summer 1981): 86.
10. Michael Walzer, *Spheres of Justice: A Defense of Pluralism and Equality* (New York: Basic Books, 1983), 211.
11. Paul E. Peterson, "Did the Education Commissions Say Anything?" *Brookings Review* 2 (Winter 1983): 11.
12. Quoted in Gilbert Y. Steiner, *The Children's Cause* (Washington, D.C.: Brookings Institution, 1976), 22–23.
13. Rush Welter, *Popular Education and Democratic Thought in America* (New York: Columbia University Press, 1962), 50.
14. Amy Gutmann, *Democratic Education* (Princeton: Princeton University Press, 1987), 11.
15. Walter Dean Burnham, *The Current Crisis in American Politics* (New York: Oxford University Press, 1983).
16. Although none is concerned with exactly the point mentioned, these works are relevant: Benjamin Barber, *Strong Democracy: Participatory Politics for a New Age* (Berkeley: University of California Press, 1984); Ira Katz-

nelson, *City Trenches: Urban Politics and the Patterning of Class in the United States* (Chicago: University of Chicago Press, 1981); and Ira Katznelson and Margaret Weir, *Schooling for All: Class, Race, and the Decline of the American Ideal* (New York: Basic Books, 1985).

Appendix 1
Carnegie Corporation Trustees
1911–1982*

James Bertram, 1911–34
Andrew Carnegie, 1911–19
Robert A. Franks, 1911–35
William N. Frew, 1911–14
Henry S. Pritchett, 1911–30
Elihu Root, 1911–37
Charles L. Taylor, 1911–22
Robert S. Woodward, 1911–20
Samuel Harden Church, 1914–43
John A. Poynton, 1916–34
Mrs. Andrew (Louise W.) Carnegie, 1919–29
James R. Angell, 1920–21
John C. Merriam, 1921–38
William J. Holland, 1922–32
Frederick P. Keppel, 1922–41
John J. Carty, 1923–32
Russell C. Leffingwell, 1923–59
Nicholas Murray Butler, 1925–45
Henry James, 1928–47
David F. Houston, 1929–34
Henry Suzzallo, 1930–33
Newton D. Baker, 1931–37
Thomas S. Arbuthnot, 1933–52
Walter A. Jessup, 1934–44
Arthur W. Page, 1934–58
Margaret Carnegie Miller, 1934–
Lotus Delta Coffman, 1936–38
Nicholas Kelley, 1936–61
Frederick Osborn, 1936–62
Elihu Root, Jr., 1937–60
Vannevar Bush, 1939–55

W. Randolph Burgess, 1940–57
William Frew, 1943–48
Devereux C. Josephs, 1944–66
Oliver C. Carmichael, 1945–53
George C. Marshall, 1946–50
Morris Hadley, 1947–67
Leroy A. Wilson, 1948–51
Charles Dollard, 1948–54
Charles Allen Thomas, 1951–65
Gwilym A. Price, 1953–67
Charles M. Spofford, 1953–73
John W. Gardner, 1954–67
Caryl P. Haskins, 1955–
Frederick Sheffield, 1956–71
C. D. Jackson, 1958–64
Robert F. Bacher, 1959–76
Malcolm A. MacIntyre, 1959–76
Frederick M. Eaton, 1961–69
David A. Shepard, 1962–75
Walter B. Wriston, 1964–71
Amyas Ames, 1965–75
Alan Pifer, 1965–82
Harding F. Bancroft, 1966–78
Louis W. Cabot, 1966–78
Frederick B. Adams, Jr., 1967–71
Aiken W. Fisher, 1967–77
Franklin A. Thomas, 1970–77
Phyllis Goodhart Gordan, 1970–79
Francis Keppel, 1970–79
Marta Y. Valle, 1971–75
Howard D. Samuel, 1972–77
Philip R. Lee, 1972–79

*Listed by year of appointment to the board.

317

Jeanne Spurlock, 1973–80   Jack G. Clarke, 1979–
Madeline H. McWhinney, 1974–81 Judy P. Rosenstreich, 1978–
Carl M. Mueller, 1975–   Tomás A. Arciniega, 1980–
Cándido A. de León, 1976–   David A. Hamburg, 1980–
Mary Louise Petersen, 1976–   Helene L. Kaplan, 1980–
Anne Firor Scott, 1976–   Margaret K. Rosenheim, 1980–
John C. Taylor, 3rd, 1976–   John C. Whitehead, 1979–
Thomas R. Donahue, 1977–   Ruth Simms Hamilton, 1981–
John G. Gloster, 1977–   Ann R. Leven, 1982–

Appendix 2
Carnegie Corporation Presidents, 1911–1982

Andrew Carnegie, 1911–19
Elihu Root, 1919–20
James R. Angell, 1920–21
Henry S. Pritchett, 1921–23 (acting)
Frederick P. Keppel, 1923–41
Walter A. Jessup, 1941–44
Devereux C. Josephs, 1945–48
Charles Dollard, 1948–55
John W. Gardner, 1955–67
Alan Pifer, 1967–82 (acting, 1965–67)
David A. Hamburg, 1982–

Appendix 3

Grants Paid, Administrative Expenses, and Portfolio Market Value
(Current and 1987 dollars), 1912–1982

Year Ending 9/30	Grants Paid	Admin. Expenses	Grants Paid (1987 $)	Admin. Expenses (1987 $)	Portfolio Market Value (1987 $)	Portfolio Market Value	Year Ending 9/30
1912	$5,518,189	$55,545	$63,988,697	$644,098	$1,467,780,004	$125,304,125	1912
1913	$4,390,369	$66,386	$50,233,989	$759,579	$1,464,164,986	$126,576,847	1913
1914	$7,787,531	$66,026	$88,224,529	$748,005	$1,440,711,798	$127,965,639	1914
1915	$3,352,791	$72,356	$35,311,964	$762,061	$1,351,619,938	$127,170,844	1915
1916	$4,059,553	$83,981	$36,409,116	$753,205	$1,171,523,435	$128,333,252	1916
1917	$9,367,194	$88,293	$71,531,300	$674,237	$988,669,492	$130,622,822	1917
1918	$6,831,699	$88,075	$45,421,566	$558,985	$850,692,607	$129,468,624	1918
1919	$5,565,902	$84,075	$31,948,277	$704,970	$735,666,744	$127,949,701	1919
1920	$4,372,019	$122,817	$28,091,853	$1,328,851	$816,633,647	$128,164,938	1920
1921	$5,123,383	$206,813	$35,149,265	$826,238	$887,777,310	$127,095,132	1921
1922	$5,416,740	$120,433	$36,507,344	$1,030,187	$880,680,438	$129,394,335	1922
1923	$13,038,018	$152,853	$87,701,043	$742,397	$873,784,283	$130,670,065	1923
1924	$4,852,401	$110,368	$31,831,751	$793,721	$928,647,717	$129,900,567	1924
1925	$6,753,542	$120,994	$43,885,280	$797,305	$932,786,372	$141,562,152	1925
1926	$6,161,318	$122,698	$40,806,883	$971,195	$962,603,663	$143,547,264	1926
1927	$6,133,217	$146,638	$41,175,047	$988,535	$1,006,535,350	$145,340,855	1927
1928	$6,224,337	$147,247	$41,786,777	$1,172,571	$986,036,776	$149,928,175	1928
1929	$5,310,583	$174,660	$36,579,296	$1,280,403	$1,099,852,572	$146,874,816	1929
1930		$185,889				$159,676,622	1930

319

Appendix 3, continued

Year Ending 9/30	Grants Paid	Admin. Expenses	Grants Paid (1987 $)	Admin. Expenses (1987 $)	Portfolio Market Value (1987 $)	Portfolio Market Value	Year Ending 9/30
1931	$5,387,107	$201,911	$40,686,834	$1,524,959	$1,090,709,513	$144,414,500	1931
1932	$6,400,079	$230,028	$53,892,108	$1,936,959	$1,155,425,606	$137,215,178	1932
1933	$5,251,340	$230,268	$46,612,410	$2,043,925	$1,243,729,146	$140,118,150	1933
1934	$4,629,653	$278,476	$39,761,908	$2,391,699	$1,293,186,366	$150,571,351	1934
1935	$4,214,948	$296,334	$35,319,418	$2,483,149	$1,332,071,434	$158,966,713	1935
1936	$8,213,178	$296,950	$68,159,482	$2,464,327	$1,445,015,993	$174,123,588	1936
1937	$5,306,958	$243,326	$42,505,031	$1,948,871	$1,359,659,283	$169,760,015	1937
1938	$5,446,809	$250,751	$44,452,157	$2,046,413	$1,356,452,795	$166,208,792	1938
1939	$4,272,633	$301,986	$35,372,471	$2,500,096	$1,353,772,595	$163,521,893	1939
1940	$4,369,468	$269,392	$35,829,638	$2,209,014	$1,336,757,645	$163,019,225	1940
1941	$3,217,001	$251,898	$25,123,246	$1,967,203	$1,279,487,640	$163,836,832	1941
1942	$3,121,542	$268,930	$22,029,899	$1,897,940	$1,125,669,120	$159,502,477	1942
1943	$1,904,886	$227,183	$12,664,918	$1,510,460	$1,130,742,231	$170,070,986	1943
1944	$6,278,081	$202,422	$41,027,915	$1,322,849	$1,107,048,797	$169,400,324	1944
1945	$1,082,424	$196,337	$6,916,268	$1,254,517	$1,154,438,755	$180,674,358	1945
1946	$9,655,933	$313,991	$56,846,211	$1,848,521	$1,023,519,511	$173,855,666	1946
1947	$2,114,079	$469,037	$10,883,241	$2,414,594	$906,854,543	$176,157,285	1947
1948	$4,786,163	$485,264	$22,862,060	$2,317,960	$818,711,458	$171,396,911	1948
1949	$4,686,297	$400,373	$22,604,491	$1,931,211	$846,337,266	$175,460,165	1949
1950	$4,929,700	$376,157	$23,547,693	$1,796,789	$871,583,259	$182,465,601	1950
1951	$5,510,601	$397,362	$24,393,972	$1,759,016	$844,301,266	$190,727,754	1951
1952	$5,695,375	$442,604	$24,672,794	$1,917,394	$830,008,020	$191,595,928	1952
1953	$5,836,616	$472,699	$25,095,263	$2,032,429	$804,480,705	$187,104,833	1953
1954	$5,158,294	$546,581	$22,068,527	$2,338,416	$930,047,772	$217,389,215	1954
1955	$6,110,868	$683,150	$26,241,683	$2,933,627	$1,034,768,982	$240,965,367	1955
1956	$8,808,312	$602,691	$37,267,600	$2,549,960	$1,039,402,936	$245,666,083	1956
1957	$7,439,690	$649,372	$30,394,178	$2,652,950	$917,735,226	$224,637,281	1957

1958	$251,015,477	$998,264,784	$2,812,213	$29,974,965	$707,136	$7,537,259	1958
1959	$261,244,471	$1,030,613,927	$2,703,718	$30,888,573	$685,350	$7,829,769	1959
1960	$255,774,424	$993,108,361	$2,738,978	$31,731,529	$705,422	$8,172,435	1960
1961	$285,617,776	$1,097,843,327	$2,892,068	$34,860,360	$752,408	$9,069,362	1961
1962	$266,173,485	$1,011,811,791	$2,874,140	$35,698,592	$756,089	$9,391,093	1962
1963	$302,129,648	$1,134,715,930	$2,849,878	$39,306,195	$758,809	$10,465,674	1963
1964	$331,177,501	$1,227,745,224	$2,849,815	$42,428,401	$768,722	$11,444,827	1964
1965	$342,337,249	$1,247,629,085	$2,887,457	$47,072,246	$792,290	$12,916,165	1965
1966	$287,927,946	$1,020,189,142	$2,817,851	$42,527,476	$795,282	$12,002,528	1966
1967	$334,651,644	$1,152,540,262	$3,257,869	$41,875,741	$945,955	$12,159,042	1967
1968	$333,695,571	$1,102,924,709	$4,255,892	$43,808,354	$1,287,642	$13,254,444	1968
1969	$301,113,677	$944,476,779	$3,906,976	$39,436,893	$1,245,604	$12,573,086	1969
1970	$282,501,318	$836,573,121	$3,981,794	$36,333,406	$1,344,607	$12,269,382	1970
1971	$317,202,778	$900,615,307	$3,894,423	$38,295,142	$1,371,642	$13,487,807	1971
1972	$351,814,948	$966,999,745	$3,834,546	$39,181,135	$1,395,089	$14,254,925	1972
1973	$336,452,962	$870,581,519	$4,138,174	$35,776,026	$1,599,277	$13,836,333	1973
1974	$198,948,833	$463,899,649	$3,888,875	$35,627,112	$1,667,790	$15,279,107	1974
1975	$239,866,491	$511,834,074	$4,053,174	$31,969,163	$1,899,484	$14,982,064	1975
1976	$280,134,116	$565,854,452	$3,906,912	$28,454,417	$1,934,171	$14,086,754	1976
1977	$271,999,617	$516,124,861	$3,544,096	$24,685,408	$1,867,751	$13,009,296	1977
1978	$284,500,744	$501,700,159	$3,297,084	$22,526,518	$1,869,688	$12,774,184	1978
1979	$294,487,245	$466,090,954	$3,327,490	$21,838,838	$2,102,386	$13,798,290	1979
1980	$345,502,059	$482,135,021	$3,099,370	$15,102,742	$2,221,035	$10,822,755	1980
1981	$334,998,550	$423,544,485	$3,216,924	$14,653,930	$2,544,396	$11,590,391	1981
1982	$380,698,909	$465,103,587	$3,872,125	$16,431,512	$3,169,431	$13,449,603	1982

Bibliographic Essay

I N R E C E N T Y E A R S, there has been a marked increase in interest in the study of philanthropy. This has been stimulated by the establishment of research institutes like the Program on Non-Profit Organizations at the Yale University Institution for Social and Policy Studies, and the Center for the Study of Philanthropy at the Graduate School and University Center of the City University of New York; by the opening of foundation files and the collection of source materials at places like the Rockefeller Archive Center in North Tarrytown, New York; by the publication of bibliographies and rosters of research in progress by the Independent Sector and the Foundation Library Center; and by increasing attention to historical questions in magazines like the Council on Foundations' *Foundation News.* Nevertheless, as Anne Lowrey Bailey noted in the *Chronicle of Higher Education,* "the study of philanthropy must overcome decades of intellectual prejudice and neglect" (21 September 1988, p. A34).

Nowhere is this more evident than in the history of philanthropic foundations. Until the 1980s, the historiography of foundations was predominantly an insiders' tale, embroidered at the margins by a few critical studies that tended to be more polemical than searchingly scholarly. The literature to 1983 is reviewed in the "Bibliographic Note" to Ellen Condliffe Lagemann, *Private Power for the Public Good: A History of the Carnegie Foundation for the Advancement of Teaching* (Middletown, Conn.: Wesleyan University Press, 1983),

195–205. Since then, there have been more studies by outsiders, although some of these have remained unfortunately uncritical; see for example Simon Goodenough, *The Greatest Good Fortune: Andrew Carnegie's Gift for Today* (Edinburgh: MacDonald Publishers, 1985). Others are more encyclopedic than interpretative, as for example A. McGehee Harvey and Susan L. Abrams, *"For the Welfare of Mankind": The Commonwealth Fund and American Medicine* (Baltimore: Johns Hopkins University Press, 1986).

Happily, however, a number of new studies are beginning to draw the outlines for a more complete and critical history. Among these I would include Robert E. Kohler, "Science, Foundations, and American Universities in the 1920s," *Osiris*, 2nd Series, 3 (1987): 135–64, and Roger L. Geiger, *To Advance Knowledge: The Growth of American Research Universities, 1900–1940* (New York: Oxford University Press, 1986), both of which call attention to the complex relationships that grew up between universities and foundations. Guy Alchon, *The Invisible Hand of Planning: Capitalism, Social Science and the State in the 1920s* (Princeton: Princeton University Press, 1985), focuses on the importance of foundations in promoting "technocratic" modes of social planning. Paul J. DiMaggio, ed., *Nonprofit Enterprise in the Arts: Studies in Mission and Constraint* (New York: Oxford University Press, 1986), includes a number of essays suggesting important connections between philanthropy and the organization of culture in the United States. In addition, though the work is still preliminary, there have been efforts to sketch the main lines of a general interpretation, including Peter Dobkin Hall, "A Historical Overview of the Private Nonprofit Sector," in Walter W. Powell, ed., *The Nonprofit Sector: A Research Handbook* (New Haven: Yale University Press, 1987), and Barry D. Karl and Stanley N. Katz, "Foundations and Ruling Class Elites," *Daedalus* 116 (Winter 1987): 1–40.

Building on studies such as these, this book attempts to describe a politics, the politics of knowledge, in which many foundations have participated, and to describe one foundation's changing engagement in that politics throughout most of the twentieth century. Although it is largely based upon primary source materials (indicated in the notes along with the secondary sources from which I drew directly), it was informed by a number of published works that I should like to indicate here.

The politics of knowledge as I have defined it has a great deal to do with the problems and politics of setting public agenda. On this point, I have benefited especially from Peter Bachrach and Morton S. Baratz,

Power and Poverty: Theory and Practice (New York: Oxford University Press, 1970); Hugh Heclo, "Issues Networks and the Executive Establishment," in *The New American Political System*, ed. Anthony King (Washington, D.C.: American Enterprise Institute, 1978), 87–124; Theodore J. Lowi, *The End of Liberalism: The Second Republic of the United States* (New York: W. W. Norton, 1969); Charles L. Schultze, *The Public Use of Private Interest* (Washington, D.C.: Brookings Institution, 1977); and Sidney Verba and Norman H. Nie, *Participation in America: Political Democracy and Social Equality* (Chicago: University of Chicago Press, 1972).

Because the politics of knowledge involves relationships between elites and the public at large, my thinking has also been influenced by studies of elites, ranging from classics such as C. Wright Mills, *The Power Elite* (New York: Oxford University Press, 1956), to more controversial works such as G. William Domhoff, *Who Rules America Now? A View from the '80s* (Englewood Cliffs, N.J.: Prentice-Hall, 1983). Sociological studies of the professions and of professionalization are also relevant, and I have found the following especially helpful: Joan Jacobs Brumberg and Nancy Tomes, "Women in the Professions: A Research Agenda for American Historians," *Reviews in American History* 10 (June 1982): 275–96; Eliot Freidson, *Professional Powers: A Study of the Institutionalization of Formal Knowledge* (Chicago: University of Chicago Press, 1986); and Magali Sarfatti Larsen, *The Rise of Professionalism: A Sociological Analysis* (Berkeley: University of California Press, 1977).

Finally, questions of enfranchisement and participation are central to the politics of knowledge. My thinking about these concepts and their meaning within the context of American politics has been shaped by works as different as Benjamin Barber, *Strong Democracy: Participatory Politics for a New Age* (Berkeley: University of California Press, 1984); E. E. Schattschneider, *The Semisovereign People: A Realist's View of Democracy in America* (Hinsdale, Ill.: Dryden Press, 1960); and Michael Walzer, *Spheres of Justice: A Defense of Pluralism and Equality* (New York: Basic Books, 1983). Last but hardly least, my understanding of the politics of knowledge has drawn heavily from a long list of works by historians, including as representative recent examples Barry D. Karl, *The Uneasy State: The United States from 1915 to 1945* (Chicago: University of Chicago Press, 1983); Louis Galambos and Joseph Pratt, *The Rise of the Corporate Commonwealth: United States Business and Public Policy in the 20th Century* (New York: Basic Books, 1988); Thomas K. McCraw, *Prophets of*

Regulation: Charles Francis Adams, Louis D. Brandeis, James M. Landis, and Alfred E. Kahn (Cambridge, Mass.: Harvard University Press, 1984); and Stephen Skowronek, *Building a New American State: The Expansion of National Administrative Capacities, 1877–1920* (Cambridge: Cambridge University Press, 1982).

Although the Carnegie Corporation has been continuously involved in the politics of knowledge since the First World War, the style of its grant-making has changed over time, usually in response to large shifts in the social, political, and intellectual history of the United States. To indicate this, I have delineated three distinct philanthropic styles: scientific philanthropy, cultural philanthropy, and strategic philanthropy. Each of these styles predominated during a different chronological era and all have relevance to the policies of other foundations.

My view of scientific philanthropy and of the constellations of beliefs and attitudes that supported it was informed by general interpretative studies of the United States at the beginning of the twentieth century, especially those having to do with attitudes toward governance and the government. Among these were John C. Burnham, "The Cultural Interpretation of the Progressive Movement," in *Progressivism,* ed. John D. Buenker, John C. Burnham, and Robert M. Crunden (Cambridge, Mass.: Schenkman, 1977), 3–29; Robert Harrison, "The 'Weakened Spring of Government' Revisited: The Growth of Federal Power in the Late Nineteenth Century," and John A. Thompson, "Means to What Ends? Government Growth and Liberal Reformers, 1910–1920," both in *The Growth of Federal Power in American History,* ed. Rhodri Jeffreys-Jones and Bruce Collins (DeKalb: Northern Illinois University Press, 1983); R. Jeffrey Lustig, *Corporate Liberalism: The Origins of Modern American Political Theory, 1890–1920* (Berkeley: University of California Press, 1982); Robert Wiebe, *Businessmen and Reform: A Study of the Progressive Movement* (Cambridge, Mass.: Harvard University Press, 1968); and Martin J. Sklar, *The Corporate Reconstruction of American Capitalism, 1890–1916: The Market, The Law, and Politics* (Cambridge: Cambridge University Press, 1988).

Studies in the social history of ideas were also useful, especially Hamilton Cravens, *The Triumph of Evolution: American Scientists and the Heredity-Environment Controversy, 1900–1941* (Philadelphia: University of Pennsylvania Press, 1978), which illuminates the racial determinism so central to many politically elitist views formulated at the turn of the century, and Edward A. Purcell, Jr., *The Crisis of Democratic Theory: Scientific Naturalism and the Problem of Value*

(Lexington: University Press of Kentucky, 1973), which clarifies the era's extraordinary faith in science.

Broadly conceived biographies such as Barry D. Karl, *Charles E. Merriam and the Study of Politics* (Chicago: University of Chicago Press, 1974), and Ronald Steel, *Walter Lippmann and the American Century* (Boston: Little Brown, 1980), as well as generational portraits like Larry G. Gerber, *The Limits of Liberalism: Josephus Daniels, Henry Stimson, Bernard Baruch, Donald Richberg, Felix Frankfurter and the Development of the Modern American Political Economy* (New York: New York University Press, 1984), were crucial to my understanding of the relatively small group of men and ideas that linked nineteenth-century mugwumpery to twentieth-century managerial philosophies of government.

Needless to say, the beliefs inherent in the cultural philanthropy practiced by the Carnegie Corporation between the two world wars were lineal descendants of those essential to scientific philanthropy. The works cited above were therefore also helpful in understanding the aspirations associated with the grant-making of the Keppel era. In addition, there is an increasingly rich literature on Herbert Hoover and the associative state, including Joan Huff Wilson, *Herbert Hoover: Forgotten Progressive* (Boston: Little Brown, 1975), and the many writings of Ellis W. Hawley, especially "Herbert Hoover, the Commerce Secretariat, and the Vision of an 'Associative State,' 1921–1928," *Journal of American History* 61 (June 1974): 116–40, and "Herbert Hoover and American Corporatism, 1929–1933," in *The Hoover Presidency: A Reappraisal,* ed. Martin L. Fansold and George T. Mazuzan (Albany: State University of New York Press, 1974), 102–19. I found standard works on FDR and the New Deal less helpful than some more specialized works, including the articles collected in John Braeman, Robert H. Bremner, and David Brody, eds., *The New Deal* (Columbus: Ohio State University Press, 1975), 2 vols., and Barry Karl, *Executive Reorganization and Reform in the New Deal* (Chicago: University of Chicago Press, 1963).

Writings on culture in the 1920s helped me understand the political significance of the Carnegie Corporation's concern with art, literature, music, theater, and adult education. In addition to the works cited in the notes, I especially profited from James Sloan Allen, *The Romance of Commerce and Culture: Capitalism, Modernism, and the Chicago-Aspen Crusade for Cultural Reform* (Chicago: University of Chicago Press, 1983); Loren Baritz, "The Culture of the Twenties," in *The Development of an American Culture,* ed. Stanley Coben and Lorman

Ratner, 2nd ed. (New York: St. Martin's Press, 1983), 181–214; Richard Wightman Fox and T. J. Jackson Lears, eds., *The Culture of Consumption: Critical Essays in American History, 1880–1980* (New York: Pantheon Books, 1983); Karal Ann Marling, *Wall-to-Wall America: A Cultural History of Post-Office Murals in the Great Depression* (Minneapolis: University of Minnesota Press, 1982); Richard H. Pells, *Radical Visions and American Dreams: Culture and Social Thought in the Depression Years* (New York: Harper & Row, 1973); and Peter M. Rutkoff and William B. Scott, *New School: A History of the New School for Social Research* (New York: Free Press, 1986). For a historian, studies such as these are often more helpful in discerning general relationships than are more theoretical works, although I was informed by some relevant sociological and anthropological writings, including Judith Balfe and Margaret Jane Wyszomirski, eds., *Art, Ideology, and Politics* (New York: Praeger, 1985); Thomas R. Bates, "Gramsci and the Theory of Hegemony," *Journal of the History of Ideas* 36 (April–May 1975): 351–66; Clifford Geertz, "Art as a Cultural System," *MLN* 91 (December 1976): 1473–99; and Amy Swidler, "Culture in Action: Symbols and Strategies," *American Sociological Review* 51 (April 1986): 273–86.

Strategic philanthropy emerged, in part, from reactions to international events, especially the atom bomb and the Cold War, and in part from the establishment of new public and private foundations. My view of the pivotal events of these years has been shaped by works such as Richard M. Freeland, *The Truman Doctrine and the Origins of McCarthyism: Foreign Policy, Domestic Politics, and Internal Security, 1946–1948* (New York: New York University Press, 1970); John Lewis Gaddis, *The United States and the Origins of the Cold War, 1941–1947* (New York: Columbia University Press, 1972); James Gilbert, *Another Chance: Postwar America, 1945–68* (Philadelphia: Temple University Press, 1981); Otis Graham, *Toward a Planned Society: From Roosevelt to Nixon* (New York: Oxford University Press, 1976); Michael J. Hogan, *The Marshall Plan: America, Britain, and the Reconstruction of Western Europe, 1947–52* (Cambridge: Cambridge University Press, 1987); Richard H. Pells, *The Liberal Mind in a Conservative Age: American Intellectuals in the 1940s and 1950s* (New York: Harper & Row, 1985); Richard H. Rovere, *Senator Joe McCarthy* (New York: Harper & Row, 1959); and Alice Kimball Smith, *A Peril and a Hope: The Scientists' Movement in America, 1945–47* (Chicago: University of Chicago Press, 1965).

I learned a good deal about the intellectual debates and politics surrounding patronage for different fields of science from David Dickson, *The New Politics of Science* (New York: Pantheon, 1984); J. M. England, *A Patron for Pure Science: The National Science Foundation's Formative Years, 1945–1957* (Washington, D.C.: National Science Foundation, 1982); Daniel S. Greenberg, *The Politics of Pure Science* (New York: New American Library, 1967); Samuel Z. Klausner and Victor M. Lidz, eds., *The Nationalization of the Social Sciences* (Philadelphia: University of Pennsylvania Press, 1986); David M. Ricci, *The Tragedy of Political Science: Politics, Scholarship, and Democracy* (New Haven: Yale University Press, 1984); and John T. Wilson, *Academic Science, Higher Education, and the Federal Government, 1950–1983* (Chicago: University of Chicago Press, 1983).

A number of biographies and memoirs provided insight into the personalities and ideas of participants, among them the portraits of Vannevar Bush and James Bryant Conant in Sam Bass Warner, Jr., *Province of Reason* (Cambridge, Mass.: Harvard University Press, 1984); Vannevar Bush, *Pieces of the Action* (New York: William Morrow, 1970); George F. Kennan, *Memoirs: 1925–1950* (Boston: Little, Brown, 1967); and James R. Killian, Jr., *Sputnik, Scientists, and Eisenhower* (Cambridge: MIT Press, 1976). On the 1960s, I have profited especially from Godfrey Hodgson, *America in Our Time* (Garden City: Doubleday, 1976); Marvin E. Gettleman and David Mermelstein, eds., *The Failure of American Liberalism after the Great Society*, rev. ed. (New York: Random House, 1967); Allen J. Matusow, *The Unraveling of America: A History of Liberalism in the 1960s* (New York: Harper & Row, 1984); and William L. O'Neill, *Coming Apart: An Informal History of America in the 1960s* (Chicago: Quadrangle, 1971).

To keep the politics of knowledge and the Carnegie Corporation's involvement in it in view, I chose to write a history that was more selective than comprehensive, and my choices in this regard were often influenced by the existence or lack of relevant literature. As indicated in the preface, for example, I decided early on not to consider Carnegie Corporation grants outside the United States. This was primarily because overseas awards tended to be extensions of domestic programs and program rationales. But my decision was also influenced by the greater scholarly attention already given to the international as opposed to the domestic side of Carnegie Corporation activities. The old but still standard work on this subject, Merle Curti, *American Philanthropy Abroad: A History* (New Brunswick: Rutgers University Press, 1963), touches upon Corporation projects. Corporation programs in Africa are described and interpreted by Edward H. Berman, *The Influence of the Carnegie, Ford, and Rockefeller Foundations on American Foreign Policy: The Ideology of Philanthropy* (Albany: State University of New York Press, 1983); E. Jefferson Murphy, *Creative Philanthropy: Carnegie Corporation and Africa, 1953–1973* (New York: Teachers College Press, 1976); and Richard David Heyman, "The Role of Carnegie Corporation in African Education, 1925–1960" (Ed.D. diss., Teachers College, Columbia University, 1970). There is less writing on Carnegie philanthropy in Canada, New Zealand, and Australia, although some works illustrate the degree to which grant-making overseas followed from priorities established within the United States, as for example Jim Lotz and Michael R. Welton, " 'Knowledge for the People': The Origins and Development of the Antigonish Movement," in *Knowledge for the People: The Struggle for Adult Learning in English-Speaking Canada, 1828–1973*, ed. Michael R. Welton (Toronto: Ontario Institute for Studies in Education, 1987), and Barry M. Williams, *Structures and Attitudes in New Zealand Adult Education, 1945–1975* (Wellington: New Zealand Council for Educational Research, 1978).

The Carnegie Corporation had significant relationships with many—one is tempted to say innumerable—organizations; in choosing which of these I would feature I was again influenced, not only by my interest in describing the politics of knowledge, but also by the availability of relevant literature. This was the case, for example, in my decision not to include a discussion of Corporation grants to the Council on Foreign Relations and instead to write at length about the American Law Institute. From its establishment in the 1920s until after the Second World War, the council received a large part of its income from the Corporation, and virtually all Corporation trustees and officers belonged to it; at the Corporation, in turn, annual awards to the council were taken for granted. Certainly an important institution, and one that exemplified the assumptions inherent in what I have called "scientific philanthropy," the Council on Foreign Relations nevertheless was excluded from this study because its history has been told elsewhere: Lawrence H. Shoup and William Minter, *Imperial Brain Trust: The Council on Foreign Relations and U.S. Foreign Policy* (New York: Monthly Review Press, 1977)—a critical account; and Robert D. Schulzinger, *The Wise Men of Foreign Affairs: The History of the Council on Foreign Relations* (New York: Columbia University Press, 1984)—a descriptive history. Richard J. Barnet, *Roots of War: The Men and Institutions behind U.S. Foreign Policy* (1971; New York: Atheneum,

1972) sets the council within a wide-ranging institutional context; Thomas W. Lamont, *Across World Frontiers* (New York: Harcourt Brace, 1951), and Whitney H. Shepardson, *Early History of the Council on Foreign Relations* (Stamford, Conn.: n.p., 1960), are examples of the many autobiographies and memoirs that clarify the views of individuals involved in both the Corporation and the council. Needing to make difficult choices in order to avoid slipping into the encyclopedic, chronicle style so familiar in institutional histories, especially old-style foundation histories, I decided to include the American Law Institute, whose history and relationship to the Corporation are equally illustrative (if somewhat differently so) of the problems associated with private institutions of governance and about which there has been very little writing and no recent secondary accounts. Needless to say, there is still need for a study of interrelationships between Carnegie philanthropy and the Council on Foreign Relations, and this might well include, in addition, some of the activities of the Carnegie Endowment for International Peace as well as the Corporation's overseas programs.

Fortunately, as should be clear from the notes to chapter 4, there is sufficient material available to reconstruct the history of the American Law Institute. But that was not the case of all institutions the Carnegie Corporation helped to support, and sometimes the emphasis I gave (or did not give) to particular grants reflects this. In investigating the various institutes of economics the Corporation supported in the 1920s, for example, I was able to locate a good deal of contextual material about the National Bureau of Economic Research and the Brookings Institution. On the NBER, there are Joseph Dorfman, *The Economic Mind in American Civilization, 1918–1933* (New York: Viking, 1959), and Arthur F. Burns, ed., *Wesley Clair Mitchell: The Economic Scientist* (New York: NBER, 1952). On Brookings, see Donald T. Critchlow, *The Brookings Institutions, 1916–1952: Expertise and the Public Interest in a Democratic Society* (DeKalb: Northern Illinois University Press, 1985), which includes an excellent bibliography, and Charles B. Saunders, Jr., *The Brookings Institution: A Fifty Year History* (Washington, D.C.: Brookings, 1966). The professionalization of economics is treated by a wide literature, ranging from Robert L. Church, "Economists as Experts: The Rise of an Academic Profession in the United States, 1870–1920," in *The University in Society*, ed. Lawrence Stone (Princeton: Princeton University Press, 1974), II, 571–609, to David W. Eakins, "The Development of Corporate Liberal Policy Research in the United States, 1885–1965" (Ph.D. diss., University of Wisconsin, 1966), and David Michael Grossman,

"Professors and Public Service, 1885–1925: A Chapter in the Professionalization of the Social Sciences" (Ph.D. diss., Washington University, 1973). By contrast, there were few primary sources and little contextual material available concerning the Food Research Institute at Stanford University and the Institute of Land Economics, founded by Richard T. Ely, and this gap in the literature was responsible in part for the emphases evident in chapter 3. Yet I doubt that my interpretation of the issues raised in that chapter would have been significantly modified, if I had recovered more material about these particular research centers, although agricultural economics and land economics are certainly areas in need of further historical work.

In addition to these institutes, there were a few lacunae in the Corporation's records that I was unable to fill. The most important of these had to do with a series of studies of Americanization that was commissioned by the Corporation in 1918. This series, originally published between 1920 and 1924 by Harper & Brothers, included Frank V. Thompson, *Schooling of the Immigrant*; John Daniels, *America via the Neighborhood*; [W. I. Thomas], *Old World Traits Transplanted*; Peter A. Speek, *A Stake in the Land*; Michael M. Davis, Jr., *Immigrant Health and the Community*; Sophonisba P. Breckinridge, *New Homes for Old*; Robert E. Park, *The Immigrant Press and Its Control*; John Palmer Gavit, *Americans by Choice*; Kate Holliday Claghorn, *The Immigrant's Day in Court*; and William M. Leiserson, *Adjusting Immigrant and Industry*. As would often be the case of foundation-commissioned inquiries, including Gunnar Myrdal's *An American Dilemma*, the Americanization studies took more time and money to complete than had originally been anticipated. In addition, and again like the Myrdal study, there appear to have been discrepancies in aim and attitude between the Corporation's trustees and the authors invited to carry out the inquiries. The trustees saw Americanization as a national security interest that required thoroughgoing changes on the part of newly arrived immigrants, whereas at least some of the authors saw it as a more reciprocal process of social reform. Although these differences would have been worthy of consideration in relation to the politics of knowledge, there were too few documents clearly indicating the Carnegie Corporation's interests in these studies to enable me to do this in detail and with reasonable certainty. In light of this, I chose as an alternative to deal at length with the Myrdal study, which also revealed the kinds of problems common to sponsored, purposive research, and to leave the Americanization studies aside.

More often than not, the example of the Americanization studies not to the contrary, there were more than sufficient internal records to allow me to deal with whichever grants I chose to investigate. My final decisions as to which to include and which to exclude therefore derived from the significance of one or another grant in terms of public policy and what it might show about the politics of knowledge and the Corporation's engagement in it. I should note, however, that there were some instances in which my work was significantly constrained by the secondary literature to which I could turn to place the Corporation's interests and actions within the context of the relevant profession, institution, or movement. I found this to have been especially the case in the domain of cultural activities associated with libraries, museums, and adult education, where most historical writing has remained narrow and professional in orientation. There are exceptions, of course, including Dee Garrison, *Apostles of Culture: The Public Librarian and American Society, 1876–1920* (New York: Free Press, 1979); Michael Harris, "The Purpose of the American Public Library: A Revisionist Interpretation of History," *Library Journal* 98 (September 1973): 2509–14; and Edward P. Alexander, *Museum Masters: Their Museums and Their Influence* (Nashville, Tenn.: American Association for State and Local History, 1983).

In other instances, I found rich literatures that greatly enhanced my efforts to discern the significance of what the Carnegie Corporation was (and was not) willing to finance. This was true of writings about black education, for example, where more work needs to be done to overcome generations of neglect, but where an increasingly diverse literature is emerging; see the excellent bibliography included in James D. Anderson, *The Education of Blacks in the South, 1860–1935* (Chapel Hill: University of North Carolina Press, 1988), or the various articles in Darlene Clark Hine, ed., *The State of Afro-American History: Past, Present, and Future* (Baton Rouge: Louisiana State University Press, 1986). It was also the case with the scholarship and policy concerns associated with University of Chicago sociology: see Lester R. Kurtz, *Evaluating Chicago Sociology: A Guide to the Literature, with an Annotated Bibliography* (Chicago: University of Chicago Press, 1984).

From this, it may be clear that the key to understanding and analyzing the politics of knowledge and the significance of foundation philanthropy generally is historical context. Viewed in isolation, foundation history is a dry, boring chronicle of men and money; viewed in context, it is a lens through which one may consider not only private, often elite, efforts to organize, reform, and govern American society, but also the vast array of institutions and people associated with these efforts as allies, opponents, beneficiaries, or victims. Approached in this way, foundation history projects one into a great variety of "histories" and the literatures that go with them. The research required is demanding. But the reward is the opportunity to think about issues and problems that are fascinating, current, and vital to the possibilities for democracy in as large, complex, and heterogeneous a society as the United States has become during this century.

Index

Abrams, Susan L., 324
Academy of Political Science, 85
Acheson, Dean, 173
Addams, Jane, 67, 132
Adler, Mortimer, J., 118
adult education, 96, 104–105, 121; for blacks, 130–132, 133; Corporation program, 105–106, 117–119; and gender, 106–108
Adult Education Association of the U.S., 121
Agriculture, U.S. Department of, 4, 168
Alchon, Guy, 324
Aldrich, Richard, 108
Alexander, Charles C., 97
Alexander, Edward P., 333
All Our Children. See Carnegie Council on Children
Allen, James E., 213
Allen, James Sloan, 327
Allport, Floyd, 156
Allport, Gordon W., 156, 159, 166, 168
Almond, Peter O., 242
American Anthropological Association, 156
American Association for Adult Education (AAAE), 106–108, 284–285n.41; and Corporation grants, 117–119, 121; and Locke, Alain L., 130–132
American Association for the Advancement of Science (AAAS), 34, 148; Committee of One Hundred, 38–41, 43, 49–50
American Association of School Administrators, 191
American Bar Association (ABA), 73, 75, 76, 84, 90; and legal education, 78–79; and nativism, 77–78
American Broadcasting Corporation, 223
American Council of Learned Societies, 174
American Economic Association, 51, 60, 156

American Federation of the Arts, 109, 111
American Federation of Labor, 60
American Historical Association, 156
American Law Institute (ALI), 3, 70–73, 124, 256, 331; and Association of American Law Schools, 73–81; and legal realists, 81–93; and restatement process, 81–83, 84–85, 92–93, 281–282n.80
American Library Association (ALA), 103–104, 106, 107, 114–115, 121
American Medical Association, 78
American Political Science Association, 156
American Psychiatric Association, 156
American Psychological Association, 39, 156
American Public Library and the Diffusion of Knowledge, The, 111, 114
American Sociological Association, 156
American Soldier, The, 176–177
American Statistical Association, 156
Americanization, 104, 119–120, 332–333
American Telephone and Telegraph Company (AT&T), 34, 42, 53, 58
Amherst College, 35
An American Dilemma 3, 7, 148, 159–161, 332; Newton D. Baker's view of, 123, 127–130; Corporation's hopes for, 97–98, 123–136, 139; influence of, 146; Keppel's view of, 145–146; Myrdal's view of, 143–145; and sociology, 123–124, 135–137, 141–145; writing of, 136–142. *See also* Myrdal, Gunnar Karl.
Anderson, Colonel James, 17
Anderson, Florence, 221, 241
Anderson, James D., 333
Angell, James R., 31, 101, 102, 154–155; as Corporation president, 6–7, 60–63, 69
anthropology, 84, 155–158, 161, 165,

335

About the Author

Ellen Condliffe Lagemann is professor of history and education and director of the Institute of Philosophy and Politics of Education at Teachers College, Columbia University, where she has taught since 1978. In 1988 she was president of the History of Education Society, having also served as vice president and as a member of the board of directors.

Lagemann is a graduate of Smith College (A.B. 1967), Teachers College (M.A. 1968), and Columbia University (Ph.D. 1978). She is the author of *A Generation of Women* and *Private Power for the Public Good: A History of the Carnegie Foundation for the Advancement of Teaching*, and editor of *Nursing History: New Perspectives, New Possibilities* and *Jane Addams on Education*.

About the Book

The Politics of Knowledge was composed on a Mergenthaler Linotron 202 in Sabon. Sabon was designed by the late Swiss typographer, teacher, scholar, book designer, and type designer, Jan Tschichold.

The book was composed by World Composition Services of Sterling, Virginia, and designed by Kachergis Book Design of Pittsboro, North Carolina.

Wesleyan University Press, 1989